WHAT ARE WISDOM
AND INTELLIGENCE

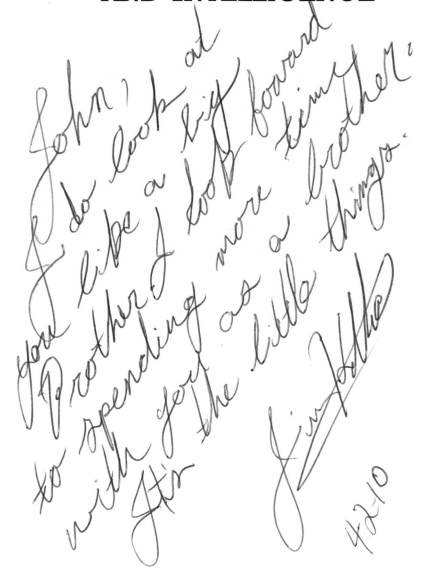

John,
I do look at
you like a big brother
Brother. I look forward
to spending more time
with joy as a brother.
for the little things.

Jim Kottke
4-2-10

WHAT ARE WISDOM AND INTELLIGENCE

by an Average Jim

James Kelley

To order additional copies of this book, contact:
Xlibris Corporation
1-888-795-4274
www.Xlibris.com
Orders@Xlibris.com
70884

CONTENTS

ACKNOWLEDGEMENT

My life was a rollercoaster of emotions. I would come to flat lands only a few times as I went on. Them flat lands made me feel grounded and content for a moment then ultimate feelings of joy would come about as I climbed to start again with each child's birth. The excitement was incredible every time and led to beautiful moments of pleasure. This excitement happened to me 6 times in my life and I would never regret or change one of them. Each one of these treasures will be a part of me forever and will bear fruit to live on forever as part of me. But without this book they will never know the man to start it all. You kids are everything to me and I hope you will have a wonderful life. This book is a dedication to all of you and an apology to each one of you. As you read these words from my past and the thinking that I should have spoke to you in person, I hope that it will help you on your own roller coaster and fill at least the knowing part of you're father's past. I did make many mistakes in my life but as you read this you'll find that I don't regret what I did in some ways. I do regret not being the father I should have been.

This book is to pass on my life to all of you. It will hopefully be a guide to help you along the paths you choose threw life. Starting from the oldest my beautiful memories are; Nicholas, Jason Ty, Christopher James, Zachery Allen, Madison Joanne, and Trenton Denver. May all you're dreams come true and my you feel joy as you go through life. Please listen to what I say in this book and do you're best in life.

Special thanks go out to Mom. She kept me grounded through all these things in life and helped make me strong enough to not get caught up in the so called "new reality." Mom, the strength you showed me in the early years of my life gave me the strength to look ahead in many times of trouble. I'll never be able to thank you enough for the things you did for me in the past. My feelings for you are heart felt and real from the bottom of my soul. My roots are strong because of you. I'll never forget were that comes from.

To my muse, Robin my fiancé, soon to be my life partner. Her Love, in some since, gave me the strength to write this book. With her in my life I found perfect serenity in my life with her. Robin, I hope you realize how important you are in my life and my future. I don't see a future without you. You gave me the urge and tenacity to sit down for 6 months and give my kids my stories. No one ever made me feel as loved as you. I'm very proud and happy to open the door for you, sit next to you in a booth, watch after you, and keep you safe. This book is you're inspiration on me. Our love will live on forever and I love you more then anything. May our future be filed with happiness and joy.

INTRODUCTION

What is wisdom and intelligence? Who is the judge of a person's wisdom and intelligence? If I remember correctly, only God has the right to judge. Why has wisdom and intelligence become like a social status? But this book isn't about religion, or politics for that matter. This book is about my life and my experiences. During this book, I'll also give you my own feelings towards things in general. It will not only be filled with my story but my thoughts about those experiences. Wisdom and intelligence, in my own mind, has given me strength to become a better person. Listening to the discussions I've heard in my life, I see that everyone has their opinion of intelligence, and some don't believe that there are many different degrees of intelligence. Wisdom arguably can be the most important and sometimes is looked upon as intelligence.

"What is wisdom and intelligence?!" I have always asked myself this same question since I was a sophomore in high school. But as I said before, who has the right to judge this question? Some of you are thinking, "Who cares!" Feeling that way is where it all starts, "apathy", which is arguably the biggest problem in our world today. Somewhere out there, someone knows you don't care; they feed on this, and afterwards, they just make whatever rules they want to. These guys want you to have apathy, it gives those people more control over you.

With one hand they will give you a piece of bread for free and with the other they're taking more of whatever income you still have, or you could get up and work a little to get a whole loaf of bread. That's what apathy will get you. Then someone is telling you that you're an idiot because someone taught them to look down on people with no education. It all had to have trickled down from somewhere. Do you have wisdom and intelligence? Do you believe or even care what other people think of you? They're out there judging you right now just because "you don't care." It can drive you crazy just trying to figure all this out. Bottom line is, shouldn't someone be able to answer this question? Well, in my life it took a long time to even think to answer it for myself.

The answer will seem simple to some people. Even though you might think it seems simple, there are still some questions to how you feel about it all, like where your decision came from. Did you read about it? Do you really think we even know the answer? Should it even need to be asked? There are a lot of people that seem to think they know the answer. As you can see, this can be quite puzzling. My life has been a constant battle trying to figure this out. It seemed my wisdom and intelligence was so important that they tested you all through school, and later in life it makes all the difference in how far you can go. How far will this go, are you happy with just a piece of bread? What happens when they start controlling the way you think, or do they already? "Sounds communist or socialist huh?" Apathy doesn't sound so great when you sit and think about it a little. Me personally, I'd rather go work to have a whole loaf of bread. Let's see how these questions took hold of my life and made me who I am today. I hope that by my little stories and reasoning, like my thoughts on apathy, will help all of you.

Hello, my name is Jim (James H. Kelley). My mother always called me Jimmy. As a child growing up, I hated being called Jimmy. Now I let people know right away that only Mom calls me Jimmy, and just like most people I've met, it wasn't good when Mom yelled, "James Howard Kelley!" That was never a good thing. We all remember having to deal with that. I didn't have a great life in the sense of being president, a star of some sort, inventing something, or anything of that nature. But I think that my story can help other people get through some of the hard times or at least give them ways to make life easier. Maybe you can answer the big question of wisdom and intelligence. This autobiography is mainly to be the father I never was to my kids. To hopefully give them the wisdom all parents should pass on to their children. So, kids, this is for you guys. For those of you who are not my kids, I'm sure you're thinking, "Jim, why should I read about your life?" Well, here's the deal. There are millions of self-help books and seminars out there to help you out in life. But look at yourself still. Did they understand your individual plight? Where they able to get into your head and understand you? I'm not putting them down. Hell, I've never read one myself. People have daily situations in life that aren't the end of the world but can be difficult just the same. Now the wise and intelligent ones that wrote these books and had these seminars sometimes—not a lot of times—have not dealt with the average Joe's problems themselves and won't have the same answers as an average Joe. Or it could be a *Jim*. Now I don't mean to put those people down; some of these people are truly empathizing with you and are truly trying to help you. I would hope that people that do have problems and search for help don't judge them also. There are some of the people out there that feel they have the answers to your problems. Do I have the answers? No. But in the past, I've been able to help people I've talked to that just need a little help with their situation. So I did my best to give them a sense of basic fundamentals that make us human. If anything, I know they felt better, may not always fix it, but they can now take a deep breath and think clearer about their situation. We can always use a little help from our friends.

I've made plenty of bad decisions in my life. I hope that by telling my story to my kids, I can help them be stronger to cope with everyday life. The simple things in life will always save you. Reading this material will take you back to a lot of your own memories. Hopefully it will make things clearer with your own memories and give *you* back to the basics of *you*. In a sense, give you back to yourself and make you strong. Maybe, like other people before our time, I can take you back to look at our ancestors. Think back to the pioneers, and remember, their so-called struggles in everyday life. Seems so terrible to us now, but back then, it was just life. They didn't have the stresses that we all have now. If I remember correctly, they didn't have TV, cell phones, or the Internet. They dealt with the fundamentals of life from the teachings of their parents. I hope to give you back your roots and help you to be strong. If you have the strength of yourself, maybe the stress of things will seem silly. This is all I can offer my kids and maybe help a few of you as we go. As I tell my story, I'll delve more into that question that haunts me to this day. "What is wisdom and intelligence?"

"I feel what I can give you is the strength to overcome bad decisions."

CHAPTER 1

In the Beginning

I was born in a small town hospital in Bessemer, Michigan. We actually lived in Ironwood. I have no memory of my early childhood except what people have told me. Even as my family tells me vivid stories, I can't recall a thing. Sometimes I'll remember things but they're like dreams to me. It was April 5, 1965. My mother's maiden name is Brownell, Darlene Joyce. My father's name is Robert H. Kelley. God forbid if you called him Bob. He hated that like I hated Jimmy. I remember coming home from the Marines one time, and when I got to the house, my mother told me Dad was at the continental cowboy. So I drove over there and walked in, unbeknownst to him, and gave him a slap on the back and hollered, "How's it going, Bob," and he just missed my face with his backhand. I think he was torn between being very happy to see me or upset about what I did. But I'm getting ahead of myself here.

My mother was only seventeen when she met Dad; he was twenty-nine. I'm not sure where we lived in Ironwood. Not that it matters at this point, but I assume it was real close by my grandparents' from the stories I've heard. I don't really even know my grandparents on my mom's side. They tell me I was close to Grandpa. He used to eat Tootsie Roll pops all the time, and he'd let me have some of his favorite kind, chocolate. So if you can imagine, I guess that's why they have always been my favorite. (Interesting how sometimes the simplest things come from your past, and a lot of times we forget why things are like they are. But look back at your family, and you'll find reasons for everything.) With the way things are in this day and age, I hope people can look back at their family and not just the day care center you were in. It's sad that it's gotten so bad that kids' parents have to have two jobs to support a lifestyle that has been instilled by TV and ads that make people think they need more than the fundamentals for their kids. It's also considered normal for people to have single-parent households. Day care centers are making a killing due to the fact almost everyone needs day care because of what I've talked about.

My mother had twelve siblings altogether. But there should have been thirteen. That's where my name comes from. My grandparents' firstborn died as a baby, and his name was James Howard. They tell me that gave me a special place in Grandma's heart. As I understand it, he died at three months old, and Mom, being only nineteen, was very scared. So till I was older than my uncle Jim, she was very protective of me as a child.

This made me think about being the firstborn. Mothers, it seems to me that there is a difference when you're raising kids when it comes to your firstborn. Mom, I can't even imagine how that felt as you lay there for the first time with a life inside you. No matter what age, it must have been scary, or maybe the word should be *overwhelming*. After all the time you lay there, rubbing your belly, talking to me with so much anticipation then go through hours of pain to look at me for the first time, must have been an incredible feeling. It doesn't make your firstborn better than the other children, but I'm sure it was an amazing experience being the first time. Even as a father myself, there is a special place in your memories of your firstborn.

The Brownells had a nickname back then, "the Calderwood kids." If you can imagine, they were extremely poor back then, not to mention raising thirteen kids. When I listen to my family's stories, I think of one of my favorite shows, The Little Rascals. They wore hand-me-downs and were picked on all the time. They weren't considered the most intelligent group of kids. See, it's already starting about the title of my book. People considered them white trash, hicks, or like I said before, "Calderwood kids." Why did they have to be treated like that? What's wrong with just accepting them for what they are? Is there a rule book that tells us to treat them like dirt because of their lack of intelligence or what the family can afford to clothe them with? Seems kind of silly when you think about it like this, doesn't it? Families of this nature, as you can imagine, become very close. The Calderwood kids were very poor so they spent a lot of time inventing things to keep themselves occupied. My mom, if I remember correctly, made us kids go outside all the time. She gave us ideas that helped us to use our imagination all the time. Cowboys and Indians, one of my favorites, in which I always wanted to be the Indian, and all I needed was a stick. We did have some cars with some Legos, and then we would build a town with roads, buildings were the Legos, and use big sticks for some of the big buildings. We used pieces of wood to move the dirt to make the roads. I'm sure you can imagine the sound effects that we had while playing.

Another adventure we had that was a favorite had to be playing with "army men." We had tanks, jeeps, and tons of army men. You see, the bags of army guys were very cheap and easy for us to afford. You would set up your roads on your side with your wood. Then you set up your Lego protection, kind of like bunkers. Once we finished setting up our forts, we pulled out the marbles. We made the rule: your hand had to touch the ground, and then fleck your marbles to destroy all of your friend's or sibling's army guys. Wow, that brings back good memories. It's the simple things in life that mean so much to your soul. See, the Calderwood kids never had much, but they learned so much more out there with just a little imagination and ingenuity. Kids can have so much fun and be completely content for hours. They were picked on a lot, but they stood up for themselves and each other as best they could. They were happy kids, and from what I've heard, they were a fun bunch to hang out with. I'm very proud to have roots come from a family like that.

Kids can be very cruel. It's interesting how everyone says that all the time, but their kids end up the same way. Well, someone is raising them, why isn't anyone changing or fixing the problem? Please tell me you don't think the government should help? Nowadays, things are very different; parents aren't there anymore, kids don't play outside anymore, and worst of all, parents don't make their kids eat dinner at the table. They're too tired to work with their children or spend time with them anymore. People today have, in a sense, gotten selfish in some instances. They have forgotten some of the basic fundamentals of raising children. We spend our childhood knowing our parents sacrificed everything for us. When we become parents, we sacrifice everything to help them grow strong. Then it's time to have fun till our parents need our help in their old age. The cycle comes back to you when your kids are helping you in your old age. Of course now, sadly enough, we pawn everything off to the government to take care of seniors and children. "Wouldn't want to take up any of their time." The other problem, as I mentioned before, is we work so much we don't have the energy to take care of being a parent. I think part of the problem is they don't get enough exercise themselves. I think I heard somewhere that a good walk or jog in the morning gave you more energy for the whole day than that latte you're drinking.

Of course if you go way back, they didn't have fast food and microwaves to shorten their time taking care of the family. They would spend time working on dinner with the whole family's involvement. Men had to work on their house or take care of firewood for the winter. The things that we take for granted in our time were just day-to-day routine many years ago. Feeding their horse, taking care of the buggy, milking their cow, and getting their kids off to school. This routine helped keep up their strength and stamina. They also had to take care of their garden, not just for fun, but to have food. Now we get no exercise unless you run or go to the gym. So people have no energy. We have all become way too lazy. Our lack of fortitude trickles down to our kids. Back then, most of the children's education was with their parents. Maybe, with a little help from their grandparents that live next door, or in your own house; and now, a lot of people barely know their grandparents, as far as I can tell. All my grandparents died way too early. I can only dream of the wonderful relationships some of you have had with your grandparents.

When we get irritated by our kids' energy, then we send them to play videos, play on their computer, and/or watch TV. Maybe next time you could give them something constructive to do with you. Now instead of working with their kids' energy, we give them drugs. Now we have a title that some wise person gave them. "ADHD." I don't claim to know everything, as you know, and I don't know too much about this title, but I disagree to some extent about the reasoning behind it. I do believe that there are some kids that have ADHD, as they put it, but I think it's way over diagnosed. I feel they just need healthier food and to get outside. Doesn't that sound logical to anyone but me? We eat fast-food and microwave stuff. Our kids never get out just running, playing, and working off that energy God gave children. I would think that every child that doesn't get out will automatically have ADHD, according to their doctors' standards. Children naturally have a lot of energy, as I said before, and need to play it off. Wake up, people, have some fun with your kids. Go get some sticks and play cowboys and Indians with your kid. Then I promise, you'll be the coolest parents in the neighborhood. Feed your kids good food, and if you don't do anything else, make a rule to have dinner at the table. No exceptions!

At this point, I need to jump ahead twenty years to tell a bit more of my birth. My first wife, Susan, and I were in a car when she blurted out that Robert wasn't my biological father. If you can imagine, this was a shock and a half for me. "Did this bother me?" Not as much as I've seen some people's reaction to it. People in this position should never jump to conclusions about the person involved in this. Everyone goes through some tough decisions in life, and we all tend to make a few bad ones. In a lot of cases, you're labeled right away as a bad person for not saying anything. Trust me though, I know there are some evil people that did things for the wrong reason because that's the way they are, but don't jump too quickly to judge or judge at all. Each situation has its own reasons behind it, and you probably don't have all the information. If this happens to you, try not to label someone just because that's what you read about in some book or were told by someone else. Listen to the ones that were actually there first. From what I've gathered from families, some not exactly partial to my dad and from some good sources, I've got a pretty good picture in my head on how I came to be.

My father was a professional thief, or I'm sure that's how he would put it. But then again, he probably wouldn't admit it. I wasn't completely surprised about this because of other experiences as a child later on. The way I understood how I was conceived starts with my dad's reasons for being in Ironwood. He was dealing in counterfeit money. He'd take counterfeit money to Canada, switch it to Canadian, come back to the States, and switch it back. Well, while he was up north changing this, he met a beautiful young girl named Darlene. At the time, I'm sure she didn't know his dealings but love later will conquer all. She fell head over heels for a dashing young man with a strong look about him. Someone a woman knows will protect her. He had money, a nice car, funny, from Texas, very charismatic, and worldly. He was in the Navy which is a very patriotic thing, especially back then after World War II. That must have been overwhelming for any country girl back then. When he wanted to take this young girl as his own, her parents were totally against this. But they were having financial difficulties and were about to lose their house. Dad came to their rescue. Well, of course there was a price for doing this; it was Mom's hand.

I lost track here, but I think they came back from their honeymoon, and somehow Dad was arrested and put in jail. A few months later, Mom was hanging out with some family and friends, smoking cigarettes while drinking alcohol. Mom had a little too much fun with one of the friends, and here I am. I have talked with my biological father a few times, but I'll keep that name out of the book. All I wanted was to let him know I was here, plus it helps to know your biological side for blood, nationality, and such. Dad got out after I was born and told everyone, "If anyone ever tells Jim about this, I'll just shoot you." Would he do it? Well, I found out twenty years later from my wife; what do you think?

Remember that I told you I have no memory of my childhood, and the stories as I remember them are not always perfect? Well, here is one of them. My mom recently told me the whole deal on where dad was when I was conceived. I remembered it wrong. The story I just told you about counterfeit money is true, but that happens later when I'm in the first grade. I'm not perfectly clear on this, but it had something to do with an ex-wife and a nice car. It was a "grand theft auto."

Shortly after I was born, Scot came along almost exactly one year later. I saw a picture of me and him once sitting on a bench. He was crying, if I remember correctly. Not long after that, we moved to Texas, which is where Dad grew up. He was raised in a little town outside of Amarillo called Pampa. I'm not sure why, but I assume there wasn't much work up there for a con. Pam was born a year and a half later. You'd think I might have noticed the difference between us, but the thought never crossed my mind. I have dark brown hair, brown eyes, and very dark complexion. I truly looked like a Calderwood kid. Scot and Pam had fair complexions and are blonds. There are other subtle differences too. I very seldom get sick. Scot and Pam get sick a lot more comparatively. We weren't babied so our immune systems were pretty good. I've heard that makes a difference.

Side note: remember, this book will be completely from my own memories. There are no references, college degree, or some weird school of learning. That's not to say I've never read a book or wasn't interested in learning. That was prevalent in my life also. It's how I interpret the experiences around me. If I'm wrong about things, then I apologize. Parents are the main parts of your morals and ethics. I didn't see this when I was young and wasn't there for you, kids. Your life and mine are about experiences. I didn't teach my children them due to bad choices on my behalf. You know the saying, "You learn from your mistakes"? I feel what I can give you is the strength to overcome bad decisions. Can't stop you from making big mistakes; you'll make them for sure. But you can fix them a lot easier. Some people are always going to try to tell you if you're wise or not and lead you around to tell you the only way to fix something is their way. A lot of people will buy into that. Suck it up, relax, and do the best you can to make it through. But like the song said, "I know what I know, if you know what I mean." Always did love that song. I sometimes wonder if half of people's problems are what someone told you is a problem. A little like a made-up reality that only exists in your mind. I'm not going to try and change your mind at all. I will, to the best of my ability, open your mind.

What, people, make you think is what makes you lose yourself.

CHAPTER 2

Early Childhood Memories

Now will talk about that area of my life that I told you I don't remember much. Just dreams and a few stories I've heard. I also have been told we moved a lot at first. Let's start with a good memory or dream, as it were. Christmas, we all love Christmas; my early years, I do have sort of like a dream that I think was around the time we were in Texas somewhere. It was a nice suburban-looking house. It had a big garage to the left side of the house. The house was brick that had light tan color. It had a nice set of hedges in the front by the window, and the porch had a concrete floor. Our dad would get anxious and get us up at like two or three in the morning to open presents. I'm sure my kids remember getting up very early for Santa also. Now you know where I got it. You should've seen the looks on your eyes when y'all came out to the tree. You guys were usually half asleep though. It is so priceless to see that picture with your own kids.

My best memory was so vivid; the toys filled the floor of the living room. Santa left all the stuff that we got from him all laid out, and if it had assembly required, it was all done so we could play with it right away. I seem to remember army men set up like in a formation all over the living room. Two colors marching to battle with their tanks and such like I talked about earlier. Pam had dolls and buggies set up to walk them with. Scot and I had hot wheels laid out all over also. It was an incredible sight for three young kids. And lo and behold, *bikes*! I can still feel the thrill from that moment. Looking back though, as a father, I see how they did it. Other than the bikes, they were all simple gifts. It didn't matter how much money they spent. You know, kids (meaning mine), I did the best I could with what we had, to make it fun for you.

If it hadn't been for that year in my past, I think I would have been really stressed out during Christmas. You kids remember it's not the price of the gift. As a kid, it was a great feeling to see that kind of Christmas. But later with all the peer pressure and the kids that got more, they made it hard for the have-not's to enjoy life. Yes that was me at times, but I did get over it; the simple things in life are what are important and made it possible. Please don't fall into the trap of people telling you what you have to have or don't have to have. Can someone tell me why we've forgotten to say, "Be happy and thankful with everything you have"? Just because I don't have something doesn't make me any less than someone else. What is wisdom and intelligence? Y'all keep this in your head as we go because it controls life to some extent. But I can make you and my family happier if you can look at life without all the negativity that is forced on us by society. Like this one moment in time of a small Christmas that overshadows anything bad for me. It's the little things in life. Christmas at that time, as I remember, was great.

The whole idea that someone is better than you really chaps my hide. I recall a story a long time ago that may sound stupid to some but very clear to others. The story was actually a skit that Bill Cosby did many years ago. I'm not sure of what the legal ramification of this is, but this is a Bill Cosby story that triggered this thought I had. He was talking about being a child when some kid in the neighborhood got to go to McDonalds to get a Big Mac and fries. The kid then was running around singing, "I got McDonald's hamburger, and all you have is a greasy piece of bread with a burger patty." I was that kid with the greasy burger. I tell you something though, that was a great burger and coming from someone who's been in the restaurant business for most of my life, one-fourth the price in food cost I'm sure. I don't know how to make that feeling clearer to you but my burger was hand-made, the bread was a thick piece that my mother had cut from a fresh loaf of bread, those tomatoes were from my yard, and the lettuce had been chilled the night before. Mom took a lot more love and care into that burger than a dollar to shut some kids up. The simple things in life make all the difference. Remember, don't make something as simple as cooking food for your kids like an irritation or chore that you have to do. Kids, you were the joy of life, not a chore.

Now for one of the times that I had a bad day, as I said before, it's like dreams to me. I think times got bad a lot in my childhood. It's been said to be one of many causes for memory loss. We moved around a lot. I'm sure that never helps anyone. I think it slowly starts to confuse kids to some extent. Those types of kids continue to have to make new friends each time, and the other kids look at you like a stranger. In some ways you lose your roots. Moving in turn makes some kids an easy target. Add to that effect a poor family with hand-me-downs, a strange accent, and that kid is in trouble. That kid was me. I don't have any ill will towards the kids in my past. At that time it was all peer pressure, and what did they know? The only thing that can stop kids from being cruel is their own parents.

Anyway that's going out of subject. I think the worst memory for me was a in a motel, I think. It could have been a small studio apartment. My thoughts are of this chicken broth soup my mom was making for dinner. I remember being very hungry, and it smelled so good I had to sneak some. Now we're talking about a little kid that knows nothing about cooking or what boiling temperature is. So I took this big plastic spoon and filled it up with boiling soup and took a big gulp. OOUUCH! Yes, as you can imagine, I burned the inside of my mouth, something fierce. I had to use straws for days to eat anything and hunger like you'd never believe. This, as you can imagine, stuck with me to this day. It gave me a big appreciation for people who have hunger. People can't continue to turn the cheek on the people you meet, especially if you have the ability to help. Please don't ever look down on them again. I don't think everyone has to go through what I did to see the obvious. You shouldn't have to suffer to feel for them but watch how you treat them; after all, they're human too. Don't jump to judge what got them in the positions they're in. "Charity is free but comes back tenfold." I think I heard that somewhere. Please don't judge.

That is truly just about it before first grade. No memories till a little later in life, which we'll tackle later on. There was a girl though. Yes a girl in my 1st grade year. I was a big man now cause Pam and Scot wasn't in school yet. Not a ton of memories but a few around then. We moved a few times, and I know one place in first grade was in Big Spring, Texas. But the girl I fell for lived somewhere else. She was a bit controlling, if I remember correctly. Her name was Amy. I remember sitting on her porch and playing some weird game where Scot and Pam were running around the house, and we'd sneak kisses while they were in the back. Corny, but hey, it's a good memory. A lot of people miss out on love. Self-confidence is a big key to love for me. People who are intelligent and wise that know who is stupid and ugly push them down. It's hard to get back up. Amy gave me a shot in the arm and I felt better about myself at least for a little while. I think a lot of that time was tough for me. Amy was a bright spot in an otherwise gloomy setting. They say if you can't remember things it's because you blocked them out. So I think I'll just hang on to the good.

Just before Amy, I had a lot of bullies in my life, and I think that's where it started. I was in trouble for something, not sure what, but I found myself in the office. When I showed up, there was a kid, I can't remember too well, but I do remember that damn pencil. Yes, as I sat down, he held a sharpened pencil underneath me. The lead broke between the groin and the upper leg. Can't say I remember the pain itself, but the humiliation was much worse. Everyone in the room was laughing hysterically, I guess, because of my facial expressions. Who is to say why people laugh at people in trouble. It's particularly sad to me because I remember adults thinking it was funny too. I can still see that pink stain on my drawers after Mom had washed them, for months. I was the oldest, so I didn't have any hand-me-downs. I'm sure I only had a few pairs of underwear. So am I to understand like those people were saying I'm stupid because I didn't see him putting the pencil under me? Or I'm stupid because I didn't think that was funny? Not sure. At the time, I didn't analyze the situation, but just felt terrible. As you'll see it's later that this kind of thing made me wonder about wisdom and intelligence.

For some stupid reason, people who look down and pick on other people don't have a clue what they do to those people. What are they, stupid? It slowly tears those people apart. It infuriates me when this happens on a daily basis all over. It doesn't make them smarter to hurt someone else. Sadly, most of the time, they don't even know what they're doing to them. WAKE UP, PEOPLE! I get so mad when I think about what goes on. I realize it's not the end of the world and most people get by anyway, but then people say I was just playing. Why play with someone's emotions? I don't get it; someone should explain why they think it's cool to some people to be like this. Maybe it is just their upbringing. There are low self-esteemed people that don't get that. That doesn't make them stupid. Just shows you some people are very sensitive. So don't jump to judge until you at least make an effort to be nice. Would that hurt so much? A simple smile or "How are you?" can go a long way. Just keep that in the back of your mind as you go through life.

We all did some pretty stupid things when we were young. I had my share. But that don't make you stupid. It is just life, and as you grow up, it will be up to you to teach your children to see these as just that, life. Don't rub things in people's face. Everyone, as you grow, can tell when the person that screwed up isn't laughing about it. Why can't people just respect that? There is no reason to judge. Just because a person thinks there more intelligent then someone else doesn't give them the right to judge. Remember the first page of the intro? No one has the right.

Here is a good one from the first grade, in Big Spring, Texas. For some reason, my father wasn't living with us at the time. I don't remember. I've recently been told this is the counterfeit situation time frame I spoke of from when I was born. Grandma

Kelley was helping us; we were staying at her house. There was this old aluminum camper shell in the backyard or alley. We played in and about it all the time. One day we got a hold of some empty Coke bottles. Then Scot and I found that they were kind of cool when they broke against the camper shell. One didn't quite break, so I grabbed it and tried again. Didn't notice that it had chipped on the top and it almost cut my thumb off. Scot was screaming, "Mommy, Jim cut his thumb off! Come quick!" And here she came running out the door with Grandma. "What did you do?" "We were just playing, Mom!" I said. "It's no big deal. It doesn't hurt at all." That was actually true at the time because I had cut the nerves. When she finally got to look, she gasped at the gushing blood. I think it was probably the first big accident I had ever had so far, other than learning to swim in the gulf, which is another story. This actually elevated my status at school for a while. The bandage I was able to pull off at anytime which, at that age, seeing the stitches was cool.

Swimming—my first real lesson, I was told, was at the Gulf of Mexico. I was five or six at the time, I don't remember exactly. My father was a lifeguard in his younger days and was very old-fashioned. Yes, the old "throw them in" routine. For me, it was standing at the shores and Dad throwing me in. He was very good at not letting you drown; he'd catch you before you went too far down. Well, as we were doing this, we had moved past where I could stand up and was holding me while I learned to wade a bit. But all of a sudden, he just let go. *Oh my God*, I'm thinking, *I'm not ready for this.* So there I was, just sinking like a log, and there was no one to pull me up. "What are you thinking, Dad?" As I was going down, thankfully I had the sense to think. *Sooner or later I'm going to hit bottom, and Jim, you better push up real hard.* Push! I got to the top and grabbed a big breath. As I did I notice Dad thrashing about. "Oh my God, he is drowning too!" Push! This time I'm seeing him walk away. What the heck was he thinking? *Where is he going?* Push! I'm not sure how long this went on, but in my mind it's an eternity. Finally, Dad grabbed me up. By now, I've drank half the gulf and that splitting headache we have all felt at the end of a long day in the sun and after swimming. Well, what about your dad? you say. It was a fishing tackle that had gotten caught on his forearm, and he thought it was a fish or jellyfish at first. That's what had him thrashing about. As you can imagine this became a funny story in conversations threw my life.

Sadly enough, that truly is almost all I can remember before I was twelve. I'm totally serious. It's a blank. People tell me they remember most of it. To me, until later, I thought that was normal. For a long time, I had no idea how bad my memory was. But hah, life goes on. Tomorrow is another day. Maybe some day it will come back to me. That seems far-fetched to me. I've heard it happens though. In a way, I hope I never get it back. If you could change anything what would it be? For me, the answer would be nothing. That was my life, my experience. Though sometimes bad I wouldn't change a thing. I feel that the difficulties in life just make you stronger and wiser. That is part of my explanation of wisdom. Changing things take away from who I am today. All the experiences we have later in life are a product of the whole. It makes me a better person to understand many different things. What, people, make you think is what makes you lose yourself. Try not to give in to what people are trying to tell you what they think is correct. It all starts with your morals and ethics. You're not going to jump off a bridge if someone tells you that it's cool. Don't take that as simple anarchy or hatred of people in general. Anarchy doesn't help anyone at all. Even the Bible talks of people following man laws. That is morals and ethics. Maybe that will be another book later. Kids, as we go on in this book, I'll explain more about this stuff and how I feel later on.

I can vaguely remember, I think in Texas, we had these plastic orange cups shaped like oranges. I'm not sure why they stick out but we went through some hard times around then. Back in the day before food stamps, we had commodities. Remember the chicken broth? I do. We also got Spam, American cheese, dried pork, and that dreaded nonfat dry milk. God, to this day I hate that stuff. Mom sometimes would get a gallon of milk and make two to four gallons with the NFD.

But out of all this, it helped me through some tough times of my own. It taught me to know lots of good filler recipes for my family when things were bad. "Thank you, Mom, the lesson I learned from tough times were priceless". Kids, now you know where all the crazy meals came from. Remember guilloché? I still think Hamburger Helper stole my recipe for cheeseburger macaroni. And I got a love for Spam. And I mean a *love*.

"If you can imagine having a whole bunch of tidbits of memories and trying to put it together like a puzzle."

CHAPTER 3

First Impression of Colorado

As I've told you, I don't have much memories of my childhood. I'm sure all of you are wondering what time frame I started to remember things. Around the fifth grade, as far as I know, this is the start of my love for Colorado. "Rocky Mountain High," we lived in Lakewood, Colorado, a suburb of Denver. Dad somehow got a job managing an apartment complex with a great pool. Gulf of Mexico paid off. I remember our summer was a swimmer's paradise. We swam all day, everyday the whole summer. This place to me was like the start of my life. My memory here is still a bit blurrier, but I can feel in my heart the happiness I had here. There was a rec room with a pool table, and I'm pretty sure I learned how to play there. This also was the first time I didn't feel the peer pressure I had felt before. I'm sure that was because we were the manager's kids, but we didn't know that. The rec room does stick out here in my mind. There are unclear thoughts. If you could imagine my frustrations with knowing something great but for some reason not remembering it. This is how Lakewood feels to me. Its funny I remember something about a neat paint job in the rec. room but for some reason I can't see it. Maybe it's the pictures painted on the wall that I remember from pictures of me from my sister's birthday party in the rec room. This is also where I think we got our organ too. All of us tried to learn, but I never quit, got the hang of it.

Christmas was fun there too. The popcorn we strung for the tree, I also think we put cranberries on them, and the *Reader's Digest* Christmas tree, took hours of folding the corners to make them. Then we sprayed them with fake snow. They were very cool I thought. It really does drive me crazy when I try to picture my life in Lakewood. If you can imagine having a whole bunch of tidbits of memories and trying to put it together like a puzzle. There were a lot of pieces, like our family going to Casa Bonita. Some of you have probably been there. The waterfall was so beautiful. Then you had the gorilla chasing people through the crowd and disappearing in the falls. They also gave you many other choices for dining rooms. I also remember a wishing well that talked to you when you tossed your fortunes inside on a prayer. I always liked the dining room in the mine's the best. These were very good times for me.

One day, we were up at the Red Rocks, I assume, just sightseeing. This is one of the times I don't remember but was told I found Finnegan up there, a Scottish terrier. "What kind of name is Finnegan", you say? Funny you should ask. *Star Trek*, one of my favorite episodes; they were on this planet where each crew member was living out their fantasy. Bonze was dreaming about *Alice in Wonderland* and was following a rabbit down a hole. I think Sulu was a knight saving a damsel. Jim was confronting his nemesis. His name was Finnegan. Just thought it was a cool name. I enjoyed it because he gets back at Finnegan. There are a lot of people I'd like to confront myself.

Finnegan became a big part of our life for many years. He was mixed colors of gray all over. He was a misfit of sorts. He was a lot like Benji. Finnegan at the time was sort of my dog. Later, it didn't turn out that way. Dad didn't like having a dog but became very attached to Finnegan. Later on in life, it was one of the few things that made my Dad cry. One big memory of Finnegan was teaching him to sic people. This became a game to the family. But we used me as the guinea pig. It was extremely funny to watch him growl and attack me. I would use a sock to protect my hand when we were doing this. He did sleep with me at first and was very friendly with me till Dad would say, "Sic him!" It was a lot of fun. Dad also taught him to play dead, or he would point an imaginary gun at him and go, "BANG!" and Finnegan would fall over. He did the stick-'em-up thing too. He was very protective over all of us. Finnegan was in a lot of our childhood pictures and in almost all of my memories.

Lakewood, Colorado, has always been this hidden memory for me, a frantic beginning for me to see my past. But it always evades me no matter how hard I try. I think the fact that we moved a lot makes it difficult to remember, and me not living around Lakewood to see the places I grew up I'm sure doesn't help. That's one reason it draws a blank for me. But then again, people in my life say that they remember growing up in other places. My love for the Rockies grew each time I thought about Colorado. Not to mention all the songs John Denver gave us. Colorado becomes a big part of my life later.

"Isn't it funny how things that happen in our childhood seem to make us who we are today?"

CHAPTER 4

Where Were You When Elvis Died?

Around this time, we moved out to Las Vegas. Now you have to realize that exact time frames escape me. So if this is wrong, Scot or Pam, at least you know about Vegas. That is really all that's important. My dad was managing a motel somewhere in Vegas. Now if you remember correctly, earlier we talked about my dad and his problem with being a thief. I also had said that it became more of an issue later. Well, this is one of the few memories that I have of this, shall we say, problem. Before I go on about our dad—"Dad, you know I love you very much, and I know you're watching over me right now but this was part of my life and I would never look down on you. You did what you had to do to watch over your family. You were not an evil person at all. You made me who I am today, and I will always remember you as a loving father. Amen. May God bless and keep you. God rest your soul."—

A few quick things about Vegas, like my map collection. You remember, Mom, the ones you threw away? Yes, I had a collection of maps. I always loved studying maps. Always wanted to travel a lot, which I think almost everyone feels that way a little. At the motel as, you can imagine, there were lots of travelers from all over. As people checked in or out, I'd ask people for any old maps they had. Back then, all the gas stations would give out maps for free, and some of you remember there was a time when mostly all we had were gas stations. I remember when they used to always service your car for you, it wasn't even necessary to get out of the car. Now it's all convenience stores, and they keep getting bigger and bigger. My collection had a map of each state according to the gas station. In my collection I had maps from fifty states in Mobil, fifty states in Chevron, fifty in Texaco, and so forth. I also got a hold of a lot of the *National Geographic* maps, like the ones that you would see in waiting areas. I was especially fond of the ocean floor maps. I realize how different that may be, but I really did enjoy those maps. Scot, Pam, and I got into the stuffed animals from Circus hotel. They were stacked all over the house.

Then one night, Dad and I were outside in a big rainstorm, setting up the pumps for the parking area. Later when we finished and were coming in from the cold, we saw Mom in tears, bawling like a big baby. Dad said, "What's wrong with you?" Mom, through lots of tears, whispered, "Elvis Presley just died." If you can imagine the shock, I started crying also, but I think it was just because I felt bad for Mom. It didn't affect Dad much. He always had this strong persona about him that was hard for anyone to crack. Mom, as you could imagine, was a big fan. He is also a favorite of mine too.

In all, I don't think we were there for long after that. I think it was a Sunday night after a big vacation weekend when the banks closed an extra day. But Dad got us up and put us in the car with all the candy and pop from the vending machines. For you younger generations, the managers from different organizations handled all the vending machines back then. And a lot of people paid cash, so we had a good amount of cash in the safe. And you know we had a lot of money to travel with. So we took off. We threw what little bit of clothes we could in the trunk and hit the road.

Things got a little sketchy for me during this time. We may have ended up in Texas for a while, but I do remember the Cherokee Chief was about this time. Some of you will remember the blue Cherokees. Well, while in Texas, my dad went to a dealership to test drive a Cherokee. He then made a copy of the key, came back home, and then went back later and picked up his new car. I remember when Scot and I were in the backseat and we pulled into the back of a store. Dad went in and came out running with a paper bag in his hand. He threw the bag and whatever was in it in the Dumpster out back, and we headed out of Texas. I remember Scot looking at me to say, "You thinking what I'm thinking?" I said, "Yeah, but I don't want to think about it." Then from the front Dad goes, "I think we'll take the back roads out of town then we can see the sights 'cause we're going on vacation, kids, so let's have some fun!" And we did have a lot of fun there. I think we zigzagged all the way to Minnesota. We would stop for days in nice motels that had pools and ate out a lot. It was great. I think this was the reason I love staying at motels. I think looking back, it's the only vacation I ever really had. Isn't it funny how things that happen in our childhood seem to make us who we are today, for instance the motels? I know what my dad did was wrong, but after the years of moving, it was nice spending so much time with my family. It was like we were in a time warp for that short period where we spent the time with each other and just had fun. So I'm depressed that kids don't get that. A lot of people out there don't get to take vacations and spend quality time together. If you ever get the chance, find a nice motel in the area and just take your kids and do something different. You won't regret doing it. Make sure it's got a pool.

"Jim, remember this if you don't remember anything else about this year. 'He who laughs last, laughs best.'"

CHAPTER 5

My Home Sweet Home and My First Nemesis

Finally we head of to Minnesota, my home sweet home. It was around 1977, sixth grade. Now you have to understand that even though I'm finally remembering sixth grade, it still is like dreams to me. People talk so vividly of there past. I'm sort of jealous of all of y'all. Well as I said, it is sixth grade now. We lived on 27th Avenue west, Above Fourth Street. We were only a block away from Lincoln Park which is the start of my adventurous side. We had skyline drive up 27th where I had my first real kiss since Amy. Elephant rock at the park and the waterfalls right next to the school. There also was a pavilion by the school too. We had a little penny candy store down on third that was very popular with the kids around there. I don't remember what Dad was doing for work, but we were surviving. The basement was kind of cold, but I vaguely remember wanting to have a bedroom down there, but I guess it was pretty nasty down there. We didn't have much of a yard, but the park made up for it. Actually, the alleys were fun too. Most of my time at first was spent in the allies around the house. Mom would say, "Stay in shouting distance." Don't remember having a lot of friends around there either. Well, there was a lot to do though, and we always had Finnegan. Don't forget the army men and such. It was kind of a hill at the house, so it gave you plenty of cool towns in the dirt.

School, as I said, was a block or two away at Lincoln Elementary. My teacher was Mr. Rodgers. Yes, it's true. "Rodgers." He wore glasses, and every so often he would play his guitar. "Rocky Mountain High" was one of his favorites. He had a thing for John Denver. Wonder who my favorite singer is? You guessed it, John Denver. At the time, I didn't know how much of an influence John Denver would have, but later it will be quite apparent. Now it's time to move along, this is also where I got my first nemesis or my Finnegan. Can't use last names in a book, so to be safe, we'll just call him Michal. Michal had a buddy too, Randy. I'm pretty sure this relationship with Michal started at the Boys and Girls Club on Second and 27th. Scot and I spent a lot of time there. It was a blast until Michal ruined it.

You all know how cruel kids can be; well, Michal was worse. Never did find out why he was like that so much. I guess we will never know why anyone would be cruel. He was constantly calling me stupid, among other things. I'm sure you can think of some of the other colorful words, but I'd like to make this book G rated though. It was a constant pushing and shoving. I was scared to death of him and Randy, his best friend. It was bad enough to have nightmares that kept going for a long time. I would go around the block if I saw him first outside, but of course, he was in my class. Have y'all ever seen the movie *Bullies*? It was like that I guess. No one will ever know the reason behind people like Michal. My thought is he was raised that way. I think the majority of the problems in life start at home. In fact I would venture to say, it all starts at home. So I hate to think what it's like to be raised by a nanny or day care. No wonder kids these days are so apathetic. Wisdom and intelligence start at home. Your parents can make you feel proud of yourself and confident right from the start. That confidence can help you learn so much faster and the wisdom to see everything around you so you can learn from your experience. My guess is Michal didn't get a lot of these things.

A defining moment in my life happened in class one day. I wasn't a smart kid in class, but I got by. One day Michal and his buddies were being themselves and calling me stupid among other things. Then Mr. Rodgers took action and called me and the boys up to the front of the class. Rodgers said, "Michal, you must be a great judge of character to be calling Jim stupid all the time. You must be very wise to know how smart Jim is without looking at his report cards. Unless, of course, Jim showed you his report cards. Jim, did you show them your report cards?" I just kind of nodded no with a face full of tears. "Well, Jim says he didn't show you his. Did you two break into my drawers to see them, Michal?" Michal hesitated before he answered. "Everybody knows that he is stupid, he said. "Look, all he's doing is crying." This is peer pressure kicking in. The whole class slowly agreed with Michal. Mr. Rodgers turned to me at this point and asked me, "Do you agree with them?" I just stood there, scared to death and thinking about what was going to happen after school. I'd have to go two blocks up and sneak to my own house. But Rodgers caught me midthought. "Don't listen to these people. They're not your judge and jury. If you listen to them, you'll just be another statistic. No one can judge your wisdom and intelligence but you and God. I'm not God. Your a smart kid and don't let them push you around like that." At that moment, old Michal started laughing again. "You're so much smarter than Jim is, aren't you, Michal?" Rodgers upped his tone at this time. "Let's just see. Should we look at the report cards?" Michal just got the smart-alecky tone. "I know I'm smarter than that baby. All he does—" Rodgers cuts him off. "Let's just see."

Michal is looking a little uneasy at this point. Me? I'm looking around the room, seeing everyone dumbfounded by this whole thing but still on Michal's side. Of course remember they're all afraid of him. A few minutes later, after fiddling through his files, he pulled out three report cards. "Well, Michal, I see a few Fs here. Oh, and two Ds. But all is good you got a C in gym. It would have been an A if you would have showed up with your PT gear a few more times. Randy, yours is almost the same, but you got a B in home ec. Good job. What about Jim? Great job, it looks like a C average, but a good effort. Michal ... Randy ... do you two have anything to say for yourselves?" They just stood there. Everyone got quiet. Rodgers turned to me and said in a lighter tone, hand on my shoulder, "Jim, remember this if you don't remember anything else about this year. 'He who laughs last, laughs best.'" Then as he smiled at me, he looked away and got Michal's attention. "Did you understand that?" Michal just stared and said nothing. A short pause and Rodgers said. "That's what I thought."

From that point on, I felt a lot better, but it didn't stop Michal yet. That day he left me alone. But it didn't take long to slowly forget that day, and he started up again with his normal regimen of bullying me. Finally one day I was leaving the boys' club, and he and Randy cornered me between Second and Third in the alley. I think it might have been fear that took over. They were punching, pushing, and I snapped. It must have looked funny when I think back on it. I just started flailing out at both of them. They both got in defensive position, and I saw them both bleeding. My knuckles were hurting later so I must have gotten some good hits in. But the sad part is when I saw the chance, I ran like hell. I could have finished them real good right then. But oh well. In school the next day they both looked like a train hit them; they made up excuses for there black eyes and fat lips. I didn't say anything, and we moved soon after that, so it ended in the alley for me. I know what some of you are thinking. "Why did you stop?" I say, "Why keep going?" I made my point. I was tired of those guys pushing me around. But I don't need to prove myself to no one, especially these guys. God or whatever it is for you will be my judge and my jury. It wasn't what Michal and Randy thought of me. Including what y'all think for that matter. During this whole time, in the back of my mind, I hoped what Mr. Rodgers was right about me laughing last. This is a book, so I'll jump ahead for a moment to prove my point.

I am, and always will be, a Marine. Semper fi to y'all out there. When I got home from boot camp, I was in my Charlies. (Marines' everyday wears outside of base. Consisted of short-sleeved khaki shirt and wool dress slacks.) That's not to say anything about my physique, which we're talking six packs, buffed out, and tan was second to none. Very clean cut and walking proud. I just had to go see my old friend Michal. Yes this is true. My dad let me drive this nice older model car. Not sure what kind (sorry, car buffs). As I stood at the door waiting to speak to my childhood Nemesis, my thought's drifted to the story I told you of Captain James T. Kirk, from the episode with Finnegan, I'm sure y'all remember my dog Finnegan? My initial thought was to bring him out and kick his butt. Then I remembered Mr. Rodgers saying "He who laughs last laughs best." My mind changed quickly as I waited there. I knew at this point that I was a better man than him.

I caught myself looking at his yard right about then. It was torn up furniture on the porch, yard that needed TLC very badly and a chain for their dog, which had worn the grass in a circle. Finally I was startled by an older lady with a cigarette in her mouth, and a musty moldy smell came from the house. While the dog was barking, I told her I wished to speak to Michal. I think the dog was a Rottweiler. She called for him, and I stepped back to my car. When I first saw him peering through an old screen door, I saw him in that scraggly-looking hair that had the matted look to it. Y'all remember the long hair of the '80s, don't you? As he stepped out, all he could say was "Yea, who are you?" He just stood there at first with a smug look. "Well, we were in the sixth grade together, and I had an urge to look you up. Do you remember my face?" He squinted a bit and slowly, the smug face went away. "No," he said. "But that was along time ago. Did we hang out? You look sort of familiar." I stepped toward him a bit, and he adjusted a little, and I said, "No, you chased me a lot though and had a lot to say about me. But we never hung out. I'm Jim from Mr. Rodgers's class, now do you remember me?" Now he had that grin like a smile on his face that I remembered so well. "Oh yeah, you were such a dork back then, how's it been." You could tell he was thinking it was a good idea to be nice to this Marine standing in front of him. I stepped forward within five feet or so as I saw the smile leave his face again. He also seemed to adjust a bit now like fidgeting, not knowing what I'd do. I leaned a bit forward and almost whispered, "He who laughs last laughs best, and Michal, I'll be laughing from now on. Thank you." As I stuck my hand out to shake his, he flinched. He slowly took my hand, and this was the first time I understood how important a firm handshake could be. His hand felt limp and clammy. I could see fear and confusion in his face. As I turned to walk away, I said, "I see you still don't get it." Thank you, Mr. Rodgers, for giving a poor kid like me that wonderful feeling. I will never forget that till the day I die. So you see, things do work out in time. This was definitely a defining moment for me. It, in a sense, gave me strength.

That's enough of the intense stuff; for now it's time to go back to some of the lighter notes in my life from this time frame. Living at Lincoln Park was a lot of fun. Sledding down the waterfalls in the winter was a blast. See, the waterfalls over the centuries at Lincoln Park had made these big rocks very smooth. During the summer I'd go wading down the river a lot. Which became one of my favorite pastimes later. There was a spot by this little bridge that was pretty deep too. This spot had a small waterfall that had made a sink hole. I never got bold enough to jump from the cliff to it. To be honest, I looked recently and it's a real small jump, but it was big for a twelve-year-old. Remember I mentioned elephant rock earlier. Scot and I would play games up there with Pam. What a neat place. Great for playing *Star Trek*, which was our game for obvious reasons like Jim and Scot: Jim Kirk and Scot the engineer, then Pam was always the girl in trouble that we had to save. Elephant rock always represented some weird formation on another planet. I also had two good friends that I remember a bit. Chris and Crystal, twins in my class. They were always nice to me. They were also one of the few that came to my birthday.

A lot of the time Scot was gone with Rodney our cousin who lived up 27th. That was my Aunt Gloria's youngest. There were four of them: Mary, Debbie, Betty Joe, and Rodney. They were in and out of our lives a lot. At that time, all I can remember is the wooden spoon. My parents would go do something with Aunt Gloria and her husband Larry. Mary was the oldest of us kids by a good amount. Debbie and Betty Joe were my age, and Scot and Rodney were a year younger. I typically wouldn't play with Scot and Rodney, so I would try to hang out with the older kids. When I did that, Mary just hit me with a wooden spoon and told me to go to bed with the younger kids. My argument with this was me and Betty Joe were the same age. Looking back now, Betty Joe was much more mature than me and was allowed to stay downstairs. As you can imagine, I didn't get along too well with Mary.

Oh yeah, my first kiss, in which it's hard to consider Amy for this precious moment in my life due to the fact we had no idea what we were doing at that time in our lives. I have to give that moment to a girl named Tina. Don't remember a whole lot about her, but that she, to me, was so pretty. I couldn't believe she had any interest in me. I'll tell you what though, I have a good memory of that kiss. Somehow, one weekend she and I had decided to go up by Skyline for a walk. I was so nervous about this I couldn't stop shaking, not to mention sleep the night before. I probably brushed my teeth five times getting ready for this day. I was very particular about where we sat down so it could be a perfect situation. It had to be somewhere we could look over beautiful Duluth. The ground behind her had to be perfectly smooth to make sure she wouldn't get hurt while we were *making out*. Above all, it had to be beautiful scenery all around us. I also wanted it to be very secluded so there were no distractions. This was going to be magic. I was slowly putting my hand behind here in that old familiar stretch move. Then to make it look even more natural, I leaned back on both arms to look at the clouds and said, "Wow, they look cool today, huh?" "Sure are pretty," she said. Of course I finally said something perfect, and it was truly an accident. "Yes, you sure are." And she gave me that perfect blush and smile as she looked at me. The perfect moment and oh my God, I missed it. I dragged it on and was beating myself up inside for missing my moment. Then I nervously fidgeted with the ground behind her, and in an awkward glance she gave me, I finally made my move. Then in all the excitement, it was way too fast; our teeth pounded together, and for an awkward moment, we smiled at each other then started kissing. "Oh my God," I'm thinking. I'm actually kissing Tina. I did finally lay her on the smoothed-out ground behind her. But never took it further than a nice long kiss. It was a wonderful long kiss, which we both could feel every inch of our lips and the tenderness in each other's heart. I'm not sure what happened later with her. I know at one point we moved to Proctor. Not to mention it was coming close to the end of our summer romance. She was very nice to me, and I'll always remember Tina who had a wonderful moment with me up there on Skyline Drive. Thank you, Tina, You have my first kiss.

One other nice memory has to be the field trips we took in Rodgers's class. He opened my eyes to the absolute serenity of nature. It is my strength. Don't worry, I'm not going to go flower child on you. I do love nature and do believe in its strength. Rodgers also gave me the wonderment of nature and all of its creatures. We did the plaster footprints, studied the trees, and learned some of the plants. But as you're slowly starting to see, I don't look at the technical side of things. Rodgers used some of John Denver words as one of his teachings when it came to some of this. I probably learned more from the words in the songs than most of the kids out there. (Especially Michal.) John Denver became a big part of my motivation in life as time went on. "Rhymes and Reasons," at the time, was my favorite

Everyone deals with problems in their life. A lot of times, as the song says, you need to stop and look at the children and the flowers too just to escape the troubles of your day. We all do truly struggle at times, don't forget to open your eyes once in a while and just enjoy life. Don't let yourself get caught up in the sadness. Don't lose you're self in the rhymes and the reasons. Follow the rainbow or catch the winds in your heart. Fill your soul with the laughter and the loveliness.

It's a sense of escape, freedom, reflection, exploration, and productivity all in your control like an extension of yourself.

CHAPTER 6

A Lot of Firsts in Proctor

Now we will move on to Proctor. There are only a few things in Proctor that stick out, like my first job, sledding at the golf course, my first drink, a love for animals, and racing. First job, I would have to separate into my first work and first real job. First work was a junkyard or something like that. I just remember picking up rocks in the field. It was only for a short time and wasn't too exciting at all. If my memory serves me right, I walked by the driving range on my way home and asked them what they were hiring for. Soon after, I started my first real job which was at a driving range. We had these metal tubs and just walked around picking up golf balls. There was hard rubber on the bottom with slits that kept the balls from falling out once you put them in. I do especially remember my first earnings. I'm sure you can imagine being from a fairly poor family; we didn't get a lot of steak when I was young. So steak was a big thing for me, and they always had a barbecue going at work during lunch. So I ran to the grocery store and got the biggest steak I could find. Didn't know what a round steak was, but it was big. Ran straight back to the golf range and cooked my first steak. I put way too much salt and it was tough as wood but I ate it proudly. I got much better at picking out a good steak later. Then every day on my way home I would stop at Bridgman's and have a mint chocolate shake. Man, was that great, and chocolate chip is still my favorite ice cream. Later that summer I also got a chance to drive the tractor and pull the cage around. I was pretty proud of myself that day.

In retrospect, I still love a good tractor and driving in general. Driving, especially at that age, was exhilarating to say the least. It's a sense of escape, freedom, reflection, exploration, and productivity all in your control like an extension of yourself. "Jim, you didn't get all that from a thirteen-year-old on a tractor." No I didn't. Think about why I'm writing this all down. It's a reflection of my life and my thoughts. That's just what driving is to me now. Then, at thirteen, it was excitement at first, of course. As the time went on, it became a place to reflect, then an escape, can't forget the feeling of freedom, and I was doing something productive which makes me feel good. Don't forget to open your eyes and explore your surroundings. Next time you're stuck in traffic, don't stress out so easily, just reflect and explore. You will be surprised what you see around you. Some will be reflecting like you. Can't forget the road rage you see in their faces. The makeup artist, the people not living in the moment on the cell phone, karaoke gone wild, parents yelling at their kids in back, people looking at their watch totally stressed, and that's not to mention the landscape around you. I hope you get the point now, its life that you see. The world hasn't stopped because you're in a traffic jam. If you are just late for work, you knew this would happen and could have left a little early. Enjoy the ride and give yourself time to reflect while you drive whatever it is that you drive. Ever hear the song "Amarillo Sky"? If you haven't, find it and you'll see my point. "Lord, I never complain and I never ask why. Please don't let my dreams run dry, underneath this Amarillo sky." Just take your vehicle another round and enjoy.

A few times I remember going up to the golf course to go sledding. Boy, was that a long run. We always set up a few jumps on our path down. Them old metal sleds were almost a dangerous fast. I'm not sure you can still get them. I haven't seen one in a long time. My favorite sled was the long toboggan. I almost lost a leg sledding down a small trail close to my house. I was sledding close to the trees one time and saw what looked like a jump so I steered towards it. Well as you can imagine it wasn't a jump, it was a tree fallen down that had branches sticking out. One of the branches caught my right pant leg, then it pulled me of my sled, and it made me crash big time. Now you have to believe it was a cool crash but that branch was thick and could've ripped way into the meat of my leg. Of course I didn't think that way myself; it was just a cool crash, as I said before. Looking back though, my mother was right, it could've been a lot worse. Kids do the silliest things.

Proctor Speedway, which was only a few blocks from our house by the fairgrounds, could get a little loud at times. I did get in a few times. That was a lot of fun for a seventh grader. Picking out a car and screaming for them as they passed another car. The nose was deafening but way cool. Then of course, there were the derbies which were the best for a young kid. Watching cars beat on each other for real and not just my matchbox cars. Of course as an adult I still love to watch derbies. What a kick in the pants. It's just like I said before about driving, "escape and freedom."

Also one time, at the fairgrounds by the track, I went to a horse show. I think my mom gave me a 110-film camera to take pictures or she took them. Don't remember but do remember having some cool pictures of a white stallion that I kept for a long while. I won a brass figure of a horse there too from one of the games. I've lost that, but I've seen others like that one during my life. You remember the games I told you about as a kid? Playing with cars and army men; I have to add horses to that. I got into horses a lot around this time. Never believed I'd ever ride one though. Wouldn't that be an exploration to ride all over the landscape? Freedom would be the key to riding a horse, I think.

There is more to mention about my childhood, but this book is not just childhood memories. What I hope you are beginning to see is how much the little things in our life that will affect our future and the future of everyone we have contact with. What we do and say affect all of it. For instance, my dad would cut his over easy eggs with a butter knife after putting salt and pepper on them. I still do that to this day. I always eat after everyone around me just like my father did. The way we treat people reflects how we were treated when we were young also. It all matters so much. You'll see that more and more as we go on. If people around you say what everything is going to be like, you know what, then you'll believe that this is the way it will be. If they call you stupid enough you will believe it. We are Americans! We have our freedom. We must believe that. We need to take care of ourselves and help thy neighbor. You know, "do onto others as you'd have them do to you." Remember the movie *Pay it Forward*? Great but very sad. Someday, in our life, we all need help. A little kindness can go a long way. I'm sure I read somewhere your kindness will be paid back tenfold. I'm pretty sure it's been said many times. People talk about it all the time but when it comes down to sacrifice, a lot of people just turn the cheek. Is that any of you out there reading this? You reap the seeds you sow I guess.

"Being drunk made me feel lonely and out of control. I guess for some that works, but me, it hurts too much."

CHAPTER 7

Scary Times that We All Go through and Starting My Singing

Scary times; peer pressure, becoming teenagers, girls, finding yourself, body changes, and so much more. Scary times, but it can be so much fun. Seventh grade is a bit of a blur though. Proctor doesn't hold much in my memories. The house we were in was smaller but a lot nicer then 27th. My room was actually, I think, the furnace or something. Scot and Pam actually slept in the living room. We had a pretty good-sized backyard with a shed. I became friends with our neighbor behind us in the alley. I got drunk for the first time back there in the alley. It was Boone's Farm Strawberry. I was staying over, and we put up tents in his backyard. Somehow after we had been drinking a while, he got caught and was told to go inside then I was left out there alone. They told me to just go home. There wasn't any way in the world that was going to happen. "That would be suicide for me." I was scared to death to let my father find out, so I stayed in the tent. As the night went on, I felt sick but always hated throwing up. Well, I thought if I held my neck real tight on the pillow that I wouldn't get sick. But I never got sick that night. Having the fear and lost feeling when you're drunk may in some way have stopped me from being an alcoholic. Being drunk made me feel lonely and out of control. I guess for some that works, but me, it hurts too much. Alcohol has never been a big thing for me. A few times I got into it, but it never stuck, thank God. Seeing it in my dad and others kept me away from drinking more than anything and the being-sick-later part was a close second.

During this time I managed to get in the Duluth Boys Choir. Don't remember trying out but I did it. I got my first acting bug here. Most people said I had a great voice and missed my calling. I just love to sing and be in front of a crowd. Don't know if Mom still has it but we made a tape a long time ago where we all sung on it. Scot even did "Rhinestone Cowboy." I was a corny performer, but it was fun making the tape. I think I did "Crying from Roy Orbison" on the tape. While in the boy's choir, I had to take a bus downtown each day for rehearsal. There was a small store by there that I'd go steal a box of red-hots once in a while and thankfully after a while, I finally got caught. *Oh my god*, was I scared! They took me to this office and put handcuffs on me. After a time they sent this guy who looked like a real cop inside to sort off interrogate me. They must have drilled me for an hour. They finally told me they would send me home, but I talked them into sending me on my regular bus line and then promised I would tell my parents what happened when I got home. Yeah, right! There was no way they were going to know. I think I was in my twenties when they found out. Getting caught right of hand I'm sure was a good thing for me, especially when you consider my past history with my father's background. I can't say I never stole again, but it didn't escalate into a bad thing. My personal opinion is that a lot of poor people at one time or another has been tempted to steal. I can't really explain my thoughts at the time, but that feeling of never having the money to get even the simplest things can lead you to it. It doesn't make people bad, but it's not good. They are the lazy, poor, and just generally bad that I would never forgive. Just don't jump to conclusion on some people.

For people out there reading this I want to explain this a bit more. Crime is crime, I realize this. I don't want this to sound like a mistake, but for some situations, people need to understand better what I'm trying to say. In my life I have become a prude to a certain extent. I drive the speed limit. I follow the laws of mankind. Stealing is a terrible thing. If each person that can would just lift a hand to other people, I feel that would help people that are struggling. When people see problem kids, they just sell them of as bad people and kick them to the side. A good percentage of the problems are their parents. Instead of helping the family or the kid himself, we just categorize the child; give them to the system, and most of the time they get worse. Talk to the child; scare them if you have the time and ability, and if you know the parents, try to help fix the problem. We are not the judge and jury for these kids. Some of these people are just flat out bad. I do understand that, but please don't be too quick to judge or generalize as I said before. Yes, some of them are just struggling and don't know where to turn. I don't mean that they have an excuse to do what they want. But be careful not to make it worse for the kids. "What does all this have to do with your title, Jim?" Well funny you should ask. In some ways, it's the point that a lot of people judge people. We forget to look past what the problem is and just judge them right off. People do the same thing with judging someone's wisdom and intelligence. Some of these people that become career thieves could've been helped at a young age. Don't rush to judge. Show them the way or dog them to scare it out of them. I know it scared the pants off me.

Now back to the choir that I started out with earlier. Duluth boys' choir was a lot of fun. I really do love to sing. Remember this all started with Mr. Rodgers. My voice was still in a developing stage, but I excelled in it. I had found something people really liked in me. Even got to be the Tin Man at one of the concerts; well, at least I thought that was great tell I passed out a few times from the heat in that getup. We did a *Wizard of Oz* sketch. I actually did pretty well with the kids there because they didn't know my status back in my neighborhood. It wasn't bad for me in Proctor either. But we were only there for a short time, so I guess they didn't get much time to figure out how easy picking on me was. Thinking back, I think the Costello and Jerry Lewis thing was kind of paying of since they didn't know me from the past. To them I was sort of a class goof instead. Singing just made me feel alive. I think back and feel it was the first thing I felt confident in. Music will become a huge part of my live. I know that's true to a lot of people. But as you'll see later, it was more of a lifesaver to me. Towards the end of that year though, my voice began to change. If you can imagine, for someone who enjoyed singing that really sucked. Soon later though we moved out of Proctor to what I think of as my best childhood memories.

"The simple things are what make it all worth it, like a good cup of coffee, a child's smile, the sound of a loon, the zipper on a tent, all such wonderful feelings."

CHAPTER 8

Best Part of My Childhood Living in the Country

Hemlock Drive, Horseshoe Lake, and all those trails was my paradise. We were out in the middle of nowhere, nearest neighbor was a half mile away; the only store near us was a bar, and I loved it. Our trailer was very small, but outside was a huge playground. A lot of people I've met, over the years, didn't like living in the country, but I was in my own element. It's like that serene place away from reality that you go to when you're down. We all have something like that; mine just happened to be real. I had a lake. We lived at the end of a long dirt road that only one car could fit down. As you drove down the driveway, it was like a tunnel of trees during the peak period of spring. If there was no moon, you could tell you were on the road by looking up to the sky using the stars and seeing a small opening through the trees. There was one turn off towards Jeff and Glens place, which took you over to the lake. You continued down the narrow street, and as you reached the end, all you saw was trees at first. Then on your left it would come into view. It was an older mobile home. We had a big yard that was shaped like a big square. As you looked at the house, to your left was a very old garage. It was usually empty. Don't really remember the inside of the garage. I kind of remember hiding from my dad a few times till he would always check there first. To the right there was a small shed that was always locked. There were also, I think, two big trees we could climb and play by. There was also the weirdest thing in the middle of the yard. Two big pipes connected twice towards the top. The bottom pipe was a little thinner and had a big bend in it. Dad said the guy before us tried using a pulley system to pull an engine and it bent it. In the driveway we had a little zigzag fence in front of the two trees.

The house itself was white. We had like a mudroom on the porch before you got to the entrance of the trailer. I remember after some of the bigger snowstorms, we had to go out the back to shovel because whoever built the porch made the screen open out. The entrance to the house was the living area, which included the kitchen and dining room. A very small hallway led you to Pam and my parents' room. The bathroom was between them. Then the back door of the trailer actually led into a small building, which was me and Scots' domain. It was pretty small, but it was ours. The beginning was a small room the length of the building. Me and Scot had our own rooms that were partitioned by a very thin sheet of paneling. My room had an old double sink for a laundry area. I also had a nice tree just out my window. Very small but cozy. On top of the sinks I had done my first woodwork and made some shelves then covered them with some nice towels, which all turned out pretty good for a teenager. It was much better than having a couple of big sinks in your bedroom.

We didn't have a "backyard," per say. Towards the so-called backyard though we did have a small basement, which was only under a small portion off the trailer. Also towards the back were an old van and the chicken coops. These also have some fun stories. The old van was riddled with a few bullet holes at first, and then I got a hold of dad's .22. For the longest time I couldn't figure out how dad caught me so much when I shot the van till I looked closer and you could tell there were new holes because the paint around them were plain metal and not rusted. Also in the back there was a small trail that only my siblings and I could find. If you looked hard enough, there were small trails all over out there. At the end of the road was the start of the main trails. These would lead you towards the lake and one going towards an old gravel pit. In general it was like my secret paths to anywhere I wanted to go. To a certain extent, I was always a secluded person. So when we got to Hemlock, I was so happy to find a bit of serenity. If you think back to sixth grade, that is where nature started to be a big part of me. Now here I was in a wonderful place, and it was a dream come true.

Moving to the country was like having my very own playground. Horseshoe Lake was a small lake that didn't have enough freshwater flowing through to keep fish alive. We did have bullheads, but that was all I ever saw there. It was very pretty until you went snorkeling. The bottom of the lake was just muck. Trust me, I went down there once. The place we all hung out was the only public beach on Horseshoe. It was on the south side of the lake. North side was just forest. You had to go through swamp to get there. West side had a few cabins, and the east side just had an old hunting cabin. The trails I told you about, by our house, gave you many different entrances to the main road by the lake. We typically would go by Jeff and Glens place to see if they were going to the lake. We got along with Jeff much better then Glen but he'd see us and come out to play. Glen was a bit of a trouble maker. I can't remember exactly why but I remember a few beatings because of him. Jeff wasn't an angel but he was a good friend. Jeff was my intro to being a red neck and I looked up to him. So I guess it's all Jeff's fault that I'm a red neck now, and proud of it. He was really good with mechanical stuff and just flat out looked the part. Never talked about it but I'm sure he was a Dale Earnhardt fan. NASCAR later becomes one of my religions. We went through the bike years around Jeff. His dad knew a bit about welding and helped us with cool spokes for are hot rod bikes.

Speaking of bikes, one year, Dad got us a pickup full of bike parts to make bikes. That was a great time. Bikes were very important to kids that live in the country. If I remember correctly, we were able to make six bikes. One of them was a big three-speed. Scot and I would take them to the gravel pit all the time. At one time I remember setting up a ramp into a water hole that was fun. We used the same bike for that. I mentioned the three-speed because I still have a scar from that bike. I was headed to the lake going down a little hill by Jeff's place and lost control. It was a nasty fall. My left leg still has a white spot from that. I messed it up pretty good on the gravel road while heading to the lake. No hospital time or anything. Remember what I talked about earlier about being on a vehicle? That's what having a bike was too. I could see and do so much with the bikes. They became my escape out there for sure. I did a lot of exploring on that three-speed bike, and it definitely expanded my paradise.

Having bikes out there in Ganesen opened a lot of doors for us kids. Some of that fun was up by Sportsman's. There wasn't a lot of concrete around, so Sportsman's became a hangout at times. The soda cans were still made of metal so we could throw them and make sparks. I know, it's weird, but it was fun. I threw one towards the trees and it stuck in the tree. I kept trying to do it again but failed. By the way, when I came back the first time after like twenty or twenty-three years, yes, it was still in the tree. It had grown around the metal. Needless to say, there were many afternoons riding bikes all around that lake.

Swimming during the summer was also a big part of living up there. Our whole summer was at the lake at times. We took every big rock we could find and stacked it out a ways from shore. We finally got the stack just inches from the top so we could use it as a cool jump. We were pretty proud of that jump, and it made for a lot of fun times out there. Snorkeling for hours on end was great; till a bullhead scared the daylights out of you. We also had plenty of crawdads and of course leeches. We always kept salt with us which we could use to take care of them. For y'all that are creeping out about this, you get used to it after a while. I have great memories of that lake. Oh, and the free tackle. We'd find tackle all over. Spent hours just looking for tackle. Listening to the loons all day just made it perfect. Always been one of my favorite sounds. I do believe I heard a wolf out there one time. I guess some would argue that, but I'm almost positive I heard him. Could you imagine a Loon singing in the background with the crystal clear lake and aurora borealis, which would be a moment to keep forever? I did see this picture one time. It was like a dream, and so . . . so . . . beautiful. I've always had a thing for lakes since then. A few times I camped out there. The sound of the zipper on the tent early in the morning is a sound that always gets me. I know that may sound strange, but it is a sound I'll always remember. Told you I was kind of weird. It's the little things in life that make it wonderful. Kids, don't forget the little things. They can save your life at times.

When things are really tough, just take a second and step back. A simple memory can cure many things. Guys, here is an idea for you next time you feel bad. Take a deep breath and walk around the house and look at things from your past. It could be anything. Something you bought or something given to you, maybe a trinket you made. Then remember the moment you acquired it. What was on your mind? How did you feel that day? Then trust me, it will fill your heart and show you "the simple things in life." Don't be satisfied with the mundane. Please don't let yourself get caught up with the wild chaos of life. The simple things are what make it all worth it, like a good cup of coffee, a child's smile, the sound of a loon, the zipper on a tent, all such wonderful feelings. Don't forget these things. A lot of people do. The basics are like the roots of a tree, they need to be strong enough to handle all the problems we face. I know it's from a movie or something, but it's very true in this case. I'm sure you've heard the saying that "love conquers all," this is a basic knowledge. A simple thing in life like love can make everything easier. Keep these simple things in your heart and make your soul stronger than anything around you, or anyone. Like Peter Pan said, "Find your happy thought." Or you could say, like Happy Gilmore says, "Your happy place."

Living way out there in Ganesen was very magical to me. Ever since then I judged a place's beauty from that home at the end of Hemlock Drive. Have you ever just sat and listened to the sound of the trees blowing in the wind? Not to sound too corny, but it was like symphonies of sounds out there by our house. It was mesmerizing to me. It was so easy to just lie there on the ground and just dream all day long. Serenity was right there in my own yard. I can still close my eyes and see that place to this day. It really wasn't much too look at, but it was home. I can see the fence that we built there in the driveway just for aesthetics. Zigzag of timbers just in front of the two big trees. The grass would grow so fast each year. So the fact that I love the smell of freshly mown grass, it was a good thing. It was like walls of trees around a square that surrounded the house. Nothing except our home was in that little square. You couldn't even see anything but the trees around the house. It was, simply put, our own little paradise. At night I would lie on my back and just stare at the stars, which were so bright you could see the Milky Way like a cloud in the sky. Here is something for you guys to try. On a clear night, find a quiet spot and lie on your back and stare up at the sky. Now pick out a star and just focus on that star. What you're trying to do is make that star the only clear thing in your mind. You will be surprised how much time will fly. It is very relaxing.

Now it's time for the bear story. "Lions, tigers, and bears, oh my." It was spring or summer, not that it matters. We were sitting at the house doing whatever when the dogs started going crazy. I forgot to tell you about my dog Champ. Champ was truly my dog. He went everywhere with me. So the dogs are freaking out, so finally we look outside, and there is a black bear playing with our snowmobile. Man, was I mad. He was ripping the set to shreds. Then Dad ran to the door and started yelling at the dogs to get in the house. Finnegan ran in pretty quick, but Champ was going to protect us. Then Dad got real smart and ran outside, yelling at the bear, trying to scare him away. I've never seen my dad run so fast to get back in the house. He took the three steps to the porch in one step. The stupid bear on the other hand lost his footing coming up the steps and fell by the door. As he recovered, he ripped the screen and I guess got tired of that and went back down and started back in the yard.

"Jim, go get the guns!" Dad said to me in a hurry. *Oh sure, that will work,* I'm thinking, obviously being sarcastic. A twenty-one-shot .22 rifles and my .410 shotgun. As we finally headed outside with our guns, he was at the side of the woods looking at us, *POP!* Dad shot a round at him and fired three or so more at him. *POP.* We were thinking later on that Dad hit him then, but the bear started running at us, probably really upset now. Scared to death, Dad yelled, "Get back in," just as I squeezed a round—*POW.* Then we ran back in the mudroom and stayed there for a few minutes till we didn't see him. Mom said, from in the house, "He ran into the woods." We both reloaded and headed to the woods. I have to laugh because we probably looked like Elmer Fud. Actually we probably looked like two idiots stalking towards the woods after a big bear with a .22 and a .410. This was when it started getting even funnier. All we could hear was this bear growling real loud most of the time. I must have shot ten stumps in fear that the bear was sitting there waiting for us. No wonder hunters have accidents while hunting. "Is that him?" we would whisper. *Bang.* "Guess not." I'm glad nobody saw us, I'm sure we looked real smart out there shooting stumps.

Thirty minutes or so later, we finally found our prey. Still scared to death, Dad said, "Shoot him in the head." *BANG.* Now Dad was thinking bear meat for supper. "Will have to drag him to the basement," Dad said. "We'll clean him up in there." We started to drag him to the house out of the woods. This, for me, was the scariest moment of all. I didn't know anything about rigor mortis setting in and making them jerk around. I must have jumped up five feet at least when his leg jerked. As we were getting to the house, I had the hind legs, and they had a huge scare on one side. "Dad, what is this scar?" We stopped just out side the basement. "wow," he said, looking at it. "I think he is rabid." The scar was like a tear with pus coming out. It was at this point that Dad went to the house to talk to Mom about the bear. Later he came out and said, "We're just going to bury him, we're not going to take the chance of us getting sick." So that was what we did. We cut a few of the claws, which I later made into a necklace. I'm not sure what happened to the necklace though. People, please don't think badly of us. We were scared and didn't know what to do. Normally, bears would always run off when you scared them. This bear wasn't leaving our area. We were afraid for us and our animals. I do feel as if we probably put him out of his misery. That scar was really nasty. Of course I was the one who had to dig the hole. It would've been nice to get help, but I guess it didn't matter, he was buried.

We did have some very poor times for a while there in my little paradise. So we did try a rabbit a few times. None of us really got used to the taste though. Then Dad went on this kick about looking for food outside like roots and other things he could find. See, he bought this book about different plants in the North Country that you could eat. Ever tried fried dandelions? I have. They're OK if you're starving, which we were. We ate some interesting things during that time.

We also tried chickens for a time. We had a lot of eggs there for a while, but in November when it got real cold, we lost all the chickens. For some reason or another, we never tried that again. See Dad was just not the country boy. He liked the city and open fields of Texas. We were very secluded out there. I'm sure a big part of him enjoyed it though. Later you'll see they didn't stay long after I left. The country life suited me very well indeed. I didn't realize that till later.

Winter was the worst time for us out in the country. Like I told you before, Scot and I lived in a building built on the side of the house. It was very small and not very well insulated. The first year was probably the worst because we didn't have as much firewood as we needed. Scot and I had to keep up with bringing firewood in for the day. Which as some of you know is hard work. Remember the story of families having to exercise to survive? There is an example for you. Dad taught us well how to start fires and keep them going. See, in the trailer though it had propane and always ran. I used to get mad at Pam because she'd always take her nightgown and cover the opening to the hot air flow and hog the air. I have very warm blood though, so it takes a lot to get me cold. Scot would sleep in the living room a lot if the fire wasn't going. But me, I just covered up good and stayed in my own bed. Just throw the covers over my head and breathe real heavy for a while and I'd be warm. For a long time, I had a broken window with cold air flowing in my room. I was too afraid to tell Dad because I knew that was going to be a beating. Yes, a beating, which I received a lot. I'm not going into that just yet, but Dad was very physical with me. Not in the way you might be thinking. My Dad was never that way. Let's just say, "Go get a stick" was something I heard a few times. So my room got really cold.

That wasn't too hard of a thing compared to the water freezing in the winter. That happened every year as far as I know. No water, no bath, no toilet, and yes, no septic. Sounds fun, doesn't it? "How did you get water, Jim?" Well, that was a job and a half, I tell you. Frank, my friend up the street or trail as it was, he didn't have indoor plumbing. All he had outside was one of them old hand pumps. He didn't have electricity either, so there was no electric pump. It was all done by hand. We took a bunch of gallon jugs up to Frank's and pump water in them, and then drag them home. We had a few big pots and ever so often, mom would heat up water for baths. Yes, we had to share the water. Remember, no septic either. We would have to take the water outside in buckets.

Our toilet was a five-gallon bucket with pine soil in it. When it was full, Mom and Dad would make me take it to the woods to dump. All this was through the snow, mind you. Can't tell you how difficult that was, but I assure you, it sometimes would spill as I clamored through the snow. But you know something; it truly didn't bother me as much as you're thinking. It was something you just did to survive. Like I said before about the way the pioneers had to live. Or even my grandparents and yours. That's just the way it is and always will be. Taking care of your own family in our time has become just a burden to some people. That is so sad when you think about it. It's so true though, isn't it? Surviving is a burden to people now. It's like they still want someone to wipe their butt or something for them. Makes you think about their kids too. It's like they're saying "Hey, it's your job to raise our kids at school." A friend of mine would say they'll ask, "Don't they have a pill for them? My kid's ADHD." I'm sure you know how I feel about that. You're just starting to get to know me and can see no one gave me pills. As we go on you'll see some other things that made life difficult for me, and it will get worse, but I'm still here and happy as I'll ever be.

People that live here in Minnesota will tell you our winters were a lot worse twenty years ago. Trust me and them it was. The drifts around our trailer would get so high we could sled of the basement side of the house from the roof. We also would be able to make tunnels in the yard due to the snow being so deep. We would always make forts out of them plastic squares you could make blocks with. We only had the snowmobile for one winter, but it was a lot of fun. It was a Speedway 340. It was a fast sled but stunk on trails. This was before they had liquid cooled and such. You remember the one the bear played with? It was a very cool blue metallic color. The speedometer went to 100 and I got it to 90 once up on Normanna road. Then the throttle stuck, and I got very scared as I was coming to an intersection by Sportsman's. I just mashed on the brakes as hard as I could, and just as I came up to Sportsman's, I started to spin. My crash ended up being into a snow bank tail first. This slammed me against the steering column really hard and knocked the wind out of me. The engine died while I was stuck in this snow bank, which was a good thing with the throttle sticking. As I got the snowmobile out and tried to start her, she wouldn't start. Then I had to push it home. I didn't tell Dad about me going 90 but that the snowmobile just died. He was OK with that, but I still got yelled at for it. I'm not sure but I don't think it ever ran again.

Forgot to tell you the tall tale, I would shovel six-tenths of a mile so Dad could go to work. Yes, by hand. We had this big metal scoop that I'd use. "'Six-tenths, Jim,' you got to be kidding?" You'd have to ask my oldest son Nicolas. He knows about it. We clocked it in my car one day. It was a dirt road all the way down and still is to this day. And we had to walk that to get to the bus stop. We were the first on the route in the morning and last at night. That did actually stink though. It was a good forty-five minutes to school. Most of the time I made excuses to take the late bus to go see friends and fool around with a girl named Lisa. But to be totally honest, those were just the excuse, it was so the kids wouldn't pick on me on the way home. The only bad part of taking the late bus had to be going through the woods by Frank's house, which at night time was pitch-black on the way home. If you think back a ways, I told y'all about having to look up to see the opening for the road. It wasn't too bad because you had the dirt road. By Frank's was a lot worse. It was just a trail, and not too big. You've also heard about the bears out there. Put all that together and you got a scared kid running down the trail singing at the top of his lungs to scare the bears or whatever creature or monster might be out there. Then you're running along and miss a step and BOOM, you're flat on your face waiting for the bear to stomp on you. It was a blast though. It would make me laugh each day because it seemed very silly to be so scared of a creature who is petrified of you. It still makes me laugh even now. What a baby I was. I'm sure you've all laughed at your own fear at times.

When I grew up out there in the country, there was some personal time that I don't think I talk about much. It gets a little spiritual to me. How do I explain this? These moments will pop up a lot later in life. I spent many hours just walking through the woods. Always had a walking stick with me that I would pick out from some dead tree, then I would play swords like any young boy did, but I was always just looking to see what was around the bend. I was always watching for something different to see, whether it be a cool bend in a tree or a creek with some pretty rocks in it. People really need this kind of time even more than they think they do. When things are tough, wouldn't it be easier to just go for a walk then get drunk and not remember why you're there in the first place? The simple things in life are the best drug out there. A simple stream, pine trees blowing in the wind, watching an animal gather food, hearing a loon in the background, a neat mushroom growing on the side of a tree, and just so much more. I know this may sound very corny, but life isn't corny. These are feelings that everyone has, but don't talk about them, and it's such a shame. There is just so much more to life. If you have to have these moments alone, then get off your butt and go explore. Who cares what anyone thinks. It's frankly none of their business.

Well, I think by now you can tell I loved living out there in the country. We still have high school to get through, but you needed to hear about why it meant so much to me. When I look back now, so much of me today started there, I just can't explain that enough. As I said before, it's the simple things that make it all worth it. That is not to say I didn't enjoy some city life too. But for now, it was the country for me. "Thank God I'm a country boy." You might find it funny, but at the time, I didn't get into country music. That happened later. To me, it was my childhood.

"I can see them in my mind laughing about the simple things in life and just the absolute friendship from all the regulars that came in like clockwork."

CHAPTER 9

Friendship in Junior High

Woodland Junior High, where I started some great long-lasting friendships. Eighth and ninth were a little vague, memory wise. Most good memories are my new friends and old, my big playground, Boy Scouts, boundary waters, and an interesting home life. Music starts to be even bigger also.

It will sound odd, but this time is a blur, but distinct. So because of this, I will have to jump around a bit. I'll start with my newfound friends. Bob was my best friend for a long time. We started out with a project we had to do for history class. Both of us were kind of geeky. But Bob was the smart one. We sat next to each other and didn't know anyone so we decided to do a U.S. map of the civil war. I told Bob about my map collection and that I could do the map if he did the looking up of the different battles. This began our friendship. Not sure how we did on our project, but I remember the map. Bob and I didn't have a whole lot in common, but we had a fun friendship. Some of you may remember Dungeons and Dragons. Oh my god, did we get into it. We spent many weekends playing for hours on end. I got into making maps and making up new worlds. And as time moved on, we become avid fans of Avalon Hill games. He also had this really cool attic with a lot of models of tanks, planes, and such. We really got into the war games. Bob also at this time introduced me to some good music. We got into stuff like Edmund Fitzgerald, Jean Michel Jarre, Moody Blues, and just that whole '70s time frame of music.

One story that sticks out was the graveyard. Sound silly? Well, we would sneak out of the bedroom late at night when his parents went to bed. Since we were into WW II stuff at the time, we would be sneaking the whole time like spy's. Every time we heard a car coming, we would hide. We always made our way to the graveyard, still sneaking around; we would read the headstones and slowly would make our way back to his house. Imaginations ran wild while we were out there. We truly got into that whole sneaking thing, like low crawling across the field, trying to stay in shaded areas. Even if we were hidden, we'd run when we heard the cars coming and try to find cover. What a blast. It is the simple things in life that make it fun.

Bob and I also got the hookups from his older brother Pete at the movie theater where he worked. *Star Wars*—a few of our other friends and I were waiting overnight to get the first tickets for each *Star Wars*, and we were also there for *Conan the Barbarian*. To the younger generation, these movies don't seem like much. But I'll tell you what, at the time they were like *Harry Potter* or *Lord of the Rings*. Huge! *Mad Max* was one of my favorites. Huge! The bottom line is, it was a big deal for me and Bob. I also became a huge movie buff later on. During this time, I learned how much of an escape from reality a good movie could be. Not to mention a little help from D and D.

I have a Bob story for you. I'm sure I told you we went to each other's house a time or two. One of these times, we were going sledding. (Sledding up north means snowmobile.) The lake was frozen over, and the trails were groomed by Jeff and Glen, so we headed to the lake. I was just showing him all the trails and having a bit of fun with speed and such, trying to scare Bob. It was working real well. I had this one trick where I'd jerk the sled from side to side while standing up and sort of put it on its side. So I get to the lake and stand up and say, "Isn't this great?" And when I looked back to see what he thinks, Bob is gone. *What the heck happened to him?* I was thinking. Well, when I was doing my scare tactics, I threw him off, and by the time I got to him, he was almost to the gravel pit. If y'all remember that's the wrong way. He was ready to go back to the house, but I hadn't shown him the lake yet. So we went to the lake and got going pretty fast to show him what the sled could do. Then as I was about to look back at him, I noticed the handle for the pull start had fallen of. I got scared and slammed on the brakes. Well, just my luck, the engine died in the middle of Horseshoe Lake. Damn it, that stunk. No tools to put the handle back on. Didn't make very many electric starts back then, so we had to push the sled all the way home. Tough day, but I'll never forget that look of fear in Bob's face. I did feel kind of bad though.

Bob was kind of a quiet person. Quite the opposite of me; I was the loud one. It was easy to make him laugh. I'm not sure what he thought about me, but we did have some fun. See, I'm a talker, and he isn't. Looking back, I see a lot of my likes started through him. Bob also introduced me to a lot of friends. Some I don't remember, but a few stuck out. I don't remember too many conversations specifically, but the memories of our friendship are strong. That is probably the closest I'll get to a close friend, but things can change in our lives. As I bring in other characters, Bob was always a constant in my life. I would call him time and again as we became men, but we've drifted apart the last ten years.

And then there was Todd. He was the funniest person I've ever known. I met Todd through Bob. He became part of our D and D group. And we became good friends; also stayed over a few times with him. He was a bit more into D and D than Bob. I can't really explain why he was so funny. He just had the expressions, I guess. Maybe it was timing. His laugh would also make anyone laugh. He also was good at playing D and D. We did some all-weekend meetings at his place for D and D. We'd get punch drunk and have a lot of fun. Todd was quiet around most people, but if you got him started he wouldn't stop as he got comfortable with new people. We would get in trouble for being too loud. I have good memories of our friendship also.

Todd brought Daryl into the picture. Now we have four of us. Bob, the quiet, smart one; Todd, quiet but funny; Daryl, the jock—and if I remember correctly, he was really into track and baseball. Interesting enough, he got me listening to John Denver again. It was the album *Wind Song*. What a great album. I wasn't as good a friend with Daryl as the others, but we also had some fun too. I was a little awkward to him I assume. I think I tried to hard to make friends.

Friends for me so far had been few and far between. If you noticed, I don't talk about friends very often. Actually, till junior high, I never had a long-lasting friendship. I don't recall any. My brother and sister were my friends. There was also Champ and Finnegan, but that was it. And to this day, I've never had a long-lasting friendship. So what I mean by trying to hard, it was new to me. I was not exactly a shy person. That tended to get me in trouble. So people would say I was loud and obnoxious. See, I was in a sense, sheltered. We moved a lot, we were poor, low self-confidence, and basically kind of weird. My idols at the time were Jerry Lewis and Lou Castillo. Some of you probably don't know them, but they were a '50s version of Jim Carrey. Sadly enough, that was me. And I wasn't good at it. I stunk at timing. I hope people around me now are at least sometimes amused. I can't tell sometimes if they're laughing at me or because I was funny. It doesn't matter much to me how they feel. I just want people to smile.

Back to junior high it was Bob, Todd, and Daryl. I have to add a name to that list, Dian. I'm not sure how she became a part of our group, but she was a good friend too. We ate lunch together, the lot of us. I assume at one time or another, all of us guys had a crush on her. But she became like the little sister of our group, and she also rode my bus every day from Ganesen. For all I know, maybe I started her in the group; I don't remember. She was a lot like Bob and very quiet at times. Till you got her started.

One of my fondest memories of our little group was Perkins. Wow. Talk about some fun. Yeah, I know. How corny is that. They had all-you-can-eat pancakes, and boy, did we get our moneys' worth. We would stay for as long as ten to twelve hours at a time. Yeah, while other kids were out getting drunk and stupid, we were sitting at Perkins, getting punch drunk. What a fuddy-duddy. Well, I bet you a hundred bucks we had more fun sitting there just laughing and talking. I wonder if they remember that as much as me. And guess what, my favorite kind of restaurants is coffee houses. I worked in a lot of them. Corny as it may be, it's one of my fondest memories. Another great memory of junior high was our ninth grade prom. "The Rose," by Bette Midler, was our theme song. What a beautiful song. I remember it well. I didn't really dance much. I'm sure I danced with Dian a few times, but that's it.

I just had an epiphany. It's about the restaurant thing. My mom and dad owned a restaurant in a downtown area when I was real young. Just a quick story my mom told me. You understand as before, I vaguely remember this. Yes, like a dream. Music was the part in my thoughts that I remember most because of a jukebox. It was a small coffee shop in a busy area. It was like a thin building. I remember a view of a bar to the left that goes the length of the building. The kitchen was in plain view behind the bar. To the right was a whole line of booths. All the way in the back was the jukebox. Like before in Vegas, the owners controlled the machines back then. So Mom could open the jukebox and just dump a bunch of quarters, and she would always have music. They also had there choice of music in the machine. I would think they were '45s. So I'm sure it was Elvis, Conway Twitty, Gene Pitney, Roy Orbison, and I'm sure much more I can't remember. But I have this distinct feeling of warmth from watching people talk and enjoy each other's company. I can see them in my mind laughing about the simple things in life and just the absolute friendship from all the regulars that came in like clockwork. A smile on someone's face after trying their meal that was cooked just the way they like it, always fresh and homemade. Now most restaurants get everything premade to cut cost in labor. What a warm feeling I get when I remember the past.

Getting back to the story at hand, this was talking about my good friends. This group of friends was another of that feeling of warmth. Just that calming, wonderful feeling I know, corny. Hey, that's just how I am. The simple things in life that keeps our hearts warm. There is a song by Faith Hill, "Secret of a Life."

"Secret of a life is a good cup of coffee." Oh, so true. As you kids grow, things will become more apparent to you later. Life will get much more difficult sometimes. That is when you need to remember the simple things in life. They will comfort you in tough times. Enjoy what you have whether you're young or old. I did have some tough times during eighth and ninth, but these people's friendship helped me. I can't begin to tell you how good having Bob, Todd, Daryl, and Dian as part of my life helped me. Thank you for your friendship.

"I truly feel for people that have never experienced the total feeling of true serenity."

CHAPTER 10

Boy Scouts and Frank

Boy Scouts. Not a lot of memories, but distinct. It really starts with Frank. He was actually our neighbor. Remember the water jugs from earlier? If you've ever seen *Grizzly Adams*, you've seen Frank. Now we're talking a cabin built by him: black powder guns on the wall; mason jars with carob, wheat, and such; and a true wood stove for cooking and heating the house. I was enamored by him. He was kind of like that old wise man or the medicine man of an Indian tribe. He was a storyteller, and I'd like to think I got a bit of that from him. He was the perfect example of what I think of as a person that enjoys the simple things in life. I can't even begin to tell you how comforting sitting in his house listening to him was like. It was amazing to me. It was like going back in time one hundred years to a cabin in the woods. There would be a fire going, a pot of coffee going on top of the stove, hearing the coffee percolating with the sound of the fire crackling in the night, the musty smells of fresh food on the shelves, oh, and that sweet smell of carob to mix with your coffee. The whole time you're sitting on a rocking chair with your favorite pocket knife, carving a fresh piece of birch. These are the things that have made a very big impact on my personality from such a short period of time. But to me it proves how simple things can make that kind of change or strength in all of us.

I had some rough times as a kid. Yes, the old sob story of your father being an alcoholic. He had some very mean streaks. I always felt that because I was the oldest, I got the blunt of his anger. Anyway, I joined the Boy Scouts and met Frank. He invited me over a few times, and I would listen to stories and he taught me to whittle. The first time I ever built something with my own two hands. Frank told me to go pick out a stick. And I would sit, for it seemed like forever, and whittle on that cane. He helped a little, but I did finish it after a few of our *sessions*—for lack of better words to explain our meetings. It was the idea of an Indian head that I tried to carve in my wood. Frank always did make me think about the Indians and their simple lives. When I finished it, I thought it looked like a chief. He took it and hung it above the door as you walked out. He said I could use it when we had Boy Scouts. Well, later I joined the Marines and left that cane there. Little did I know the effect it would have on Frank's son and me.

Four or five years ago, when I came back to Duluth for the first time in a long time, I stopped by Frank's house to visit. When the man answered the door, I thought at first it was Frank. I was wrong. It was his oldest son. I never met him as a kid. He was a bit older than me. I did meet his youngest brother, and I think there was a little animosity towards him. I guess there were some problems when Frank married a much younger wife. She was the one I knew. His son and I talked for a long time about his father. Frank had passed a few years before. As you can imagine, it was slightly intense. Actually, there was a lot of laughter and tears between us. Come to find out he really loved his dad but was very upset at him for leaving his mother. He didn't really ever get to know his dad because of this. In some ways, I felt terrible that I got so much close time with his father. But in some other ways, we were both happy that I did because I was able to share the real fatherly type his dad was. After many heartfelt hours, it was time to go. Guess what was still hanging above the door? You guessed it, my first cane. The simple things in life had come back to me. Sadly, I lost that cane, but the memory will always be there in my soul.

Our Boy Scout troop was filled with misfits. Frank made us all good friends and taught us well about survival in the outside world. Of course the way he taught was like living in the 1800s. We followed our Scout guide to a certain extent, but he made it more real than the guide did. He also had these books called *The Fox Fire*. These were made in the late 1700 or early 1800 for the pilgrimage west. They went through everything you needed to know about survival. How to build a house, how to build a latrine, and how to plant a garden—even had a section on how to clean a game kill. I should try to find them. I'm not really sure that's what they are called, but the name sticks out when I think about it. You truly could survive life in the country with them books. Maybe one of you will look it up for me and give me the information someday.

We got a pretty good second education from Frank. He was very clear that he felt someday this was going to save the human race, which was a little strange but good education. I feel if something did happen, God forbid, I think I'll be OK. For all of y'all out there, it wouldn't hurt to know some survival skills. Would it hurt you to at least look some stuff up? We are so dependent on technology that it's sad. I can't believe how many people don't know how to do some very simple tasks. Like for instance, how to drive a stick, how to change oil, maybe build a shelter, where to find food, or even just knowing what can be food. Do you know? Pretty sad thought when you think about how many people wouldn't survive long. Oh, and something that came to my attention a few days ago. Some cookbooks nowadays aren't even from scratch anymore. They will say stuff like "mix one box yellow cake mix." People don't know how to make cake from scratch. When was the last time you made a loaf of bread? 'Course I can't spell *loaf* though. Which do you think is more important? Spelling it or making it? You decide. Makes you think what intelligence without wisdom is. Frank gave me my own answer to that question. A lot of the other troops at that big meeting we had were a lot more book smart than our group. But we won most of the hands-on competition that weekend. We did look like a bunch of misfits though.

While we were there, I had whittled this really cool sword. I remember late at night I did the hiding thing like me and Bob used to do. I swear I could touch people with my outreached hand, and they wouldn't even know I was there. It became a game of sort, and somehow people found out I was out there and started searching for me. That was so much fun. Guess who caught me? Yea, it was finally Frank who found me. He was a bit mad, it seemed at first. Later he was proud of me. What a lot of fun that trip ended up being. Like I said earlier, we did well on the hands-on stuff but stunk at the so-called important stuff.

Our training for this started at the Boundary Waters, before the get-together. I couldn't tell you what part of the Boundary Waters it was, but it was beautiful. We did a lot of traveling. Or at least it seemed like it to me. Before this, I don't remember ever going camping at all. Like I said, I stayed out at the lake a few times, but nothing like this. Frank had given us a list of things to bring. I can't recall this being a problem with my family, but if it was, I blocked it out. We took just the essentials. This was a big adventure to me. Portaging was even fun. Frank never pushed us too hard, and we took a lot of downtime. There was a funny moment while we were canoeing. The sun was either rising or setting and was right in my eyes, and I couldn't see a thing. While we were paddling, just as we hit the tree line, we got the sun out of our eyes. *Boom!* Right in front of me was a huge moose. "Holy smokes!" We paddled as fast as we could backwards to get away. Then we were back in the sun again. We went back a whole bunch till the fear subsided, then slowly floated ahead with the current till the sun fell again behind the trees. Finally, we realized he was just as afraid as us and saw him taking of in the forest. He was huge. The water must have been five—or six-feet deep where we saw him. When we first saw him, it was mainly just part of his back and his head. That became the story of the day.

I truly wish I could remember more about this trip, but like before, it's an overwhelming feeling when I think about it. The feeling is very serene. Canoeing down the peaceful river with no cares except were to stop for lunch. It was so peaceful. I truly feel for people that have never experienced the total feeling of true serenity. At one campsite, I remember a picture of a canoe on the side of the river with a huge rock that took half the picture just on shore. A small campfire at the bottom of the rock, we had enough firewood to last for days. Just after these big boulders was an open area on the river that was a good size. We did our first canoe training at this area. We would intentionally tip the canoe over and learn to flip it back without going to shore. You obviously had to have the basics of swimming, which we remember my lesson in the Gulf. "Thanks again, Dad." I'm actually a very good swimmer. I was on the swim team at Woodland. Sorry, almost forgot about that. Seemed silly at the time, but it was part of our competition at the rally later. Yes, we won the canoe part. But as you can imagine, it was a lot of fun learning it too. You never know it may help me out someday.

Cooking fresh walleye out in the bush was also a great experience. Best fish I ever ate. One night we made a big pot of fresh wild rice. Getting the wild rice was the fun part. We came by a lake full of rice that day. Frank taught us to get the canoes going pretty fast and steer them in a sharp turn. The momentum would make the rice slap the side of the boat, and the canoes filled with rice. Got to the campsite and there you got it, wild rice and fresh walleye. Boy was that good. The stars were magnificent up there, with an aurora you wouldn't believe. What a magical evening. Frank went over a lot of skills out there. We read a lot from *The Fox Fire* and our handbook. You'd be surprised how much they were the same. I did forget a lot of the knots, but I get by pretty well. You already know I love to whittle. Had a quick lesson on trees, but a big part of me was just enjoying the scenery. I was in awe with the water, trees, and not a soul around. I can't remember the conversations, but they went on for ever. This was probably my first campfire. And by far one of the best things about being out there or on any camping trip will always be the campfire. And for me, it started in the Boundary Waters. What a place to start. I'm sure I'm not a pyro, but I feel mesmerized by a campfire. It was always more wonderful when you could share it with your friends. I've sat around many more campfires in time through my life, but the first was very special. Having the sound of the river behind us was pretty cool too.

"I do see the good in technology as we see it now, but it has become a distraction from reality."

CHAPTER 11

Becoming a Teenager

Here we go off to Central High School. There are some people who can't wait to get to high school, some who don't care about anything, and then there are a few that are scared to death to go to high school. I was scared to death, and it started right off the bat with that stupid bus. Yes, I'm the one that got spitballs ever so often on the bus. I guess you could say whenever they needed a laugh, I was their Huckleberry. You see, someone a long time ago decided that the freshman should get razed in school, and it stuck. Oh, but it's OK because you get to do it later to the new freshman next year. Kind of like a tradition I guess. I'd like to meet that person in a dark alley. I'd tell them a thing or two. Do you remember me talking about some people are just not made to be picked on and are better left alone if you have a nice bone in you? This is another one of those moments where it was kind of fun to play a little bit, but if it's bothering someone, then set them aside and just be nice to them. Of course people say, "That's just the way it is, why change things?" To me that just sounds stupid. "What is wisdom and intelligence? Who the heck made up that stupid rule?" It's just not funny to me, to be mean to the obvious people. I was the obvious person that just had a target on him that, I guess, gave the people the right to pick on me. Y'all are saying, "Quit your whining, you big baby." That right there is my point. These people are put here on earth for people to push around? I wouldn't think so. Could it just be someone in the past that just made it so and everyone followed suit? I guess we're all in the process of jumping off the bridge. I don't know about you, but I'm not ready to give up and just jump.

Bus ride kind of stunk, but I did later get into high school a little. It was tough at first until I made some friends. I didn't do so well in school education-wise. I think in junior high I was a C or D average, and that didn't change much at first. Don't remember all my classes, but I did get in the white choir and, believe it or not, got on the debate team for extracurricular class. "The debate team, what are you nuts, Jim?" Actually, that class was my saving grace. It helped me to be a little smarter and make some good friends. In some ways it kept me out of any trouble. In a weird way I at least had a gang to hang out with. For a little while I was the "lord of the nerds." What a title. This was before the movie, by the way. Like the song "Hip to be Square." Even had a girlfriend of sorts, who was my debate partner, Megan. She was taller then me, skinny, and wore glasses. She was infatuated with me from what I remember. On our bus rides to debates, we would sit together, and she would always sneak her hand on my knee and rub it with her finger for what seemed hours. She was very pretty in her own way and very sweet. Some would say, "What a nerd." Kissing was still scary in them years, but we did. She and I weren't ready for anything else in this stage of our life. Oh, I'm sure the thought was there, but that's all. She was very good at studying and putting her thoughts on paper. I was good at just talking, so we made a good team. I'm pretty sure we did well at the debates. We even won a few times. Our relationship didn't last long, but she was very nice to me and was a lot of fun.

Choir was starting to become my thing. I loved to sing. It was also one place I didn't get picked on, so I loved that class. At first I would say I was apprehensive in choir, but time went on, and I got confident in my singing. I was actually better than a lot of these kids. Sometimes Mr. Roby would use my singing as an explanation of what he wanted. People were actually nice or I should say tolerable of me. (Remember my favorite comedians were Castillo and Jerry Lewis, and my timing stunk, so I wasn't very funny. Maybe I was just irritating at times.) I had good intentions. I remember it being so much fun in choir. The rest of my schoolwork was terrible. I was so afraid of people pushing me around that it would always hold me back through school. Fear has a strong affect on kids. I know it made it very difficult to me. It can be hard to concentrate while someone is intimidating you in the class. I think it is more of just the harsh words than anything. "Oh, you stink, who's your tailor? You're so ugly." All the silly ones were not a big deal. Pushing into the locker, spitballs in the face, things of that nature really get to you after a while. But choir was different.

When I got to high school, all the natural changes were almost complete. I went from a soprano to a baritone, girls were a lot more interesting now, and luckily, acne wasn't too bad. I was a little too dorky for the girls so far. Megan loved me though. Getting a home run with Megan wasn't a big goal for me at this point. To me she was more like my first girlfriend other than Dian, and I do mean friend. Sorry, Megan, it's not a bad thing. We just never really got that way. Don't get me wrong, those feelings were starting up for sure, but I was very shy about that stuff.

I didn't do very well at first in school, but after being in debate for a while, I did pick up my grades. It may have been the studying aspect of debate that gave me the boost in school that I needed to do better. I had too much going on around me to pay attention to my schoolwork. Bullies in school, worrying about my dad, and many other things, I was so distracted. Not stupid like so many of them would say. At this stage in my life, now when I look back, I didn't enjoy learning. I see that a lot in the kids I meet today. Actually, kids now are much worse then they ever were. There are so many distractions for kids today that it's become too much for them to just have fun and enjoy learning. Life is now controlled by computers, being online, cell phones, politics, gangs, music, TV, movies, peer pressure, and the list goes on. Kids now are so confused. They don't even realize how far they are from true reality. "What do you mean by that, Jim?" True reality, what an epiphany, what a concept, and I don't think God had cell phones in mind when he made humans. I'm sure that they weren't part of true reality. Can you imagine not having your cell phone? "Jim, cell phones are just reality." I beg to differ from that.

True reality is back to basics instead of that long list of distractions. We are controlled by many questions like wisdom and intelligence. A simple man like me is a dinosaur of sorts. I didn't comply and worry about my wisdom and intelligence. I just lived. The only reason I have this computer is for this book. I stay as far away from credit cards as humanly possible. I don't believe whenever I have a question I should Google and listen to God knows who explain something to me. I love watching movies, but to me it's my drug of choice, my escape from reality, the keyword being *reality* in this sentence. What happens in a movie is just a movie. I'm not going to run out and use magic or have a sword fight. As you can imagine, *Lord of the Rings* is my all-time favorite. Music is an escape, not reality as some might say. Our freedom, right now is all we have to hold on to and that is getting tougher each day. Reality is not what everyone tells you, it just is. We live and breathe on our tiny planet as we use our biggest instinct . . . to survive. The simple things in life are what give us strength to survive. Water, food, air, and companionship, I added companionship myself. This goes back to my chapter on the Boy Scouts. If you didn't have all the technology around you, how would you survive? This is true reality to me. The very basics of life in a roundabout way have been forgotten.

Now because of them people that tell you what wisdom and intelligence is, we have become what we are today. I do see the good in technology as we see it now, but it has become a distraction from reality. True reality, to some extent in my mind, has different degrees. There is your very basic, sort of Neanderthal reality—that being what I listed above: water, air, food, and companionship. By companionship, I sort of mean there has to be family to continue on the human race. The next step and what I believe is missed the most are your basic realities that make us human. Compassion, love, and patience, they just seem to be gone.

I told you at the beginning that my sophomore year, I started wondering about the title of my book. Reality, as I see it now, was an afterthought later in life. But the feeling was there that I didn't need to listen to what other people thought of me. It started at the end of my sophomore year. Choir tryouts, which I dreaded for weeks, I really wanted to be in the red choir. See, we had the two choirs. Our white choir was for sophomores and juniors who don't make red choir. So there I am ready to try out, and Mr. Roby pulled me aside, "Jim, I want you here for seventh hour to try out for the Mob." "You're kidding, right, Mr. Roby? Those guys won't let a dork like me in Little Mob." I said this with fear in my eyes I'm sure. "No," he said laughing. "Trust me and be here tonight." Talk about anxiety. I was scared to death, so I sucked it up and showed up.

The Little Mob back then was only fourteen of the best in the school. I think the red choir had like seventy-five to a hundred singers. So it was a big deal to make the Mob, especially for a dork like me. I don't recall details of that day, but I was in the Little Mob. Now this definitely boosted my self-confidence. This was the beginning of my future of paying attention and learning how to read people and to relax my mind. Most of my stress was all about being different and people making me feel bad about it. Now this change in me is definable now as I look back at my life but not at that time. I knew something was different and I reacted to it. As a fifteen-year-old, I didn't analyze this like I can now, but I felt great at the time. I had fallen in the rabbit hole. I had been accepted in a whole different society. Now I'm speaking of "what is wisdom and intelligence?" I know; relax, I'll explain.

We've been talking about the people that started this idea that they are the brains, they know everything and became controlling over what people think of others. That false reality that I've been talking about that has clouded people's minds. I was nothing and unwise to them, the perfect target to pick on. Now in all that pressure, I had become that way too. I started to lose my friends and lose touch with myself, but I always felt good when I sang. This was towards the end of my first year in high school, so I lost contact with some of my first year friends.

People now were encouraging me to become cool, don't hang out with them idiots, this is how you should be, and basically just change myself. Becoming this new person, no matter how I felt, was reality. You're smarter and wiser than them people. How did this become reality? I still don't know who made it this way. Looking at the big picture, I'm not sure how all this came about, but it's been this way for a long time I'm sure. What do I think made it worse than ever? You won't agree with me at all. Technology has changed it all. Being smart and knowing technology is reality now. I disagree wholeheartedly. That is, now I disagree; then, I didn't know better. So here I am writing this book and hoping people will become better for it. For now I need to move on with my story. But don't forget I have fallen in the rabbit hole at this time.

I'm going to have to tell my high school story in different situations instead of following a time line. I can remember situations and friends better than I can follow time. Trust me, it will be easier to understand that way.

"There is an awesome power about music. It defines the times to a tee."

CHAPTER 12

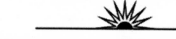

The start of Passion for Music and Drama

This actually started in a small way with Mr. Rodgers from the sixth grade. Remember him? He was the one who gave me John Denver, loving the outdoors, and my first boost of confidence during the Michal situation. I can also attribute my love of music to my mother. She always played a lot of music while cleaning house and that jukebox from my early childhood. I knew a lot of songs and would sing to the radio all the time. Still am pretty bad about that to this day, which anyone who knows me would say the same. Also, like any kid, I loved my cartoons on Saturday and Sunday. Friday night, I would also stay up late and watch old movies. If you can remember me talking about Abbot and Costello, also Jerry Lewis was a favorite. When it came to me singing, I just liked to sing and can hold a tone. Good music to sing with was very uplifting. It became more of a passion when I was with the Duluth boys' choir. I was actually good at something. Mr. Roby just solidified that for me.

I didn't think much about acting at first. To be honest, I can't remember why I tried out for my first play when I did. I think it had something to do with some people from the Mob. It was *Lilies of the Field*. I ended up with a small part toward the beginning of the play and the end. I played a Mexican restaurant owner. That's actually very funny to me looking back now. I ended up learning some Spanish later in my life. I had a mustache and was supposed to have a Spanish accent. I guess I did OK; all I really remember was the main character was having problems eating eggs and doing his lines at the same time. I started laughing, and he just got mad at me for it. Completely took him out of character. See, he was one of the ones who never really accepted me into the Mob in the first place. I'm sure he hated doing that scene with me. He was very popular at the school. He would act like he accepted me around some of them, but alone around me, he would literally just ignore my presence completely. I personally hated that in people. It would almost be nicer if they just picked on me than ignore me, especially due to the fact that around other Mob members, he would be nice to me. That was the way it was though with a lot of people. I figured this out later as time went on.

Thankfully, that play gave me the drama bug. If I'm not mistaken, my next play was a one act in which I got to play a lawyer in a wheelchair. This was a lot funnier due to the fact that Mr. Popular wasn't in this one. The thing I remember the most was opening night, full crowd, major butterflies, and that fear of messing up. I had this really important line that I just can't remember, in which I was suppose to be turned away and spin the wheel chair fast toward them and yell it out. Well, the wheelchair didn't stop and kept going around. When I tried to stop it, I caught my fingers in the spokes. That wasn't the real problem though. We all started laughing and couldn't stop. We had the whole crowd laughing. They knew this was supposed to be very serious time in the play. Unlike the situation in my first play, it wasn't taken so seriously. After a long pause, we continued and had a great time. The play went very well. You know, I wish everyone could do at least one play in their life. What an experience it was to spend a month with strangers and become really close friends toward the end. It was just so much fun that I can't explain.

Then the first musical for me was *Alice in Wonderland*, a small part with no singing. I played a foot soldier guarding a gate during the first part and a little speech during the trial. I was so afraid of that speech that I just kept reading it over and over so many times. I kept messing it up in rehearsals, but finally opening night, I got it right, and it made her cry perfectly. See, I was supposed to make Alice cry then. It was to be loud and demanding. The words were screwy though, so it made it hard. I still remember it though. "Impenetrability, that's what I say!" Then Alice said with a hint of fear, "What is that supposed to mean?" With an angry yelling tone I said, "By impenetrability, I meant just now, we've had enough of that subject, and it would be just as well if you'd hold your tongue, as I don't suppose you stopped here, for the rest of your life, interfering with our trial! Soooo."

It was perfect. I hated all that green makeup.

My next play was a musical also that I had a blast with. During this one, I even had a girlfriend that got me into guitars for the first time. She was a cute redhead that did "Time in a Bottle" very well. For you guys that don't know that song, you may remember the name Jim Croce. He was very popular in the '70s. She was a very sweet girl. The musical was *Seven-and-a-Half Cents.* Also was called the *Pajama Game* when they made it into a movie. I played the part of the president of the union. My character just went by Prez. I was a fun-loving, flirty guy who was always trying to pick up on the employees. Yeah, he was kind of a pervert. In the musical, he was just stupid, and dingy was a nicer way to play him. I was perfect for stupid and dingy. It was actually a good part. I was even the main comedy of the play in a slapstick kind of way. The first scene which I was in also was me looking for my lunch box under girls' sewing tables. Obviously, I didn't particularly have to look under their dresses, but that was the comedy of it. I played a dork.

I also got some real fun musical parts in the musical. First one was the opening song. "Seven-and-a-Half Cents." I still have that almost down in my head. There were plenty of lines for me too. There was this company picnic scene where I had this huge speech to union members; then on opening night, I forgot the whole thing. I took a four-minute speech and made it a thirty-second speech. It was my first adlib. Everyone was OK with it though. I sang a song called "Her Is" twice in the play, which was almost a solo. The girl I was chasing while I sang it would answer back, "Her is," each time, which was all she'd sing. It was funny. The first time I did it was me chasing some girl that was way too good for Prez. The second time, a different girl was chasing me around at the picnic. They said I was perfect for the role in the papers. What I thought was my best singing was singing in the back with the main character. Nobody knew that it was me due to the fact I was his conscience singing back to him. The song was called "Hey There." It was a blast to do that musical, not to mention a great party the last night we were on. Lost touch with the girl when it was done. She went to East High.

The *Pajama Game*, I think, was the summer of my junior year. I'm pretty sure because I also did the Spirit Mountain Festival during and after this. Later I'll explain more about Steve, one of my friends from high school and my D and D time frame, which deals with Steve also. Anyway, Steve was held back a year or two in high school, and he introduced me to his friends who talked me into tryouts at Spirit Mountain. They had a guild they called the Thieves' Guild. The idea was to have a new recruit they were training to be a thief. This guy was a bumbling idiot. Yes, I was perfect for the part. Being a Castillo and Jerry Lewis fan actually paid off. My character's name was Les Dexter, less dexterity. That was very challenging, to say the least. Having my character gave them some knew skits to add to what they already had. One was us just sitting, around teaching me how to sneak while they ate their lunch. At one point I would use a hay bale to move as I snuck towards my prey. Well, somehow I fell backwards and landed in a very pretty girl's lap. "What an interesting pickup line," she said while I was looking up at her. "Hi, I'm Andrea, what's yours?" She said as she pushed away the hay from my hair. I turned red instantly while everyone was laughing hysterically. But like before, we ended up adlibbing, teaching me how to be a gentleman. See, she was a tourist who became a girlfriend later. Funny thing was her friend Beth we used as the other subject for our adlib. The head of our Thieves Guild was my instructor during this. He and Beth became lovers as time went on. Andrea and I may have gotten a lot farther, but she was going to England on a trip the next week, which postponed everything for us.

I did fall for her big time and held up for her while she was gone. Even wrote a song for her while she was gone called "Sitting on the Lakeside." Can't remember the song now, but I did sing it to her when she got back. It was extremely corny but a loving song. She loved it. Later that evening, at her house, she freaked me out and got very aggressive, wanting me to take her. Scared me at first, but being the dork I was, I chickened out. I felt so stupid at the time this happened, and she cried at first then later thanked me for being a gentleman. We slipped apart, and nine months later, I found out she had a kid. I don't know if she knew that when she was trying to get me to sleep with her or just wanted that feeling again. I guess I'll never know.

As you heard, I had started my guitar playing by this time. My first song was "Gentle on My Mind." See, singing had become such a part of me while in the Mob; I couldn't live with just singing at school with my new so-called friends. Thought about learning the piano, but you can't take it with you. So the natural course was the guitar, which little did I know that that would affect me so much later on in my life. Some of the seniors in the Mob were nice to me. A few just ignored me, as I explained earlier. All in all, they were good to me. I did have a very good voice, and they couldn't take that away from me. A few times I'd get picked to do solos, which they didn't like too much. The girl they teamed me up with was basically nice to me, but we weren't friends of any sort. She tolerated me because of my voice. I think her name was Shelly and thinking back she was probably the only one that never really made me fell bad. I thank you for that if she ever reads this book. I do remember Roby put me with a different girl for a song called "Loving You," and the whole time she never looked me in the eye. I realized I wasn't her type, but come on already.

My junior year, we did 167 performances. We did everything from malls, old folks' homes, business meetings, concerts for school, a Christmas video, and even did resorts. At the resorts, when we'd stay overnight, we sometimes would find Roby getting drunk playing piano for the ladies. Regardless of that, it was a lot of fun, and I will never forget what Roby did for me when he told me to try out. Having that in my life was priceless. Choir and drama gave me an appreciation for the arts. There is an awesome power about music. It defines the times to a tee. Kind of makes you wonder, doesn't it? Each generation goes through its seasons. John Denver talked about this in his record "Rocky Mountain High." Also came up later in an album with the same name "Seasons of the Heart."

When you start of in life, you're very vulnerable to everything around you. You, for a short time, are in what I called "true reality." Sleep, food, and water is all you need. Then like in the wild, you're trained about things by your parents and surroundings. Then the next phase begins: learning compassion, love, and patience. Or like I said, the next season of the heart, which is a scary thought in the new reality that we are suppose to follow. Can you imagine a five-year-old cranking music we hear now about busting a cap, time in jail, degrading women, or just talking about how terrible life is. Then there is the terrible stuff that has no morals at all. Don't get me wrong, there is some good artist out there giving out good messages to the younger generation. Not all new music is bad. Some of it is quite good music. My point is that the seasons are different in their own way. If you don't have solid roots, it's very easy to manipulate a young child.

It would be very easy to start going over some of my favorite songs right about now. This chapter is about my high school years though. My generation's music was pretty good, if I do say so myself. We were right after Vietnam or the late '70s. Economy was just OK, but it was kind of laid back since the war. The time of the singer/songwriters, like Jim Croce, John Denver, John Cougar, Eddie Rabbit, Don Henley, Bette Midler, Chris Ledoux, George Strait, Barry Manilow, and the list goes on and on. Our music never died. People are still singing our songs like "American Pie," "Time in a Bottle," "Country Roads," "The Rose," "Edmond Fitzgerald," "Horse with No Name," All

My Ex's Live in Texas," "Cadillac Ranch," and many more. People are still singing them to this day. They were songs about compassion, love, and just plain fun. They were about true reality. Music was more personal; it had deeper meaning to it, wasn't demeaning to woman, and wasn't so destructive. That's not to say there was none of that in some music. But it wasn't as prevalent back then. Now it's normal for someone to say, "Oh, it just makes me feel better when I listen to it." "Makes me feel better" to shoot down life, that just sounds stupid to me when I think about it. But then I'm being like them people that tell you whether you're wise or intelligent. What I'm saying is you need to understand how immoral and unethical that kind of music can be. If you look at it and say, "I'll never be like that" while you're listening to a song, then maybe I can understand why you might listen to something like that. But when people start reacting to the music they're listening to, then your morals and ethics are discombobulated. Wake up, people, stop listening to them. They want you like that so they can take control.

The second part of true reality is gone, and that makes it easy for someone else to tell you what to do. Compassion, love, and patience are so important to the survival of the human race. With them telling us our intelligence and wisdom, they have disrupted our true nature and replaced it with what they want. Now music just gets worse and worse each generation. Like before, I'm not talking about anarchy, I'm talking about wisdom and intelligence. We are talking about true reality, morals, and ethics. That's all, don't ruin yourself with anarchy. Next time you listen to your music, ask yourself a few questions. Is this a moral song? Is this music ethical? Would I want my children treated this way? Especially if it were your daughter. Is this truly the world I wish to see? Try these questions and get back to yourself about them. Don't get sucked in to what they want. You can be a nice person, with a good head on your shoulders.

"I had a big imagination that never stopped. I salute all you D and D lovers, *Star Trek*-watching, all-around misunderstood weirdoes."

CHAPTER 13

Dungeons and Dragons: The Rebellious Teen

Does playing D and D make me a hypocrite? Some people might say that I am. But that would tell me you're missing my point so far. Trust me, I've heard this before. Some of you are not familiar with D and D, so I'll give a quick lesson on Dungeons and Dragons. Basically, it's all about imagination and using that part of the brain. It's all done in sort of the middle ages. Just like *Lord of the Rings* being middle earth. Everyone knows orcs, goblins, elves, and dragons don't exist. We know that it's just fantasy. So why does everyone worry about people playing an imaginary game? "Jim, wasn't there some weirdoes who took it too far?" Yes, there were some of them out there. With that, I have to think back when I heard the saying "You always have that ten percent." There will be that ten percent in anything in life. There are some good people out there that grew up with D and D, and they are well established. D and D was just a lot of fun to a lot of people. At the time when D and D came out, there were a lot of kids looking for an escape for themselves. D and D has been a part of movies for a long time. This was one of the ways to portray dorky kids like the geeks being portrayed as *Star Trek* fans. I'll defend D and D till I die. We weren't bad kids, just geeks and dorks, I guess. Remember the statement I made earlier, "lord of the nerds."

Lord of the Rings will always be my favorite movie. I had a big imagination that never stopped. I salute all you D and D lovers, *Star Trek*-watching, all-around misunderstood weirdoes.

D and D has changed a lot since I played it in high school. We just had basic rules to go buy. A dungeon masters guide, a player's handbook, and a simple monster manual. The rest was our imagination. No distortions to cloud our minds. Everything was basic evil and good. I'm sure you remember Bob, Todd, and Daryl? Now it's time for high school friends; Jimmie Johnson was my best friend. We played a lot of D and D together. Yes, we even skipped school to play at times. It was so much fun to us. It was our escape from reality. It was a rebellion of sorts I guess. When things were at their worst, it made us relaxed to play. We could do as we pleased for them few precious hours. I could search for a lost artifact that had been stolen from a small village. Go after an evil dragon that took sacrifices every month. I could search a ruined castle in the hills that had a hidden dungeon somewhere in the ruins. I could chase a centaur across the valley to an evil castle. It was just our escape. We didn't do drugs or even drink. Y'all know the only time I had drank so far. We didn't need anything but our dice and imagination.

Jimmie Johnson was my best friend through high school. He was the one constant that I had in high school. I can't remember if I met him right away or if it was as a junior. But that doesn't matter. He lived fairly close to the school, so on many occasions that was our destination. Sometimes we'd skip and go to the arcade downtown and play for hours. Yes, I do like a good video game. Tron, at the time, was my favorite. We were both dorks, so we got along pretty good. I kind of liked his sister too, but she was two years younger than me. We flirted a lot; I think I even kissed her. Nonetheless, that was it. I know I was the bad influence on Jimmie, sorry about that, Jimmie. We did have a lot of fun. Due to the fact that we were dorks was probably a good thing. Never got invited to wild parties or anything else of that nature, so I guess that made Jimmie and me the not-so-cool ones. I'm glad of that fact; I've seen what happens to that kind of people, firsthand.

It may sound odd, but that was really about all I can explain about Jimmie right of hand. We made real good friends. Spent a lot of time playing D and D and video games, this was our way of being rebellious. We were bad kids, weren't we? Jimmie followed me around, and like I said, I did get him in trouble sometimes.

Steve would play D and D with us later in my junior year. He really got into the whole thing a bit much, but he was OK. If my memory serves me right, his adventures were very detailed and fun. Still have to thank him for getting me into the Spirit Mountain Festival. We played a lot of D and D at night a few times during the weekends at Spirit Mountain. But the campfires were the best. (Remember the campfires?) There were guitars all over during these campfires. I did that a few times later in life as an adult. That is something you'd never forget; every one sitting and just reminiscing about life in general while the fire is just mesmerizing to everyone. I enjoyed the crackling of the fire, the smell of the wood burning, and that glow of the things around you with the fire's light. Always enjoyed the popping and crackling sound while you lie in your tent. It was a very serene feeling.

People always say it's the reality of things to have your teenager rebel. I'd love to know how that started out; you know, a lot of kids don't have problems as teenagers. Don't get me wrong, we all do make mistakes as teenagers, but that doesn't mean they're rebellious. There are many ways to keep your kids from starting off wrong. I'm sure you've heard about my favorite one: having dinner every night at home. That is a big one. I recently have seen the commercials on that one so I can't say that is my own idea. But my kids, most of you, are grown-ups now. The few of you that remember know we always ate at home at night. Talk to your kids about things. Give them as much confidence as you can. Let them know how you feel about drugs and alcohol. As a parent, you're supposed to teach them, not their friends, TV, music, or other sources. You are there guardian and mentor. Some people should start acting like it.

My mother was a great mentor. As people would say, "She was my biggest fan." She gave me strength and confidence all through my life. She was always there to pick me up. She was very good at reminding me about the positive things in life. We spent many hours in the summer with her great music. That music to this day soothes my soul. People like Jim Reeves, Gene Pitney, Roy Orbison, Andy Williams, and of course we can't forget Elvis. There are many more that I hear from time to time that will take me back to that old café as a kid or doing my best to help on clean-up day. She always had a smile on her face and hid any pain she might feel till I was older, and then I knew when something bothered her. A lot of my strength was born from my mother. She always made you feel loved. Mom would hide my rebellious side from Dad.

Dad was my father, and I will always respect him as such, but he had some anger issues when it came to drinking. Mom kept him in check most of the time by taking the brunt of his anger on herself. That doesn't mean he didn't take a lot out on me too. Let's say the sound of a belt coming of and sliding through the loops of his pants made me cringe. Those belts were very painful to be sure. They made me damn afraid of my father as a child; that during this time of my life, I couldn't react to any pressure whatsoever at school. My parents couldn't do anything about that because I was too afraid of what he'd do if he found out I was the dorkiest kid in Central High. He had so much power over me that when he yelled, I would freeze. Then he would spank harder for not jumping when he said jump. Honestly, when he was sober, I often wondered if he remembered how bad he beat me the night before. He never said anything till later on in life which we'll get to later. When he was sober, he was fun when he was around. I will say he would never drink at home unless we had family over, then he'd have some with them. I was very glad of that. I couldn't even imagine what he would have done to me if he would have caught me drunk and I was too afraid to find out. I'm glad I never did or I could've become a drunk myself with all the problems I had.

D and D he never had a problem with. That ended up being my rebellion. Other little things I'm not remembering may have popped up, but Mom kept as much as she could from him. I know she saved my butt plenty of times. I do mean that quite literally, as you can imagine. My fear of my dad was so strong; I did my best to stay out of his way and out of trouble. "Was he mean?" Hell, yes; he was very mean and very abusive mentally too. "Was it hard on you?" Very much so, especially at first in my life. "Did it help you at all?" I can't tell you how much it helped me yet. At sixteen, in a way I hated him. I truly felt I would never forgive him. I was so afraid of him; there was no way in hell I was going to give him any reasons to get mad at me. That kept me from partying, coming home late, not telling him where I was, breaking the law, talking back to my mother—big no with my dad—basically staying at home and doing what I was told. Debate, drama, and music were my escape from my prison. He let me do them things.

"There I was, soaked to the bones, crying like a baby; and like a rush through my body, I felt warm."

CHAPTER 14

Friend or Foe

Can y'all think back and remember the guy that did the play *Lilies of the Field* with me? I'm pretty sure his name was Phil. He was a senior along with a few others that didn't believe I was Mob material. I can't remember all they're names, but in general at first they were very nice to me, I guess because they were told they had to. When it came to singing, I was right there with them. They were the cream of the crop as class and status go. You know the type: president of class and all together most popular in school. In a way they sort of took pity on me in class but ignored me outside due to my status as a dork. As time went on, they started to talk with me in class and on some of our trips. We had a working relationship at first.

Now before I go on with this story I need you to understand something about me that will only come up in this chapter. I only do this because of reasons you will understand as you read on. This book is not to force any politics or religion on any of you. The decisions about them things especially should be from your own free heart. I apologize ahead of time to all of you.

After a little while I was invited to a Bible study by Phil, and I think it was Tim. They were born again and said before you decide I should listen to a tape they loaned me. The tape was by a guy named Keith Green. The tape was called *No Compromise*. I had a few favorite songs from that album that are still in my head today. Keith, not them, was a big influence in my life. I thought he was an incredible musician and had such a gift of really getting you to feel what he was saying. So it was making me feel like I was being called up. Nothing at this point in my life made me feel too good, but this made me felt loved as much as the love I felt from my mother. My self-confidence was boosted up around my new friends. We would sing for hours with one of the members playing guitar. I got my first Bible at this time. My singing just seemed to get better as I sang with my Keith Green tape that I never gave back. I started playing the guitar during this time. I was starting to feel very good about things outside of home. bANG! It all ended just as quickly as it began. A defining moment was all about my Bible and inability to memorize the verses. "Sounds a little over the edge, don't you think so, Jim?" No, I was there, and it was a terrible thing to feel from a bunch of born-again Christians. What is wisdom and intelligence? Ask them? They made me feel so out of place. It was like I don't rate to be a Christian because I don't have the intelligence you need to understand or be one of them. Laughing at someone for something like this just doesn't compute to me. You have to remember that being picked on and pushed around was just the way it was for me. As some might put it, this was my so-called reality. I hope you are getting the point here. It's not in me to whine about being picked on. I was fine in my own world and in my own way. But I was feeling very good about myself before this happened. Self-confidence is a big problem for kids like I was. It makes life difficult.

So there I was, feeling like you know what; Phil was my ride home, and I couldn't stop the tears from starting. I felt like God had forsaken me. Religion was supposed to be this wonderful thing. But I was guessing only for the smart ones that could memorize the Bible. In school, this wouldn't have bothered me at all. This obviously did bother me. After a while, this jock named Tim finally pulled me aside and said not to worry about what they were saying. "I'll give you a ride in a few minutes," he said. I didn't speak to anyone in the Mob or red choir ever again about my Christian side. I didn't tell any of them what happened that night when I got home.

Tim just dropped me at the front road to the house. Y'all remember the trail by Frank's from earlier? Anyway it was dark and very cloudy when I got out of his car. I just stood there for a few minutes, contemplating asking Frank about what just happened to me but decided against it due to the fact it started to rain. I love the rain so much that as soon as I got a little in the woods, past Frank's, I sat by an old abandoned house to listen to the rain. Typically, I would be running and singing at the top of my lungs to scare away the bears, but not that night. For some reason, I had no fear whatsoever. As I sat there getting wet, I thought maybe, I should just pray like everyone says so. Then some simple words came out like, "Why did you do this to me?" We have all asked God, or whatever we believe, this same question. No answer I guess. A little frustrated and upset, I got up to finish my walk home, got back on the trail and the old saying started, "raining like cats and dogs." It was like taking a lukewarm shower.

There I was, soaked to the bones, crying like a baby; and like a rush through my body, I felt warm. I was completely and utterly relaxed. I looked to the sky and out of nowhere just said thank you. The utter pain and humiliation had just disappeared completely. To this day, I still think that was me being baptized by the Holy Spirit.

When I got home, I think my mom knew that something had happened to me that day and was very surprised that I never went back to that Bible study group. Mom and I may have discussed this, but I can't remember. If I didn't, Mom, I'm sorry. It was a great moment for me.

Don't worry, that's all I have to say about my belief; I'm not here to talk of religion or politics. I had to tell the story because of the significance of wisdom and intelligence. My belief, as you can imagine, is strictly between me and him alone. As Forest Gump would say, "That's all I have to say about that."

"Why can't we just stick to the basics and forget all the hoopla of the new reality that leaves so many behind? Who said we have to do all this?"

CHAPTER 15

My Slow Decline from Education

It had always been tough for me in school from that first memory of the pencil. I saw it in one of my step kids clear as day and now understand it in my own mind perfectly. His name was Alex. Alex was picked on daily just like I was from the day I met him. His grades were terrible, and he would just shut down when things were bad. In a short time I saw myself in him. He didn't have a father in his life till I came along. I began quickly to work on his self-esteem. As he got older and stronger mentally, he started to do much better in school and indeed up having some good friends.

Now back to my schooling. (Don't worry, Alex, you'll be back later in the book, I promise.) Like Alex, I was picked on and pushed around a lot. I was never, as they would put it, intelligent growing up. My grades stunk all through school. My mind was always worrying about who I had to pass by through the next period. Should I bring everything I need till lunch hour so they couldn't get me at my locker? If I did that, then while everyone was at lunch, I could sneak back and get my other books for the afternoon. This became my normal routine. The last thing on my mind was class itself. It was enough for me to survive the day without incident. I bet there are a lot of kids thinking, "I know how that feels." Choir was the best part of my day. We were too busy singing for anyone to say anything to me. The fact that I was pretty good at it probably helped a little.

During high school, I became a part of their reality and just started acting weird on purpose, so it was them laughing at me instead of what they made me out to be in their minds. "Abbott and Costello, Jerry Lewis." And later that character I played, Les Dexter. Here is a good example; I learned how to juggle with lacrosse balls, running around the common area chasing my balls when I dropped them. Yeah, that is very funny. Do you see the idea now? It made it much easier to deal with. Kids like Alex find something for themselves to get through it. Alex just shut down; I tried to make them laugh. Some do drugs, some play D and D, and now there's so much out there it would make anyone insane. Don't forget the title; this all started with people telling each other what their status in society is. It's almost like someone or something has complete control of people in general. Your wisdom and intelligence is your strength now. It has nothing to do with people's morals and ethics, or so they think

Don't misunderstand me. I'm not speaking of just this generation at all. I'm in my forties, this has been happening since the dawn of time. Like I said earlier, reality has become this very interesting new thing. Morals and ethics are getting worse and worse with each generation. It seems to me that in all generations, sooner or later every one has to get back to basics to make a new start. Why can't we just stick to the basics and forget all the hoopla of the new reality that leaves so many behind? Who said we have to do all this? Where did it all start? Nobody knows. In high school, I was so confused about all this, as you can see. But after my rainy day, I just dealt with it as best I could. Things did change slowly during my junior year from that time.

I did have Jim Johnson, as you remember. D and D, Steve Ward, the Spirit Mountain weekends and a few short-time girlfriends in there also that was nice. I'm sure you remember Megan, Andrea, and the girl from *Pajama Game*. But nothing ever got serious though ... yet. During the summer, things got a little difficult at home also. I was growing up and getting a bit bolder with my father. In some ways, I guess that was a good thing, but in others bad. Getting in trouble was getting worse than ever before. I think in some ways that was getting Dad wondering about things a lot more. He was in a way starting to understand that I wasn't a little kid anymore. At one time when he got really mad, he was yelling so loud it got very scary. "I just can't deal with you anymore. I have no idea who you are or what you want anymore. I can spank you, tell you bleed, and it just doesn't get to you anymore. Sometimes, I don't even know if you like girls. All you care about is your music and drama. Why can't you be a real man? Are you gay or something?" To remember something like that after all these years, I'm sure you can see how bad this was to me. During the rest of the summer, we didn't talk much.

Towards the end of the summer, my parents were going somewhere for some reason for a few weeks. Now as you can imagine, I wasn't really mature enough to be alone with a brother and sister for two or three weeks. Even though I was the oldest, I would say my brother was more mature than me. So my parents asked a very good friend of the family to house-sit while they were gone. Let's call her Samantha, for reasons you will understand later. She was very pretty, and I knew her well. We liked the same music, and we hit it off a little to well while she was there. Sam was in my brother's room next to me because Scot had gone over to our cousin's for the weekend. Well, as you can imagine, I lost my virginity to Sam. She was two years older than me, and I became infatuated with her as you can figure out, I'm sure. She was pretty, she was the first, and she was a family friend, which made it easier.

After my parents returned home, we kept the relationship quiet behind family and friends' back. She was a graduate, and I was still in school. So this was not exactly a smart move for either of us. It was like playing family for a very short time for me. We both were in love, but it was like a puppy love of sorts.

A short time later, Mom was sitting in the kitchen as I came in from playing outside. She had a cup of coffee and a pack of cigarettes in her other hand and said, "Jim . . . we have to talk." We both stared for a moment then started laughing at the same time. "Son, I'm serious, we have to talk about something!" "This is about Sam, isn't it?" I said. She stopped smiling and said, "That's true, but I don't think you know about why I'm talking to you about this. Sam is pregnant with your first child and you're not even out of high school." "Mom, I love her." She got very upset now and said, "Jim, that's crazy, no one in their right mind is going to let you two teenagers raise this child alone. You're definitely not going to quit school to support her. Her parents are not going to let this happen and don't want you to have anything to do with Samantha or her child."

I was very upset at all this. Sam I think moved in with her parents or something 'cause I was kept away from her. Her family and mine weren't going to let me have anything to do with any of this. At my young age, I was devastated by all this. At that time, I didn't understand what everyone was saying and tried many times to contact Samantha. I'm glad they did what they did at this time in my life, but then I was very confused.

Then it was back to school again for my senior year. I was still in the Mob, of course, and Jim was even more of a friend. We'd skip the whole afternoon to play D and D or go to the arcade downtown. Always made it back for the Mob of course, that was more important than anything in school. I had failed some of my classes earlier, so my morning classes were like basic English and basic algebra. Now I was worse than last year in the sense of learning. I was no longer being picked on or anything, it was much worse. A sixteen—going on seventeen-year-old who hated going home, was having a child, whose father thought he was gay, had regular beatings, was failing school, had cold friends, and was probably going to have to come back next year to graduate from high school. Like I said, I was really confused. Mom did the best she could, but I'm sure this was very overwhelming to watch her son deal with this.

Think back and remember; Mom, you were also having some tough issues with you and Dad during all of this, that must have driven you insane worrying about me. This would've been a bad time for me if I also would've known about my biological dad. I hated my dad at this time, and it would've driven me over the edge. I was losing it so badly. Day to day was becoming insane. Now don't think of this as a pity party, it's not. This is just what I was going through at the time. I was sick of people trying to tell me how stupid I was. Sounds familiar to some of you, doesn't it? Who started this sick so-called reality? Even still, I was a big dork. I didn't have the gumption or wisdom to do anything about it.

Then something happened that no one could've predicted. True reality hit my family like a brick. Dad had a heart murmur or something like that. They said it was very close to a heart attack. If this wouldn't have happened, he soon would've had a bad heart attack and probably fatal. They were going to have to do heart surgery. I was so mad at my dad before this that I hated him. Now what do you do?

I freaked out big time. This was a breaking point for me. I didn't know how to accept this. I loved him and hated him at the same time. I think it was the look on his face when I saw him at the hospital. We had broken out of the past and were only thinking as father and son. I just couldn't handle all this pressure. I was too young and naive to know how to do this or what to do. A teenager shouldn't have to make these kinds of decisions. But there I was anyway with way too much going on: father is sick, can't be around your own child, don't have the wisdom or intelligence to be a part of society, the dork of the school, and no possible direction for me to go. What would you have done? Should I just stick around and let society put me where it wanted me? Why did it have to be me in this situation? What did I do to deserve this? I felt like that little kid with a pencil still stuck under me all over again.

Now just think; I didn't have the maturity to handle anything like this. I only drank a half bottle of wine when I was twelve. I still couldn't handle having a girlfriend at all. I can't even organize my schoolwork. Now I have to grow up real quick. High school was supposed to be the best years of my life. In a roundabout way, I guess they were. Society had dealt me a hand from hell, but at least I hadn't fallen yet. I can't even imagine how hard it is now with how bad it's getting. A bunch of these kids don't know who their parents are or don't ever see them. The parents are too worried about themselves I guess.

So here I am and I don't know what to do and somehow I get the military in my head. Oh, there's a smart move for the lord of the nerds. At the time, it seemed logical to me to make some money and go to college. My dad was in the Navy; maybe he would think more of me if I go in and do like he did. What other choices did I have? I loved my country, and those army men were a lot of fun. My first movie that I didn't mention was *Midway*. Iwo Jima was a favorite also. So I got it in my head and went to the recruit place I think on Central Avenue.

I was mostly thinking of the Navy because of Dad when I got there. But I was open to suggestions. The first door had, in big letters, THE FEW, THE PROUD, THE MARINES. Cool uniform was a first thought. Then in a window was this beautiful sword. Seemed like an ivory scabbard, an ebony handle, and beautifully shined brass for the fittings. I had to see what that was all about. Dad always said he looked up to the Marines. Their camaraderie was second to none. Well, that would get his goat and show him a thing or two. I would go one step further and beat him at his own game. I'm going to be a *United States Marine*.

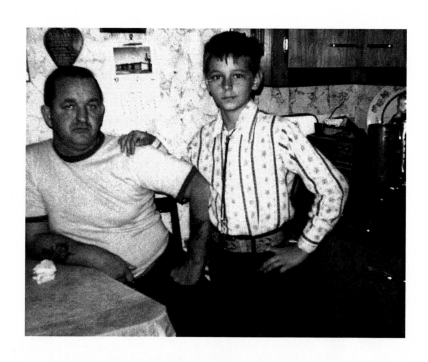

"I missed just lying in the grass, playing with my army men, cutting the grass at home, leaning on a tree listening to the wind blowing through the trees, and the feel of the grass in my palm as the wind blew it away."

CHAPTER 16

U.S. Marine Base in San Diego
Boot Camp

They called it Hollywood Marine base. They always joked that we were issued sunglasses at San Diego. They didn't tell you it was right next to the airport and the Navy boot camp. I also didn't know you had to be an NCO to get that beautiful sword I saw at the recruit station. Looking back, that was the main reason I chose the Marines when I went to the recruit station. Remember, I loved D and D, so that sword would be really cool hanging on my wall. See, I had actually signed the papers and took the ASVAB test a bit before Dad had his heart problems. That and Sam being pregnant just made me decide not to wait till the next year to go in. If I remember correctly my scores, were quite good for a so-called idiot. I can't remember what I initially signed up for, but I'm sure it was much better than open contract. Open contract means the Marines decide what my job will be when I finished boot camp. When everything happened with my dad, I freaked, as you know, and waved my guaranty. The recruiter told me my ASVAB was good, and I shouldn't have to worry too much. So I went to MEPS and did my physical down in Minneapolis, and away I went.

I'll try not to go too much in detail about boot camp; you could write a whole book on it. But I'll give you my feelings towards it. Some details will make it interesting to y'all that always wondered how bad boot camp was. One question Marine's get a lot is, was *Full Metal Jacket* close to the real thing? In some big ways, yes, it was a lot like it; in a few ways, no. The food part was a lot like the real thing. My recruiters were clear on the physical things just not on how they achieve the physical things.

When I got to boot camp, I weighed about 165 pounds, was five foot ten, could only do like five pull-ups, maybe thirty-five sit-ups in two minutes, fifty pushups, and did the three-mile run in twenty-nine minutes at the recruit station. My last week in boot camp, I was 195 pounds, six feet tall, did like endless pull-ups or say fifty, 120 sit-ups in two minutes, endless push-ups or say a hundred, no problem, and did my three-mile test in eighteen minutes. So you could say they changed me. It was incredible. It was a lot of work, but it was still incredible. No, I'm not pulling your leg on any of this at all. The Marines out there know exactly what I am saying. But I digress.

Let's start from the beginning. My first plane ride was to get to San Diego. When we got there, we had been instructed we're to meet the bus to go to MCRD (Marine Corps Recruit Depot.). It was a very short ride that was very strange indeed. As I entered the bus, it looked like every walk of life was there. Country boys, city boys, farm boys, and every lifestyle were present. I wasn't sure where I fit in to that, but it was very strange. One guy I guess thought it was cool to have a toothbrush hanging out of his mouth. There were a few baseball caps on sideways and backwards. A cowboy hat from one of them did kind of stand out. It was the melting pot of the Marines. We were about to get our worlds rocked when that first Marine walked on that bus, or should I say, ran on the bus.

Everything just got nuts. There were plenty of drill instructors there, and each one's voice was louder than the next. People were getting pushed and belted if necessary to get on the yellow footprints on the pavement. I admit I was scared to death. Remember, Dad was like this at times, and

I was definitely afraid of him. What the hell was I thinking? "Get on the yellow footprints. What, are you to stupid to follow directions, maggot?" This is insane; what is wrong with these people. They never stopped yelling or pushing you every second. No matter what I did it wasn't fast enough. You got to a point were if you took two seconds to think, someone was in your face. Some of the new recruits were stupid enough to be very nonchalant about getting on the footprints. Big mistake for them; they got an early lesson on thrashing. (If you can imagine doing every calisthenics you can think of while an instructor is screaming in your ear, "Faster, maggot!") That was thrashing to put it lightly. They finally got on the footprints. I thrashed a bit for laughing at the guys thrashing. "Oh, you think that's funny, huh, boot?" One of the instructors screamed to me. "Well, if it's that funny, drop down there with him!" Or "Do you think you're too special? Mom's not here to go crying to now, so I guess we'll just sweat those tears out of you!" This was very tense for a seventeen-year-old dork. I had such a baby face too, not to mention a part in the middle which was popular in the '70s, but this was 1982. So that was like having a bull's-eye on my head.

It seemed like we were there for many hours, I'm not sure, but trust me, it seemed like forever. We had people passing out while we stood at attention. As you can imagine, if you wanted the drill instructor's to leave you alone, you just did what they said and everything was cool. Our first night was getting issued all our gear and standing or sitting at attention waiting for our turn. It seemed to take all night. They split us up into platoons, which consisted of fifty or so people in each. My platoon number was 3118. We were given platoon leaders because of the holidays coming up. It was December 15, just before Christmas obviously. We were getting are drill instructors on the third.

I'm sure you're thinking it was going to be a cake walk for two weeks, but trust me it wasn't. In a way I guess it made it easier for a seventeen-year-old to get used to boot camp, but it was very hard for me. We did a lot of drilling, learning about our foot lockers, where chow was, learning how detailed hygiene was in the Marines, basically just getting used to life in the Marines. Getting our shots was a bit of fun. One of the corpsmen thought he was cool and was hitting us after some of the shots and saying, "This is really going to hurt later." BAM, he would hit where he gave the shot full force. "You're a Marine; you can handle it, OH RAH!" OH RAH is the (Marine sound for motivation.) Boy, did it hurt later. It was very hard just to lift your arm. See the Navy takes care of the Marines' medical. Sadly enough, the Marine emblem has Department of the Navy on it. Corpsmen are stationed on Marine bases. They also have a hospital on each base for the Marines. Plus the Marines are amphibious so they give us our ride.

A few weeks went by, and it was time to meet our drill instructors. For some reason, we thought we were starting with a guy named SSGT Armando, but we ended up with SSGT Pierce for our senior drill instructor. My other two were SSGT Rainier and SSGT Marmalejo. Marmalejo was a Vietnam vet and had Agent Orange all over his face. He was very short and not loud, but intense. Rainer was a dark green Marine, and we called him Pretty Boy. (Dark green was the Marine way of saying he was black.) Rainer was very loud and always in your face. Pierce was the calm and collective one. I guess he should be due to the fact he was actually picking up gunny when he finished with us and was the senior drill instructor. We also met our commanding officer, and as soon as he left, the stuff hit the fan.

If we thought the first two weeks were bad, the next was hell compared to it. What in the past would be two minutes to get outside in formation took us till lunch. We couldn't get out there fast enough for SSGT Pierce, so we thrashed and did it over and over again. The first few weeks were a lot like this. Getting up quick enough, getting information, using the head (the bathroom), setting our beds fast enough, basically everything we did we screwed up on. All of this has its purpose I learned later. Reaction time is the key to a good Marine. If, God forbid, we ever got to a wartime situation, a split second of misdirection or misguided move could kill you and everyone in your platoon. This training of serious urgency has made people think I'm a spastic person now. When a task is set before me now, my subconscious takes over and keeps me focused most of the way through. When I manage a restaurant, I've been told I'm distant especially during the rush. I guess that's what I got from the Marines.

During these first few weeks, I was so bad that I kept crying to my mother on Sundays when I called home. For my drill instructors, it was obvious that I was having major growing-up problems. Think back and remember that I hadn't really grown up much in my teenage years, so things were bad for me. Looking back, I have to thank my first sergeant the most while in boot camp. I was very lost while I was there, so this next story had a completely different perspective then now.

At the time I wanted out bad! I was dead straight on getting out of the Marines before they could break me. Why should I have to deal with these people anyway? Of course as you know, I'm always running away from problems. But these guys weren't going to let me out at first. I don't know the inside track of this, but I was sent with SSGT Pierce to see the first sergeant. I didn't know why till the first sergeant started asking me all kinds of questions that would get me kicked out of the Marines. "Have you ever done drugs, do you walk in your sleep, are you gay, do you have flat feet, have you ever wet your bed?" That's when I said "Yes, sir, if that will get me out of the Marines, yes, sir!" *Oh*, was that the wrong thing to say. He got up so fast I think it even startled SSGT Pierce. He came across that table so fast it would make your head swim. "BS Private Kelley, you signed a contract and said you wanted to be one of the few and the proud. You told your parents, 'I want to be a Marine.' You gave Uncle Sam your word. Does that mean anything to you? Well, it means everything to a Marine. You may not have been a man when you got here, but I'm going to make you even more of a man then you could have ever been." Then he said, "SSGT Pierce," "Yes, first sergeant?" SSGT Pierce replied. "Get this little s—out of my office and make him a Marine. I want him to be a squad leader when you get back to your platoon." The first sergeant then looked at me while I was standing there, crying at attention and started poking his finger in my chest as he talked. "Don't make me come down there and beat the crap out of you because you're not doing your job! Next time I see you I want to be talking to you on that parade deck when you graduate. You get me!" "Yes, sir!" I have to remind you, as the first sergeant was saying all this, he was poking his finger in my chest, which was something my dad did a lot to me growing up. In a way it made me fell better about my dad now. He was a tough man and wasn't really sure how to tone that down when he was trying to get his point across.

I'm not really sure why that worked, but it made me proud to do my job and be the best Marine I could possibly be. It turned into a blind passion of sorts. I wasn't great, but I became more motivated in turn. First faze was still tough, but it started just being a normal day after a while. I actually got really good at drill pretty quick. (Drill was marching, in case there are some of you that were never in band or the military.) I loved the sound when we were all in step. It became my favorite part of boot camp. It was a thrill indeed to hear that crash of our boots on the deck. "Let me hear the sound of thunder!" The drill instructor would holler as he called his cadence. "Your left, right, left, right . . ." It was a song to all Marines. We all came up with our own songs as we marched with each other. It was very motivating when you see Marines marching on the parade deck on a crisp morning, when the sound echoes through the air, all of them in perfect unison. It brings a chill down my spine when I really think about it. I guess it sounds lame to some of you, but to you Marines out there, all I have to say to y'all is "Semper fi." If you look at my shoes to this day, you see the heel worn out to the outside of each foot. This, for me, is what made life in boot camp bearable knowing we would march everywhere we went. Not to mention it was almost like a downtime for the platoon. Remember as the squad leader that also gave me the chance later to do some cadence at times. My mind wondered a lot while I marched too.

A thing what sticks out the most for me while I was in boot camp was grass. Yes, grass, which I missed so much at times. The parade deck was concrete, there were no vehicles, but we marched here and there on concrete paths; our barracks was surrounded by gravel and concrete, and the one place we saw grass we were to busy doing the course to notice it. The slide for life was on the obstacle course. While we were marching, my mind would wander to the grass. As you can imagine, it was very well kept. Remember I mentioned the love of freshly mown grass? "The simple things in life are what are important to all of us." I missed just lying in the grass, playing with my army men, cutting the grass at home, leaning on a tree listening to the wind blowing through the trees, and the feel of the grass in my palm as the wind blew it away. Corny, I know, but very true. I wanted my spare moments back. I still essentially had three phases left in boot camp. Technically two but we also had our work week to go. We were split up into three groups, one did chow hall duty, some worked on the grounds, and the third, which included me, went to different stations to do basic cleanup duties in different buildings. I was at a company office to just clean brass and do other general cleaning. Looking back, I wish I could have been in the chow hall; I was way too bored the whole time. It was like trying to find something to do all the time. It was only two weeks, so it was a nice break I guess.

Second phase, if I remember right, was rifle range. That was also when we got our rifles for the first time. We were about to head over to Pendleton to do combat training and rifle range. We went by bus, which was very interesting. We haven't seen girls in a long time or normal people for that matter. It was a very short ride though and for the most part we were excited about being in the field. This is where the infamous Mount Mother was, that we had been made to fear for a long time. A long hill we had to climb while in boot camp. That wasn't the biggest thing on my mind though. Grass, open fields of beautiful grass. We finally got to sit on the grass most of our days while listening to lectures on combat and wilderness survival. I can't begin to tell you how many times I would just hold it in my hands and run my fingers through the grass. It was so rejuvenating, I just can't tell you enough about how much help this was. I'm not sure I understood it at the time but figured it out later. A lot of things that happen to us are new and misunderstood while were growing up but is very apparent later in life. It sounds corny to you kids now, but someday you guys will get reminiscent and get it later. Growing up in the country really made an impression on me as you can see now.

Second phase, they started letting up a little mainly because we didn't screw up so much anymore. It was also time to learn the heart of it all; we are a fighting force, and we learn to kill here. We shot different weapons, learned basic hand-to-hand combat, combat formations, how to work as a team, work with claymores, lots of combat first aid, the gas chamber, and even threw live grenades. I'll tell you what, holding a live grenade for the first time was very intimidating to be sure. As we waited our turn, we watched from a glass bunker, and they were so powerful, the ground trembled. Those were all interesting training days to be sure. There was never a dull moment. At this point in our career as Marines, we weren't shooting .50 cal, .60 cal, or .45s yet. There was also the anxiety of knowing this was the time for our trip to the gas chamber. I'm sure you guys have seen documentaries of the gas chamber, right?

Well, I'm going to tell you about it anyway. Gas chamber was something you did once a year the whole time you were in the corps. Each year when you qualified with your rifle, you went through the chamber. We also did war games during rifle range. The gas chamber is very scary to anyone with a brain. We called this NBC or (nuclear, biological, and chemical). We got our gas masks and could still feel a tingle from the mask that had just been used last week by another recruit. So they still had the gas on them. I was scared enough as it was, but to have this smell and tingle didn't help much. We spent a lot of time downing and clearing our masks so it became second nature to us. "Make sure you know how to don and clear because you will be taking off your mask while in the chamber," the instructor said while he smiled. Now I was feeling much better about this ... not. They kept saying, "it will be over before you know it." I wasn't buying this.

As we sat waiting our turn, you could smell the gas from a hundred feet away. The sheer terror on the faces of the Marines coming out made you want to run to the hills. "Attention!" our drill instructor yelled. It was Marmalejo, who had been gassed in Vietnam. "Time to see what it's like," as he pointed to his face and gave us a big grin. Reluctantly, we donned our masks and headed to the chamber. Our turn was sort of in the middle, so she was stout by the time we went in. (Amount of gas in the chamber.) We rushed in and stood in a plain room, which was very clouded inside. In the middle of the room was a Marine with full NBC gear playing with a can to stoke it up a bit more. There were a few other people in the room watching over us with flash lights shining on individuals as they checked everyone. Also towards the middle was a guy going through the instructions on taking of the mask in a few moments. "You're going to take off your masks till I instruct you to don and clear your mask. My signal will be the uniform signal for gas. Flapping my arms and saying GAS. At this time, you will don and clear, if someone jumps the gun, we will do it over and over till you all get it right. Do you understand these instructions as I gave them?" "Yes, sir!" We all screamed in fear I think. I'm sure just like me, everyone was thinking the same thing. Leave it off or get jumped later.

Before we could finish our thought we heard, "Gas, gas, gas!" I pulled it off after I closed my eyes and took a deep breath; man, did it sting. It felt like thousands of pin needles poking at you. It was almost as if you could feel your nose burning. I'm not sure if it was fear or what, but time went very slow. I didn't have a big enough breath so I took a little air. That was a big mistake to be sure. The shock got me to open my eyes and make things worse than they were. Now I can barely see and was breathing hard in fear. Guess what though? Once you got used to the pain of it all, it was tolerable. As the pain wears on, you just get used to it, just then. "Don and clear your mask! Come on, get it back on before you die, you big babies." (That's not the words he used but you get the point.) Little problem at first, but it went pretty good for me getting it on. You could hear people, including myself, gasping and breathing heavily all over the room.

"Now when I tell you too, I want you to turn towards the door and place your left hand on the recruit in front of you. Go! Now when I say *gas*, use your other hand and take of your mask, head to the door, run outside, hold both hands up, and walk fast in the air to get the wind to blow the gas of you. Do you understand?" "Yes, sir!" "When I say *gas*, I want to hear, OH RAH!" "Yes, sir," "GAS," "OH RAH, Marine corps!" Talk about clearing your sinuses. Frankly it was gross watching everyone blowing two-foot long strands of snot as they ran through the woods. Actually, it was pretty funny when you look back though. It would stop you from having a cold, I'll tell you. After a few years, you did get a little used to the gas.

Now it was time to shoot the M-16 for the first time. The average person, when sitting in the Indian position, will put their right foot over the left. Go ahead and try it but trust me when I say it, we saw it a lot at the beginning of first phase. We had to put our opposite leg from our hand we favored on the top. I'm right-handed, so it was left over right. This was very uncomfortable when you sit like this for very long periods. But now we understood the reason behind this. That gave our left hand a good stand when we shot from the sitting position. It made it much more relaxed when we shot, which gave a smoother pull when you fired your weapon. In boot camp, I was who they called a toilet seat, or marksman. That's what we needed to qualify for the Marines. Later on, I always qualified as an expert every time. I think I was just more relaxed, and it made me smoother when I fired. We had a lot of downtime out there, which was a nice break for a change. It still had its moments, but as long as we kept our urgency, everything was left alone. Like I said before, that urgency has always been a part of me.

For you Marines out there, this will bug you a little. I never climbed Mount Mother. No I am not kidding about this. It was a major downpour and our company called it off due to safety issues. Trust me though, it was dangerous out there that day. I'm sure it was a smart and safe decision. Just like everyone in the Marines, we did plenty of running, humping, and thrashing. I don't feel less of a Marine for not doing Mount Mother.

Mainly the rest of phase two went very uneventful as far as I can remember. It truly would be a whole other book to go through more detail about boot camp. Constant movement and constant wearing you out was a norm in boot camp, and we were surviving it just fine. The physical part was becoming much easier day by day. We were getting tougher and tougher with every pushup and sit-up. Now it was time to go back to MCRD and be the big boys on base. We were now coming to third phase.

Freedom bird was starting to sound really good. If you can think back, I told you we were by the airport where we saw planes take off all day long. Now we could truly see ourselves on one of them planes on the freedom bird home. Now it was time to start testing what we had learned these past seven or eight weeks. We had the rifle range out of the way, and now it was time for swim qualification.

We all remember how I learned to swim in the gulf, I assume? Not to mention having an avid swimmer for a father. Then there was all the time swimming in Colorado in the fifth grade. As you can imagine, I did very well at swim quail. You had to have a class 3 to be a Marine. I don't remember the specifics of each class, but I passed the first two each in one try. Class 1 was much more difficult to be sure. Treading in full gear for like two hours, a sort of save-yourself thing where they dropped you with too much weight and you had to get to the service before drowning. Well I passed that with no problem. Now I'm a class 1 right of the bat. I was given the option of the highest rank, which I can't remember what it was called, but it made me a lifeguard. Well, what the heck, why not, I've come this far.

Well, after a full day of practicing saving techniques and finishing grueling tests, my final test came. I had to save one of the instructors to get my license. I do know that aside from all this they said I would be the youngest they had ever seen pass this test and get my license. I was pretty excited now; mind you, there were only three of us left at this time. The first guy did OK and he passed the test. Now here I go, so I jump out there in the deep end and swam to the middle.

When I give the thumbs-up, they said turn around. Without question I did so and started going through my head what I need to do to save someone who lunges me from behind. I'm all set when suddenly he comes from behind me, underneath me, and grabs me very hard around my neck from the front. I lost myself and was very close to drowning when I gave the signal to give up. Man, did that stink. I was so close to spending my time at swimming pools; it wasn't funny. God, I'm sure, had a different plan for me, or they just didn't think a dork like me should be a lifeguard. Remember, I didn't fit that profile very well.

I am still an S1 from the Marines, and it wasn't easy, I assure you. It was a very cool moment in boot camp to remember. Never crossed my mind to go back later on and retest later. Of course I don't think I ever really thought about it in the past till now. It just never came up, I guess.

Boot camp was coming to an end and now it was time to learn what I would be doing for the next four years. Remember the ASVAB test I spoke of earlier that I did fairly well at? That score kept me from being a grunt. "What's a grunt, Jim?" In the military or at least the Marines, the backbone of the military, also known as the infantry, is the grunt. I was going to be a radio operator. That to me didn't mean much at the time, I just wanted to graduate and go home.

My mother told me my cousin David was going to come and see graduation. The only problem with that is me and David had never met and don't know what each other looks like. I never did find David that day though. This was it; I had made it through Marine Corps boot camp. Essentially, no one except a cousin I didn't know could make it to my graduation. Money, as you know, was something we didn't have a lot of. See, I was still thinking like I was home with my family. As young and naive as I was, I hadn't realized that I was stepping out away from home and soon it would just be me. Very soon I was going to get a big wake-up call. For now, it was all about becoming a Marine.

One weekend before graduation, we got to eat a big breakfast, and we had a day with family. I guess it was like a family luncheon; I basically just spent the time relaxing. This is when I think it finally hit me that I was becoming a Marine. That seventeen-year-old kid three months ago that was at the brink of destruction and was about to lose it. I have no idea what would've happened to me on the path I was on. I definitely changed that with this big move. On the last night I was there, I pulled fire watch, but it was totally cool. No one slept that night. We were all looking at them planes; our free bird. We were about to take off to freedom and live out whatever dreams we had. Of course the Marines had control of where we would do this. I was heeded to 29 Palms California. They told me it was the biggest land mass base in the Marines, but first I had a date with Michal, prove myself to Sam's family, and to my dad.

It was time to put the Eagle globe and anchor on for the first time. Our drill instructors were the ones that gave them to us. SSGT Pierce had given us a motivated speech about it that I can't remember, but I do remember the feeling almost brought us all to tear up. He was the first one to call us Marines. Then it was graduation time. For the crowd that must have stunk sitting there while we all did a parade of sorts. It seemed to last forever. Finally, it was over, and we got to say good-bye to our drill instructors. SSGT Pierce said something about how proud he was of me and he wasn't sure if I'd make it there for a while. But he made me feel real good when he said he was proud of me and to "hold your head high, Marine." Then I shook his hand and never did see him again.

I tried for a while to find David but then decided I was too anxious to just get away from all these people. Went to the barracks and grabbed my bag and got on the shuttle to the airport. Yes, it did seem like the same bus from fourteen weeks ago. I remember as we drove away seeing new recruits and for the third or fourth time, tears fell from my eyes. It was like seeing myself again when I came here. Boot camp meant a lot to every Marine you'll ever meet in your lives. To this day, it was always one of the proudest things I've ever done in my life and will always be in my memories.

When I got to the airport, I was starving but got checked in first. Did that feel weird or what, people were staring at me all the time it seemed like. See, I'm still in my Charlies like I explained when I went to see Michal. Not to mention a fresh haircut, Marine style. Even still I headed straight to the restaurant by my gate. That was probably the best plate of spaghetti and a Coke I've ever had. If you can imagine in my life, I didn't get much soda, and at boot camp we got none. This is not to say the Marine chow wasn't good; you will never eat better. But I didn't have anyone screaming at me to finish in four minutes. I got to relax and enjoy food for the first time in fourteen weeks. This was a good day for a seventeen-year-old kid that fourteen weeks ago had no future. But trust me, I was still very confused about all this. It was very fitting that the Marine Corps would help me with many decisions from now on. I'm not sure where I would've gone or what I would've done on my own. Now I had a purpose in life, something to look forward to, a sense of direction, I was now and always will be a United States Marine.

"People thank you for serving, but do they really mean it?
Do they really understand the sacrifice?"

CHAPTER 17

Coming Home, as a Marine, for the First Time

This was a big day for me, as you can imagine; I couldn't wait to get off that plane. In a way it was your normal routine of hugs and kisses and "Oh, I'm so proud." But the first moment I looked in my father's eyes was the part I remember the most. It's very difficult for me to explain something so minuscule. I got this rush of sorrow and glee and "God, I was so wrong" when I looked into my father's eyes. I don't know how I saw all that in just a look from his eyes, but I did. Remember, Dad was in the Navy, so he knew what I just went through. Think back to four or so months ago, Dad asked me if I was gay. He didn't know what to do with me, as he put it. Now there is this Marine standing next to him, arm around him, and not looking at the past when he beat me. I know he was wholeheartedly proud of me, and he did say that. But it wasn't in him to apologize to anyone ever in his life. See, Dad was a very proud man. He would never admit to any mistake whatsoever. This is what I saw in his eyes. But he would never admit it to anyone, including his family. I felt for the first time in my life he saw his mistake and felt very bad about this. The heart attack may have had a lot to do with it. Maybe it was just the realization that his kids were growing up and he missed it. I could see the difficulty in this to him. Now because of me, he was thinking about his life and what he had done or not done.

Mom was just crying the whole time I left and now since I got back. Remember what we talked about just before I decided to go in the Marines? Mom, I think, was just crying happy tears because I had made something for myself. Now she could see that I was going to be fine. It was very fulfilling seeing me get past my past and watching our family getting together in a wonderful moment for all of us. Driving home was kind of weird for me, considering where I was for fourteen weeks. As Dad hit that gravel road, I felt such a rush driving down Hemlock Drive, that ultimate rush of coming home. At that particular moment, I didn't see the meaning of all that nature surrounding me again. Don't forget my whole page just on grass. It was the whole simple things in life that I've been telling y'all about. It was slowly becoming apparent how important that is to me. I hope this is the first of many moments I can show you, to help all of you see how clear this is. The basics of reality and the simple things in life are so important for all of us. After that day, when I was lying there on my bed from my childhood, I just can't tell you how relaxing that was for me. Looking out my window at the tree I looked at for so many years and watching it blow in the wind was priceless. This was the first time it really hit me that I was now a Marine, and I was leaving here to start a new life for myself. It was a bit scary but naively, I thought it was going to be so easy, and everything will be fine.

For now I was at the top of the world. The next day was my meeting with Michal, which you already know about. I also drove down and said hi to Bob and Todd, which was fun. I think we went down to Perkins and did one of our long nights. Things were much different now, mainly because of my new way of thinking. I guess in a way I was becoming a man, and they were about to graduate from high school. They had no idea what I just went through. I told them stories, and we mostly just laughed about things. They don't see things the way I do now. I heard a lot of "Oh, there's no way they could've made me do that." Or the one I liked, "Why didn't you just walk away?" It was a sense of pride to me now or maybe just a sense of responsibility that us, as Marines, feel. I gave my word to protect Bob and every other American out there. The civilian world was so sheltered and is even worse in these times. People, to some extent, only know what they are told on TV, and their blessed computers.

This is that whole idea of wisdom and intelligence. People thank you for serving, but do they really mean it? Do they really understand the sacrifice? I think they do, but sometimes you wonder with the media the way it is. Now think about this; I'm a high school dropout now, so that means I have no education. Does that make Bob or Todd smarter than me? I would agree yes to some extent but no in life experience. I'm already ahead of them and I'm not even eighteen yet. Does that make me smarter? Who cares is what I say. We live our lives through experience to some extent. Or we can go to school and learn about someone else's experience or at least what they tell you to believe. I guess I choose the hard way. I don't think at that time it was a conscious decision but a survival decision. I guess it could be looked at as running away from the reality thing but y'all know how I feel about that subject. Bottom line is I made a decision and now, whether I wanted to or not, I had to go through with it. This took me from a path of my own destruction to another path that I had very little control over.

Which one was the right decision, I've wondered many times. Bottom line, as I said before, I wouldn't change a thing. With my background, it was a good thing to let the Marines make my decisions for now. I don't like to speculate what would have happened to me if I wasn't a Marine. I was way to immature to go anywhere without this. Actually, I really enjoyed the unknown at this age, and the travel was fun to me. Remember the maps?

If you're wondering about Samantha, I tried to see her, but her family and friends kept that from happening. She had found a boyfriend while I was at boot camp, and they lived together now and were getting married. I think he was a truck driver or something like that. A little later I got a hold of a picture and she was beautiful, holding our son there with her husband standing behind. She named him Nicolas, or Nick as I later found out. Nick, I'm sorry I never got to be there. Things happened that I had no control over. We can't change the past. Nick, you will be back later on in the picture.

All that said, this left me in a state of depression for a while. But soon I had to go back to the Marines and learn my new job. I spent a lot of time with my family talking about things and just being a family. It was very nice to feel that. Yes, I did spend plenty of time out there in the woods just exploring. I gave everyone gifts, if I remember correctly. Dad got a camouflage wallet that he seemed to really like, which is something you'll have to remember for later on in my story. Mostly it was just T-shirts and stuff that said USMC on them. I was starting to get excited and scared at the same time. I was about to embark on a whole different life for myself. I don't think one year ago I would even dream of doing what I had done in such a short period of time.

It was just a short time ago I was playing with army men and tank models up in Bob's attic. Who would've thunk it. I still had a lot of my old army men from my childhood. I also had my maps to see where 29 Palms was, right in the Mojave Desert. "Smart move, Jim." But it was that time now. No more thinking about what was happening. See boot camp was such a flash due to the severity of the urgency distilled in each moment. I was told what to do every second of every day. At least now it would be more like a job or at least that's what I hoped for. Of course looking back, I was so young; what did I know about anything to judge what would happen. My new life or big adventure begins.

"If you don't feed your soul, it will die. You become cold and distant from everything around you."

CHAPTER 18

29 Palms, Otherwise Known as the Stumps

What can you say about the Stumps Marines? It was hot, dry, sandy, middle of nowhere, and very windy at times. It's the largest base, land mass-wise. Marines used it for live fire mostly. One of our tank battalions was here. Sorry, Marines, I don't remember what battalion it was. The reason I'm here was communications school. It was a big school, I tell you. My school was for radio operators, which was a 2531, for you Marines out there. I was supposed to learn about the different kinds of radios the Marines used and all the right wiring for each one. Then we were going to learn how to take and give messages. I'm not going to bore you with the details of the school, but some of the things that happened to me at 29 Palms.

For a little about the school, so you see a bit of what I did in the Marines, I'll tell you a few things. The main radio at the time of my enlistment was the PRC 77. Semper fi, to you Marines that remember that thing. For you that weren't in the Marines, this was a *major* lifesaver, especially in Vietnam. You can see this radio in a lot of movies that are out there. For instance, *Platoon*, *Hamburger Hill*, *Full Metal Jacket*, and I think even WW II movies. It was very durable, easy for anyone to use, batteries did pretty good, and depending what the receiver was using to hear you, it went pretty far, for its time. We learned about some others, but for this book this should be OK. Military people know the PRC 77 very well. We were instructed, very efficiently, on preventative maintenance and use of all the radios of my time.

Then after that phase was over, we went into how to send and receive messages. I'm sure you have seen movies were they talk about fire missions and such. Alpha, bravo, charlie, delta, echo, foxtrot, and doing cryptic messages also. That I can't talk about, of course. It was very simple in a lot of ways if you had the aptitude for communicating with people. Also there was a bit of mechanical skill when it came to wiring and the radios themselves. So that should give you an understanding of what my job was without too much time involved.

"Enough of the military garble for now, let's hear some more stories, Jim!" I think it was maybe Palm Springs that the plane I flew in went to and then had to take a bus to 29 Palms. Heck, I can't remember, but it seemed like a long ride to get there. I was very nervous the whole way I guess. There were other Marines, and it seemed there was only a handful of us that wore our uniforms like we were told for checking in. Later I learned the ins and outs of the whole thing, for checking in. We could travel in civvies till we got to base then change just before. No big deal though. We smelled like boots anyway, every one of them knew we were just checking in. When you said "smelled like a boot," it means our uniforms smelled fresh of the shelves of the PX. PX being were we bought our new clothes and such. A "boot" just meant someone new to station or just out of boot camp, key word being *boot*. I was very naive and wasn't sure what to expect when I got to school. I checked into the company office and found out what barracks I was going to be in and headed that way. I tell you what, it was hot as hell there on that parade deck. There was only a small spot of grass in front of the officer's area. But everything else was desert. I have to tell you though it was beautiful.

The ride in was so interesting for me. The last time I did anything in the sense of traveling was sixth grade, remember? I don't know who else did it, but I remember looking out the window of the bus during the rides to school and when we traveled as a kid and pretending to be on a horse or a motorcycle of in the distance. Sounds weird I know, but trust me it was fun. As we drove around the desert, I remember thinking how many jumps and such there was. I guess you really need to use your imagination to see what I did. I could see myself running around gates in fields and jumping across creeks. I admit there was a part of me that was totally worried about what I was going to be doing. As I sat there on my way to my new life, my mind wondered out in them fields the whole time, even got to see the big windmills outside of Palm Springs for the first time. Desert beauty has a way of creeping up on you. First impressions are as I said earlier with the heat of the day, dry skin that just dries up like sand, and that eerie feeling of being desolate. As you start to look around and just experience the sights without blocking yourself of your feelings, it slowly starts to glow. The incredible vastness begins to grab your soul and makes you feel humble. I would learn later that as desolate as it may seem, it's full of life.

When you see the vastness of the world, it's like your soul. The saying "Seeing the forest for the tress" comes to mind like a rush. "What the heck are you talking about, Jim?" I'll try my best to explain. I'm sure you remember my thoughts on the simple things in life? Well, taking care of your soul is a simple task when you think about it. I don't know all the biological or chemical parts of the body, but I know in my heart we all have a soul. If you don't feed your soul, it will die. You become cold and distant from everything around you. Please, kids, don't leave your soul empty. Open your mind and look past the obvious. It's obviously a desert, but when you look closer, you see magic in every corner of the desert. A beautiful cactus which holds water as we all know, an interesting rock that somehow the wind blew around grinding it for God knows how long to give it it's shape, or just a simple bug crawling across the ground looking for food to survive.

Kids, your soul is an open book, and a lot of people will try to close it so they can lead you along the way they choose. Don't miss the forest for the tress. A destructive soul would just kill the bug for fun. Remember, we were all given an evil side and a good. You as a human beings have a choice to pursue either way. I had this discussion with a friend at work once, and he said, "People are going to think you're crazy talking like this." He is probably right to an extent, or it could just open their eyes. So next time you're in the desert, contemplate about that bug or before you push that dorky kid around in school. Hurting that bug or that child may not seem like a big deal to you, but to the child or bug, how does it make them feel? It's really easy to hurt someone and just walk away, isn't it? Look at it this way, you're walking in the desert and you see a beautifully formed small tree. That tree has been a part of that beautiful scenery for many years. An evil soul comes by and decides to destroy the tree. Now that has changed that scenery forever. Do the same thing to a child or human being and you've changed them forever. Breaking that tree or tearing the child's soul isn't going to make you better in any way. Now for the big question: why do it in the first place? Give the tree some water or the child a simple smile instead. Would that be so difficult? I hope in the future some of you think twice.

"Jim, you got all that from a bus ride?" When you've had the life I and many others have had? Yes. It was time to move on, and the ride to the stumps was very fulfilling. Now here I was standing in front of my new home, for now. I had met another Marine who transferred here from the same company in boot camp as me. His name was Wilke. He became a good friend as we went on. We were on the bus ride together and checked in at the same time.

Well . . . here goes nothing, and then we walked in the barracks. Soon as we stepped in, they started in. "Attention on deck! Get on the line, maggots!" Everyone we could see was running for their bunks to stand at attention in front of there bunk. There was a guy standing at the entrance to an office with a Smokey Bear cover on. (Smokey Bear cover is what the drill instructors wore.) As soon as Wilke and I got in front of two empty bunks, he started down the line. "What a sorry bunch of wannabe Marines! You idiots are so slow, my grandmother moves faster than all of you! And you!" He stopped in front of me and was screaming about my chin having stubble since I was in a plane all day. "What the hell is your excuse, Marine?" I was speechless, and he had me do fifty push-ups for my stubble. I'm thinking, *here we go again*. I felt so low right then I could just give up.

This went on for a good while till I noticed someone laughing in the corner of my eye, then another, and another. Finally the whole room was breaking out. Wilke and I were dumbfounded. For the first time in my life though, after they all got a hold of themselves, they were patting us on the back, shaking hands, and saying "Welcome to the stumps." It wasn't the same feeling as in my past; we weren't being picked on and such. In a Marine Corps way, they were welcoming us to the platoon. The Marine Corps is full of tradition. For the first time I realized we weren't at Central High. This was a new beginning for me. They accepted me as a fellow Marine. I passed initiation in fourteen weeks in San Diego. This had just been a ruse to welcome me to the platoon. For the first time I felt the true camaraderie that all Marines have. Semper fi was everything to us Marines. (Semper fi, meaning "always faithful.")

So there I was finally at the barracks waiting for Monday and orientation to school. I barely slept a wink the whole weekend and not because I was excited. There were radios everywhere you looked, and everyone had to turn up to compete with the next radio. It made me insane! I just didn't get it. Some of my kids will remember how I feel about this. Everyone thought their music was better than someone else's. This constant battle was very childish, I felt. It's the same thing as someone driving down the road with woofers vibrating their cars to make everyone listen to their music. I see the point of a loud radio for tailgate parties and such. That is simply what they want to do. Blaring it in the middle of town and making everyone listen to it is just flat out disrespect. That is how I felt in that barracks over the weekend.

I was pretty broke when I got to the stumps, so I couldn't buy a radio. So I just spent most of the time exploring the base and unpacking. When Monday came, it was a fairly simple day of checking in and learning where our school buildings were. When I went to payroll, I got a good check so later that evening, it was off to the PX. Over the weekend I had found the E-club, which was a bar and lounge of sorts. The restaurant part was going up to a counter, ordering your food, and then just paying out. But like a lounge, they had nice tables and a music box. Monday after work, I went there for dinner and had some fried chicken that was to die for.

Then I had to get a radio and some headphones before I went to the barracks. I got me a real nice double-tape cassette player and some pretty expensive headphones to drown out the other people's music. But then I was stumped. I don't remember buying any music as a kid due to lack of funds. This will lead me into a side story real quick before I can finish this thought.

A few years back when we first moved out to Hemlock, I have a memory of our first music other than the radio. It was an old phonograph that I think my parents got at a rummage sale. It also had a few records with it. Remember "I'm Henry the Eighth I Am." That was one of the records. I had either *Van Halen 2* or *Van Halen*, I'm not positive, but I think it was 2. Then there was *Even Now* by Barry Manilow. *Van Halen* and *Even Now* became my favorites right away. Scot had become a big Beatles fan, and me, I still wasn't quite decided what I liked. I did still have a taste for John Denver that I got from Mr. Rodgers. Remember Daryl? One time when I stayed at his, place he found that I liked John Denver and gave me the *Windsong* album. "The wind is the whisper of our mother the earth. The wind is the song of our father the sky." That was a great song, by the way. Somehow later, I got a hold of an old Roger Whittaker album too. One of my favorite songs from him was "I Don't Believe in If Anymore." His voice was very clear and baritone. I listened to all these albums over and over again till I memorized almost all the songs just so I could sing with them. To this day, I'm pretty bad about singing with music all the time. To say the least, I seriously overplayed those albums growing up.

There I was, looking at music to find something to listen to that I could sing with. The first place I went to was country, thinking that's were JD (John Denver) would be. No JD, so I tried easy listening from a suggestion from a store clerk, no luck; well, I tried pop. There it was; I didn't realize how many albums he had. I can't tell you the specifics of how many tapes I bought, but I had all the JD I could find. I found a few Roger Whitaker, Barry Manilow, Kenny Rogers, and for some reason that escapes me, *Dr. Hook's Greatest Hits*. I was set now; with my great headphones, I never had to listen to what they all wanted me to listen to ever again. With all that aside, I would also go on long walks at night to get away from the barracks when I could, listening to my music the whole time.

Right by the base was this small hill that I spent a lot of time going to at night. If I went a little way up, it was neat to look down on the base while listening to John Denver. "The Boy From the Country," was among my favorites at the time. I guess my thought, as I looked at the base knowing that there were Marines in every barracks doing their own thing, was like an eye opening to life. Life to me had been my little square of land there on Hemlock. As big as this seemed to me, I know even this was just a grain of sand compared to San Diego, for instance, were I had just been. Let's just say John Denver was freaking me out. His music was hitting me on such a personal way. Y'all have been reading this book; I was seventeen, in the middle of the Mojave Desert, and had just become a Marine. My peers were still in high school. That's not to mention Nicholas was about to be born. What the hell was I thinking? I had said that I made mistakes in life, but looking back, this wasn't one of them moments.

"Boy From the Country" talked of people laughing at him because of his views. This was very true in my case in high school, if you think back and remember. I was happy with the little things in life that are all around us but seemed to be forgotten. As I looked at the base, it was apparent that I still was the only one looking at life this way. Another song that sticks out in my mind as I tell this story is a song called "Eclipse." The difference in what I see and what those people on the base see, it puts smog between us. That smog can also be seen as the smog of industry. I have always felt bad that people don't see the simplicity in the little things in life. Then you start to wonder why it's come to this. That song playing for me sitting on that hillside was intense. During the stress of school, inspections, and life in general, my visits to the hill became a drug to me. Now I wished I could learn more on the guitar, which does become part of my life later.

Well, like I told you, music became a big part of my life as time went on. John Denver, I have to say, was like a father or mentor for me. Everyone that knows me was very clear on that subject. I was just saying to my fiancé that I could write a whole book just on what he did for me. She said that should be my next book. I do like the idea a whole lot. Will have to see where we are later. My love for music was kindled by Mr. Rodgers for sure. But that tape player took it to a whole new level. I don't think it's ever stopped. Being kind of a singer helped out I'm sure. My voice just fit the music that he did, I guess.

Time for some other interesting tidbits about 29 Palms; for instance, it was hot! Just kidding, it was very hot there; we even had to wear gloves to touch any metal in the heat of the day. If you didn't, it would burn your hands. Yes, I saw many rattlers and scorpions while I was there too. There was always some nasty-looking needle they kept around in case anyone got bit. During our weekly inspections, we did big cleanups before we got any weekend time to our selves. I don't think we ever messed that up. We always kept our barracks yard racked real pretty. Yep, that sand and dirt was always kept in perfect lines and the rocks in perfect formation. I know I said it was beautiful, but we had our days when we hated that place. Especially after a three—or four-mile run where that weather would kill you on a run. I forgot to tell you that we PT (physical training) on Monday, Wednesday, and Friday. It was always at four in the morning so it would be cooler. I bought a little fan to keep me cool at night. The barracks stayed fairly cool, but there wasn't any AC blaring to keep us cool. Some of the classrooms were nice and the ones with a lot of equipment, which were like warehouses, were a bit worse.

School itself, I was doing real well in considering I was an idiot, according to high school. My scores were high—eighties to low nineties. Did seem very simple work when you can concentrate on your schooling instead of worrying about who was going to jump you at the locker; of course they're still in high school as I'm learning my trade. I suppose in the light of things, I thought about why I did this and didn't just stay home like a normal kid. I have told you before though that I wouldn't change a thing in my life, and I'm sticking to that.

Father time keeps moving on, and I turned eighteen out there in 29 Stumps. Not much of a celebration. I treated myself to some fried chicken with Louisiana hot sauce and a large diet Coke. I was never a big Coke fan. The sugar thing was not for me. I would say I was probably ADHD on steroids when I drank Coke or anything with sugar. Nicely enough though, Wilke showed up and celebrated a little with me. I and he weren't drinkers; we'd just watch the idiots at night getting stupid. Wilke was also a religious man. They'd get in so much trouble in the morning with alcohol breath, and they would dog them the whole day. That would cure a lot of people in the civilian world. Hangovers in the Marines were not a reason to call in sick. In the Marines, you learned real quickly that there was a time and place for everything. Drinking all the way up to two o'clock in the morning, like it made you cool, knowing you were working the next day, was flat out disrespectful. If you needed a little stress relief, then Friday and Saturday was your time. Then on Sunday, you rested got ready for the next week, and things went smooth. Seems kind of simple, doesn't it? It s just a matter of respect. I'm not saying drinking is terrible, but not respecting yourself and others around you is bad. Someone has to pick up your slack, and that just doesn't seem fair to me. I did my share of drinking later on in life.

If by chance you're wondering about Marines getting around at a base, we used taxis a lot. Whenever you wanted to get away, you just called a cab. Everyone ended up with favorite cab company. All the Marines out there are thinking "I remember that now. It kept us out of trouble a lot having the cabs there all the time." My weekend cab rides were mostly to the movies or Pizza Hut. All you can eat to a Marine that gets plenty of exercise was awesome. Mainly it was to movies. I hope you also remember the motels from earlier, which soon I'll get to the first time I did this in the Marines. I truly loved watching movies though. As I said before, I'm kind of a movie buff. I'm sure a lot of you can remember *The Cable Guy* with Jim Carrey? I was that kid at night on the weekends at home. Remember I told you about Jerry Lewis and Abbot and Costello? Well, I kept my tradition in the Marines.

First time in a motel for the weekend to get away, but this was a special time for me. Dad was coming to Palm Springs to meet with me. I set up a bus ride for myself and plane ticket for Dad. I think it was a plane, though that doesn't matter. For some reason, it was a four-day weekend for me. In Marine Corps terms, it was a 96. I'm pretty sure Dad came in on a bus from Barstow so I was at the bus depot to meet him. It started off real nice; we hugged, said our hellos, and went to have lunch. We didn't have a whole lot of money, so I think we just ate at McDonald's. That was a mistake though; since it's a tourist town, they hype up the prices. Our conversation the first few hours was catching up about home and talking about what I've been doing in the Marines. It was very simple and nice for us to just sit and chat. I'm sure you can imagine we didn't talk like this much in the past. I could tell that his heart attack was really bothering him bad. It was making me feel he truly wanted to fix our relationship. He said a lot of really nice things about the fact that I had made it in the Marine Corps, and he knew what kind of accomplishment that was from him being in the Navy. Then he was the first person to joke around about the Marines being part of the Navy, which I've heard a thousand times from the squids I've met over the years. A "squid" was the Marine nickname for the Navy. All in all though, he had a pretty good idea of what Marine boot camp was like. He made it abundantly clear that he was proud of me.

My dad, I hate to say, was very abusive with me and my mother. He had some big moments with Scot and Pam, but I felt a lot of his anger was taken out on me. Scot and Pam, I'm not saying that y'all had it easier, but I seem to remember the spankings ended up on me a bunch of times because, as Dad said, "Jim, you're the oldest, and you should know better." I hated hearing that so much. In a way, it was a good thing that his voice was so intimidating, because at my age, when I got to boot camp, I was able to handle that. We didn't talk about that though. That isn't something you talked about with Dad, but in his own way, he was very apologetic the whole time we were there in that motel room. He made me feel loved as he told me stories about his time in the Navy, his father's heavy hand, and how hard he tried to stay on top of things to take care of his family. In a very roundabout way, he was apologizing to his oldest son before anything happened to him. In a sense it was just like me talking to you right now. He was giving reasons behind his life so I would understand him better. I was finally getting a heart-to-heart talk from my father. I'm sure you can imagine how great this was for me; it was helping me let go of my childhood. We know how great that was. I needed to move on though and enjoy my life now. This is probably the best moment I ever had with my father.

The last day he was with me got a little weird to some extent. We went to bed late the night before, listening to John Denver. Dad had to catch his bus kind of early that morning, but it was hard to stop talking with the thought that he was leaving in the morning. He was being much quieter that morning, and when I asked him about it, he said almost in tears, "No, I'm fine, but I'll miss having you at home. It is your time now, and you're my oldest, so it's difficult to see you become a man. When you think about it, Jim, you're the first to move on, and me and Mom are always going to be worried about you. But we are very proud of you at the same time." He didn't break down in tears, I did. At that moment, my tape player was playing "Boy From the Country" just as he went for the door. Dad had come with just a small duffle bag that he held at his side. "Well, son, will see you in a few weeks when you finish your school." It was me that made the first move to hug him as he left. I said, "Love you, Dad." He answered back the same. The song got to the chorus as he stepped out the door; he walked toward the corner of the building as I saw him pull his duffle over his shoulder, and he was gone.

I listened to that song a hundred times if I didn't hear it once that day. I admit I bawled the whole day with the thought of seeing him shuffling that duffle as he walked away; it just really got to me. My bus wasn't leaving till the next day, so I had way to much time to contemplate the past two days. I guess that's why that day sticks out in my memories so much. For me and my dad, that was the end of a very long road for us. This also affected him because it got him to stop drinking for the first time that I remember. It didn't always last long, but he was beginning to see that he had a problem. He wouldn't say that, but that's what I felt in him. This marked the beginning of a much better relationship with him even under the circumstances of our past. The past in my eyes, that day, were forgotten and forgiven. The man I spent time with that day was very humble. Scot and Pam, how I wish I could give you that memory of our father. The feeling I had that day I hopped on the bus and headed back to the stumps will last me the rest of my life. Thank you, Dad, for that time, and may God rest your soul. Till we see each other again.

That, as you'll see later, was my first visit to the stumps. The rest of the time there was normal day-to-day routine that would probably just bore you to death. I graduated in the top 25 percent and was excited to go to North Carolina for my first fleet duty station. (Fleet duty was the ones that go to war and such.) I had been through six months of training now, and it was time to be a Marine. In a lot of ways, I hoped never to see 29 Palms again. As I said, it was pretty, but it was too hot for me.

"Who in their right mind would drink, forget where they are, get sick, not even be able to walk straight, feel like crap the next day, and then after a long day at work, do it all over again?"

CHAPTER 19

Camp Lejuene, N.C.: My First Duty Station

I did go home for a little while before I went to North Carolina. I tried again to get with Sam, but to no avail. Everyone said she was happy with her fiancé and that Nicholas would be fine. Of course at eighteen, I thought the world was still over.

Real quick, we need to discuss the person writing this today against the person you're reading about. My life, as you're reading this, has come full circle to me. As you get older, you look back and reminisce all the time about different things. It could be a smell, an old letter, a favorite song, and maybe even a favorite shirt. But we all look back at times. When I'm writing, at first it's just a story, but then it turns into a feeling for me. You've heard me say a lot that "my memories are like a dream," that is still true; but like a bad dream, you still feel the same psychological feelings you were having when you wake up. That goes for that nice-looking guy or girl in your dream that made you feel wonderful. You'll still have that feeling for a while. The whole Sam thing is still a feeling for me, but the hurt isn't as strong 'cause in time, you turn it off, move on, and wake up. When you're in the dream, there are things you don't see around you; but when you look back, it seems clearer to you. That's how I feel now as I tell you my story. I feel wiser and wish I could change the dream, but I can't now. But I'm not going to let my past be my life now; that's not a dream, it's today. I hope that all makes sense to you as you read it.

Now it's time to head to North Carolina for the first time. My orders were to Eighth Communications Battalion. Lejuene was actually very beautiful. There are a lot of trees, and the ocean is very close by. Jacksonville is a pretty big town, so lots to do and really nice movie theaters. But it's also a big base with great facilities like the great e-clubs, swimming pools, gyms, racquetball, and a great PX. My barracks, finally, wasn't a squad bay. We shared a room with one person. We did all share bathroom and showers, but they were individual, which was nice. My roommate was a big guy that thought he was an Indian or something. He didn't believe in deodorant. He actually had that stupid joke look about him, and he was definitely a corn feed boy. He had a nice enough personality, but the bad part of him was he was racist. Myself, I was oblivious to that due to lack of experience either way. Duluth, for some reason or another, never had many dark greens as I grew up. (Dark Green in the Marines was a black man. Light green was a white boy. WM was a woman Marine.) Racism was not a part of the Marines in any way. But for my roommate, it was instilled in his brain from his childhood. Knowing a little about me, you can imagine my feelings. I just didn't care what color or what type of person you are. I'll talk more about my first roommate in a bit.

This unit that I was in is what the Marines call FSSG (field service support group.) Just like it says, we are support for the grunts, tanks, artillery, and basically any of your forward operating people. We obviously handled all the communication support for what we called division. I was the boot here for now. Wilke made it here too. I don't remember the specifics of my platoon as it pertains to my company or numbers of any kind. Hopefully like the rest of the book, I'll remember things as I go on in my story. Names and situations resurface sometimes. Initially, things were fairly quiet, checking in, and getting used to the base. I fell in love right away with the chicken at the e-club and could be found there almost every day. Most days it was just a jukebox for music, and on the weekends, we had a DJ Friday and Saturday. At this point, I still didn't get into the whole drinking thing at all. I will admit watching these guys getting stupid drunk was very funny. I guess that was part of the reason I didn't drink. Who in their right mind would drink, forget where they are, get sick, not even be able to walk straight, feel like crap the next day, and then after a long day at work, do it all over again? Just didn't make a lot of sense to me. People talked about it all the time like it was the coolest thing or coolest night last night. Was this that whole peer pressure thing starting all over? It makes you stupid if you don't party all the time? Because everyone else did it that made it cool? I still had my own fun doing other things or just laughing at them. I can't say I never drank, mind you. As I told you, that story from seventh grade of Boone's farm.

Before all of this, I did start playing the guitar after buying one the first month or so here in Lejuene. It was a cheap Gibson six-string with a nice case and of course John Denver music. Seems logical, doesn't it? I already had all the songs memorized, so what the heck. I had learned a little from the girl that I dated while doing the *Pajama Game*. "Time in a Bottle," "Gentle on My Mind," and "Country Roads" were the first songs I started doing when I was still at school. The John Denver anthology became my favorite book there at Lejuene. Have you ever played a guitar in a racquetball court? "What does that have to do with anything, Jim?" Well, if you've ever played racquetball, you know the acoustics are great, so that became my study room. I couldn't play in the barracks because it would be worse than playing my radio loud enough to make everyone listen to me. The acoustics made it real easy to make tapes for my mom to listen to, and it made me sound real good in my own mind. A good percentage of the time people would stop and listen. This really got me in to playing a lot for a long while. I'm sure some of you have heard the phrase "I got blisters on my fingers," or "playing till your fingers bleed." That happened to me many times in that racquetball court. Sometimes I'd take the guitar down the trail behind the barracks to find me a place to myself to play. Then other times I would just take my headphones to sing with my tapes to memorize new songs to play on my guitar. In a roundabout way, it probably kept me out of trouble. I wonder what people thought when they walked by that racquetball court while I was in there? Must have been kind of strange to a lot of them, but to me it's a very distinct memory.

One Friday night while I was eating my chicken with my Louisiana hot sauce, a guy named Phillips came over with a few of his friends. I recognized them as part of my platoon. He seemed to know me pretty well as he spoke to me as a good friend. "How are you doing, Kelley?" With a bit of surprise, I said, "I'm doing pretty well here with my chicken, how are you?" "Hey, we are great, you mind if we join you?" "No problem." Now remember that I truly had only just met a few dark greens, but I'd never had a conversation with a dark green. He started in some small talk about the day at work and I was acting a bit shy I guess, and then I told him in almost a whisper. "Phillips, I've never talked to a dark green before." He and his friends just burst out laughing so loud, I practically jumped out of my seat. "Dude, you got to be kidding me?" I was laughing myself now as I told him about Duluth a little. When I finished, he had a big smile and said, "Well, now that were good friends, you got to let me buy you a beer." Well I had to tell him the truth. "I never had a beer except maybe a sip of my dad's when he wasn't looking." "Waitress, get my new friend an Old English 800!" Little did I know at the time how potent malt liquor was. I think I only drank two or three, but I was a serious lightweight. Thankfully, my first buzz was a fun one. I had a great time with Phillips and his friends. From that day forth, they watched over me like big brothers. I didn't hang out with them of sorts, they were just good friends wherever we'd go. I'll always remember him.

Speaking of Phillips, that reminds me of a situation that happened with him and his friends, after our first meeting a few weeks later, they pulled me aside after formation to ask me a favor. "Kelley, around twenty-two hundred, we need you to be at the e-club till around twenty-four hours." I think I was actually broke, and I agreed without a question, and they gave me a twenty to get some chicken, and I headed over around twenty-two. At first it didn't bother me, but as I thought about it I realized that my roommate was about to be in serious trouble. If any of you have seen the film *A Few Good Men*, this was a code red. We never called it that as far as I know; we called it a blanket party. Did he deserve it? I guess you'd have to decide for yourself, wouldn't you? To me, as I sat eating my fried chicken, I guess it would depend on the severity of the contact. My roommate was definitely morally wrong for calling them the names, which he did many times; it was even worse when they weren't around, meaning the dark greens. When I got back to the barracks, he didn't look as bad as I thought he might. He didn't speak a word though. The next day he had a fat lip, black eye, and a little purple around the cheek. At formation, people just joked about it like saying, "What was her name?" He would just smile back and joke with them. When I saw Phillips saying, "Good morning," he smiled and said it back. Nothing was ever said about it after that day, and things got a little better with him. He even started wearing deodorant after that night. Was it necessary? Maybe not. Did it work? Yes, indeed.

"Jim, how does this fit into your feelings about being picked on?" Wouldn't you say that violence is a bad thing? Good question to someone like me. I'll answer with a question. Should I just take my beating or fight back when I'm cornered? Most of the time in my life I was picked on, but typically never cornered. Well, if you have been paying attention you know what happened when I was cornered in the sixth grade. Phillips and all his friends were cornered in the sense that if they did something like fight back, in our world, they're looked at as the problem. So they did what we were trained to do in the Marines. We take care of our own. We don't go public with our problems, we just handle it. My roommate was morally wrong and was stopped for being that way. Phillips, in a war, could be in the same foxhole as my roommate, and they needed to be a team. There was no color in the Marines, we are all green. There shouldn't be color anywhere in life; we all have a different pigment, that's all. People are pushed by someone labeling different races, and each one does it among their own race also.

This is along the lines of what is wisdom and intelligence. Someone is teaching them to be racist or treating them that way so even when they try to stop it, they will get it again somewhere else. This vicious cycle was started way before our time. Remember the song "We Didn't Start the Fire" by Billy Joel? What a great song. Only by going back to the basics will this stop. We have to erase all of these things that have been placed by TV, media, politics, music, movies, online, cell phones, just that whole push by someone more intelligent than me or you that knows the answer. No, I don't think there is conspiracy about this. Even the intelligent or wise ones, I don't think see how destructive this can be because they only see the answers they read about in school. A lot of people have never been in a racist situation themselves. Take care of yourself, help the people you can on a daily basis, and watch after the things that you can control around you. That is all we as human beings need to do. Phillips was a nice guy whom I know didn't let racism get to him. He was a good friend to everyone he knew. He was just cornered and took it upon himself to teach somebody that what he was doing was just wrong. My roommate was just one of them people that used his physical side to get his way, so they had to show their strength to get the point across. That turned into a long story. Hey, after it was over, at least I didn't have to wear a gas mask in my own bedroom. He stunk pretty badly.

Even though I didn't hang out with Phillips much, we were friends, but the one good friend that I did hang out with was Wilke. We both were from Minnesota, both had religion of sorts, and we both became lovers of Chinese buffet. Yes, one of my fondest memories of Lejuene was the Mai Tai. Oh, our beloved Mai Tai restaurant. I don't remember how we found it; I think it was our cab driver one weekend that said it was great. Well, I guess so; we ate there almost every week. That was my and Wilke's favorite spot. They had great ice tea; you wouldn't believe the atmosphere, and they have a mouth-watering buffet. I think Wilke had a crush on one of the waitresses too.

Our cab company by the way was the Blue Diamond; we'd call, and they knew exactly were we wanted to go. Remember how we've been talking about the simple things in life are the ones that save us? In Jacksonville, for me and Wilke it was the Mai Tai. Yes, I even learned how to use chopsticks there. It became a ritual for us that started with egg drop soup then a little fried food, a place for rice with sesame chicken then the moo goo gi pan and top it of with some rich vanilla pudding. Oh, the simple things in life, how sweet they are.

After a great meal, he'd head back while I found my favorite Motel Six, which was right by the grocery store and KFCs, and go shopping for my night of TV. I'd pick up a gallon of milk, some chips of course, whoppers, bucket of chicken with mashed potatoes, and a large two-liter of diet Coke. I was all set to relax. It was mostly old movies on the regular TV listings, but this Motel Six had cable with HBO, so I was set for the night. Next day, I'd check out at eleven on the dot so I didn't waste any of my time there that I paid for; then back in the cab. This time it was the movie theater. They had ten theaters, and I'd pay to watch three; then the owner would let me stay the whole day if I wanted. Yes, I would watch, I think, five or six movies before they closed. At that point, I'd hop back in the cab, go back to the barracks, and Sunday would be my rest day before the week. Of course a rest day in the Marines was laundry, with my guitar, shoe shining, ironing, and basically just getting ready for the week. I did go roller-skating and do the Pizza Hut thing ever so often. Sounds exciting, don't it? No? Hey, that's just the way I was. That was my young adult life. I never got invited to parties or to go to Myrtle Beach. In a sense I felt a little distant from the so-called norm. It still wasn't the same as before though. People were always nice to me, and we'd talk at times, but they didn't judge or treat me different. They knew that was just the way I was. What a difference in my life. As Marines, we were all in this together. There was no reason to put someone down or to be mean to a guy that you know you may be sharing a foxhole with in the future.

In the civilian world, things were, and are, much different. Our world has gotten greedy. People are taught to always want more. The commercials are scandalous. "Oh, you need this outfit so you'll be in style." "This car is all you've ever wanted, and it's all yours if you just screw someone else over to get the money to buy it." "Hey, instead of helping your local shelter, you should buy this beautiful purse so every one will think you're cool." "Don't be a dork and buy the simple home to raise your kids, no, buy this beautiful five-thousand-square-foot home so you and your wife have to work all the time to pay for it. Come on, it's a beautiful house. You don't need to spend that much time with your kids. They got great video games, computers, cell phones, great music, and good movies to teach them about life. Go ahead and buy the house." Don't get me wrong, I don't think the whole world has gone greedy, but if the shoe fits. For me it's just all the stuff that's crammed in our face. It changes people at times, and then it trickles through their heart and gets spilled on to other people they're in contact with.

In the civilian world, I felt like I was an interruption to the natural flow. I didn't give in to the true reality that they believed in. There is a big world out there, of military people that weren't smart or wise enough to be part of theirs, but they believed in their country enough to be willing to die for it. That world, which we believed in, was our reality. One thousand years ago, they had hunters and warriors to protect their kind, and they didn't worry about their world because they knew they were looked after. Jump forward to now, and some people take what we provide for granted. That was OK to us, military people. We did what we thought was right. That gave us a camaraderie that civilians don't understand. I sometimes wonder what would've happened to me if I had stayed in this world we all look at as reality. Looking back, I'm so glad I had these opportunities; they made me a much wiser person as far as I'm concerned.

When they came up and told us we were headed to cold weather training soon, it definitely got my heart racing. That meant we would go to Norway in February or March I think it was. But right now they needed volunteers for Beirut. Travel and the chance to do what I was trained to do made me jump to take the challenge. My age and the fact that I was new in the fleet and needed more time training kept them from choosing me. We lost seven Marines that day. They never came back from that mission because they were sent to Twenty-fourth MAU, which was where the troops that were in the barracks on that fateful day in Beirut. I didn't know the seven people very well, but it was definitely felt they're at our company. Being young, I just wanted to go get revenge for our fellow Marines. If you can imagine, after all of this I was extremely excited to go to Norway, first it was going to be training in the field here and a trip to Minnesota in December. Fort Ripley, just south of my hometown, was our destination in Minnesota. This was going to work out well for me and Wilke being from Minnesota. My first sergeant set it up before we went to Ripley so the Marines that lived near by Ripley could just go home from there. Now I was even more excited. This was going to be a truly interesting endeavor. I was truly ready for intense training.

"When I felt comfortable that the Cong wouldn't hear anything, I lunged at him and got a good hit just behind his shoulder."

CHAPTER 20

Fort Ripley and Some Intense War Stories

So it was off to Fort Ripley and some cold weather training. We did this training because it was towards the end of the cold war with Russia, and we trained in Norway due to the fact that it bordered Russia. The training mainly dealt with movement skills in the snow and to familiarize us with the cold. Trust me, it was very funny to see some of the Southerners in cold weather for their first time. A lot of these guys had never seen snow, so in a little way, they were very excited to see the snow. I will say the clothes they issued us for cold weather was very warm. Even with all this great equipment, some of them acted like big babies about the cold. If my memory serves me right, it was only like negative 10 or negative 20 at night which for all you Northerners, that isn't that bad. During the day, it would be in the 10s or 20s, which is a light jacket for some people. During the day, I was sweating the whole time. I've always had very warm blood. Some people would say I'm like an electric blanket. For Wilke and my friends, after being here in Minnesota a few days, they thought we were crazy to live here. Trust me, even at my age, I love the cold still. I heard somewhere that "in a warm climate, you can only take off so many cloths, but in a cold climate, you can always put another layer on." I personally think that makes perfect sense. They had it lucky too; there wasn't much snow that year. The Mississippi wasn't completely frozen but had huge, like icebergs, flowing down.

"Time to grab the skis, Marines!" The first sergeant yelled as he entered the barracks. "Here we go, off to do nothing, in a nothing base, and none of our radios to mess with." This was like a fieldtrip to us. We were just here to learn to use the cold-weather equipment. We even had these stoves that we were going to use in the tents that were quite cool. I guess we were using the taxpayers' money very wisely. *Sorry*, I promised no politics in my story. The reason I mentioned these things is due to the conversations between all of us during the three days we sat there. I also think there were just a lot of them that just hated the cold, which just intensified the whole situation. All of them admitted to Wilke and me that it was a pretty state. After a few days though, once the honeymoon was over with first-time snow guys, they began to really hate the snow. For Wilke and me, it was all just good memories. We both loved the snow. That was probably one of the many things I missed since becoming a Marine. First it was San Diego, then 29 Palms, and then hot and muggy East Coast. Finally, here I was, back in the snow. It was great for me being here as an eighteen-year-old kid that left home for the first time.

The training was kind of fun to a certain extent. I had never skied before, even though Duluth has a ski area. It was just never my thing. This was only cross-country too, so I didn't do to bad at it. The stoves I told you about were lifesavers a few of the nights especially. We also learned about these nice tent liners for cold weather that worked really well. Water was a big part of the training for obvious reasons. Melted snow that was boiled for at least two minutes was good for you. You always tried to boil enough for the next day so you didn't eat snow. I would assume you kids know about the snow being bad for you if you don't melt it first. It is also very important to boil it for a bit to kill the germs that may be in the water. At least now someone learned something new. Wilke and I were very familiar with the layer aspect of dealing with the cold, but since this is for my kids, here is a quick explanation for all of you.

Sweating in the cold can be deadly for anyone. If you jump in forty-degree water, it will kill you very fast because that water is touching you. If you sweat that turns into ice and cools you very fast also. The way you can fight this is by wearing layers so you can peel as needed to keep you from sweating. They went over this with us during this training. Guess who I learned it from? You're right, it was Frank. That guy sure did teach me a lot.

All of you will have these types of people in your lives, especially at a young age. For you young people out there, try to learn as much as you can from your elders. Having respect for them can go a long way. Looking at the younger generation, I worry about y'all. I don't want you to grow up and have to look to your computer to know how to get a tic of you, to get rid of the hiccups, to make snow good to drink, to survive in the cold, or to just have fun. As for you, adults, teach your kids about things from your experience. Don't make some of the same mistakes your parents might have. Tell your kids stories that could possibly have a message for them. Do what I'm doing now and teach your kids through your own life. Life has been passed down for thousands of years before us. They didn't have a computer or TV. They just taught their kids the important things in life. You see this every day on *National Geographic* in the stories about animals. Like my personal favorite: wolfs.

Wolfs teach there cubs on a daily basis all the simple survival skills. They teach them about respect for each other and their elders. You know the head wolf won't eat till the whole family has eaten? Zachery, I know you know this one. Zach is my third child that spent four or five years with me when he was twelve. Zach, I remember you got in a lot of trouble for doing what you were taught, remember? I had gone to the store for a can of chew while Zach, Alex, and Jesse were at their aunt's house. My aunt's family had just made them lunch for everyone. They were starting to serve the kids, and Zach said, "I'll wait till everyone's served." Mind you, Zach is the oldest boy in the house at the time. My aunt and cousin were older, but he was taught to be the last to eat in that situation. Well, long story short, Zach got in trouble and was yelled at even after he explained why he wanted to wait. "Your dad's not here, so you eat this or you don't get anything at all," my cousin said. Zach said, "I'm sorry, then I have to wait till you two eat, so I guess I don't eat." Well that was kind of pushing it, but he stuck to his teaching and had to sit in a corner at sixteen years of age. When I got there, he was almost in tears, and when I got the explanation I backed Zach totally and made sure he knew I was a very proud father that day. I've told you before, Zach, but "good job." What I'm saying is learn from your parents. Parents, teach your experiences to your kids, not the computer. I made a hug mistake in my life and will never totally fix things, but hopefully my mistakes will help all of you.

The training, as I said before, was kind of fun, but the nighttime was even funnier. We were all hunkered down for the night and would begin telling stories and jokes to take our mind off the cold. Now a lot of the jokes and stories I can't say in mixed company. Which by the way, I've always had a terrible time remembering jokes, so you won't get much of that out of me. A few stories did stick out for obvious reasons as you'll see. Before I tell you these stories, I have to say some of the stories are very upsetting. "Then, Jim, why write it out?" Because there are many of you that didn't have the background to be around our soldiers or to be in a position to hear about the terrible things that this courageous people dealt with, because they believed in their country. It's a shame that some people treat them the way they do. These men and women did the best they could in the situations they were in.

The first story was about a gunnery sergeant that was in our tent. He never talked about Vietnam to us ever before. Somehow someone snuck a bottle of Vodka in a box and it was the right time for it. Well, we drank the whole thing that night. I had a few just to be part of the group. Well, Gunny was very relaxed now, and he had this scar that was actually quite gross looking. There where some signs of bite marks on some of it. To be very honest, it looked like it went through a meat grinder. "Gunny, come on, where did you get that scar from?" He got real quiet for what seemed like forever. "I got that in Vietnam."

"I'm sorry to ask, Gunny, but how?" I had said without thinking whether he really wanted to tell us. "Kelley, I'm going to tell y'all so you don't get someone killed someday in combat. It was a tiger. We had set up an ambush, and my whole platoon was in hiding, waiting cautiously for the dreaded moment. You've never had butterflies till you see them Vietcong moving towards your position knowing what you were about to do." It got as quiet as it could be as he choked a bit on his words. You could hear the regret in his voice about the people he probably killed in plain view as he looked down the barrel of his M-60.

"Out of the corner of my eye, I saw a tiger of all things walking right towards me through the woods. As he was sniffing my leg to see if I was dead, I could see in the distance the Vietcong moving close to the position for us to start with our claymores. Then it was a full rush of pain shooting through me as he bit at my leg for a taste. Then CHOMP, he grabbed my leg and started to chew. When he heard the Cong in the distance, he set his teeth better and started dragging me away from the Cong. The pain was making me nauseated and making me feel like passing out, but I knew I was too close still to do anything, so I started reaching for my bayonet while he dragged me. When I felt comfortable that the Cong wouldn't hear anything, I lunged at him and got a good hit just behind his shoulder. With a bit of struggle, he laid quiet, and just then I heard a shot in the distance and then claymores. I quickly threw a makeshift brace and struggled to stand and run back to my post. I kept falling then running on my knees for a bit then running again. I fell right on my M-60 and started in with a burst straight away. We survived the ambush, and the core man got to me as I passed out. I don't remember getting back to camp, but I've been having that dream of trying to run from that tiger ever since."

We were all speechless as he wiped a few tears hoping, we didn't see them. I don't really remember how we got to a different subject, but I did know that gunny had a Silver Star for his bravery by not giving up their position. He also gave us some pointers on how to make some interesting weapons, which brings me to another story from there. A lot of their ideas were things that the Vietcong had done to them. See, they didn't have a lot of money so they had a lot of makeshift weapons that were brutal. One that sticks out is taking a fifty-five-gallon barrel of crude oil from changing oil in jeeps then throwing old parts, screws, bolts, crankshafts, and a bit of diesel mixed into it. After that, you hide it in the woods with a claymore in it with a trip wire. I'm sure all of you can imagine how terrible that would be. After that evening, I felt a sense of pride that I hadn't had before. Sure I was proud to be a Marine, but this was something new. Now I knew the difference between me and a civilian that had no clue what a sacrifice these soldiers have made for them. Not only do they not feel the burden of watching a fellow Marine be killed, but they never went through the pain that lasted a lifetime with the evils of war that we as Marines witnessed. Don't forget their plight, people. They volunteered for it, in some cases, because the rest of the world had written them of. Most of us don't want handouts, we just want respect.

During the day we spent a lot of time hopping from campsite to campsite so we could also learn the dangers of hypothermia. Drinking plenty of liquids during the day can help your body fight any hypothermia. By the way, water can also keep you from getting altitude sickness, which I've seen myself. Basically that's all for Fort Ripley. At the end of that, I had set it up to have Dad come down and pick me up. It was very cool for Dad to meet my platoon. My platoon was a pretty good group of friends, from what I remember about them. Now it was time for a little rest and relaxation in my own bed instead of a fort.

"If you thought seeing the ocean gives you humility, try going through a storm on a ship with thirty—to fifty-foot swells."

CHAPTER 21

First Time on Ship, Norway-Bound

When I returned to Camp Lejuene, it was business as usual. Regular PT, cleaning equipment, and of course my extracurricular activates like the Mai Tai. After a short period of relaxation, it was time to prepare for our big trip. I was headed to the Atlantic Ocean. At the time I don't think I really knew what to expect. Being as young as I was, the big picture was not there. In a way, it just wasn't real. Now looking back, I had an experience that very few people would ever see. I don't believe that that makes me a better person, but I, like the others that seen it, should share that with my kids. Being out there was a defining moment to say the least. This experience gave me and others like me a camaraderie that will last a lifetime. It is something that will live in our memories till the day we die. I hope you all can see how wonderful the world is through my story of the biggest trip of my life.

I actually got separated from my platoon to be sent to the communication ship for the operation itself. This ship they put me on was a beautiful ship called the *Mount Whitney*. Now first I have to explain the fleet of ships that typically carry the Marines to their deployment. Not only are we the first to fight, we were amphibious too. This fleet had a nickname, Gator Ships. The rest of my platoon was on the Saipan. The *Mount*

Whitney was the flagship of our fleet. She handled most of the communication for the whole fleet. That put me in a position to have a secret clearance for this operation, which would be ending up very close to Russia. It wasn't as big a deal as it may sound. Nothing juicy happened on my watch.

Hopefully someday you all will get a chance to at least go to a show and see the inside of a Navy ship because they are very big and beautiful, especially inside. Being on the command ship, we had a lot of brass on board, so this ship was immaculate inside and out. We basically had an outside deck full of high tech antennas everywhere. The inside floor was like glass, it was kept so clean. During our shift, we were in the war room, as they called it. It was always dark in there like you see in the movies. The atmosphere was always very military at all times. We were giving all the orders to the troops on shore during the war games from commanding officers onboard our ship. That was actually very empowering in a way. I guess, other than my stint as a squad leader in boot camp, this was my first leadership position in my life. Remember, I'm still just eighteen during this time. Nobody ever yelled at me for anything, so I guess I did OK.

A berthing area on any ship in the Navy is your sleeping quarters. Our berthing area, like everything else on this ship, was perfect. Our common area had very nice gaming tables for just sitting with your friends or just for relaxing. We also had a very nice TV room with very comfortable chairs and a few couches that you could lay on. By are double bunks, we had a very nice writing table with drawers on each side for you and your bunkmate. Typically we had opposite shifts, which gave you that space to yourself on your off time. It was here that I finally learned how to play spades. That is a great game for two couples or four good friends. Of course it can be very competitive.

My favorite part of this whole journey, hands down, was standing at the back of the ship and just looking out over the ocean. All of you know how magical moments like this are to me, so you can imagine the wonderful feeling of all this for me. Holy smokes would be one way to put it. Some of you have had this experience, and I hope you share that with any friends that have not. The movies and pictures of this scene really don't give it justice. I can't even begin to tell you about the smells of the ocean. The view is breathtaking. It definitely gives you a sense of humility out there in the vast world at sea. On the back of the ship, you constantly hear the waves of your propellers pushing this huge ship along its way, and on the deck the wind can be mesmerizing at best. The ocean had a way of making you feel like a grain of sand. When the day was calm, it was very relaxing to look out over the ocean and just dream. Getting caught up in the moment just made everything disappear from your heart. The entire constant worrying about things that I can't change just disappeared. The strength of the moment which took control of my heart just like the idea that I have any control over the weather or how at any moment a storm could swallow us up. In other words, I felt the moment was more important than any constant worrying about my life or my future. I realized that there is something else that controls my destiny and gives me the opportunity to take care of that moment itself. Take care of the ship, and it will take care of you. Take care of your family, and they will take care of you.

That makes me think about the times we have now in our world. People have lost trust in life and the people in our life. No one is taking care of the ship anymore, and we all need to look after it or face the consequences. It's very interesting to look at it that way, but it also makes a lot of sense. That brings me to the rough seas that I went through while I was out there. If you thought seeing the ocean gives you humility, try going through a storm on a ship with thirty—to fifty-foot swells. As the ship rises up and then falls, your heart drops with a loud bang on the hull of the ship as it lands in the water. Jump off a bridge that's only ten-foot high with you only weighing 160 pounds, I have no idea how much that ship weighed, but I'm sure you get the picture. This was a strong ship and well maintained, which gave me complete trust while we were in the storm. A strong ship or strong family can weather a storm. I know I'm weighing on the metaphors pretty strong, but I think you see why. Each one of us makes their own decisions about what kind of ship we build for ourselves and who we build it together with. Anyone can choose their type whether it be a small sailing ship, a yacht with a crew, to be on a cruise line letting other people control your destiny, or any other large boat for that matter. The bottom line is, it's your choice. You have to make that ship sound so it can last the storms. Remember me saying about strong roots? Same thing in a sense they have to be sound also, like the frame of the ship.

During this trip, I also crossed the Antarctic circle, which they call the order of the blue nose. It was an initiation of sorts for all us Marines and Navy. Now I can't really tell that part of the story in case one of you decides to go into the military. Let's just say it was very cold out there in our PT gear. Norway itself, when I saw it the first time, was incredible. It was a little cloudy that day with a hint of fog as we watched to see the first signs of the beach. To my surprise and amazement, I saw small mountains or hills if you are from Colorado. It was so beautiful to see after being out at sea for so long. As the day unfolded, we saw some small villages that were postcard-like. It was definitely a sight to be seen. I can tell you from experience though that seeing it with your own two eyes is a lot more magical and memorable than any postcard. People constantly talk to me about how wonderful the Internet is and how much can be seen online; but personally, I'd rather see it for myself. I will never forget the things I've seen or the things I've done in my life and hope to continue for a long time.

For me, this operation was going to be spent outside the war room, giving information to the troops in the field and passing information for the platoon commanders. As I said before, it was very dark all the time in the war room, and the brass was everywhere. We worked ten-hour shifts and had ten hours off. So as you can imagine I got to spend plenty of time watching the horizon. I don't remember how long this went on, but when the time came, we were sent on a mike boat to the Saipan to go back to the States with the rest of my company. I did get to go ashore for a few days to help with cleaning and loading just outside a small village. Compared to our trip to Minnesota, it was like springtime in Norway. It was a nice twenty-five to thirty degrees out, and sunny. A few friends and I went out one night, which was very uneventful for all of us. If I'm not mistaken, it was like a Tuesday or something and pretty quiet. I can still say I was in Norway, but on land, it was just a few days. It didn't take long to finish up, and we were headed back to the Saipan.

USS *Saipan* was an LHA, which I have no idea what the nomenclature meant. To us Marines, it was a helicopter ship, and a flat bottom. Compared to the *Mount Whitney*, it was huge. The *Mount Whitney* was a cutter, I think that's what it's called, which was much nicer in a storm. As a cutter, it had a point to cut through the waves and the flat bottom rolled through them. I think I remember someone saying it was one-fourth or one-third the size of an aircraft carrier. It was like a bunch of big warehouses and a big bay full of helicopters. The top was flat like a landing pad, which also was used to land the OV-10 reconnaissance plane for ordinance and refueling. If you can imagine the chow hall was big also, and it was my first time working in the chow hall during the trip back to the States. Actually it was very nice working there while out there because it gave us something to do. Don't get me wrong, I had plenty of time of to just sit in the berthing area playing risk or spades. I even had plenty of time playing D and D with a few Navy guys I met at the chow hall. That actually happened after our time in Belgium and England.

"It also gave me the sense of pride for my ancestors, that they gave me my life in the United States because of their struggles on a ship so many years ago."

CHAPTER 22

My Only European Tour

Portsmouth, England, was our first stop before we headed back across the Atlantic to go home. This first time was going to be for five days of R and R. Wilke and I decided to just go to town for shopping and some English food. No one would've even dreamed of what happened to us then. We were by a very nice water fountain, having a drink and kicking back when five young kids came up to ask us for American souvenirs. They obviously had a very cool English accent. Wilke said, "Hey, if you can answer a question correctly I'll give you a dollar bill." The kids answered with a little hesitation and said they'd give it a try. "Who is Jesus Christ?" I don't remember the answer they gave, but it started a very nice conversation with the small group of kids. The conversation went so long that we bought the kids lunch at McDonald's. We mainly told the kids about life as an American kid back in Minnesota. The youngest I figured was around five or six. The oldest had to be fourteen. All of these kids were a little on the poor side I assumed. Their manners were very good though. They were all very respectful and polite. Trust me, you can't even imagine how cute the little boy was. All of them looked after him like he was their prize or something. One of the two girls was the youngest boy's sister. Wilke invited them to eat dinner with us in two days at a Chinese place we saw earlier, and they accepted. We had guard the next day, which is why we said in two days. That was the first day in England.

We truly did have guard the next day, so we both just took it easy till our turn for the shift. Our shift consisted of guard duty in the different holds. See, as big as the ship was, we had different units all over the ship. That means a lot of different equipment that we could acquire for our own unit for when we get back to the States. It was, to a certain extent, a friendly thing because in a way, it belonged to all of us. It was a friendly thing in a way, but you tried hard not to let them get a chance to steal yours. Hence, you always have a guard watching all of your equipment.

The next morning was calm, clouds were thick, and we had an interesting day ahead of us. The town of Portsmouth was very quiet this morning, so we decided to walk some of the side streets that typically weren't traveled by Americans. This was very interesting to see these small homes that were hundreds of years old. It seemed as if every house had a little garden in it. People here took a lot of pride in their homes unlike some places and or people I've met. Like everything else, I was experiencing all of this and it was a postcard also. I'm sure I'll never smell or hear some of the things in these alleys. Of course I guess I can look on the computer and see the sights again, I guess. We all know that won't ever happen with me. Like I said, I'd rather see it with my own two eyes.

After getting lost for a couple of hours we made our way back to the water fountain, which that day was full of bubbles. Someone, the night before, put what smelled like dishwashing liquid into the water. What a silly thing to remember, huh? The kids showed up an hour early and what a sight they were. Try to remember movies like *Oliver, Annie*, or even Shirley Temple movies. That is the closest picture I can give you of these kids from two days before. Now as they came around the corner, they were dressed as well as they could be with what I assume were their Sundays best. It was such a neat thing to see the trouble these kids went through to dress up for a big lunch with two Americans to learn about what

167

being an American kid was like. We took them to a very nice Chinese restaurant that was near the water fountain. We were a bit early, so we talked a little outside as we waited for our table for seven. The kids all worried so much about their outfits that it was hard to get them to relax. I remember a few of them talking about never being in a nice place like this. I assured them not to worry about their education so much in front of a couple country boys from Minnesota. I will say that showing these guys how to use chopsticks was a lot of fun. I truly wish I could remember more of the conversation from that day, but like before, the memory of sharing with them kids instead of going out and getting drunk with the guys was a cherished moment.

The last few days Wilke and I spent looking around adventuring before we went to Belgium. The only thing that sticks out was a cool tour we took of an actual old sailing ship. That's probably why I enjoy pirate movies so much. Those ropes they used were huge. They have a big huge wheel towards the front also that brought up the anchor. They stuck these big live oak boards in the square holes, and two guys on each would rotate the wheel to drag the big anchor up. It was a sight to see. One thing that struck me was the size of this ship compared to the *Saipan*. The thought of being on that ship for four to six months at a time in them tight quarters was incomprehensible.

Think about your ancestors. It sure made me realize the struggles they went through to start a new life. Kind of makes your worries seem pretty small, doesn't it? Would you sacrifice that much for your wife and kids? Now people worry more about themselves than their family in a lot of cases. That beautiful thirty-thousand-dollar car is more important than a future for a child. "How much time do I get to spend on my computer or cell phone tonight?" These are the problems of our generation. How about back then when they had to decide how much corn they needed to plant to make it through the winter? Believe it or not, those thoughts crossed my mind as I stood in the bowels of that ship, seeing the swinging hammocks, listening to the creaking sound of the bulkhead, and smelling the old wood. It also gave me the sense of pride for my ancestors, that they gave me my life in the United States because of their struggles on a ship so many years ago. That's why the kids cared for their parents as they grew old back then. I just can't imagine their struggles for what they were. Situations like this are all but forgotten at this point in time. If you would take a moment to think about this, it can overwhelm anyone and be very difficult to even imagine. Of course you're reading my book, so maybe you're already thinking about it. That is the point, I guess, to make you guys think.

It was time to head to Zeebruges, Belgium, for the ship cleanup before heading back. We couldn't have any dirt on the equipment for customs. Luckily, that wasn't going to be me cleaning. A few guys that I had made friends with on the *Mount Whitney* wanted to take me out for my birthday on the second day that we were going to be there. That just left me with the first day we were there. Zebruges, like all of it, was astonishing to say the least. It was another murky, cloudy, and yet tranquil day. The small village was a resort like beach town, but it was during the off season. All the pubs were very quiet that day. I had one of the best-tasting beers I ever drank called Juniper. I'm not sure if it was the serenity of the moment or the actual taste of the beer that made it so good. Maybe it was both. As you grow up, you'll find moments in your life that will be so special that everything will be a better flavor than at a regular time. For instance, remember my plate of spaghetti at the airport after fourteen weeks of boot camp? That could've been what made that beer so good. I didn't drink when I was in England, so it had been a while. Not that I was much of a drinker at this time. Trust me though, it was a good beer. After the few beers, before the sun went down, I went for a walk down the beach. You know me, and I'm sure you know this was a very picturesque moment to me. It wasn't my first time on a beach, but it was the first time in this kind of weather. Because of this moment, I find myself enjoying a beach in inclement weather much more than a sunny beach. It's just so undisturbed with only the sounds and smells of the ocean filling up your senses.

April 5, 1984, in Zebruges, Belgium, I turned nineteen and hopped on a train going to Antwerp, Belgium, so I thought. Don't ask me how or why, but we ended up in Brussels. This was a great mistake for us. When we figured out what train we needed to be on, we had a few hours to kill so we went for a small walk which later on we wished we would have just stayed there. Brussels was a very deep-rooted beautiful city, with magical cathedrals all over, it seemed. Some of the old cities even had bullet holes in some buildings. The history of this town just spilled out into your heart around every bend. I could've spent days just wondering around taking in the scenery. The excitement of a new city and new adventure put us back on that train to Antwerp to celebrate my birthday. What's the saying, "Hind sights twenty-twenty?" All we did was spend a whole lot of time finding a hotel that wasn't booked and find a pub to get drunk. Then we were all so tired, we couldn't get into the whole parting scene and went to bed. I wish I could change that a bit. Brussels made the whole trip worth it though. The last few days I just relaxed at my little beach. After a few uneventful days, it was back to Portsmouth for five more days of leave. Because I did duty the last time we were there, I got to stay the whole five days off ship. This was not good.

I had decided after my trip to Belgium that I was going of the beaten path when I got to England, so here I was by myself, taking a cab to the nearest small town. I don't remember the name of the town, but I do remember the Red Horse or Red Pony was the name of the pub he dropped me off at. When I walked in the place, it got a little quiet for just a moment. I think it was because my haircut, which was a dead giveaway for the Marines. They went back to there drinking when shortly after I sat at the bar, a small group of college kids came and introduced themselves to me.

At this point, I only remember one of their names. D-O-T, yes that was how she explained it to me, with a few slurs I might add. That was her initials, so she always went by the name Dot. She was a very beautiful young nurse in training. I think she was just as turned on with my accent as I was with hers. Not to mention she loved military men. We obviously hit it off really well. Being a little wasted I think kind of made things a little weird for me. Not being a big drinker and watching this people getting very loud and obnoxious was strange to me. Frankly, I didn't get it at all. I was trying to be nice and fun to Dot. It was fun being as touchy-feely as we were, though, I admit, but this was kind of new to me. Sam was the first real thing for me, and that was like playing mom and dad at my age then. This was very exciting but in the same thought, "awkward." My thoughts were of romance and quiet nights, not partying and such. Granted, I did have a lot of fun, but this girl thing was very new for me. Finding girlfriends for me was a difficult thing all my teenage years. I think I watched too many chick flicks I guess.

Dot found out that I hadn't set any thing up for the night and, in a seductive way, invited me to go and stay with her for the night. Well I'm not going to turn that down. So we were able to just walk to her place due to the fact she lived right by there. It was a college town, so as we got closer to her dorm, I began to wonder how we were going to pull this of. "Oh, I've done this before, don't worry," she said. "Yeah, right" I'm thinking. This is nuts. But she was a girl that was interested in me as much as I was in her. She was right, we got in with no problems, even saw a few girls in the halls, but nothing was said. Now in her room, scared to death, I sat nervously as she got into something more comfortable. Dot looked like a dream when she came back to the living area and invited me to her bedroom. Figures; it's a double bed, barely room for one adult. She said its OK, she likes to cuddle. She did seem very relaxed at first, but as we lay there I, felt her become a little nervous as she asked if I had protection. She did, if I didn't.

Then all of a sudden, I think it hit her that something was about to happen. She seemed very scared all of a sudden. "Are you OK?" I asked as she shook just a little. With a completely different voice then I'd heard all night, she said yeah. Now at this point some of you men are going to give me a hard time because she was perfectly happy to let me do my thing. But to me it was obvious that she felt like she was in trouble and was just going through the motions to be nice like she owed me something. Wrong. "Dot," I said. "You don't have to do this if you're not comfortable." The kiss I had after I said that was a very passionate make-out kiss that lasted for what seemed like hours. It was not the right thing under the circumstance to just take advantage of a new friend.

Is this how it happens and I'm just too naive to know? I hoped not. I have more respect for women than to just take advantage. We had a very nice time that evening just making out and holding each other. In the morning, she had class, and it was time for me to say good-bye to this pretty young lady that almost made a big mistake. I assume under other different circumstance we could've had a relationship very easily. "Dot, I hope the best for you for the future" was the last thing I said to her. I don't think I ever told anyone about her due to the fact that I let her go. Not to mention I don't kiss and tell.

There I was again just walking around, enjoying the countryside, when I heard cow bell from around the next bend. Imagine my surprise when I saw a man walking down the street pulling a cart, or at least that's what it looked like at first. There were the bells on the handle which controls the electric motor to run the cart. What the heck kind of hick town have I run into? Now you have to understand that I love milk and had some fresh milk from a family named Solums. This guy with the cart was delivering milk to all the people in the neighborhood I was in. I said some hi's to him and asked if he had some extras he could sell. He said sure and sold me a bottle. Just like the beer earlier in Belgium, this was the best milk I had ever had, hands down. There I was a in this beautiful old village, perfect cloudy weather, nice small cottage-like homes, and a very nice old man selling me fresh milk. It was great milk. So good, as I finished the first, I had to get two more. Like I had talked about before, I can't say which was best, the milk itself or the atmosphere around me at the time. When I sat down near a small ranch, I remember thinking about home and that NFD milk from my childhood. I also started thinking about how tough things have been since I joined the Marines, and I'm sure Sam came up in my thoughts that by this time had the baby, Nicholas. I was thinking how nice it was here and thought why not just stay here in England. Yes, go AWOL. What the heck, why not stay here and enjoy myself? The heck with everyone else in my life, it was all heart aches anyway, right? I was too young to think about anyone else but myself.

With this on my mind, I decided to take the last of my money and head to the same pub from last night. I was welcomed with open arms and greedy wallets. I bought one too many rounds that night. I was the king of the pub though for one night. I guess that was fun, and I did make a few friends. Two in particular hooked me up with a place to sleep that night. As they closed the bar, I remember this one girl that had been hitting on me all night was standing in the doorway, and out of no where I reached over and began a very sensuous kiss that seemed to last forever. Then I just walked away and said, "I'll see you, tomorrow." She just smiled as I walked away with my new friends. That's another chance for love, which bit the dust. That's OK; I had plenty of time to find love.

So off I went with these two idiots that almost got me put in jail over a stupid moped that we were going to steal for some money to head back to the pub. I'm sorry; I shouldn't be calling anyone idiots considering the title of the book. They were friendly enough all together. If I remember correctly, we did have some good laughs while I was hanging out with them. We did try to steal a moped, but it ran out of gas minutes later before we got too far, and they knew the alleys very well so we could get out of town before we got caught. That night we had problems finding a place to sleep and basically just stayed up all night. As you could imagine, these didn't last for me, and the next day I literally ditched them in a public bathroom and went back to the ship to go home. To be perfectly frank, that was a great meal that night on ship. That was the first feeling of being totally lost without clues where to go or what to do. Being homeless wasn't what I call fun. Those guys just felt so nonchalant about their predicament. It was sort of exciting at first, but that ended real quickly. I hope to God none of you ever have to feel that way in your lives.

Well, that in a nutshell was my experience with Europe. I have to say my accidental trip to Brussels stands out with the kids in England a close second, and can't forget that beautiful day at the beach either. Did I learn anything? Well, I guess I could ask you the same question couldn't I? A few things kind of stick out for me I guess. Women do get themselves in some awkward positions where men can't show respect in some cases and just back off. Fresh milk is definitely one of them simple things in life, to me. Keep your mind open and eyes peeled to see the world for what it is. You are an American so you are given the freedom to live.

"I wonder if you made a new rule that we take everyone in the US, take the land mass we have, divide the amount of people here into that, and give each American that amount of land and tell everyone to learn to survive in harmony would we survive?"

"My thoughts, as I stared out at the sea, subsided of pain, then turned into feelings in the present, and what I was doing now."

CHAPTER 23

Long Trip Home

In all my time in the Marines, this was probably the most relaxing time I ever had. It made for the most relaxing few months in my life. I had done my duty time on the *Mount Whitney* being on the radio and doing some time in the chow hall on the *Saipan*. So my trip home was completely free of all time. I spent all kinds of time in so many different ways. We had some time on our hands due to naval exercises that would be going on for a while. Our time off started with plenty of stories about all of our trips and experiences while in Belgium and England. Some of the stories consisted of Norway too, of course. This only lasted for a short time but was a lot of fun to hear how other people had spent their time. As you can imagine, I didn't stick my two cents in very much due to the problems I could've faced with humiliation. You know what I'm talking about. They would have crucified me for letting Dot get away. I can't even imagine what they would've said about me staying in England. That isn't even mentioning getting lost in Brussels. I shared bits and pieces especially when it came to scenery and such. One big mistake I did make is in all that time being in them beautiful places I never took one picture. What an idiot I was. I can't tell you how much that bothers me now. One of the guys did give me a few pictures from Brussels later on that my mom has. I hope when I get the book edited, I will get with mom and see if I can put them in.

Y'all remember watching toward the end of Forest Gump when Jenny was dying, and he spoke of all those things he saw? I guess that will be me trying to explain to all of you the pictures in my head. I'll do the best I can. I've kept you up to date so far as we've gone through each location. I think I need to explain a little about being on a naval ship.

Almost everywhere you go on the ship there is like a constant hum from the equipment around you. Stem pipes, electrical wiring, and tons of fans for atmosphere. The whole ship was obviously gray and kind of boring, but there was so much around every corner. This ship was huge. It had all the amenities that you found right there in your own town. We had a very nice library with all the plush couches and chairs. The chow hall was set up to be used twenty-four hours a day for anything that people wanted to use it for. Writing, studying, meeting with friends to play D and D, playing cards or anything else you might think of. In our berthing area, we also had a common area to do these kinds of things. You could get in with the art department and do art if you want to. It, as you can see, had endless possibilities. People were on ship for very long stints of time and on the Navy's side stationed on this ship for years at a time. The Navy does a great job giving them a since of home to make what they do easier for them. "Jim, did you have a favorite place on the ship?" Of course I did. At first I started with the risk playing, a little spades, and an occasional game of D and D. I did actually when one of our Twenty Four hour Risk championships. Not to mention a good stent with a good team for spades. When all things calmed down I did find a spot to contemplate.

At the rear of the ship was a watch spot that was always quit in the since of no people. You did have the propellers there though. I'm sure you remember the Mount Whitney and talking about ships as a metaphor for the life we build for our self. This was one of the reasons I loved it so much back there. This had become my place back there. The water churning was a very calming sound that was constant. To this day I still slip with a fan and love the sound of water. I loved taking afternoon naps back there. Watching the water was like watching the waves on a beach for hours. I especially loved it back there at night. The stars are so bright out there on the ocean. It obviously reminded me of my yard back in Duluth. Not to mention sitting at Horseshoe Lake and staring at the stars from the spot at the beach.

Now here I was sitting on a ship as big as a football field, in the middle of the Atlantic, already had a child I couldn't see, and I'm only nineteen. For some reason, a lot of my childhood hit me in them times in the back of that ship and not to mention all the time walking around the deck during the day. If you've never done it before, it's a very surreal feeling to be out there in the middle of the ocean knowing what's below you and how far real life is from you. All those problems that I felt as I joined the Marines and everything you've been listening to so far kind of hit home out here were I had no control, but did I ever have any control over any of it? No, I would think not.

I can't think of any way to change the people around me or what they did or said to me. Were they worrying about me right now? No, their life went on without me being there with them, and I'm doing fine without them way out here in the middle of nowhere. Why should I lose sleep or feel pain all the time when out here I can't change things? My thoughts, as I stared out at the sea, subsided of pain, then turned into feelings in the present, and what I was doing now. I can't say that from that point on I changed, but it definitely helped me grow up a little from my childhood memories. I needed to decide who I was. I had started being a man for the first time.

This time was a big step from the depression I felt the first year I spent in the Marines. Granted, a lot of the times I didn't have much time to think, but during the downtime, life haunted me something fierce. I had already been home a few times as you know. When I was home though, I held on to some of the woes and took them back to the base with me each time. Then I would do things wrong at work sometimes because I always had my mind somewhere else. We all know things like John Denver music were helping me through, but I shouldn't need that stuff all the time to survive. It was finally time to put my worries behind and listen to John just for fun. This trip finally gave me that spirit that I had locked up inside from all my exploring as a kid. Forgive and forget so I can move on. This is my time now and I was really loving everything about the ocean and loving life.

Another very cool memory from my little hideaway was seeing something glowing in the water one night. At first I had no idea what it was but it was very pretty. There comes another one from of in the distance. I started to notice that as they swam towards the ship, the light from the moon seemed to give them a tail of sorts. When they went faster, the tail seemed to get longer. A few more joined in what seemed to be a dance to them in the foam of the ships propeller. Then it happened the first time one of them decided to jump from the water. Oh my god, it's a dolphin. It was a whole school of dolphins frolicking in the foam of the ship. This was an incredible thing to see for the first time. There were a few other people out that night because of the beautiful full moon we experienced. "The tails you see are the stalagmite that feeds of the dolphins, it fall's off as they swim and gets reflected in the moonlight leaving a beautiful tail behind them. The faster the dolphin goes, the longer the tail. It was a very magical moment as I'm sure you can imagine. I've seen a lot of dolphins in pictures and TV since then but none as vivid as real life. I would assume some of you have heard the saying "seeing dolphins frolicking in the foam" before. Well, now you know what they're talking about. They are a picturesque sight.

This reminds me of the whale we saw up near Norway that I forgot about. I just happened to be finishing up lunch one day and heard over the intercom that we had come up on two whales. I got to the deck just in time. The people around me were pointing in a northern direction and saying they were there a second ago. Then it happened so suddenly if I hadn't known where they were seen, I might have missed one of them jump just enough to cause a wake from it. As they went under, the other poked his back a bit and stuck his tail up a little, and they both swam away. No one seemed to know what kind of whale they were, but they were very majestic to see just the same. What a thought when you wonder about the size of the whale then think about how much waters is underneath your ship. The vastness is dumbfounding. As you're mind sees that, then look up at night and see the stars . . . That gets you thinking. I have to say though, being there at the moment was bigger than your imagination could ever be. Oh no, I'm having them weird thoughts again.

Think about the whale that I saw and how nonchalant he was as he went by us. Why would he bother us out there in the middle of nowhere in this vast venue? The world is so big around us, and he's the biggest one. I don't see him wanting more than what is provided to him. They say the whale is very kind to its offspring and protective, but yet gentle at heart. They are completely content beings and show us a bit of humility due to their size. No different then an elephant I suspect. As big as this world is, with these thoughts in your head, why do we tend to want more than we need? Like the whale being a wandering soul, why can't we just want the experiences in life instead of the greed we see every day in our life? Does that mean we all have to be that way or can we just live and do what we can for each other?

Remember our heart-to-heart about reality or should I say basic reality? Where does it all end? We've already been to the moon and spend a lot of time exploring the oceans. For y'all that don't know, where do you think all of the trash on ships goes? Yes, right there in the whales' backyard. Think about reality and what you want in life. Think about the size of the US and we all realize the largest populations are in the city. I wonder if you made a new rule that we take everyone in the US, take the land mass we have, divide the amount of people here into that, and give each American that amount of land and tell everyone to learn to survive in harmony would we survive? I might have to look that up to see how much land we would have to survive. Talk about reaping what you sow, how many would survive? Of course if we all helped each other, there wouldn't be a problem. Wow, what a concept, helping your neighbor.

The rest of the trip was basically uneventful till we got down towards the Mediterranean and right into a bigger storm than on the *Whitney*. I had done really good about seasickness and hadn't been sick at all for the past few months. This time, I did get sick, but nothing compared to some people. I happily didn't worship the porcelain God, but very close. Let's just say I was queasy. One cool thing happened during the storm. I and the squids met in a room that they knew about were the anchor holes were; of coarse it was to playing D and D. This was about the time the storm was starting. The anchors were up of course, and to say the least, they were big. The holes were covered by these heavy duty glass plates, which they pointed out earlier to see the ocean as you were looking down. As the waves got bigger, actually, I should say the swells got bigger. It was very cool to see this through the glass. Remember this ship was a flat bottom, so as you lifted up in the air, you would see the ocean sort of move sideways a bit each time you fell back down. This is what almost made me sick.

As time went by and the storm got closer to its peak, looking out the portal got real scary. The ocean would seem fifty feet below then fall with a bang. Luckily, we weren't by the portal when the water popped it open, and jets of water ended our D and D real quick. When we got to the doorway heading away from the anchor room, some of the lights faltered as the water splattered them, and one of my friends got on of the phones that are in every room and called safety to get them in there to connect the portal. We decided it was best to just get back to our berthing. By the time, I got back I was feeling pretty sick and decided to get to my bunk, which was like a hammock, and tried to sleep through this storm. It had been an exciting enough day already.

A short time later we had a long day on a Mike boat from ship to shore and my wonderful journey was over. Then it was another wonderful feeling seeing my bed again after three or four months away from home base. If the military does anything, it takes you from your home for long periods and gives you such a high appreciation for what you do and don't have. You cherish the simple things when you're not in the field.

I've been in the field many times and do think about home a huge amount of the time. Kids, if you never go into the military, that is great, but think about this as you go through you're civilian life. I'm sure you guys remember camping a few times, same with all of you. We'll exaggerate that into survival skills, machine guns, war games, no showers, no hot food, no candy, high stress, working most of your days, no TV, no phone, and you start to see some of the feeling of being out there in the field. Now add a war like Vietnam, Iraq, or Afghanistan, and then you'll see how important freedom is. Even if you go in the Marines without patriotism, trust me you'll come out a true-blooded patriot. I know I've told all of you to respect the military men and women before; this may give you more reason. I spent I think it was three or four months on them ships and you better believe we sacrificed our selves to learn our trade to protect us from evil, foreign or domestic. I thank all you military people out there for your sacrifices and you're dedication to the United States. Semper fi!

"How can anyone out there think they know the answer to someone's situations if you personally weren't with that person every moment, haven't experienced that person defining moments, or know that person's childhood?"

CHAPTER 24

Father Moves Family Back to His Own State—Temple, Texas

When I got back I still had some time remaining for leave, and my family had moved down to Texas over the last six months or so. I decided I should go down and see what they got themselves into. I guess they had moved to the center of the state in Temple, Texas. For some reason, I vaguely remember their house at that time. Not really the point I guess. But I was interested in seeing the new restaurant. Actually I think they were living in a trailer. So a little time later and my leave went through, and I was back on a plane. This isn't a big point, but I have to let you know I still don't have a license to drive yet. Remember, I've been traveling and using cabs in North Carolina so far in my life. When I was in high school, we couldn't afford to put me in driver's education, which was I think seventy-five dollars at the time. This was becoming an issue when I went on leave and had to depend on my dad for rides.

About my dad; you remember that wonderful day in Palm Springs? Well, our relationship was still pretty good, but I could see that he was drinking again, and his life was a little scratchy right now. A little catch-up is in order here. Scot had moved out shortly after he graduated and was going to school to be a teacher in Temple. Something I didn't know was Pam was headed down that bad path of drinking and drugs. One thing my family did very well was hide things from me since I started my new life. For me, she seemed a lot more adventurous but no different than any other sixteen-year-old as far as I could see. Boy was I being naive. When all this was going on with Pam I had no "civilian" street-smarts. If you think about it, before now I had no experience with drugs, being underage for alcohol, big parties, lots of free time, casual sex, and not to mention, I never went to a prom. So in some ways, I was an idiot again to her age group. My experiences were in life now. I dated a few times and had my rebellious side, but we all know mine was fairly harmless. Scot and Pam had experiences that I, to this day, never had. At the time this made my relationship with them a little weird. Remember when I came back from boot camp and spent some time with Bob and Todd? This was happening with my siblings to. Right now the only person that had any idea what I was going through was dad, the one that was in the Navy. The only problem was I had no idea what he was going through. Not to mention the last few years that they hid from me.

See, you kids think you know so much about others, and you couldn't be more incorrect. I did the same thing to after my trip abroad. Remember the bus ride from Barstow, California, the story about the bug and the tree? Did you ever travel to another person's desert? How can anyone out there think they know the answer to someone's situations if you personally weren't with that person every moment, haven't experienced that person defining moments, or know that person's childhood? We each have our own experiences that we will share with our children in the future, hopefully. Granted, you're learning about my thoughts, but are you psychic and can read everyone's mind? If anyone out there is truly psychic, you'd be the richest person on earth. None of us can truly judge someone's wisdom and intelligence. What gives anyone the right to say you're wise? I feel my father was wise, and I only heard a few of his experiences. He wasn't very good at expressing himself though. He definitely gave into his evil side a few times growing up, and he could see the same thing was happening to Pam. This was making him very frustrated because she was too smart for him, and felt he had failed her deep inside. This drove him back to the bar again. I can't tell you how deep his desert (soul) went. I couldn't tell you how many times he was stepped on or if he was the stepping-type himself. He kept his past very well bottled up from us kids. During this visit, I was starting to judge his behavior, and it backfired one very sad evening. All of you, as you grow up, will face memories of your mother or father that you questioned them and felt you were right.

One of the toughest days in life for me was in that trailer I told you about at the beginning of this chapter. I don't really remember much else of this visit because of this. It overwhelmed the whole trip. Dad, like I said, seemed a little on edge while I was here this time. Something was so different, and at the time I just shrugged it off. I tried to be cool now because we did talk a lot about my trip. After I had been there awhile, I was getting strange vibes from Pam too. She was very distant, and we didn't have much to say to one another the whole time I was there. Sure there were heartfelt hellos and some small talk about simple things, but she always had somewhere to go or someone to talk to. Other than that first day, she felt like she was on a different planet. Think back and remember at the time I had no experiences like hers, so I couldn't, at the time, see her dependence on drugs and/or alcohol. Now looking back, Dad was in a bad state of mind. Mom, I can't imagine how difficult this was for you. Your little girl was losing control fast. I'm sorry I was so naïve at that age that I wasn't able to help. I truly had become a dork from the peer pressures that I had growing up around all those intelligent people in school. Of course, I'm pretty peaceful with what I've become. I hope they're happy with what effect they had on people and their experiences. It would have been pretty profound if Pam's big brother could have stepped in then though.

The last week or so that I was there, Mom and Dad had somewhere to go and said this would be a good time for Pam and I to spend some time with each other. Before they left to go out, Dad stopped and said, "Jim, don't let Pam go anywhere, you're in charge while we are gone." "No problem, we will be just fine." Boy was I wrong. Some of you know how manipulating a drug user can be when they want to go have some fun. Pam's friends were young Mexicans that swore they were just going to take their new car around the block, and Pam was saying, "It will only be a few minutes, and I'll be right back." God, I was so blind! It infuriates me to think about how naive I was! You see how such little things in life can just hurt people in ways you can't even tell at the time.

"Did she come right back?" Of course not, it was hours before I even saw a car. After it got dark, I heard a car door slam and jumped to the window. The blindness of the light hid what kind of car was in the driveway, but I assumed it was Pam. I ran to the front door, ready to give Pam the big angry speech that I had plenty of time to think over. I could hear the screen door open as I unlocked the door and began to turn the handle, yelling, "Were in the f—have you been!" Then the door opened so quick from one pushing and one pulling, then I lost my balance as I heard my father's voice screaming, "No, where the f—were you when the police called me!" **Bam!** The first fist hit me across the top of my head due to me catching my balance from the door, and I fell back against the couch. "Who gave you the right to put my daughter in a car with a drunken idiot! You're not getting off that easy!" As he spoke, he grabbed me by my shirt to drag me away from the couch and threw me with ease across the living room, slamming hard into the wall, which gave way easily to put a huge hole in the wall. As I got myself together, looking at him walking across over to me, all I felt was fear and anger at the same time. I think he felt the anger in my eyes and said, "You got something for me, Marine?" Then the second blow, this one didn't miss though, right across the face. This startled me, and in that second, I was being thrown again toward the couch. Surprisingly, the couch didn't fall back on the floor. He then came at me with the dreaded pointing finger then switched in anger to his fist and started pounding on my chest as he spoke, "You son of a b—, when you make a promise, you better keep it, no matter what the consequences! Your sister, not that you care, was in the hospital from being in a car crash!" I was dumbfounded and didn't know what to say to him. His anger was way beyond fear for me right now. I did feel bad about not standing up to Pam, but it was hard to get over what just happened with my dad. In some ways, I had gotten it a lot worse growing up with the holy belt, sticks, and basically anger spankings that were brutal. This was something else that I had never seen in him. At that moment, I wasn't scared of a father, I was scared of a man. But in the other hand, I understood the look on his face. He was protecting his daughter. Remember, I'm not a biological son, not that I ever felt that way, but this was different. This had a long-lasting effect on me for sure.

Would you die for your family? You know I would. Why wouldn't you? My father was in an instinctive situation of protecting his offspring. We all have the instinct of survival. We also have an instinct to protect. Remember basic reality from earlier? We have a very good survival instinct. But how can you survive a car crash, a gunshot, chemicals in food, plane crash, pollution, basically anything unnatural and or man-made. Is this basic instinct? Is this the way things are supposed to be in a human's life span? Are we truly headed down the right path? Do the people that tell us who are wise or intelligent have the answers, or do we even still have basic instincts? I'm sure someone out there thinks they have the right answer. I know I don't have the answer. When all this took place, I believed that I knew the answers. My father was very mean in his own way; it's only my place to feel the way I choose about the situation on that terrible night. He was very stressed at the time I'm sure. I didn't help the matter by giving in to Pam. Things would have been a lot easier that way. I see that now. If I would have had a bit more street-smarts, I may have been able to help my sister more. We all can look back and find things that we could have changed if we just knew better. I guess we should just listen to our parents who have been around you your whole life, they know your defining moments, and they've seen you through your whole childhood. Does this sound familiar to you?

For the rest of my time on leave, things were much quieter and I believe we were all happy to go our separate ways at the end. Dad never did talk about that moment ever again. It was something better left unsaid I guess. I wish I could've talk to him a bit more later in life or to Pam, but I was too afraid to bring it up. Time to say good-bye to my old life again, but I will say one thing: I hated the humid and hot climate of Texas. Sorry, Texans. All things aside, I'd rather be in 29 Palms where it's dry and hot.

"Ozzy Osborn became my favorite rock and roll during this time."

CHAPTER 25

Seeing a Bit of the Wild Side

When I finished my trip home to the trailer, I went back to Jacksonville to start back to normalcy. My first visit was to the Mai Tai. The next few months were basically uneventful and more of the same things. I played my guitar as much as possible, went roller-skating a few times, movies as often as possible, rifle range one time, and among other things my first stint of mess duty. Little did I know how this would affect my future. I never felt comfortable being a radio operator and being around the antennas. When they first told me about having mess duty, I was slightly upset but it grew on me real quick. I'm not sure what this work did for me, but I do know to me it was very exciting. You have to remember the restaurants that I was around as a child to see where this came from. I guess part of it has always been seeing the smile on someone's face when you cooked for them. I think doing something then seeing firsthand the product that you've made being eaten right there was a good feeling. I guess I was tired of just cleaning radios all day. Working in the chow hall just felt rewarding and more productive.

After a while there they let me do some of the cook's jobs like egg grill and a product now and then. I was having such a good time that when my month was up, I requested to stay on again, and they let me. Well, at this point, we got a new crew, and they made me the chief mess man. This became a lot of fun. This was the first time since I'd been out of boot camp where I was in charge. I wasn't great at first but slowly started learning how to get the most out of each individual. It did kind of get to my head a little I guess. One thing was for sure though, I learned very fast at everything I was learning to do, so I became very knowledgeable of everything in the chow hall. I wish I would have realized my gift of learning a lot quicker than I did.

A little side note about the differences in civilian life and a military world. Right then, I was only nineteen, and in the civilian world, I'd either be in college or working a low-paying job. College students, when they get out, are partying at someone's house or in a fraternity. The average worker underage is partying at a friend's house. Marines, we just head to the e-club. The way it's figured is we are only eighteen, underage, but we can die for our country. So on base, we can drink at eighteen though we were limited to only beer and wine, but its still alcohol. At this time in my life, I was still looking for friendship in weird places. That made the e-club an even bigger thing for me. In the past, as you know, I would go down during the late afternoon and just relax with my chicken. Now we didn't get off work till after chow was over. That put me at the e-club late, which put me into loud music, dancing, and chasing girls. John Denver was not exactly e-club music, but if you remember, I had a Van Halen record back in junior high. Now I wanted to fit in, so I began my stint of hard rock for an interest. Ozzy Osborn became my favorite rock and roll during this time. Then the drinking began for me. It was just the thing to do, and all my mess men did it a lot. Most of the time when I was with them at the e-club, I kept very responsible, most of the time.

Then something happened that blew me away. After being at the chow hall as long as I had been, I had made a lot of friends. Maybe, acquaintances would fit better in this situation. A few of the girls were showing me some interest for the first time in a long while. There was DOT, of course, but that was one day in a different country. Well, the night in question, I was hanging out with my friends, listening to loud music, and drinking way too fast. I have to tell you, this was my first experience of having no memory of the night before. That wasn't that big of a deal until I found myself lying in a motel bed, naked, head pounding, and a female looking at you with a mustache saying, "What are we doing tonight?" Don't jump the gun; yes, she was a she. She wasn't terribly attractive but a nice person that worked for me. Because of the Marine inspections, she had shaved her face once and now had to all the time. I played it very nice because I didn't want to hurt her feelings at all. I really didn't remember coming to this motel with her and vaguely remember her pawing on me all night last night. "What do you do?" Heck, I was nineteen and never really had a steady girlfriend; I don't know what to do. I still to this day don't know whether I slept with her or not. But I wasn't as excited as her about that next night. In hindsight, she was very nice, and if it wasn't for the mustache, I don't know.

That morning I had to go to work, so she said, "Can't wait to see you again tonight. You're so wonderful and very sensitive." She then, as we both stood there naked, came up and gave me a very nice kiss and said, "I'll miss you." "Me too" was all I could think of. I didn't know what else to say at that moment. It was a very awkward moment for me, but it seemed very nice and comfortable to her. When I got to work that morning, I got some snickers and strange looks at first till the ice was broken. Then they began to all laugh and joke about what happened to me while I was drunk and how stupid I was acting at the e-club. It's there that I feel very bad about the things that happened later. I fell into the stupid ranting about her being ugly and what they felt about her. I did what this whole book says not to do. I didn't think about what she felt since I had spent some emotional time with her. One of the girls said I shouldn't just dump her but try to act innocent and make something else with it. "You should just have a party without talking to her about it, and she will get mad and leave you alone." This girl said. Great idea, I thought.

That night after work, we all showed up at the motel. Talk about things getting worse. When I turned the key and opened the door, there she was all dressed up looking very pretty with a picnic set up on the bed with KFC. Did I feel like crap or what? Startled was the best way to explain what I saw in her face. I gave her a quick kiss and started yelling like an idiot to get the party started. We threw a bunch of ice in the tub and just poured every bottle we had in the ice. Then we put a few gallons of punch in it, and there you go. I remember trying to get drunk quickly again to stop thinking about that nice picnic she had for us. If I could put some curse words in the book, I can think of a few for me for what I did to her then. I forgot about her later, and the police made us stop partying, so we went to someone else's house. It was so bad I gave my keys to the room to another couple since I was leaving anyway. Man was I a big a-hole to her. This isn't the end though.

She didn't work the next day, so my friends that stayed the night before told me what happened after I left. "Boy, Jim, you are lucky to be alive right now." That was the first thing they said. "She never left and you're going to get a bill for some lamps and a coffee table." "I hope you're not serious?" "Oh yeah, she cried, threw things around, swore to kill you, or cut some things off you. She was mad and very sad at the same time. Not a very good mix." When I asked what I should do, they said, "Leave it alone and time will heal it." Thinking about how I would feel about this, I swore to myself I would never get that drunk again. I stuck to that most of the time in my life. This was definitely one of those bad decisions in my life, to say the least. Kids, I hope with this story, you'll never make the same mistake. For the girl out there, if you remember me, I do apologize in the deepest parts of my soul to you. What I did was just, flat-out mean. Guys, just keep in mind all the things about making people feel bad. I only did this to stay cool with the idiots around me. Don't get caught in someone else's world. You can make the right decisions on your own.

Later on we made friends in a very strange way. It was in the middle of a hurricane. I don't remember what the name was, but if you really want to know, I guess you can look it up online, right? I think it was the summer or fall of '84. Yes it was a hurricane, during then they used the military buildings for shelters, and we were in there for a couple of days twiddling our thumbs. We just sat and talked it out so we could see each other's side. To her she was ready to get married, and to me it was just not time for that as young as we were. I didn't tell her about all the comments about her or anything; she didn't need to know about that. We became decent friends after that hurricane. At one time it was like a bomb went off, so we all were looking outside and—BOOM—another one hit right there in front of us and split this huge tree right in the front of the building. Man was that a sight to see. Just like you might have seen on TV, but we were fifty feet away. I think I can almost say it scared the "you know what" out of me.

After my long stint on mess duty, they called me back to let me know I had orders to Okinawa, Japan. Oh my God, Okinawa. Boy, they do get us Marines around a lot. Guess who else got orders; yes it was my old friend Wilke. He was going to the air wing but I stayed with FSSG. That also meant another good leave, before going to Okinawa. I wasn't totally excited about leave after last time with Dad, but I hoped for the best.

"Your experiences, as I said before, give you your personality, wants and needs, what makes you happy, and in general makes *you* who *you* are."

CHAPTER 26

In Retrospect

This chapter is a quick thought to my past relationships. Nothing I did in the last twenty-five years will ever be thought of as a mistake to me. All of my children are a blessing to me. If I changed anything, they wouldn't exist in this world. I know that my decisions weren't very sound, but I did them in the spur of the moment as I saw them. I'm not proud of the fact that I had many relationships at all, but I hope you kids will see the other side of my decisions. Jason, if I hadn't left your mom when I did, then Christopher and Zach wouldn't be here today. Chris and Zach, the same for you, or Mattie wouldn't be here. Mattie, after me and your mom, there was Trenton. Then there's all of you're children in the future. Please don't any of you feel like another child is more important than you are. You are just as much a miracle as the others in every way.

For y'all that are wondering who I'm talking to, here is a quick rundown of my miracles. Nicholas is the one we have already discussed. He was born in Duluth before I went to the Marines. Jason is the second who was born out in Fallbrook, California. Christopher and Zachery were both born in California also. Madison was born in beautiful Steamboat Springs, which is also were Trenton was born. I was a terrible father to each and every one of them due to reasons sometimes out of my control. Please all of you, including you kids, don't jump to judge me yet. We will go through this one at a time. I will give you all the important information for each one of you. I hope I can make each of you a better person from reading about this. Maybe each one of you in these roles—fathers, mothers, wives, and especially the children—can make something of my thoughts. Kids, this is not made to be an excuse, but to give you reason. Y'all remember Forest, "I'm not a smart man." I was very young and not ready to do some of the things I had to. All you teenagers out there need to think about things before you jump the gun. I tried my best to tell my children and people I met to relax till they're at least twenty-five. For now, just have fun. Most of you have no idea what you're going to be like in five years, not to mention deciding to be with someone forever. I can't change my story, but you kids' story isn't written yet. Learn who *you* are first. Then the right one will see you better for what you are and you'll be much happier. This all reminds me of a song. Please let me explain.

Everyone out there has "Seasons of the Heart." We have all heard this saying time and again, but how well do you understand it. For y'all that live in an area of snow, it's more apparent to see the metaphor. Spring, you're a new born and your life is just springing up. Everything is beautiful and new to you. It is all fresh to you. Summer, this is the meat of your life, the longest part, filled with bright sunny days, and enjoying life in general. Fall, life starts to slow, things sort of die down, and we began to settle. The point of change is upon us all at this time. Winter, a time of reminiscing, retrospect, rest, and when things come to a close.

We all go through these seasons in our life. It seems to me that the younger generations want to rush straight to the summer of their life and skip the spring, which is our most important growth time. That doesn't mean our size, but our mental growth. Spring is a wonderful time of wonderment, experiences, learning, and it is all fresh and new. Skip that and you may never be able to get it back. You also will lose out on the adventures of life in general. Your experiences, as I said before, give you your personality, wants and needs, what makes you happy, and in general makes *you* who *you* are. Would you skip that with a little knowledge of what you see in the US? A lot of divorce out there, isn't there? Why not just wait a little while and have fun. One of John Denver's first albums, **Rocky Mountain High**, has five songs dedicated to the seasons. Then later when he made his mistakes with Annie, his wife, he did a song called "Seasons of the Heart." This will come up for a lot of people if you don't find yourself first. Enjoy your spring before you jump into something.

Some of the simple things in life may become very difficult in a relationship, if you don't explore your thoughts before you get very serious about someone. Think hard about this so it doesn't bite you later. How many times have you heard "irreconcilable differences" without any real explanation? More than anyone could ever count, I'm sure. Knowing yourself is the key to them differences. Granted, we all make some compromises in a relationship, but you don't want that to change who you are. You've all heard that saying I'm sure. "You can't change your spouse." Then why do we do it anyway? Maybe if we listened to our parents at least a little, people wouldn't divorce so much. I'm sorry; I forgot that most people just go online to find out about relationships. I'm sorry; y'all know I hate computers.

I'll give some simple explanations of what I'm trying to say here. Music is a good example; how does a hard-core country girl feel about a guy listening to rap all night while they're sitting around the house, relaxing? If your wife loves to party at a dance club, talking to all her friends, dancing, and men trying to pick her up every time her husband goes to get drinks; but her husband hates a room full of people, getting drunk, don't like dancing all the time, and really feels insecure about the men trying to pick up his wife. Husband loves Southwest art and wife loves a gothic setting. I'm sure that's enough to get you to see my point. Make sure you know who you are before you fall head over heels and get so far that neither one of you knows what to do.

As you read the chapters on my relationships, you'll see a lot of these problems came up for me. It would've been nice to grow up a bit more and enjoy my spring. I was too grown-up to listen to anyone about my relationships. I refuse to get into any detailed about "behind closed doors" situations with my relations because this is for you, kids. I also won't be giving complete detail of breakups with any one. That is between them and me only. I don't want to say things about myself or my relations that might hurt my children's feelings. It just seems a little counterproductive to be arguing over things with a child in the middle. Sometimes I bet the child is wiser than the parents. Arguing and screaming at each other doesn't solve anything. I learned that the hard way.

There were a lot of things I did during the beginning of all this I'm not very proud of at all. Guys, please just bear with me through some of the dim-witted times in my life till we get towards the present. Just remember this chapter and some of the problems of growing up too fast can bring. Kids, this is the part you have been waiting for, I hope someday you'll forgive me for my misgivings.

"I wish I would have known the difference between love and lust. It's really hard to see the difference when you haven't had your spring yet."

CHAPTER 27

My First Romance

My excitement about going to Okinawa outweighed my worries about Dad big time. When I got home, it was as if Dad forgot about the whole thing. I guess that was a good thing and thinking back, I don't think it was ever mentioned again. This definitely made me feel better about things. I was only there for a few days when Scot called to come visit, or I called—don't matter either way. He was meeting Rodney at the Taco Bell there in Temple by the mall, and as I sat waiting, this pretty girl came in. She was a friend of Scot's and Rodney's. Her name was Susan, and she was a student at Mary Harden Baylor. I did still have my Charlies on so she could see right away that I was a Marine. "Who is this?" she said to Scot with a fascinated smile. "That's Jim, my brother." "So you're a Marine, huh?" She was saying as she sat herself at the table I was at. To be honest, I don't remember the whole conversation, but we hit it off real well. Passion mounted very quickly between us, and we eventually ended up at a hotel that night. Susan wanted to be a teacher and was quite intelligent. She was very pretty and seemed to know what she wanted in life. Unlike me, I think she had her life planned out to the T. She was definitely a country girl at heart. She was driving one of them Mustang LS, I think it was. Not the real sporty model. We had some very intense nights that first week we knew each other. This was very exciting to me, which I'm sure you know.

On that second Monday, for some reason, I hadn't been sleeping much and was having a whole day with Susan Tuesday. Mom let me have a few sleeping pills to get my mind off Susan to get some sleep. I remember waking up Wednesday. You're thinking, "What happened to Tuesday, Jim?" Don't know honestly. But Mom reminded me that I asked Susan to marry me and she said yes. If you remember correctly, I was headed to Okinawa in what was now three weeks. Everyone thought we were crazy even thinking about this at such a young age and in such a short time. We convinced everyone that this was the right thing to do and even convinced each other after arguing with everyone else about it. I was so infatuated with passion that I never thought about whether we were right for each other. It did seem right at the time, but our minds weren't ready for this, I should say our hearts weren't ready. "Love conquers all," they say. I wish I would have known the difference between love and lust. It's really hard to see the difference when you haven't had your spring yet. This feeling was new to both of us, but we should've let it just be fun I guess. I'll admit I couldn't get my mind off her back then.

We decided getting married at her mom's house would work out perfectly. It was a beautiful home to say the least. Jason, I assume you know about us getting married there at Grandma's. If I remember correctly your aunt played the piano for the wedding and your mom surprised me with her talent too. It was a very traditional wedding right there at Grandma's house. Somehow my dad got a hold of some spray paint for your mom's car and Susan was truly ticked off. On the back, like always, it had, "Just Married." In one corner it said, "What an idiot." Your mom didn't like that at all. It was all in fun though. It was really nice getting married in a house. I think it was her dad that set up our honeymoon. It was a real nice resort south of Temple. After the reception, we headed down I-35 to the resort as mister and miss's. Something funny about the honeymoon for everyone; Susan and I were very excited but very tired when we arrived at the resort. We got a little romantic as we got to the room then Susan interrupted that with a very strange request, "Jim, it's been a real long day and I never got to read the paper today. Is it OK if I read today's paper before anything happens?" Maybe I should've said no, but I didn't want to be pushy right at the start of our relationship. She usually got her way after that. I sort of followed her lead. Other than the paper, it was a very nice holiday, to say the least. Soon we knew I'd have to go. "Leaving on a Jet Plane" comes to mind. Mom hated it when I'd play that song on the guitar.

Well, Jason, that's what I remember when I met your mom. I stared at the pictures of her on that fifteen-hour or so plane ride to Okinawa almost constantly. I remember one in particular where she was looking up to me with a very loving smile in a light blue blouse. I think you've seen that picture, Jason. She did have a nice smile when she wanted to. It was a quick stop in Hawaii for fuel, which we never got out of the plane, then next stop, Okinawa.

"One of my biggest arguments for drinking, you kids, is to understand about getting sick; it isn't very smart at all. It would seem to me if your body gets you that bad, wouldn't that tend to reason that it's not good for you to get that drunk?"

Chapter 28

Alone in Okinawa

If anyone is being curious, Okinawa is just south of Japan, and a little to the right. That was the karate kid's teacher's home in **Karate Kid II**. The Marines helped take it back from the Japanese in WW II. I was stationed with Ninth Motors Battalion. We were at camp Butler right by a town called Naha. This was on the east side of the island towards the bottom, or south. I may be wrong, but I think it was close to the holidays when I arrived. I have to say it was very beautiful there right off base by the seawall. "Seawall," this was the only defense against typhoons for Okinawa. Try to imagine a whole bunch of big medal **X**s piled on each other to slow the flow of waves, and you'll see the "seawall." You could see it from the base, and when you got close, they also had a big concrete wall. Ninth Motors was actually quite cool. I had a lot of old salty Marines with my platoon. Our coffee was made the day before in a three-gallon coffeemaker and reheated for the day's coffee. You could say it was slightly strong.

Work was daily routines of cleaning equipment and rifles. We did PT three times a week here. That was a nice break. We had a pretty big e-club there on base. Drinking was legal in Okinawa though, so the e-club stayed much quieter. Here's one for you, beer machines in the barracks. Trust me, that wasn't really a good idea. Yes, it was back to squad bays though. Here in Okinawa, the radios were watched after a lot more. You always had an NCO on duty to watch over the squad bay. NCO is a "noncommissioned officer." I was still a lance corporal or E-3 at this point. An E-4 is when you become an NCO. The point is it was a lot nicer than being in 29 Palms. Our base PX was also very nice too. One thing that all Marines know about was the technology of the day when it came to sound systems. Yeah, I know all you old Marines remember how big a deal that was over there. We always had a big choice of sound systems in Oki. A lot of Marines will remember the restaurant in Naha with the water system on the windows. What was that place called? Can't remember the name, but it was a Mongolian barbeque. You went down a line and picked out the food you wanted. Had choices like beef, pork, chicken, lots of different vegetables, and then what kind of sauce. Put all of it in a bowl, hand it to the cook, watch him cook it on this big half-moon thing with a wood fire and, **boom**, dinner. Susan liked that place.

During these first few months of being by myself, I was able to take care of a few things that I hadn't done yet in my life. I still didn't have a license for one. They sent me to a two-week school for a jeep license. It was Ninth Motors after all. This was a lot of fun and kept my mind off my new wife, which was a very difficult thing to deal with. Those jeeps were incredible, they seemed to go anywhere. Have any of you been fording? Fording is driving in the water. You could literally drive the vehicle totally submerged. The motor and such was waterproof, and the muffler was six-foot high while fording. Pulled the hand throttle, stuck it in first, and steered with your feet. Very cool thing to do and also learned how to drive a stick. After that it was forklift school. As I'm sure you know it was quite easy to pick this up. A little while after that, we needed a new MIMMS clerk. This was a school to learn the paperwork for all the equipment in the Marine Corps. So let's send Kelley. It seemed to never end. But it did keep my mind working and not to mention it was strengthening my brain. I forgot to mention getting my GED, which had become a regulation since I got in. I had been too busy to lose sleep over my separation. I was definitely falling deeper in love every moment without my wife.

Off duty time had become very spiritual a few times out. In some ways I always felt bad if I had too much fun. I think the favorite part for me had to be the ocean. The serenity of the ocean, like times before in my life, was something that made me feel good about life. Its beauty was undeniably breathtaking. Susan was always on my mind out there. I also used to go to a town called Nago on the weekend to get away from the Marines a few times. It had this awe-inspiring bay right there in town. The mountains all around town just added to its already magnificent look of splendor that I've already mentioned. Because of the landmasses in the area, there were a few islands in the bay too. As I'm sure you can imagine, this just took it over the top. The people were always so nice to me there. They could see the love of their home that I had in my heart as I traveled around sight seeing. Nago will always be in my memories. It's was something else.

Do any of you know the difference between a hurricane and a typhoon? Simple enough it is the direction of the spin. Hurricanes turn counter clockwise. I'm sure you remember I had already been through a hurricane; well now it was time for my first typhoon. I actually was put on security for this typhoon, which meant I got to be outside making sure no one was stuck outside during the typhoon. We had to wear our flak jackets in case of flying debris. That was very exuberating but not the part I remember the most. It was an idiot that I was going to be on duty with. You see, we weren't allowed to drink eight hours before our duty, and this guy loved to drink. It was thirty minutes before we hit that eight hours. So he just grabbed all the change he could and started downing them .55 cent beers. You remember the beer machines? Well, just before that eight hours, he had drank fifteen beers. Yes, fifteen beers in thirty minutes. If you can imagine, he passed out. An hour or so later, he woke up and started freaking out. It was funny at first, and then he started hurting himself on the bunks and slamming into the walls. We finally had to catch him and tied him to the bunks with belts. We did this when he started bleeding from many cuts and bruises. In a big way it went way too far, but you can trust me when I say he was hard to catch.

I should have paid more attention to that moment before I started drinking tequila later.

Time seemed to tickle like watching snow melting in the spring. Knowing Susan was now a part of my life was eating away at me having to wait till we can be together again. Looking back from now, I know it was more lust and puppy love, but for me then I was thinking about her all the time. One of them days that I just wanted to stop feeling this, I went to a favorite watering hole to drown in sorrows. I liked their jukebox, the best of any in town, and it was always a little quieter there. I started the jukebox up, grabbed a blue Hawaiian, and started writing to Susan. Blue Hawaiians turned into seven and seven. It was then that I started talking to the pop-a—son and listening to different music. Somehow he talked me into a drink called "snake bites." This has tequila and really creeps up and bites you. I have no idea how many shots I did, but it wasn't good.

I remember leaving the bar and grabbing some "Yokatory," (BBQ chicken on a stick.) Actually it had a teriyaki taste to it. Trust me, they were great. So I grabbed my little snack and that was about it for me. Next thing I know I'm laying on the side of a "ditch," trying to make my hand move. As I lay there, screaming at my hand to move, I couldn't help but laugh. This was a very good thing because my hilarity is what made the MPs investigate the noise and find me. "What the hell are you doing, Marine?" they said as I continued to laugh hysterically. My answer started them to be quite amused, "My doggone hand want do what I tell it to, and I can't move my legs." "Will take you back to your barracks so you can sleep it off," they said as they lifted me into there jeep. As you can imagine that was not an easy task I'm sure. I truly couldn't move an inch to help them get me up. If I remember correctly, I didn't drink tequila for a while after that. I can't stand getting sick and I do everything in my power not to. One of my biggest arguments for drinking, you kids, is to understand about getting sick; it isn't very smart at all. It would seem to me if your body gets you that bad, wouldn't that tend to reason that it's not good for you to get that drunk? Seems pretty logical to me, wouldn't y'all think the same? Drinking is fine in moderation. I kind of wish someone would've told a few stories to me to help my decision making.

It got worse before it got better. Mess duty again there in Okinawa. It was actually a very nice chow hall, by the way. I don't remember how it came about, but I ended up in the scullery. Washing dishes for close to 750 people a meal. Sounds crazy? It was a blast busting your butt to keep up with the line. I'm not positive where I got it, probably the Marines, but I always did whatever it was that I was supposed to do, to the best of my ability, no matter what it was. Trust me I could sling some dishes. I met two friends that I actually remember their names: Paddock and Chief, who became my best friends while I was there, in Okinawa. I kind of hope they read this and try to find me. We became the comedians of the chow hall. The majority of the time we had hangovers. But then that second wind kicked in around dinnertime, and that was all she wrote. We were like the three amigos, or maybe it was the three stooges, I guess it depends on how you looked at it.

We kind of got in trouble once and they stuck us in the pot shack. I'm sure you can figure that one out. Man, we were awesome in there. We weren't supposed to like it, but it became our home away from home. You see we had a schedule that we stuck to pretty well. We were so fast that we were always done before everyone else. Around six or seven, we ran to the barracks and took a power nap till around nine. Then we'd hurry over to the e-club and close that down at two, run to the barracks drunk, take a quick shower, get in our whites, and crash in the GI shack till formation at three thirty. We wouldn't be very productive till around seven when they brought back this huge bowl with ice water that they used for the milk. This kind of started as a bet and turned into a routine. We stuck are heads in the ice water to see who could last the longest. This is where we found our hangover recipe. Ice water on the brain. Head hurt for a bit, but then, **boom**, felt great and we started kicking tail. Six or seven rolled around, and we would do it again and again. Chief and Paddock, thanks for all the fun, it was a blast.

"Think about them boys waiting for an ambush in the middle of Vietnam, hearts pounding, can't move an inch or you get caught too quick by the enemy, can't even cough for fear of giving up your position, and back in the States someone's, upset because it's taking too long to cash your check at the bank."

CHAPTER 29

A Short Trip to Korea
Twentieth Birthday

To be honest with all of you, I can't remember if I went to Korea Before or after Susan got to Okinawa, so I'm going to do this short chapter on Korea. I was sent to Korea on what we called TAD, (temporary assigned duty.) I was put with a medical battalion as there radio operator. We were assigned to the USS Durham. LSD, I think it was. It was a supply ship; yes, she was part of the Gator fleet. Funny enough, the USS **Duluth** was with us to. This group also had the LHA **Tarawa**, Like the **Saipan**, and the flagship was the **Blue Ridge**. Remember I was a radio operator and part of a naval unit this time. We were helping them by setting up their communications.

Our group was going to be the BES or "beach evacuation station" for the war games on the beaches of Korea. The operation was called Teamwork 84-85. The group I was supporting was what we call a West Pac. They did all of the orient areas like Korea, Thailand, and Japan. I was just TAD for the evacuation station. I was communications to the ship hospitals during the games. We would go to units and tag Marines with problems. Frag grenade, gunshot in the liver, basically any kind of wound you can imagine. The corpsman in the field would field dress them and they sent them to us to process through our field hospital. I sent reports to the ships and would send for medical evacuations. After the Marine went through that process as a guinea pig they got to take a shower on the ship and come back as troop replacements. This was very good training for all of them, from the ship hospital to the field corpsman. This is also how I got to spend time on all those ships I mentioned earlier. Yes, I did have the hookup for that one.

First things first, we had to hit the beach like we would in a real war. We were sent of ship on mike boats later in the morning after all the grunts secured the beach. It was high tide, or so we believed. When we started circling we were just told the beachfront had heavy seas and we had to wait for a while. At first we just stood around talking and twiddling our thumbs. "Sorry, guys were going to be out here a little longer now," we were informed, and then they said we should go ahead and eat our lunch. A few more hours went by and we headed back towards the **Tarawa** to get fuel. We haven't had confirmation on when to hit the beach so we have to take on fuel and were getting some bottled water for all of us. This was getting ridiculous, but we're Marines and don't complain. It had already been four hours when we got the water. Back out to sea we go. Some people were starting to get sick now, but again I missed out on that feeling. Thank God, they looked so miserable. Well, long story short, we circled around out at sea for eight hours all together. So as you can imagine, as a civilian, waiting has never been a big deal to me.

Think for a minute about all those times you get so upset about waiting in line for something. What would you have done while you were out there on the mike boat just going around and around? Think about them boys waiting for an ambush in the middle of Vietnam, hearts pounding, can't move an inch or you get caught too quick by the enemy, can't even cough for fear of giving up your position, and back in the States someone's, upset because it's taking too long to cash your check at the bank. Seems kind of silly when you look at it like that, doesn't it. "Didn't it bother you sitting on that boat for eight hours, Jim?" Of course it did, but what difference would it make if I got upset? We all stayed calm and just dealt with it.

If anyone would've gotten upset, it would just make it harder for everyone. You start screaming at the teller, you just stress everyone out, and that makes a bad situation worse. Take it easy and just relax when it happens. You have plenty of time.

We went to "Po Hang" for liberty, which was uneventful, to say the least. Now you Marines are out there, saying "Jim, what about the liberty, didn't you go crazy while you were there?" "No, absolutely not, I had a bet with all the people I hung out with." For all of you that have never been there, the place is a "red-light district" with no rules, except the ones you give yourself. This book still is and always will be G rated. The stories that Marines can tell y'all in private are endless, yet very true. I was too afraid to lose Susan by doing something stupid just to have a good time. Granted this was a great place for a birthday, but she was my whole life and this was just a few days. It wasn't worth it to me at all. None of my friends believed me when I said I wasn't messing around. I bet them each $50 that I would stay faithful while I was in Po Hang. We won't be with you the whole time. So I came up with the idea that one would stay with me watching me the whole time. They agreed, and it was on. Well I have to give them an A+ for trying while we were there, but when it was all over I was $250 richer.

South Korea was a very pretty country, and the people were all very nice to us all the time. But I thought the Marine boot camp was bad till I met the "Rock Marines" or (South Korean Marines.) It was the law there that they all had to serve at least two years in the military or you got no benefits from the government the rest of your life. The paycheck they received was a joke. I think it was like $200 a month or so, they got two bottles of sojue (rice wine) and a carton of cigarettes. If they didn't smoke or drink, they could trade for other things. We would trade MREs for the sojue all the time. It was very strong on your stomach, but the ones that did it didn't care. These guys were some very tough Marines. Their training was much more abusive then we ever saw on anyone. They were beaten with sticks, batons, and basically anything their superiors could find. You learned to just not make any mistakes or they'd make life miserable. As wild as they trained in person, they were very different. The way our "seals" were best explains it. The silent types will always surprise you. Kindness surrounded them on their off-duty time. Even the superiors were nice to them while they were on downtime. Like I said though, don't make any mistakes. Let's just say I hope we never face them in battle. They may be small but there very deadly.

That's really all I can say about Korea. It was very neat to get to see all the different ships. I was scared but enjoyed the helicopter rides. I thought our training was very productive also. I learned a lot about the medical side of the military. Yes it was a little like seeing MASH in person. It was definitely nice to visit another country. Twenty years old, and I had already seen five countries, not bad for that age.

"The Declaration of Independence gives us the right to have an opinion and gives you the right to choose your side of things. What it doesn't give you is the right to make someone follow your beliefs. I can't make someone be thoughtful and kind, as much as they can't make me be mean to others"

CHAPTER 30

She Finally Arrives

You can imagine this was going to be a big day for me. Before I get to her arrival, we have to discuss our living arrangement. Now remember, I haven't been on my own yet. In a way maybe, but I was always in a barracks at this point. I got the permission I needed to live off base, and I started looking. The only thing I found was an older model home that needed some TLC before it would work out for my Susan. I had found Wilke, and he helped me clean the place up a bit. I got a few things from friends and got some essentials, like dishes, a bed, kitchen table, couch, a few other nightstands and such. It was very hot around that time, and I had gotten used to sleeping with a fan, as you may remember. She had sold her Mustang and got a civilian flight to Naha, I think it was. I hadn't found a car yet, so I took a cab to the airport to pick her up. Seeing her again and smelling her perfume was a great moment for me, but she did seem a little scared at first. Some small talk ensued, and we got in the cab and headed to our first home together.

Susan wasn't exactly impressed, but she seemed too calm a little once she freshened up and sat to take it all in. She got up to do something and asked me to get something from her bag. This was not a good moment for me. Now in defense of the situation, I have to say that our meeting was brief at best. We fell in lust right away but wasn't sure what was going to happen. As I reached in her bag, I found a letter, which at first

I thought was mine. Then as I read the note, it was from her previous boy friend. Like I said before, I won't go into detail what was written in this note but will say I was devastated. This was all new to both of us, and I didn't know what to do or say. I was dumbfounded to say the least.

As I read the last few words, my heart was sinking and the tears started to fall. Just then she came from whatever room it was, and then started yelling that that was none of my business and ripped the letter from my grasp. It started off with yelling at each other through tears; soon after, it had turned into complete silence. I can't say I know what all was said, but I know some of it was about being unsure, almost not coming, had we made the wrong decision, and a little about knowing him much longer than me. I decided to jump in the rabbit's hole, just work it out with her, and see if this can work. Mind you, Susan is a very intelligent woman. I was infatuated with her from the start. She learned very quickly how to push my buttons. This, as you can imagine, made for some interesting times for me. It didn't take her long to get me to forget about the letter in her bag. I was devoted to Susan in spite of it all. (Remember Korea?)

Sometime soon, if not that night, Susan was making some spaghetti of all things. (Spaghetti at the airport.) What a coincidence, spaghetti being our first meal, or so we thought. One thing I have to tell you that you won't like is about roaches. More specifically, flying roaches in Okinawa. That's what was flying right at Susan as she headed for the table with the spaghetti pan. It was really funny at first, but she was distraught for the rest of the evening. "You didn't say anything about flying roaches, did you? I can't live like this. If you want to be with me, get us a nicer place and get me away from them roaches. We can't live like this." Needless to say, our dinner was all on the floor. I promised to do the best I could to find a new place as soon as possible. Mind you, lance corporals didn't make too much money back then. What we had was what I could afford. Life was already starting to be difficult.

Things did settle down a bit shortly after our spaghetti incident. She slowly learned how to at least tolerate flying roaches, to a certain extent. We bombed the place and cleaned it up real good. The previous owners weren't too clean, as I'm sure you can imagine. One notable thing happened while we stayed in this house. Remember Wilke I'm sure. Were both in different units at the time, but we did have some time together. He knew about Susan coming and was a big help getting things set up for her, also had him to dinner a few times, and became a friend to Susan too. Well, one night we were sitting, relaxing and a knock came at the door. I'm sure you all remember that Wilke was very religious back then? As I opened the door, there was Wilke, supporting himself on the hand rail, looking of into space with a blank stare and whisky on his breath. When he finally realized where he was, he had that exuberant drunk sound when he said hi to me in the doorway. "How's it going, my best friend of mine, with a wife in a small town and a family and an escape from the BS of the Marines?" His voice was slurred, and his tongue kept sneaking out as he smiled through his speech. That's when Susan popped in the doorway and Wilke started to fall as he reached to give her a friendly hug. I caught him and struggled to get him to the couch.

After around an hour or so, he woke up in a daze. As he looked around to get his bearings, he began to realize that he had done something totally against his character, and not to mention his beliefs. Wilke was devastated. Through his sobbing I was able to get him to relax and to know that he would be forgiven. I also was able to get him to see the good side of experiencing life so he knew what this all felt like. It would help him to see others' points of view. "Wilke, you're a good man, and this moment in life is not a terrible, life-changing thing. You just drank too much." I said this to him' he began to relax a bit. "Life is about experiences, it's about living to its fullest, and how would you sit and preach to someone the evils of alcohol without the experience of it?" "Jim, I think you're so right. If I do become a preacher, this will help me in the future. I see that now. God works in mysterious ways I guess." Sadly, after this time, we very seldom spoke with Wilke and lost contact with him during my time at Okinawa. I'm sure he remembers the good times we spent with each other. If you're reading this, Wilke, it was a lot of fun.

In the process of trying to find a nice home for Susan, we realized that one of the only ways to do this was going to be getting a roommate to help with expenses. Luckily, there was a guy in my platoon who had just recently gotten married also and was moving his wife over there too. I don't remember him as well as I should, but it was a funny story all the same. Can't think of his name, but I can explain his personality a little. He was a very big man in a lot of ways. The big character on **Everybody loves Raymond** matches his description very well. Raymond's big brother, the cop, who was big and tall. He was a little naïve comparatively, even to me. People at work sort of picked on him a lot, I guess you could say. He was just a little slow but a real nice guy. He was actually a little older then me, like his early twenties, maybe twenty-three or so. We helped him to get the paperwork set up and flights for his wife. Then we found a very nice two-bedroom apartment that was perfect. It was a few floors up and seemed to be roach-free clean. Susan was ecstatic once we moved in.

Our new friend's wife was flying in shortly after we moved in and Susan was excited too because this would give her someone to hang out with while I was at work. Mind you, for some reason we hadn't seen pictures of his wife or knew her age or anything yet. We were shocked to say the least. He was probably six foot two or three, and when we saw her she was barely five foot. That wasn't really the shock though. She looked like a twelve-year-old girl. I swear to you she still had braces and a ponytail. Oh boy this was just too weird. We stayed very cordial and didn't ask her age right then but found out later she had just turned seventeen and her parents loved her husband. One of the first things we noticed was our friend was like a big puppy following her around. She wasn't too happy to meet us at all. After a very short embrace, all she had to say was, "Get my bags, and take this bag right now." She was barking orders at him every step of the way. It was a little on the embarrassing side, we thought. She wouldn't hold his hand and when he did try to kiss her, she looked irritated, more than excited. It was truly a sad sight to see. I thought Susan was a little this way, but this girl was ridiculous. I knew right there at the airport that this was going to be very bad.

As you can probably imagine, the sleeping arrangement was not to her liking at all and almost turned into an all-out war. Luckily that warmed over later on in the evening. As we watched them in the few days to come, it was very apparent that she was a spoiled little brat. I truly don't remember her even lifting a finger once in the whole time we were around them. My friend was very nice to us before she arrived, but now it was Dr. Jekyll and Mr. Hyde. It started slowly but got very apparent very quickly that Susan and she didn't get along while we were at work. It must have been terrible for Susan, I'm sure. I don't remember how long Twiddle Dee and Twiddle Dumb were with us, but I assure you it wasn't long. Yes, that's what we always called them. It seemed to fit real well. Once that was over, the first thing we did was get a puppy.

There are going to be some people that really don't like this book. Dee and Dumb are the perfect example of that fact. There are a lot of people that just don't care what other people think around them. I'm not saying these are the people that started the whole "what is wisdom and intelligence?" I would say they're a product of what I've been discussing. I would hope people take a good look at themselves as they read my book but I don't expect all the ones I want to read this will. Dee and Dumb-type people are set in their ways. I can't change people. I can help them open their eyes a little like I said at the begging of the book though. But if you're not willing to look at things from another perspective, then that's just the way it goes. The Declaration of Independence gives us the right to have an opinion and gives you the right to choose your side of things. What it doesn't give you is the right to make someone follow your beliefs. I can't make someone be thoughtful and kind, as much as they can't make me be mean to others. Like I said, I can't make you be an ethical and moral person.

After that incident, we started just living with our newfound friend. Tenshi was our baby's name, which meant love in Okinawa language. I can't tell you what kind of puppy she was, but she was very cute. It became a tradition to take her for walks around town each day when we could. In general, things were very newlywed like right then in our relationship. Thinking back, I think this became an escape from Susan's reality that she needed. Her whole family was teachers, and that's what had been imbedded in her mind that she had to do. I feel she had done everything in her life because that's what she was made to do. She played piano, but I don't think it was a choice for her. Now she was free to do as she pleased. She was very country girlish, and I was rock and roll. But I did what I was told to do like my friend Twiddle Dee. So I listened to country while she was around. I didn't want to rock the boat. We did really start enjoying our life now. Things kind of got into a routine with us. We liked it so much, and she was so happy being away from her reality that we asked for a three-year hitch in Okinawa. It came through without any problems. It cost the Marine Corps a lot of money to move us away from Okinawa.

Then the shock happened without any warning. "Jim, I'm pregnant." Oh a happy time; how wonderful is that? In a normal sense, this was all wonderful. But after a visit to the doctor, it went bad. Susan was a high-risk pregnancy. Her iron counts were dangerously low for having a baby. They had another term for it, but I don't remember what it was. "Bottom line, Jim and Susan, we don't have the facilities to handle this safely," the doctor said. "We will have to send you back to the States to have a safer environment for your wife." This turned into more paperwork and a hardship transfer. We weren't exactly happy about this. We liked our new life here. But we did what we had to do to make sure she and the baby would be just fine. They had made it known to us that this wasn't a risky thing at all with the right equipment. They just couldn't do it here.

So a few months later, our orders came in for Camp Pendleton, California. I think things got a bit scary for us around then. We were twenty years old, in a foreign country, pregnant, and now we were going to San Diego to have or first child together. Sadly enough, it was a rocky start to our relationship, though we had come to love each other in our own way, our love had not been tested outside of the comfort of our small island. Was this going to work in the real world? We found a good friend in our landlord who found us a good home for Tenshi. One of the many reservations I had at this point was getting stationed with a division unit at Pendleton. Being in FSSG for so long made me lazy. Wasn't sure what to think; Susan and I also had a lot of issues with starting a family this early. I have to admit that Susan was the one that made it work by doing all the planning. It wasn't that easy. She had to fly home a few weeks before me and would plan our first family trip to California. If you remember, she sold her car to get to Okinawa and come to think about it, I didn't even have a license yet. I did get that jeep license, but that was only for a jeep. In a way we had been on a vacation the whole time we were here.

She took off, and the depression hit me hard, the last few weeks there was going to seem like forever. I was so busy thinking about my depression, it didn't even hit me to think of her ex boyfriend in the letter. I guess I'll never know. It truly doesn't matter anymore either. The second to the last week was fairly boring, and there were my orders, time to check out of my unit. I could only check out of a few things which included dental. Then it would be PT and this ten-mile hump, which was going on that week. That is when dental gave me a parting gift because I needed my wisdom teeth out. Then my last three days would be light duty and pain pills. Only bad thing was the actual getting them pulled. See, they thought since I'll be having it done anyway, they might as well take all four out at once. I wish I would've said no and just had the two out. That was a very painful hour or two. One of them was stubborn, and they had to break it while it was still in. At that point, they pulled it out piece by piece. The one good thing was two days of bed rest.

I was so excited to be getting back to the US that it was like forgetting all the wonderful times I had there in Okinawa. Including both, when I was alone and while Susan was there. I hope my stories show you how nice it was. The beautiful ocean views I think stick out the most. Favorite being my trips to Nago. It was all, definitely, an experience never forgotten. As I write this, I do see the pictures of Okinawa in my head very vividly, some that I haven't mentioned. Now it was time to get back home.

"I'm sure you don't have to be reminded that my memories can be distorted, and chronology is not my strong point, so if I get the time frame wrong, in my thoughts, don't jump me for it." "Where were you when the Challenger blew up?"

CHAPTER 31

Our First Home in US
Camp Pendleton

I have to admit I wasn't sure how this was going to go with me being Susan's husband, staying in a perfect strangers' house, and sleeping with their daughter. Yes, we had been a couple for a year, but this was very new to them, and us. They were very nice to me though while I was there. Think back, a short romance, and then she was gone. To them, the last year didn't seem real. It was like a time capsule. Not to mention I had taken their baby out of college so we could be together. (Remember, this was a big deal to them, they're all teachers.) I think you get the picture of what I felt like. I don't think we spent any time at my house while we were there. Looking back, that must have been very difficult for you Mom. I'm sorry I was so naïve, that I didn't demand some time with you. We did have a lot to get ready for all the same.

I didn't have much control over the goings-on about our trip. All I had to do was get a license real quick before we left. Not much of a problem, I came to find out. They basically just used my Military license to give me a Texas license. That was very easy. I didn't even get much choice on the car we got. It was a Chevy Chevette. Of course I think her parents got it for her. They also set it up to help us with our furniture. My pride went out the door at this time, but not that I knew much about it at the time. All in all, I guess it was necessary. We were determined to make this work, or at least that's the impression I got from Susan. She had control of our checking account and money. I don't know if I even had one when I met her. Probably not, I think I just had an empty savings account. But it doesn't matter yet to me at this point. I just let Susan do as she pleased so I didn't get her upset.

The trip must have been uneventful since I don't remember it at all. San Diego was so big to me, it wasn't funny. We got to base, and I checked into my unit. I was with artillery at Las Pulgas, which is a small base at Camp Pendleton. Luckily someone pointed us to a small town of the back side of Pendleton called Fallbrook. Very nice quiet little town, which they say is the avocado capital of the US. It was quite pretty to say the least. Actually Camp Pendleton was very beautiful too. I've heard it's a very prime piece of property in southern California. It had rolling hills all through it. Pendleton was also were we came for rifle range in boot camp if you can remember. Remember Mount Mother in which we got rained out? Don't believe the hype, as it were. Finally got to run that while with this unit, and the beach nearby was oh, so perfect. Beach runs were a favorite of our platoon commander since we were an amphibious military. Bottom line was that it wasn't as bad as I thought it would be, meaning, being with the division part of the Marines. Remember division was our grunts, tanks, artillery, or the main part of the corps.

I kind of lucked out you could say. With my little bit of background in maintenance management, (MIMMS) from Okinawa, I became the MIMMS clerk at my new platoon. My so-called office was up a makeshift wooden later above the equipment. So as you can imagine, it wasn't a great introduction to working in an office. It was a good distraction from my home life and everything around me. "Where were you when the Challenger blew up?" I was in that little office getting ready to go back to 29 Palms. We heard it on the radio after someone had called to tell us that it just happened. That was a very sad day indeed. John Denver later wrote a song about that called "They Were Flying for Me." Very nice song if you've never heard it. Yes I still listened to him quite frequently, and yes, I was going back to 29 Palms again.

Susan, during all this was doing OK as far as I could tell. Our first home was a small trailer with the bed in the living room. Yeah, not much to look at but it was nice. The pregnancy was a little tough on her body though. Jason, you were a big boy. I would have to say that we were excited and scared at the same time. She, I feel, was a little disappointed with her predicament. At one time or another, I started working at Taco Bell for some extra money. We got most of the things we needed for Jason, found a nice crib for Jason, and was making it work like she had said we would before. Having to struggle was not something she was used to. As you know, it was no big deal to me, yet. At one point or another, Susan was also working as a secretary I think. I sort of remember this because of a bad memory. I guess you sort of block things out in your life. I surely did. Now don't get me wrong, I'm sure I did some things to irritate Susan, but this really did make me feel bad.

Susan's job was having a picnic, and we decided to go to it. Like I said before, Okinawa was a good distraction for Susan, and I basically had her to myself the whole time we were there. She would go and get the mail on base all the time and knew more people in my company over there than I did. I say all this to let you kind of see my perspective at this party we went to. Susan is a very intelligent person in her own right, and we all know where my education came from. Everyone at this party was a little like what I was saying in the beginning of the book. They were the wise and intelligent ones, and I was just a stupid Marine. Sadly, that's the way I felt. Susan didn't even introduce me to a lot of the people that I saw there. That would have helped tremendously to say the least. Instead I just hung out in the corner till dinnertime came. It was honey-cured ham and for some reason I got sicker than a dog. I never understood that saying but you know what I mean. I didn't say anything about being sick because I didn't want to bother Susan and her friends. As a matter of fact, I don't think I ever told Susan how I felt about the cold shoulder she gave me around her friends or family. Thinking back that was part of our problems later on in the relationship.

I'm sure you don't have to be reminded that my memories can be distorted, and chronology is not my strong point, so if I get the time frame wrong, in my thoughts, don't jump me for it. I can't remember if I went to 29 Palms right away or worked at Taco Bell first. Well, Taco Bell was actually a good experience for me for the time being. I personally always loved Taco Bell, especially at that time when everything was still made from scratch.

Yes, kids, even at Taco Bell. All the vegetables on the line were chopped by the salad prep person. We also had a fry person who fried fresh chips, taco shells, tostadas, and the taco salad shells. We even used real grease then too, which gave it a lot more flavor. Yeah, I know, "Jim, that fat will kill you." I think I heard it said somewhere that everything in moderation isn't so bad for you. I would also think that if you're lazy, you're not going to work it off, any way you slice it, if you're not working out you still gain wait. None of these even mentions the fact that all the new chemicals they put in food to make it better for you is, essentially, making it worse and causing cancer. Now people are starting to think it's OK just because they used some chemicals to make it better, so now they gorge themselves instead of just enjoying the flavor.

The taco meat was also freshly cooked each day, and boy, did it have a great flavor. Beans were probably the best of all of the fresh food. They were the first thing the cook would do in the morning. We cooked them with fresh onions; some canned chilies, great seasonings, and of course some lard before you refried them. Believe it or not, we used an industrial drill with a paint-mixing blade on it to mix and blend it with the lard. Boy oh boy, was that good beans. I still make my own refried beans the same way now. Man, I'm really getting hungry now. So Taco Bell was awesome back in the day. It did give us at least a little extra money.

The sad thing right now is trying to remember which came first, 29 Palms operation or you Jason. It's truly making me feel bad, but I think it was the stumps. I do remember that we went through a lot of time making sure everything was perfect for Jason's arrival. The crib, the clothes, the changing table, car set, and decorations galore. You know that old saying about "woman glowing"? It came to fruition right in front of my eyes. She was so excited about your arrival and always seemed to have a smile. Unless you were kicking at her, but even then that just let her know you were excited too.

A little more on the unit I was in. We were a battery of 155 Howitzers, (Other wise known as PIGS.) They used them five-ton trucks I told you about before to carry them. Communication was an intercut part of keeping things going. Not to mention the Forward Observers (FO) sending co-ordinance for the targets. Training before we went to 29 Palms was imperative. The wrong word on the radio could get someone killed in friendly fire. I'm sure you may have seen movies with those big camouflage setups they use over equipment. Lots of practice with that stuff, which as you can imagine is important to be very fast at setting up. That can keep them from finding you. We learned to put that up extremely fast before we even went to 29 Palms. I think deep down I was very excited to go back to where it started for me but just felt like the timing stunk. It was time to go play war again.

"The Marines changes you to just take care of the task at hand and don't think about it, you just do it."

CHAPTER 32

Return to 29 Palms

Well if you remember back the last time I was here, I was seventeen going on eighteen. Nicholas was born the last time I was here. My new life was becoming a reality for me. This time was much different. Twenty years old, been overseas twice, seen five countries, one hurricane, seen storms at sea, one typhoon, got married, having another child, and now I was traveling in a jeep, instead of a bus. "A lot can happen in three years huh?" Being in a jeep was an interesting change, to say the least. I'm sure you can remember my bus ride over. Looking out the window and seeing myself on the horizon. Yep, still doing it, but in some ways my thoughts were distracted from enjoying what I was seeing again. The distractions in life we talked about were in full force now, as seen above. Of course mine were deferent than most. We hadn't gotten to computers and cell phones yet. At that time, it was the guys in the vehicle talking up a storm with me, the occasional moment to remember my family when things were quiet and not to mention the twenty-four-hour a day job ahead of me for a few weeks. These were good life distractions I guess compared to computers, cell phones, and such. It was more real-life experience. Sights, sounds, and smells.

All of you, maybe at one time or another has seen the windmills and the big dinosaurs on the highway around the area of Palm Springs. I didn't talk about them much before.

The windmills seem to go on forever on the horizon, they are so big that they stick out and take over the view completely. I say this after seeing this big four-by-four truck driving down a dirt road next to the windmills. Kind of made me wonder what kind of life that would be, taking care of all those things on a daily basis. I guess the reason behind the thought was having my first real job other than the Marines at Taco Bell. As I grew up, I can honestly say that I never put much thought into work growing up. To tell the truth, even at this point, it was a fleeting moment to think about work at all. The Marines changes you to just take care of the task at hand and don't think about it, you just do it. This will help me a whole lot later in life.

The other thing on that road that is popular is the life-size dinosaurs at a truck stop, which actually ends up being our halfway mark for our trip; hence we had our lunch break and fuel stop. One of the few times you're ever around civilians in your camouflage uniforms. That's a big problem with the Marines, unlike the other branches. The Marines are much stricter about a lot of things, I would have to say. Some of the dinosaurs you could actually go inside to look out of their mouth, I think it was. I remember trying to call Susan to say a one last good-bye while we were there. I'd be in the field soon and like I said before, "no cell phones." Then it was time for some lunch. I think it was the first convenience store burrito I ever had. I assume some of you know the ones I'm talking about? They were really good for some stupid reason. I still love them things. I know a lot of you out there who have been on there way to work, in Middle America, have had them. Then I washed that down with a tall soda for the last time for a while. Caffeine is just coffee out there in the field. Unless you brought an extra container of instant tea mix in your vehicle. I have to say though, the amount of strain on your body each day takes good care of the lack of caffeine. Working out or working hard puts out more endorphins and keeps you strong. Water becomes the key to life again out there in the desert. Not that latte in the morning or the thirty-two ounce soda sitting next to you.

When we got to 29 Palms, the memories were strong from when I was there for school. The base looked so different this time though. I'm not sure why it was so different, but my thought would be experience. As we get older and wiser, things change. You look at things different. I hope you can remember me speaking about kids thinking they know their parents real well but learn later how wrong they were? The more you know, people, the more you understand, and then the easier things become. This was part of the change for me there. Twenty-nine Palms was becoming a comfortable place to me. I never liked the weather, but it was a fun place to see and or visit.

Once we got our camouflage stuff set up, it was off to the desert for us. We were very good at setting up as I told you before. This was very exciting for someone from FSSG to see the guns a-blazing for the first time. I still have problems with my ears to this day because of them PIGS. They were very loud, and that was with our ear plugs. When the guns would fire, the dirt around a fifty-foot square would jolt up every time. I would hope you have all seen pictures of this. It was incredible to say the least. They even let me pull the trigger a few times while I was out there. At the moment, it was all real exciting, but humility kicked in when you see the devastation of one of the rounds as it blew up. You would all be surprised how exact the technology is with these guns. Of course this is only possible because there is a forward observer on the front line, giving the info at times. Other times they just use satellite images to give precise locations for targets. The many different rounds also make the devastation even worse with the right ordinance for the task. I won't get into them because I was only a radio operator. I knew the names of the rounds but not all of there properties. It all definitely made for an interesting training experience for us all.

Most of this trip was very intense, so personal time was scarce to say the least. Nights, unless we were doing night stuff, was your time of reflection, but you were so tired that, typically, you fell right to sleep. Susan and the baby on board were always in my mind though. This time I was able to be the father. Jason was going to be a very exciting moment in my life. All of us had that worry of how we would be as a father. Of course, now in a lot of cases they're more of a distraction and an irritant than a blessing. Please don't let that be any of you. Susan and the thought of being a father was a bad distraction from work because I was so happy. Work has always been important, to an extent, but family was the ultimate reason for living. At the time, my work ethics weren't so tuned in, so I did go a little overboard with distractions of home during this trip.

One of my first lessons in work ethics was there in that hot desert. I was distracted and left the headquarters bunker without my flak jacket, which, as you can imagine, is a very bad thing. My Marine Corps punishment was to build a bunker by myself with my e-tool. For you nonmilitary people, it's a shovel you can fold up into just the size of the shovel head. This bunker was 6 x 6 x 6, and I can't remember how long it took to build it, but it was most of a day. Never took that flak jacket of after that, I tell you. What the first sergeant drilled into me that day was that at the workplace rules are rules. At one time or another, they were implemented for a reason. Doesn't make the rule right, wrong, or indifferent, it's just the rule. He had witnessed himself, a gun misfire that killed the whole crew in a few hours of pain, when all they needed was there flak jacket to survive. By gun I obviously mean the howitzers. In the Marines, when you're given a task and a set of rules, there is no questioning, you just do the job set in front of you to the best of your ability. That trench was a great teacher to me out there in that desert heat. Also in the Marines, you always have the right to question, but in the moment, you just do the job given to you by a supervisor. If you did exactly what you were told and didn't feel comfortable at the time, then bring it to someone's attention later and work things out. Then you did as instructed, and if it's wrong, you did what you were supposed to and your supervisor will answer for it. Remember to always be the best you can be even if it's digging a ditch for nothing.

To be honest, that's about all I remember from the trip. I did ace qualification while I was there and was sent on a long day looking for gun line. I can't talk about that so I don't mess up things for future Marines. I learned to always have a bottle of hot sauce for your MREs. I also kind of got used to rattlesnakes out there in the desert from seeing that they're more afraid of you than we are of him. You leave them alone, they'll leave you alone. All in all, it was an interesting trip for me. Hard being away from my glowing wife, I just couldn't wait to see her and have our first child.

"A child's birth is a wonderful thing, and I hope none of you have to miss that."

CHAPTER 33

Jason's Tough Beginning

As I had said before, I wasn't sure when the trip to 29 Palms occurred, but I do remember the long two days ahead when Jason was born. The trailer we had wasn't working for Susan at all, so we started looking for a new place for Jason's arrival. With both of our extra incomes, we could finally afford to get a nice apartment. I vaguely remember the trailer, but this apartment I can still see in my head. It was huge to us compared to what we've had up to this point. If I remember correctly, it was only a one-bedroom, but the living space was ridiculous. It was perfect for us. I think this is also when Pat, her mother, came out to see us and helped us with the nice furniture that we had now. We have to remember this all kind of went on without my input, which was OK with me for the time. When she met me, I wonder if she could see the dork in me. It doesn't really matter I guess. It's the past. It was all very nice though. They used a mauve color with pastels to decorate the house. Almost forgot about the precious moments that she collected. They were all over the house. I don't think I had ever heard of them before Susan. They are really cute I guess.

The glow I saw in her was most apparent when we got close to the due date. She was so excited and couldn't stop thinking about you, Jason. We both kept rearranging your bedroom stuff. We couldn't wait till you came. People always think about what we are supposed to do in this life, and I can't truly answer that question. I don't think anyone can answer that question, but as I sit here in retrospect, all I can think of is the people around us, like our children and family, become our reason to be here on this earth. That, personally, has become enough for me. It's because of my life now that I see that more clear.

"Here he goes again." Sorry have to put this in. "Why are we here?" Our minds are the building block like the picture of the desert that I gave you in 29 Palms. In a sense, "the ground in which we walk on." Our setting is the place we choose to live when we become adults. Some people choose familiar settings and stay close to their family. Some move on to explore new world and see other settings. The people around us are like the tree in the desert or the bug that I mentioned. The way our life grows from that initial setting is up to us. Some may destroy parts of your world, but you alone can fix and repair it. You don't have to let people hurt your surroundings.

When we have children, we in a sense are molding our existence and our setting. It's an existence that we mold for ourselves and the ones we love. As we grow, how you finally mold the scenery is up to us. The actions of other people's worlds can have the effect of changing our world but only if you let them. Growing old, we begin to sit on our own porch enjoying the world that we make for ourselves. Then we sit on our porch with our feelings and memories, in which we molded in our own minds. As I sit on my porch looking out at the world, which is my life, I share my view with the girl sitting next to me and the world she created for herself. And with retrospect and contemplation, we live out the rest of our days. You won't meet her till close to the end of my book. Just remember that only you can make this life for yourself. You all will hear that all the time in your life, but trust me when I say that it is so true. Sorry, Jason, for getting sidetracked.

Thinking about all of you kids makes me think about the meaning of life. You are my world, and I dropped the ball on all of you in the beginning of your own world. I'm so sorry for that, y'all. Jason, you were a tough one to say the least. We had a due date, and it was going past it now. Susan was beginning to look miserable all the time. One of her problems was her not getting enough iron in her blood so she felt real weak at times. Finally the doctors decided that they needed to induce her labor. So we came to the hospital, and they gave her something to start the contractions. Then a little later, they broke her water. This was it; we were going to have a son soon.

I'm not going into detail about this, but the labor was horribly long. It was around thirty-two to thirty-five hours long. At one point they gave her some strong pain medications to help her and the baby sleep for a little while. "Jim?" The doctor said. "You're going to have to watch the monitor and wake her just before each contraction so she wouldn't wake up in a bad way." No problem, I'm thinking. At first it was fine, but after a while, things went south a bit. See, there was a fan in the room to make her more comfortable. Like I said, at first it was fine. I'm sure all of you have stories of woman hitting their husband and/or going off on them. Well, it was no different for Susan.

During one of the contractions, she woke up screaming, "I told you to turn that f—fan off!" "I'm sorry, honey, as soon as we get you through this contraction, I'll turn it off. Now just breathe with me." "How am I supposed to breathe with that damn fan blowing in my face?" She said as she started her breathing exercise. All I dare say at this point was "yes, dear." OK, I'm thinking, that was fun. Her time between was around ten to fifteen minutes at this point but steady. Here comes another spike. "Honey, it's time again," I say in a nice whisper so not to startle her. "Oh my God, I told you to turn that fan on a minute ago!" Again in her angry voice as she begins her breathing. "I did what you asked, honey, but I'll turn it back on for you." Not a smart thing to talk back to a woman in labor. Trust me on this one. "I can't believe you're lying to me in the middle of this whole thing that *you* put me in! Turn that damn fan on now!" Now I'm thinking "this is crazy." Obviously a little later it was time to do it again. "Susan?" She darted her eyes at me with a deer-in-the-headlight look and WHAM! She hit me square on the face with a slap that almost knocked me from the side of her bed. "What the hell are you doing? I told you to turn that f—fan off!" After the last time, all I could say was, "Yes dear, I'm sorry." The slap ended up being a one-time deal but as you can imagine it was very funny conversation later in life. She did go back and forth between on and off for a long while, but she was as tired as the night got longer.

Early the next day, it became scary and they finally had to do an emergency C-section on Susan because you were in distress, meaning you, Jason. This as you can imagine stressed Susan and I even more. Not to mention I wouldn't be there when Jason was born. They assured us that it was fine and told me to put a smock and such on then led me toward the operating room. Sadly enough as I headed for the door, they stepped out with you, Jason. You where a bit messy, but you were so incredible, seeing you for the first time. They gave you to me and said "Congratulations, Dad, on your new baby boy." A son. How wonderful is that? Nick, I always wished I could have been there for you too, but hoped you understand from the circumstances that lead to you. A child's birth is a wonderful thing, and I hope none of you have to miss that. In some ways I felt cheated by missing Jason's birth, but I was still the first to hold you. It's hard to put into words that feeling when you hold your child for the first time. One thought was the movie **Hook**. They did a great job showing the emotion of that moment. It's a very happy thought.

Once we got Jason home, things were pretty normal for a long time. Susan, at first, seemed to always be in a good mood, and having Jason around was so much fun all the time that it always made me laugh. After a little while, things did get a little difficult financially, and we had to move out of the one-bedroom for a two-bedroom. The first few months were fine, but we needed to give Jason his own room. I don't remember all the details of why we had to move to the new apartments, but I liked them. It was nice to have our own room again. Still, Jason always wanted to sleep in our bed for the longest time. It was cute and fun at first, but it's a hard habit for a one-year-old to break. Kids, don't make the same mistake.

Another job that helped us out for a little while was "Sizzler." I think it was that time I spent on mess duty that helped me land that job. I learned a lot about steak while working there. I was a broil cook. "Talk about packed." We were always full, and my huge broiler would fill up real quick and stay that way most of the night. I thought the chow hall was busy. That was nothing compared to cooking for a bunch of civilians. Not to mention how picky they could be. It was a great experience and gave me a skill I have been able to use all of my life. I love working in restaurants, always have, and always will. It's your fault, Mom; the little restaurants you worked at gave a lasting impression. Didn't know at the time how true that was going to be for me as time went on.

Well, like I said things were fairly good for now in my life. It was kind of funny how things crept up on me and Susan though. Neither one of us seen it until it was too late. I felt out of place sometimes as much as she did about the positions I put us in. Positions, meaning the small apartment or the trailer we stayed at for a while. Her family wasn't rich or anything, but they never wanted for anything either. Now we struggled to make rent sometimes. We did OK, considering. But it was a worry.

This was around the three-and-a-half-year mark for me, and it was almost time to get out of the Marines. It was a resounding big "no!" from Susan when it came to the thoughts of getting out of the Marines. It would have been a bad idea to get out under the circumstance that we were in at the time. Plus, I still hadn't bought a sword yet, remember? It bothered me a little that I never became an NCO during my tour of duty. This also gave me reason to want to stay in the corps. What stopped me, thus far, was a new contract that came out in 1983 that gave anyone who signed up E-4 in twenty-four. All of us that got in before '83 were basically put on hold because of these contracts. In the Marines, other than these contracts, we had what they called a "cutting score." This was points given by many things: time in service, time in rank, your PT score, rifle score, and such. Because of the contracts, these scores to pick up rank were outrageous. This made me a very salty lance corporal.

In talking to the career planner, I found that the only job out there in the Marines that would give me a cutting score low enough to pick up corporal was the baking field.

Yes, I'm serious, the baking field. To pick up the rank that I wanted, I had to become a baker. As all of you know, this was not such a bad thing to me. Remember, I loved being in the chow halls, and now I could be working in them all the time. Susan obviously didn't care what I did for a job but wanted to make sure I was still a Marine. So what the heck, I thought. Not to mention I'd get my rank, finally. As soon as they drew up the papers, I signed them. Now it was four more years in the Marines, corporal, and a trip to North Carolina again for school. That week they told me to bring Susan to formation one morning and they pinned my strip on while she was there, which was very nice. Right about the time I was going through the gauntlet, it started pouring down rain. Lucky me, I guess. The gauntlet is an initiation into the ranks of NCOs. The Marine uniform has a lot of symbolisms all over it. Our blues pants are either plain blue or they have a red strip down the side. The red strip symbolizes the blood we shed as Marines with some time on the lines. I won't go into explanations about the gauntlet so people don't call the Marines and stop them from doing it because it's too mean.

So there I was, sitting in the car with my family as a corporal now. Shortly after that it was off to North Carolina. Jason was just a baby, and I felt bad about leaving her alone to care for our son. We all make sacrifices of sorts though in our lives. That strip was a nice raise for us and put us in a lot better situation financially. I felt the need to make a better life for Susan and Jason. Remember, this life was unexpectedly hard for Susan considering were she came from. She had no real worries till she married me. It wasn't terrible in my mind, but it weighed down on her slowly but surely.

"We also got a little carried away at one point. It ended up giving are platoon a nickname, MacGyver Platoon."

CHAPTER 34

My First Real Command Camp Johnson

Camp Johnson is a small training base right by Camp Lejuene. It was first built as a boot camp for dark greens many years ago. Now it housed the cook and baker side of things in the Marines. I think it also had some administrative classes to. The school I was about to go through was a basic baking course, which will be mostly Marines just out of boot camp. I knew this would be an interesting trip for me. One of the things you have to think about with the Marines is a corporal is the main troop leader. Us Marines, if we do anything, we do it with pride. That also goes for how we treat our rank structure. It is pushed especially hard in boot camp. When I met my platoon, they were locked up in formation and waiting for my instructions. Now I've become pretty relaxed about things with my three years in and don't really have that kind of spunk anymore. I wasn't that motivated about being stuck in a barracks with all these kids, as I would put it. I obviously didn't have any choice in the matter.

I did have one lance corporal in my platoon. I can't think of his name anymore, but I guess he just got the rank out of boot camp for enlisting some other people while on delayed entry program. All the rest were private and private first classes. (PFCs) I have to say that the barracks was in a cul-de-sac, nestled in the trees. It was very pretty back there. You know very well that was very nice to me. I had to march my platoon everywhere, which ended up being a lot of fun. I got really good at calling cadence. This ended up being a good training ground for me and my rank. I can also say it was throwing gas on a fire.

I have to admit something here to all of you. I have a tendency to like being the center of attention now and again. I always had fun with that to an extent. When you just think about it, it makes perfect sense. I was the oldest child in my family. I did all the plays and musicals in school and out of school. Spirit Mountain was a blast for me. It was singing in front of all those people in concerts and shows, playing the guitar late nights and weekends in the racquetball court, and not to mention juggling lacrosse balls in the common area. Susan had changed that a bit with our relationship. She didn't look at me as the center of attention. I would think after a while I was more of a nuisance to her. Now all these guys looked to me for everything. But I have to say we ended up being a very tight unit. They weren't exactly the smartest tools in the shed, but they were good people. Part of there respect for me came from my rank, but I like to think that after a while, they accepted me for how I treated them. Though I have to admit, we were a motley crew.

A little bit of my management skills probably came from Frank, I would assume. I would think y'all remember him. Frank gave as much respect as he received. Good leaders, I think, have to have humility and morality. As I said before, we learn from our experiences as we go through life. The Marines, if it did anything, taught you to take care of the people around you and they will take care of you. I think I heard it said somewhere that "we reap what we sow," and "give kindness and you will get it back tenfold." It went something like that. I may not have worded it right, but you get the point. As you kids grow, I hope you can learn to respect people at first glance, and they'll either give it back or not. If they don't give it in return, don't judge them, but instead let it be. Being nice to people that aren't nice in return will hopefully get them thinking. You will be the better person in return.

We became a very tight-knit group in the few months that we were together. I was also able to instill a great sense of pride in them. They tried so hard on a daily basis to do as well as they could on barracks inspections and marching skills. In a little bit of time we became the platoon to beat when it came to all the inspection competitions. We also got a little carried away at one point. It ended up giving are platoon a nickname, MacGyver Platoon. It was a fun name, but it came to us in a dangerous way.

Each week we had a big inspection on Thursday of each platoons barracks and had a cup that you kept in your barracks for the next week. This became very competitive as school went on. We had it a few times and then lost it. I told them, "I want my trophy back." Well, what stopped us in the last inspection was our shower walls had a cleaning film on it. What we did was mix some chemicals to stop that from happening. Like I said earlier, we were short a few tools in the shed and did something very stupid. "Don't ever mix ammonia and bleach. The chemical you get from mixing the two is extremely toxic. It will burn your lungs if you breathe it." I didn't know that at the time. I failed chemistry in high school, and the guys with me didn't do so hot either.

Remember what I said about the people in the military? In some ways they were the so-called non intelligent people that didn't do college. Don't get me wrong and think the whole Marine Corps were idiots; I don't mean that at all. I don't want to judge or generalize the people in the military. I'm just saying a lot of them probably don't remember or care about chemistry class from high school.

As we were cleaning the showers with our great cleaning solution, very quickly it hurt to breathe. We opened all the windows right away, as fast as possible, but that didn't make any difference whatsoever. There were five of us in the room at the time. For some reason, I remember one guy's name that was in there at that time, Ipsen, who was a redneck and a half. He was definitely corn fed and became a good friend while we were there. I sent him to tell everyone to get out, and the others helped me try to hurry and clean. That didn't last long;

we all had to leave and couldn't stop coughing. The coughing didn't subside, so I told them to call the base corpsman. They came very quickly and were extremely mad at us for mixing the chemicals. They even had to call in the NBC people to clean up after our little chemical experiment. The NBC guys couldn't stop laughing at our stupidity. Three of my guys ended up in the hospital overnight. Thank God no one was hurt long term. Yes, we did lose the inspection that week. We did get it back after we were named the MacGyver Platoon.

Off duty time was fairly quiet. I was never a big partier so things kept pretty quiet for me. A lot of my time was thinking about my family. I would call every chance I could get, but things seemed to be drifting apart for me and Susan. I was really starting to think I might lose her soon if I didn't do something to make her feel better about us. One night I was out with a few of the guys from the platoon when the lance corporal said, "Why not just get a tattoo for your wife to prove your love for her?" "Dude, I can't afford that kind of money while I'm raising my son. That is the problem in the first place. I can't give her the security that she was raised with." Then he said something real stupid if you ask me. "If you get one, I'll get one and pay for both of them." Well, who could turn that down? You never know, maybe it will work. At least I was real picky about my tattoo. It was a beautiful cross with a ribbon wrapped around it. On top of the cross was a rose. The ribbon had "Jim and Susan." It was very nice and not too big. I also made sure to keep it above the t-shirt line so I don't have to deal with questions during inspections.

Now a quick lesson about this lance corporal I mentioned. Talk about your suck-ups. He was real bad about kissing up to me all the time. I really didn't mean to take advantage of him when I got the tattoo. We were all drinking and having a lot of fun, and he knew I couldn't afford the tattoo. No, I didn't fight it either. I should have, looking back. For anyone of you that might feel a little naive about what a suck-up is, I'll explain. There are a few names that come to mind, "Suck up, brown nose, and of course the bad one, kiss a—." I do believe a lot of people like this don't realize they're even doing it sometimes.

It is pretty simple; suck up being someone sucking up to the boss. It can be kind of embarrassing to the people watching you do it. It's even worse watching the boss that uses it against them. This lance corporal was a brown nosier to the corps. I tried real hard to get him away from that while I was with him and hope it worked. I also, in some ways, felt bad for taking his offer for the tattoo, but I was young and drunk; and about the tattoo, sooner or later they fade away to where you can't really see too much of it.

When I told Susan about the tattoo, she wasn't too impressed and our conversations got smaller and smaller. I'm not sure we talk much at all towards the end of my time at Camp Johnson. "What was she doing?" I wondered each day. Time will tell. That was about it for school; I was officially a baker by trade now. It was time to go home and try to fix things with our marriage.

"Kind of hard to show real pride on a computer, isn't it? There are some out there that think things like pride are useless. I say it is one of the many reasons we are losing things in life now."

CHAPTER 35

A New Unit and More School

During school I got my new orders which happily kept us at Camp Pendleton and also put me back with FSSG. I was now part of supply battalion, which was in area 22. (Places in Pendleton went by numbers.) This also housed the helicopter units, so we had an air base right there across the road. This would become my home for a long time in Rations Platoon. We were otherwise known as the "Rat Pac." Our platoon was made up of embarkations people who warehoused the MREs for Pendleton. (Meals ready to eat.) It also housed all the bakers for the base. All the chow halls had our people working for them, but since we had equipment for the field, they were originally assigned from Rations platoon. We had two types of field bakery units. One was very old but made outrageous amounts of bread for the troops. The smaller was the one used the most. It was all kept in the same warehouse with the MREs. Nicely enough since I had a forklift license from Okinawa, they kept me at the warehouse at first. As you can imagine, we kept real busy with MREs coming in and going out regularly. I have to say there are a ton of memories of this place in my life. I have no idea how to begin.

I guess the best place to start is my first impression of the Rat Pac. I have to admit my first thoughts were this was going to be a bunch of lazy Sergeant Bilko's platoon that I'm going to be with. I figured this was going to be a skate job. **Skate**, in the Marines, this meant you were going to roll right through things, skate around work, and/or I guess you could say this was a nice way to call someone lazy. "Stop being such a skate and get back to work!" Boy, was I wrong about Rations Platoon. These guys were borderline "gung-ho." We did PT every day in the Rat Pac. They were very proud to be part of the Rat Pac. Don't get me wrong, they weren't mean or anything, just proud. Oh no, here we go again.

What a lesson this unit was to me. The last time I felt this way was in boot camp. Actually, being in baker school and having my own platoon I think set me up for this. When people try to peg your wisdom and intelligence, they bite down on your pride. I don't see a lot of pride very often anymore around me. The love of the game has turned into love of money. Now I do realize there are people that have pride still, but it just doesn't seem widespread as much anymore. Kind of hard to show real pride on a computer, isn't it? There are some out there that think things like pride are useless. I say it is one of the many reasons we are losing things in life now. Pride isn't only about sports though. It is so much more. It's not conceded its excitement. Being proud just means you truly enjoy life to its fullest. You care about what you do or don't do. It makes you whole and human. Makes us healthier, fit, gives us emotions like crying and laughing with joy, and fills our senses. Pride also doesn't mean arrogance, in my book. Arrogance, I feel, is someone who thinks they're better then someone else. They are above us. Pride is feeling good about you. Having pride makes you a better person. Some people with out pride tend to be lazy in their endeavors. Not being proud of yourself tends to make a person's hygiene go to pot. Picking on kids makes people lose their sense of pride also. As you look back at my life, I was that kid with low self-esteem, and even when I was good at something, I had no pride to pursue what I was good at. Please don't be the one who holds people back.

I don't remember a whole lot of names from the Rat Pac but a few stands out. SSGT Bolt, CPL Newman, CPL Parish, CPL Knowles, LCPL Ipsen from school, LCPL Vasquez, LCPL Sears, and there were a few sergeants that I can't remember their names that had lasting effects on me. All of these people had some lasting impacts on me through this part of the book. Susan seemed to be slipping away slowly but surely while money was beginning to be a big issue. Susan was very good at budgeting and was able to keep us afloat. I had become more stressed not knowing why things had changed between us then what was going on financially. In some ways she kept me in the dark about them things. I should have taken more pride in my family in retrospect. She didn't have the passion for me anymore and really seemed more irritated by our conversation than anything. My unit's pride kept me away much more than ever before. Running PT every morning at four thirty and then working till four thirty really drained me. Thank God I was young, I guess. We spent a little time in the field and went out on ship once for maneuvers at Del Mar beach, but other than that, we just always trained hard to stay at the top of our game. That gives you a quick overview of things. Now some stories.

One of my favorite stories has to do with Parish. Parish was very short and very excitable, if that's even a word. He had a bit of a temper as you can imagine from being short. He was very tough for his size. I'm not sure why, but we made good friends anyway. Routinely in the Marines, each year you go to the rifle range to qualify with your rifle. It's at this time that we do basic combat training for people in the Marines that aren't grunts. While you're there, you also do the gas chamber. I'm sure you remember my story from boot camp. They also give us time with weapons like the .50 cal, the .60 cal, and don't forget them loud grenades. For right now, this was about the combat training.

In the Marines, there is a lot of squad training during this time, for instance things like troop movement, hand signals, and such. Well, because of that stupid CPL in twenty-four thing that I told y'all about, we had a lot of corporals in our platoon, which explains a bit of Parish and I getting along so well. We both got our strips the hard way. In training, Parish and I were given the task of setting up flare traps behind the enemy in our war games. That also meant a little climbing for us since we figured they wouldn't think of our unit coming up through there. This had given him and me a lot of time to talk, which made us even better friends. Do y'all remember that game I played in the Boy Scouts where I was hiding on people and moving around there campsites? If you can picture that, that's what we decided to do when we got up the hill. See, we lost contact with the rest of our platoon so we had no idea where they were. We found a good spot as a makeshift drop zone and took our packs and such off to get into recon mode. Then we moved into the camp.

One thing we didn't count on was practically the whole platoon up there was asleep. Yes, I'm not kidding. Most of them were dead asleep. So now we are thinking, "What do we do now?" Then we noticed that all their rifles are not with them; they're hanging on trees, sitting on rocks, or stuck up against their tents. That's when it hit us, take their rifles first. It was almost a game to us at this point. We snuck around taking rifles and setting them at our makeshift camp. We almost got caught a few times, but now it was early morning and still our platoon hadn't arrived yet, so we started getting a bit nervous. Not to mention in this thick woods, we didn't have any idea where there COs tent was yet. Then we came up with a plan.

Parish decided one of us should get caught while the other waits to see where the COs tent was, then at that point, pounce on the CO. Sounds smart, huh? Well the bad part was I drew the long straw and had to be the one that pounced. I personally would have been happier getting caught. Well, there goes Parish. Now I'm all by myself in the enemy's territory, watching him get captured by a half-asleep enemy with no rifle. "How did they do that?" Someone ran out of the tent he was guarding in the commotion with his rifle. A few others joined in, and they headed for the COs tent. See, the plan was to jump in right away so we could surprise the CO. By the way, he was a lieutenant from supply platoon, who happened to be at the other end of our warehouse back at base. While Parish was being dragged to the tent, he was laughing at the sight of a bunch of idiots who can't find there rifles. I was doing my best not to laugh out loud since I was still hidden. Well, just like we planed I jumped in the tent right after they went in and surprised the, you know what, out of everyone in the tent. The look on their faces was hilarious.

Well, at first it was really exciting, but that ended fairly quickly when they realized we stole like twenty rifles. Believe it or not, we ended up getting in trouble for taking the rifles from the troops. Still not sure why, but the fact that this was a rival platoon didn't help. Not to mention how embarrassed the platoon commander must have been when most of his troops were asleep. It was nothing big to Parish and me. They just screamed at us for a long while, and we went back to the barracks. We did win the takeover award for the weekend. It was all good I suppose. It was definitely a lot of fun for us. SSGT Bolt was real happy too and told us not to worry about the butt chewing. "Nothing will come off it. He will just have to answer to the battalion commander later, so he is pissed."

After boot camp's toilet seat, I always qualified expert. Also each time we did the rifle range, we would do a PFT (physical fitness test). This consisted of sit-ups in two minutes, pull-ups in which twenty was a hundred percent, and then the three-mile run. If you'll remember correctly, you had a cutting score for rank in the Marines. Well, rifle range and your PFT score was a big part of that, and with expert rifle and one hundred percent PFT, that was very helpful indeed. I was very consistent on both of these while in the corps, even as I started getting a bit of a gut.

Parish and I did well that day but another reason we got along was while he was out there having fun, his wife was leaving him. Parish was maybe a few years older than I but he spent a lot of time on a West Pac before I met him. He met his wife in Korea and went through hell trying to get her and her family to the States. They had I think two children, and she brought her mother and younger sister to the States. While we were in the field and after she had her paperwork for staying in the States, she just moved out without any notice. Parish was devastated as you can imagine. His child support was like six or seven hundred a month. Susan and I were very upset for him. Everyone told him that it was possible it could happen to him. He eventually would move on. Parish was a good friend the whole time in Pendleton. What happened later between me and Susan brought me and him closer too. It was all close to the same time frame.

There were a few people I didn't get along with at the Rat Pac, and SSGT Bolt was one of them for sure. He was a know-it-all idiot when it came to tact and knowing our field. He was passed over for gunny a few times. He had some good moments, I guess, but he didn't seem to like me much. The sergeants in our platoon tolerated him to say the least. When it came to the moments we all were just B.S.ing, he was actually quite funny. To be honest, I'm not really sure what he did there at the Rat Pac. He really did get on my nerves at times, but he was my superior, so as a Marine, I gave him the respect of his rank.

Corporal Newman was another interesting character, to say the least. You see, he was one of them twenty-four corporals who believed everyone should respect him because he was so smart. I remember he always used to carry a stick when we were in the field like his scepter. All of us corporals used to have many discussions about respect, and most of the time it was because of something Newman had done without any tact whatsoever. There was a little truth to what he said. "As a Marine, you have to have respect for rank no matter what," he would say. That is very true, and most did have plenty of respect, but that didn't motivate them to work just a little harder. If you gained even more respect, they worked that much harder. See, Newman didn't believe in that way of thinking. Parish and I believed earned respect was better than automatic respect.

Vasquez was from Puerto Rico and had some big issues with taking orders. We also found out in conversation he was a boxer and apparently very good from what we gathered. My take on Vasquez was totally different than most. He had respect for people automatically, but not for people that had attitude about it. If he thought someone was an idiot, then he'd just ignore them as much as possible. In all actuality, it wasn't authority that bothered him but irrationality and blatant stupidity. Newman had a situation with Vasquez out in the field once, and Newman even tried to write him up, but it never got past gunny.

We sent Vasquez to school to learn about generators for the field bakery. One time out in the field, Newman decided he didn't like the way Vasquez was doing things, and he changed the dials or settings on the generator, which ended up shutting us down for a while. Vasquez was levied to say the least but kept his cool. The old saying three strikes and you're out came into effect. We told Newman to leave him alone a few times, but he wanted his respect and believed he knew everything about generators, so he did it a third time. Now this was all out in the field so we had plenty of downtime, and I remember us all sitting around the NCO tent, playing cards, when Newman came up to us. "What the hell happened to you Newman?" I said this as we saw him walking over to us with blood on his face, holding his nose. We also could see a black eye once he got closer. He began to speak in obvious pain, "Vasquez started the gen—" Gunny interrupted by saying, "I told you to leave that damn generate alone. I sent Vasquez to do a job, and you couldn't leave well enough alone. Get away from me and get clear.⁻d up. You look like you fell from a cliff. Have Doc look at it." "But Gunny, this was Vasquez." "I'm sure Vasquez did see you fall from a cliff, now go see Doc, and I don't want to ever hear about this again!" Gunny said as Newman finally walked away. "Always treat people with respect, and most of the time they'll return it." I honestly don't remember if that helped Newman later. As you can see, I learned a lot about pride and respect while I was with the Rat Pac.

Another person had the effect of pride and respect but added a bit of arrogance to it was Corporal Knowles. Knowles was a very tall dark green who I think was on the embarkation side of our platoon. He actually had the most time in grade of all us corporals. He was a very proud man to say the least. He took pride to its deepest levels physically and mentally. He wasn't arrogant in a bad way but in a hidden way. He didn't run around telling people how great he was, but you could see it in his face. Knowles was all-around a good guy, but if you wasn't in his circle, he only tolerated you, but at least I didn't feel like he was one of the people telling me whether I was intelligent or not. He did have a good amount of intelligence and wisdom.

One of the more intelligent people I met in the Marines had to be Sears. This guy was silly smart. You wouldn't know by just talking to him, you had to get to know him. Sears was always very quiet. I did make good friends with him and learned some interesting things about him. Everyone in the Marines, just like any other military person, has a reason for being here. I mentioned mine and told you earlier about the people in general that joined. I also told you there were many of them that where very intelligent. Sears was one of them. Funny thing was that it wasn't his idea to join the military. He did choose the Marines though. His grandfather, I think it was, passed away and left him like three million dollars, but he only got it on one condition. He spent four years in the military and got out with a clean record.

That wasn't enough for Sears though. He was very active in his of duty time, getting a pilot's license. Every weekend he would spend at the airport taking lessons. Mind you, all the money for lessons was what he got in the Marines. He always stayed at the barracks, and he saved his money. I don't know, maybe it was wisdom that he had and not intelligence. I do know that we got a long a bit because in general, we were both quiet. Sears was not the motivated type at all, and I don't think he even picked up E-4 while he was in but instead had his license and instructor's license by the time he got out of the Marines. I think that was also very smart for his grandfather to get him to do that and learn humility. I still have a lot of respect for Sears and what he accomplished in the corps. No, I don't think he was part of the Sears family at all. I asked that question and he always denied it.

I don't want to get into Ipsen stories till I get back from school for NCO baking. He definitely stays a good friend for a while. It's time to get back to Susan a bit. During the course of all these stories, Susan and I seemed to just get worse. Because of all the hours I spent in the field, working late to get a load of

MREs out, PT at wee hours of the morning, and constant worry of my next day even when I was home, I didn't leave much time for her and Jason. At one time or another, she seemed very nice to me but very distant at the same time. I suppose I didn't notice why she kept wondering when I was going to be home, but because of Jason, we won't delve into that subject. I know now it was also because of me when everything went to pot. Just before I was to go to school, again for baking school, we started fighting a lot more than what could be considered normal. But these was the Marines, and when you have to go, trust me, you have to go.

The last time I was here in Johnson I was at the top of my world and had a platoon to deal with. This time, my life was falling apart right before me, and we had our own rooms because we were NCOs. For that we didn't have to deal with the crap I did before. The first time I was here, I didn't bring a guitar with me, but I was so depressed before I brought it along to help me through some lonely times. I'm so glad I did. You see, Susan never really appreciated my singing and guitar music, so I had stopped playing for a while. Y'all remember how important that was to me towards the beginning I'm sure. Playing with that girl at the play, while I was in the festival at night around the fire, long nights in the racquetball court, and in general anytime I could before I met Susan. Don't get me wrong, I played a few times around her, but it was more of an irritation to her than anything. I compromised and stopped. Now I had some time to myself to get back into it. Little did I know what kind of effect it would have on all the other students.

School itself was OK, I guess, we spent a whole lot of time on "faults and causes." The one big thing was the tournament that we had while in school. I did a Neapolitan desert and some whole wheat bread. My Neapolitan placed and gave me a solid one hundred percent for my desert project. That was definitely a moment to shine, but it was nothing compared to my laundry concerts on the weekends that grabbed everyone's attention. See, these barracks were like a big apartment complex with a big laundry room. The first week there I was doing laundry and pulled out the guitar. By the end of my laundry, everyone that had not gone to town was listening. Talk about getting my mind out of depression. It was almost as if all them times playing were preparing me for that time in my life.

Each call from Susan devastated me to the fullest extent. Looking back, she was trying to get me to break up over the phone and I refused, saying nothing could break our love for each other. As you can imagine, I was wrong. Playing my guitar for everyone made me feel so much better. When I was alone though, all I could think of was Jason, and the thought of losing Susan. I had already lost a son to the problems of age. Now losing Jason was threatening me. I really wanted things to work for us. The guitar was a blessing to my sanity while I was away, and I can't tell you how excited I was to go home and try to fix things. Then that time loomed over me, and we found out we were going early, and I couldn't wait.

"As I was driving, I saw a sign and smiled when I said, "Here we go, 25 mph, hold on." "Don't even think about it!" But it was too late; I hit the corner at around 50 mph and felt her slipping from under me."

CHAPTER 36

Breaking Up Is so Hard for Everyone

We originally were leaving at the beginning of the next week, but for some reason we left early. Boy, was she going to be surprised. After a long flight and a taxi home for the big surprise, I arrived home. That's as far as I'm willing to share with you guys in this book. What happens between me and my exes should stay between me and them. My kids don't need long-drawn-out stories of breakup in their minds. Let's just say we argued all weekend and decided that we should split up at this point. I guess in some ways, it could be considered mutual, but to me it wasn't. Even after that day, it was hard to let go. Jason was the one suffering the most. We would move on in time, but the memory of me will stay with Jason. Well, at least I hope my memory stays with all of you kids. That's why you're reading this book, Jason. It was a tough decision, Jason, and I'm sorry we didn't make it through. I'll always love you and hope the best for all of you.

Breaking up was a tearful thing, then to add salt to the wound we had to stay in the same house at first. In one aspect, this was great for the sake of Jason and the amount of time I'd spend with him. At first I dreaded the thought of moving in the barracks, but being around Ipsen a few times made me think it would be fun again. Me and Susan spent many nights at first going over things and sadly arguing. At one point, right away we knew I needed my own vehicle. We still had our Chevy Chevette between the two of us, but I really needed my own. For some reason, probably Jason, we kept very civil about the whole thing. After a short period, it did become a little weird, and we knew I was going to have to do something else.

The first thing had to be a car. Ipsen and I had been hanging out a bit, and he was the one who drove me down to Oceanside to find a car. One thing y'all have to remember at this time, I had never had my own car. This was going to be fun. Now other then stealing Dad's Chevy Nova and driving our little Chevy, I had never even had a thought of what kind of car to buy. Nova kind of just became my favorite car. But no one had one I liked. We must have spent that whole day looking because my memories say it was dark when I signed for my first adult loan. "What kind of car was it?" Wasn't a Chevy, but it was a sports car. Light blue T-Top 280ZX, and boy was she fast. Almost killed me many times and almost killed Ipsen once too. This car took the place of all my transgressions. I hope you remember what I told you about driving. She gave me sheer freedom and a great release of depression. She became a passion for me in time. I admit buying a car like this, with so much inexperience was probably not a good idea, but she was so pretty. Having the 280 also became my escape from arguing during this time. Whenever it got bad, I would go out to wash and wax the car. On the weekend, I soon started going for drives.

One of the things me and Ipsen did was look at a map to find a country drive to get away. I lived in Fallbrook, California, just northeast of Camp Pendleton. We were looking for a lake or something to go to. Ipsen was starting to get a little upset with me after a while. I had learned that if a sign said "Caution 45 mph" I could double that and add ten mph and feel safe on her suspension. Ipsen didn't believe me at first, so I had to prove it to him. Then when he got scared, his knuckles turned white with fear. I feel bad now but then that just edged me along to go faster and scare him more. Sorry, Ipsen.

One thing I didn't know was the double thing doesn't work on anything less then a 30 mph sign. "There's a lesson for you."

Well, Ipsen and I found out the hard way. As I was driving, I saw a sign and smiled when I said, "Here we go, 25 mph, hold on." "Don't even think about it!" But it was too late; I hit the corner at around 50 mph and felt her slipping from under me. Then as I heard Ipsen yelling a colorful word or two, she slipped and headed for the ditch. In my own defense, I was able to slow her just a hair before I hit the small hill on the side of the road. My first thoughts were a ditch but as the car buckled up and was lying on the passenger side, I realized the highway department was smart and had a small natural hill of sand to keep us from crashing into the field. That was all well and good, but Ipsen was not exactly in a good mood. See, normally, Ipsen didn't use colorful words ever, but as I looked down from the driver's side on him, it was like the cartoons with steam coming out of his ears. I think I heard every colorful word in the book as he lay crushed against the ground in his window. As he spoke to me, I realized the car was still running and pulled forward to get the car back on level ground. Soon as we leveled out, Ipsen jumped from the car and stayed upset for good reason.

Looking back, that small hill was what saved us. We did end up staying for a long time just waiting for a tow truck with a compressor and some tools to reset the seals on the driver's side. Yes, that's all that happened to the car, thank God. When I slid into the hill, it popped the seals, and Ipsen slowly did calm down, but only after I promised to drive normal from now on when he is with me. Obviously, I was very apologetic. I'm sure you can imagine that was a fun story for everyone but Ipsen. I did slow down a lot after that incident, except maybe when I was alone.

A few weeks later, things kept really building up on me and Susan. Her father was talking about coming to California to help her get ready to come back to Texas. I was in no position to argue about her going back even in the sense of Jason being my son. Jason, even you know that you were distending to be a Texan, and trust me and your mom, we truly tried to fix things, but it just wasn't meant to be. You were so little and vulnerable. Children, in most cases, should always be with their mother. Not that I would've ever thought about that, but in retrospect that's true. Sadly enough, Jason, I was also a Marine and couldn't follow your mom to Texas. The time was coming soon to say good-bye. I was spending as much time as possible with Jason as I could without the fighting. Sadness was becoming overwhelming, and the open road was becoming my only escape.

"Now in my forties, in retrospect, I realize what mistakes I made in the past with my situation with you. I can't change that, but Jason, I am truly sorry for missing your life."

CHAPTER 37

Funny-Tasting Chili

One weekend I decided to go the farthest from base I ever had. I saw a lake called Henshaw, which was past Palomar Mountain observatory. Which, by the way, was were we hit the ditch. Seemed like a good idea at the time. Maybe something like Horseshoe Lake would make me feel better. Palomar Mountain was just a twenty-minute joint off the road to Henshaw, so I went there first. It was truly beautiful when I got there. Though it was a beautiful place, I spent little time there because I wanted to see a lake again. Got back on I-76 I think it was and headed for the lake. When I got there, the scenes were overflowing with serenity and joy. There weren't as many trees as a Minnesotan, but it was a vast sight to see a lake again here in California. There was a marina right there off the road and what seemed to be a restaurant up a small hill. Behind the restaurant was a small trailer park with small trailers winding up a small hill. It was much quieter than I thought it would be for a small resort lake, but very picturesque. At first I parked over by the restaurant and walked over to the docks at the marina and spent some time running my fingers in the water and reminiscing about my childhood at Horseshoe Lake. Then my stomach reminded me that I'd been driving all day where there isn't much in the way of food.

At the time, I hadn't experienced much in the sense of restaurants types, and all I had was the memory of my parents' stores. So far in life, I had not seen a mom and pop's that made me feel quite like that in a long time. Not only was the lake making me melancholy, but this little café gave me a rush of memories also. It had the added sense of scenery as you looked out on the lake. I can't really remember if there was anyone else there or not, but my memory says I was alone that day. It was one of them places you order at the counter and the sit down, and they bring you your food. That's when I saw her for the first time. She had a faint smile and was very cordial with me as she spoke, "What can I help you with?" I was awestruck for a moment as I used the menu on the wall to help distract my obvious infatuation with this lady. "What's good on the menu today?" She answered back with a bit of a giggle and said, "All of it's good, I made it. But I really like the chili. It's my recipe." That's all it took for me. I was hooked.

It's all a bit of a blur for me at this point, in the sense I don't remember the conversation or how it began. I do know we talked a long time while she worked here and there. At first I think talking about the chili may have started our conversation. I told her it was really good but different for me. I told her it seemed like a very tomato like taste to me. "It's good, but not what I'm used to, is all." She jokingly said, "You just haven't had good chili before, is all." "Oh, you're talking about mom now, not nice." This was all said in fun. Her mom was there, saying hi also. I saw them time and again out of the corner of my eye looking at me and talking in a whisper. But I do think she knew I liked her too. I think towards the end of my time there we were talking about seeing each other on a date of sorts very soon. Might have even been the next day, I can't remember. Heck, I'm not sure what we did that day. If I'm not mistaken, she was living in Santee, California, which is by El Cajon. Her parents owned a house right next to the fairgrounds. It was a huge house and had a wonderful view. How far it was from the base wasn't a concern at first, but it was sixty-five miles from Camp Pendleton.

Her name was Dina, and she had two little girls: Tiffany and Stefanie. Dina's mother was the owner of the restaurant I met her at, and she lived in the trailer park behind it. It didn't take very long for me and Dina to fall in love with each other, and very soon after that I moved, in with her and the girls. My thoughts now are logical that we should have spent more time together and got to know each other better; at the time though, she was pretty and very friendly with me. We had a lot of fun together at first and were always laughing. It actually took the girls a bit longer to get used to me being around. Especially you, Stefanie, It was as if you were afraid of me. Jason was my only experience in raising children before you, and I wasn't sure how to be a father figure to you and your sister Tiffany. I hope, in time, you feel I did a good job for you and Tiffany.

Before I get too far ahead of myself, I wanted to share my first ticket with you guys. All of you know how much I loved my car, but you have to hear this story about how stupid I was for a long time in that car. One stupid thing was driving at an average ninety miles an hour on a daily basis. Remember that sixty-five miles a day I had to drive? I think my best time was forty minutes. If I seen a car even a mile in front of me, I chased him down and passed him before we would hit one of the spots that had a double yellow line. God forbid if I got caught behind them before I hit the mountains and wouldn't be able to pass them. Here is a stupid one for you; you know them reflectors on the side of the road? I would get in the dirt on the straightaway at 100 mph and swerve to miss them to get the feel of the dirt if I started to lose it sometime. I probably did it for fun too or even to keep myself awake. I don't know whether it helped me later in life or not, but I like to think so.

One day I was running late and going even faster then normal on Interstate 15, just outside of Fallbrook going approximately 105 mph when I saw lights catching up to me. Well, I have to say that I had raced many people on the road in the past few months and thought this was just a challenge for me and my baby. So I stuck her into fourth gear and took off. At first I was doing good and noticed I pegged the speedometer, which was 130. That's when I saw the lights for the first time. Yes, I mean cop lights were catching me at over 130 mph. "Holy smokes" I thought. What kind of car was he driving? The only thing so far to beat me was a motorcycle. We all know I'm not the criminal type, so as you can imagine, I pulled over as soon as I saw them. Probably one of the smart things I did in life. Because of that the officer, while he handcuffed me because of protocol, was very kind to me the whole time. In fact as we walked away from the car, he said, "Your ticket is for in excess of 137 mph but I noticed you had Firestone Firehawks for tires. Well, if you got some Goodyear's, it would be over 142 mph in that car." I couldn't help but chuckle and say "Thank you for the tip."

As funny as that may seem, that's not what makes me remember this whole ordeal but it was the funniest part for sure? After a night in jail, my fine was $650. Even still not a terrible part. SSGT Bolt made a suggestion to the gunny that I should pay for this by not being able to drive down to the shop after morning formation. See, formation was at the barracks a half mile away. A lot of the troops didn't have cars, so I marched them everywhere for two months. That was very humiliating for me. I did enjoy doing cadence again, but I tied up a lot of my time, not to mention having to eat at the chow hall with them. I always brown bagged it back then. As you can imagine, I didn't get along too well with SSGT Bolt. It did slow me down a bit though. At least for a little while, but now we need to get back to the story.

Towards the beginning of our relationship, you have to remember that Susan, in a sense, was still in the picture for a short period of time. So there was a few times that I got to spend with Jason. I still can see her and Jason getting in that car to leave for Texas with her father. But I was happy that Susan was going back to her family even though I was torn up about losing Jason and her. I would be very confused about things for a while after that. I was truly falling in love with Dina but couldn't get over all the things that had gone wrong over the past few months.

Dina seemed to have a lot of patience, not to mention, she was very understanding during all of this. She stood by my side all through it. It was now coming to a point of what were we going to do about us. Real decisions hadn't been solidified yet between us. While this was going on, I decided to go to Texas to see Jason and spend some time to think things through. Dina and I spoke of her coming, but her work schedule conflicted with my trip. So we had a tearful good-bye, and I grabbed a map and headed out.

I'm sure you remember my love for maps? This was also my first road trip on my own. Under the circumstance, this was the perfect time for stress relief and contemplation on the road. My love for driving intensifies. I have to tell you now that having a sports car on the I-10 late at night became very intense at times. It's a miracle I didn't get a speeding ticket that day. Not to mention in the little time that I was with Dina all the way in Santee, she was getting used to me driving way too fast. See, the road to work was a much quieter highway during the week than during the weekend with Sunday drivers. Needless to say, I pulled into my parents' house in just twenty-one hours. Man, I truly loved that car! When I got to my parents' I got some sleep and called Susan to set some time up with Jason, and that is were the trouble began.

"I don't know if I can trust you by yourself with Jason," she said. Her attitude towards Jason's father changed for some reason. To this day, I don't get it. "I don't think he knows you enough now, and I'm not comfortable letting him stay with your parents." This, as you can imagine, was a complete shock to me. She wanted me to meet her at McDonalds so she could watch over me while I played with my own son, Jason. I'm not sure what made her feel this way. I guess, in speculation, it had to be partly her knowing my father's background with me and my sort off naïve ways in life. I have to say though, she knew I had reconciled with my dad as all of you know, and what little time we did spend with my parents, he was a perfect grandpa. Could it have been the status difference, or was it something else that I don't know about? Was I not smart enough to be with my own son? She knew I had just reenlisted so she wouldn't have to deal with me unless I moved to Texas. This became very disconcerting for me, and under our laws, I could have maybe fixed this, but I was to naïve to figure this out at the time.

Dina, as you can imagine, really didn't like Susan. At the moment, Dina tried to get me to go to a lawyer, but for someone with my fears and being very naïve, I thought it would be best to just let her be with this and later things would work out. Because of this situation with Susan, it became one thing that started many arguments with Dina and just escalated in the future.

This, as I'm sure you know, was a big mistake like I said at the beginning of the book. Jason, you were my son, and I let people manipulate the outcome of our experience together. I should have listened to Dina when she and my parents told me to go to a lawyer. When all of this came about, Jason, I was too naïve to know the right thing to do. Susan took everything from me the day she left for Texas, including you, and my pride. Not that I had much pride at the time. Now in my forties, in retrospect, I realize what mistakes I made in the past with my situation with you. I can't change that, but Jason, I am truly sorry for missing your life. For all of you that may be reading this who might be in the same situation, don't make the same mistakes I did. For the mothers out there that are saying, "You don't know my ex." I know there are certain men out there that are abusive, alcoholics, having drug problems and not to mention anger issues with some of them. By all means fight them for the rights of your children. Please, people don't use children to your own advantage. Be civil and moral with your decision.

In this time of my life, I was still very young and had no real education, not to mention much street-smart. Things, that are left unsaid with Susan, were devastating to me, and I really hadn't been alone enough to give myself some sense of personality or a sense of self. Fear also was my guide in life too. Boot camp did make me a little stronger in that sense though. Remember when I spoke of seasons of the heart? I was still in the spring of life with no real background. I was what people made me. You guys remember the dork of Central High, don't you? Then it was straight in the arms of the Marines. I had a little time to grow up and then Susan. I became what I thought she wanted me to be. Now I was trying something a little different. Dina hadn't seen the real me, in such a short period of time. Don't get me wrong though, Dina helped make me who I am today, but so did Susan. I was becoming what my surroundings were making me. Admittedly, I was way too far behind in my maturity to be in the situations I was in. Trust me though, this isn't a pity party for me, it was just how things were at this time in my life. At that age and maturity, I just wasn't aware of myself as much as I needed to be to make the right decisions for me and my children.

Dina proved to me when she came out to Texas that she was very interested in me, and when we got back to California, things took a big leap for our relationship. That tomato chili became a staple for me on a weekly basis. This was our honeymoon time in our relationship. We were in love.

"Will I hold up against my enemy? Do I have what it takes to use the training that I've had to help my fellow Marines, or will I cower in the eyes of my enemy?"

CHAPTER 38

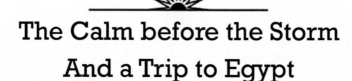

The Calm before the Storm
And a Trip to Egypt

After Susan left and we spent some time in Texas with my parents, it was time to really get down to being a couple. Like in any relationship, it was wonderful in many ways at the start. I have to say that after that time in Texas, things were very nice in the passionate and romantic way. At home with the kids felt so much different to me with Dina compared to Susan. At first I felt I had more say-so in this relationship than before. It was a team effort with Dina, at first. I have to admit that the long-distance travel for both of us was a little difficult though. It was becoming very mundane in this routine that we had no escape from, for the time being. After a while, I have to say we sort of got used to it. We got up at around two thirty or so. We both would get ready and then get the car set up. We tried not to wake the girls then put them in the car. We headed to her mom's restaurant and needed to be there by three so I could do the last forty-five miles to Pendleton. Once we took the girls in the back room of the restaurant so they could sleep a bit more, I would leave with the music blaring in my fast little hot rod. Two tapes that stick out in my memory were **Slippery When Wet** and **Ronnie Millsap's Greatest Hits.**"

Other than the long drives each day, our relationship was going real well. Obviously the drive was getting bad after awhile, and we knew we'd have to move somewhere closer to the base soon. Our life together was fairly uneventful, but the people around us made things interesting. My family, for the most part, wasn't too much of a bother because they were still in Waco, Texas. Dina's family was right there with us. Dina's father, who loved a cold beer, was in a sense our landlord, and her mother was her boss. Her brother was in construction, and her sister was going through a divorce with her ex, and he was a cop. Tiffany and Stefanie's dad had some issues with drugs and always tried to see them. Not to mention he knew where we lived. As I write this, I have to laugh a bit. I'm looking at the future of the book, and it's interesting how many things happened to me from my relationships' families. Don't get me wrong, it's not like a bad thing, just an observation.

When you kids start new relationships, remember what I'm saying here. As you bond with your newfound love, you must accept everything about them, including their family. Don't forget that their family knows a lot more about your loved one than you do. Be responsible and show them respect because you are taking care of their life's blood. Now obviously, there can be other circumstance that would make things difficult, but do your best to get along, and most of all, don't hide yourself and the loved one from their own family. Remember before, I talked about how your parents know more about you than you think? Give their family credit as long as they don't prove you otherwise.

It was very obvious, looking back, that Dina's family could see the fact that I was a little naive when they met me. To their credit, they were very good to me except maybe a little razing now and then. Her father and brother were probably the worst of them. They both had a background in construction. I didn't realize at the time how hard that job is but later learned the hard way. Her dad was all about trucks and beer. He was a pretty nice guy to me I guess. I'm not going to go too much further about Dina's family or anyone else's for that matter. This is a book of my experiences, and what I saw of them is more of a private thing.

My chronological order may be wrong, as you know, but somewhere during this, we finally moved to Fallbrook to a decent apartment. The only bad thing there was some interesting neighbors. Started off fine as you might expect and even became friends to a certain extent, but it went south and became a major problem. The typical problems existed like loud music, paper walls, arguing and or fighting became louder and louder. I'm not sure how our decline in friendship started, but it became a big stress for us as time went by.

One thing I can't get over is how difficult it can be for people to just be neighborly. Treat them as you'd have them treat you seems pretty logical. Respect each other's privacy doesn't seem to hard to do to me. Makes you wonder what's happened to this world. Does anyone think you should have to listen to someone else's music? Just doesn't seem fair to be so rude to each other. Neighbors can be so mean to each other at times. You would think they'd just get along for the sense of peace, but that's not the case at times. As I've said before, this isn't something that is just starting to happen; it's been around all my life. Even in the barracks, as you may remember. Later in life, as I matured, I realized how stupid things where and can say that a little kindness can go a long way. "Why should I be nice to them, Jim?" that may be what you're thinking, but all I have to say is "why not?" I did have many situations in my life with neighbors that where fixed with just a little kindness. I do say that with experience.

Other than our friends, it was pretty nice being close to base. This is where things, as far as I can remember, started going south. It always starts with money, doesn't it? Just like every American out there, we were living beyond our means and we kept digging the hole deeper and deeper. In a way though it started with the 280 Z, and after that, the credit started rolling in. Not to mention the checking account.

This is an area I have always wanted to tell people about. Some of you out there had some good teachers in your parents when it comes to finances, but like me, a lot of you didn't listen to your parents about your money. I personally think that credit and such has become much worse than when I was little. Now it seems that it has become a way for the rich to get richer. It is a very vicious cycle that no one wants to see through the BS. Do your best to follow me here. There is a long list of people that benefit from every red-blooded American's misfortune. When I was younger, it started off OK to a certain extent. Investors put their money on the line to lend people money and then the banks give them a good return on the money they put in because their charging the little guy tons of interest on the money they lend to you. Now you're OK with that because the media and TV shows make you think that you need something right now. The credit cards give you the ability to do that. In a way, that is a good thing, but in a way, you're just helping the rich get richer.

You might be thinking in a way that the risk isn't worth it for them, but that's not true at all. Admittedly, there is a percentage that always pays their cards off, but the small amount, that doesn't, just help in other ways. That opens up even more money being spread out to other rich people like the insurance companies, collections, and not even to mention advertising. This vicious cycle destroys families over and over. Then we spend all of our money on counseling and blame everything on the alcohol that we started drinking to get over the stress of it all. That puts money in someone else's hands. This also helps a lot of other people that make more and more things that we don't need but put it on the card because it's easier than paying cash for something that we know we don't really need. A false sense of security, as it was. Then we need a bigger credit line because we feel we have to have the security again because the card is maxed-out. After a while our credit dips down because we have too much credit and, our rates go up and don't even realize it. Now the banks and investors are taking more of your money.

Only you can stop the insanity! Wake up, people! They rob you blind and then say "Sorry, you should have budgeted better before you got even more credit." Dina and I fell very deep in this hole, to say the least. It was the beginning of the end for us, in a roundabout way. We always wrote it down as a necessity as time went on. Our hole of dept got bigger and bigger but our pay never grew with it. After awhile we just weren't making enough money to pay the bills.

During this initial time of credit, we needed another car for a family car. The 280s just don't cut it as a family car. I had also grown a liking to the Toyota pickup as a favorite truck because of one of the sergeants at work's little Nissan pickup with the carpet kit installed. The Toyota idea came from a little push from Dina's dad who owned a Toyota. So on top of all this other debt we bought a nice red Toyota with the carpet kit. It was a beautiful truck to say the least. It was actually the same truck as her dad's truck.

I got a chance to go to Egypt with the Marines. It was basically just a short trip for the operation called Bright Star '86/'87. The bad thing, if my memory serves me right, was that at the same time frame, my father had another surgery for either his heart or aorta bypass. This hardship situation has sent me back early and gave me a trip to Alexandria for a phone call. I'll get to that in a moment.

Part of me was really excited about this trip, but a bigger part was worried about Dina and the kids. This was one of the few trips in the Marines that I didn't have a two-month ship ride to get there. Instead it was a long plane ride with a quick fuel stop in Hawaii. So in a way, I can say I've been there but we never left the plane. Now for all of you that are younger then thirty or so, the eighties was the time of peace for the most part. The grunts and some special forces did some things around the world, but for our little group the only thing we had seen is a flak suppresser and the rifle range. (Flak suppresser was what we used in training when shooting blanks to stop people from getting injured in your line of fire from the flak.)

Quick note: when I first went to the field and used them stupid flak suppressers, I couldn't wait to shoot my weapon as much as possible. One thing I didn't get was all of the salty guys were giving you their blank rounds away. So I thought this was awesome for me until it came time to clean that damn thing. They suppress all the carbon as you're firing, and it builds up very easily. It took me days to clean that thing. Needless to say, I always gave my rounds away after that.

Things were made to sound very difficult in the Middle East at the time, and we took many classes during the preparation of this trip to make us very cautious and suspicious of anyone while we were in country. So in layman's terms, we were scared to death as we landed in the undisclosed location in Egypt. As we started looking out the window while taxiing around, we saw Egyptian troops with AK-47 lined up all over on both sides of the plane. This just made things even tenser for all of us. When we started coming to a stop, we noticed many tents with the sides rolled up all over the field away from the main terminal. They instructed us that the tents had color codes with numbers for each platoon and told us our individual platoon colors and numbers for our section. When we arrived at our exclusive tents, they had two MPs at each tent that told us each Marine had to put their name on two gallons of water and were told to drink both before we could leave to the field. This obviously took awhile but was extremely important to hydrate each one of us.

After a few hours of that, we took Egyptian transportation, which was a little comical in itself. If you can imagine having a bus full of Americans who have a plethora of different music in their heads like rock, rap, country, and don't forget the big-hair bands from that time, sitting there cautiously listening to Egyptian religion music. No offense to the Egyptian driver and his choice of music, but it got some really interesting looks from all those Marines. We also had a slight situation with the driver wanting to know what we had in the foot locker on the floor filled with M-16s that we weren't suppose to have with us. He was told that it was food and water in case we got stranded on the way to the field. Once he let that go, it was loud Allah music riding through the Egyptian desert. "What is it with you and bus rides in the desert, Jim?" Yeah, that is kind of a funny thought. Like all the other times it was very pretty out there. A little different then the Mojave Desert, this was a lot of sand dunes too.

The operation itself was fairly relaxing for me. For some unknown reason, I ended up with the special services platoon, which I think SSGT Bolt had something to do with that. It actually ended up being very simply the guy who handed out water bottles, MREs, and watching after the ice machines. Yes, that's right; we had ice machines in the middle of the desert. Some of the higher-ups' tents had plywood floors and carpet. It was that green carpet you use on the porch, but it was nice. At one point I had a kidney stone and ended up in the field hospital for two days. See, we use chlorine to purify water in the field. That was paradise for two days. They had AC units in the hospital. After that, I had a newfound respect for AC.

The one other nice thing was giving every person the opportunity to go to the Mediterranean at least once for a swim, which was interesting having more Egyptian soldiers as guards around the perimeter again. I have to say the one scary moment that tops them all was the night we were on alert. Everyone was getting set for the evening when the alarm went off, and we all were sent to our foxholes with the fear of being attacked. "Was this an exercise?" Well, in an exercise they don't hand out live rounds to put into clips, we never locked and loaded through the night, but as you can imagine, it was a long night for all of us.

This was the closest I had been to any kind of combat in the whole time I was in the corps. I can't even begin to tell you the feeling of fear and excitement that you get in that situation. Like I was telling you when I was at Fort Ripley, you military men and women out there, I have more respect then anything for all of you. I was lucky enough to be one of the guys that never had to deal with the memories that all of you will carry forever in your heart. That long night in my life was nerve-wracking at best. Will I hold up against my enemy? Do I have what it takes to use the training that I've had to help my fellow Marines, or will I cower in the eyes of my enemy? A million scenarios flooded my brain like a dream. I found myself looking at my foxhole in great detail, making sure that it was safe to move around so I didn't trip or fall in a fight. I found myself even wondering how close my canteen was if I needed some water. I also worried about taking my eyes off of my fire line for even an instant to blink. Now I only had to deal with this for one night, and even then nothing significant happened. Some of you did this as a daily thing in Iraq and Afghanistan, so knowing what little I do; I thank all of you from the bottom of my heart. All of you people that haven't been there, including me, shake someone's hand next time you see a military person.

A bit after that a message came over the wire that my father was sick and was going to have surgery, they set me up to go to Alexandria and get a landline to the States to call him in case something happened before they got me home. What little I saw of this town was a bustling market and a small apartment that a plain-clothed solider was staying in. Yes, I guess in a way it felt like some cloak and dagger place, and the market looked like something out of a movie. Except there you could smell it. I can't really explain the smell very well, but it wasn't real pleasant. Of course it wasn't terrible either. I guess I would say "you could smell the poverty." That is the best I can explain. For anyone that lives in the city, in certain areas you would know what I mean. Even here in Duluth, we have an area of town that has that musty smell. Of course in West Duluth it's because of the sewer plant, from what I've heard. Remember I was in the sixth grade there. Now when I go back there, it is such a familiar smell that it doesn't bother me at all. In fact it makes me reminisce when I'm down there.

I was only there for a very short time, and they sent me back. They couldn't just send me, but a lot of the brass would be leaving soon after the war games with the Egyptian soldiers, and I would be heading out with them. The war games were very trivial to a certain extent. We showed them what we could do then they ran down the field yelling and screaming for their show. I think all of us felt they held back on what their ability was for some weird reason. We had air strikes, helicopters, tanks, artillery, mortars, saws, and cleaned up with ground forces. They had a few helicopters, a tank or two, and their little band of soldiers. In the training when I got to shoot the M-60 and the M-50, we were just playing around a bit. Then when it was the Egyptians turn, they turned the fifty-five-gallon barrel into mincemeat. They were pretty serious then. It was as if they had to prove something to us. Kind of like a dog with Napoleon syndrome.

Well after that, it was time to hit the road. The plane they sent me on was a supply plain, C-130. We were on board with a bunch of con ex boxes. The only service we had was the MREs they handed out for lunch. My bed was my sleeping roll and a rifle box. It was actually a comfortable ride. Don't remember the flight time, but it was fairly long. All in all, I just slept the whole way.

When I got to my father, he had already had the surgery and was in the recovery room. I may have this time frame wrong, but I do remember seeing him with tubes going in his body, and he wasn't able to speak. I'm not sure why my mind blocks this memory so much, but I didn't handle all of this too well from what my brother tells me. I like to think I'm a very sensitive person, but I also know that I keep my bad feelings away from people, and sometimes they never see that side of me. When I stood there looking at my father with a tube down his throat and some going in his side to his heart, I just lost it right there in ICU. My stomach got queasy, I felt sick and basically started bawling. It was like living my whole life with Dad in a rush of memories and feelings. It was so devastating to see him like that. That picture will always be in my memories. He pulled through that tough surgery very well. That is definitely one of the many good uses of technology today.

"Having dinner at the table was always the perfect way to end my day no matter how stressful the day was. In my eyes, it is like reaping what you've sown."

CHAPTER 39

Christopher Is Welcomed to this World

Dad did get better, and life began again for Dina and I. Dina, you and the kids will have to accept my apologies ahead of time for the next little bit of the book in the sense of chronology. I know around this time we got the exciting news of our first child together. But I'm sketchy on where we lived at the time. I think we were either in Fallbrook still or Ramona. No, not Pomona like in **Die Hard**. There was a Ramona, I think, to the east of San Diego. Bottom line was Christopher was born in Fallbrook. I know at one time we moved to Ramona to have a middle point for Dina and me for our commute. From the little I remember, I really liked Ramona. It was my first hick town of sorts in my adult life. It was also a little cheaper to live out there too.

Things really started to get rough for us during this time with a new baby on the way and falling into the trap of credit debt, not to mention having the feeling from the media to just want more. I do admit a lot of this was due to my being naive and not knowing how to say no. Ask my fiancé now or anyone who knows me well; you send me to get milk, and I come back with a hundred dollars' worth of groceries. That in some sense wasn't the big problem, but my inability to priorities was. If it was a choice between bills that were due or food for the kids, the food came first. Having that guaranteed paycheck from the military gave me the ability to just get more credit. Credit card companies are like vultures when it comes to the military. That all goes back to that vicious cycle we spoke of earlier. Trust me when I say to try your best not to use credit if you can. They already tax you enough and then we go and pay all the extra interest on credit debt.

When you were born, Chris, it was like having a candle to get you through the night in the dark. You brightened an otherwise drearier time for us. We were struggling but surviving. This is when all that stuff we talked about in the beginning of the book with my mom's recipes came in very handy. We always sat at home for dinner and had a nice big meal every night. Chris, we couldn't wait to have you there with us. Even in all the difficulties that we faced, we were happy. As you came into this world this also gave me and your mom a time to finally settle things at the justice of the peace and we married just after you were born. That day was one of the best and at the same time one of the worst.

After I finally got my divorce settled and Dina's also, it was time to make our family official. Chris was a newborn, but he came with us to go to the justice to get married. We had the girls looking perfectly pretty, and Dina had just got a beautiful turquoise dress that was perfect on her. I know you're probably wondering why I remember the color of the dress. I'll get to that in a moment. We were getting married somewhere around her hometown, which was Lakeside. I knew this road very well and was traveling up there at a pretty good speed in the red Toyota. In the hills, there are a lot of spots that are no-passing zones, and out in the country we got a lot of Sunday drivers, and that day we happened to find one. We were doing 35 in a 55 mph all the way through the hills, Dina and I were both a little upset. We knew about this half-moon section of road that for us will be a left-hand bend. There was a car behind us tailgating us also. This half-moon was a blind right turn as you came up on it. Trust me, when I hit that corner and saw no cars, I took off.

For any of you that remember those little 22 R engines in them pickups were pretty fast. We got up to 55 really quick, and the car behind us pulled to pass behind us. As soon as we started passing this vehicle, they speeded up so I had to go in the 60 to 70 mph zone. No sooner did I do that than he'd speeded up too. Now I'm getting upset and accidentally woke the kids in my anger. Then out of the corner of my, eye I saw a semi coming at me from the top of the bend. The guy behind me slowed to get behind the car we were passing. Now to give you what kind of picture I saw in my eyes, I'll go through my choices here. If I brake, the car behind me gives me a further distance, and by the time I get behind him, I get hit by the semi, which by the way, is coming downhill with a load, not to mention he's in the middle of a turn when he gets to me. I can't just turn to the left because there is no shoulder and a drop of around fifty to a hundred feet. There is also a big tree right there that I would definitely hit. The guy I'm passing is still going as fast as me at first, and if I just push him to the right, there is a rock cliff wall right there.

I was committed to the pass as you can see. The kids are screaming at me from the back, Dina is wailing on me with her fists, the semi's blaring his horn with the other cars, and the idiot I'm passing is flipping me off. Not that I'm stressed out or anything. Well, here I am writing this book so I obviously made it. I'm sure I only cleared that semi by inches because the air from it pushed us as we passed him. That was the other close call I mentioned from my swimming lesson from earlier. I can't begin to tell you what went through my mind at that moment. I can tell you I hope to never feel it again. Actually, I can give you some of it. Has any of you ever been on a roof or tall ladder and just slipped for a second? Those gut-wrenching feelings you get before you get control of yourself? It's a terrible feeling to say the least. Multiply that by ten and make it last for a minute or so, then you will know how it felt.

After that, it took a while to get over that fear, but it was time to get married anyway. We picked some Barry Manilow for the back ground music then needed to change Chris before we started. Dina put her legs together and sat him in her lap while she changed him. Remember, Chris, you were small then. That's when we found out Chris wasn't done yet.

All over Dina's beautiful turquoise dress. Don't be concerned, we just laughed about it, and it cleared the air of the almost accident that we had experienced moments before. Thank you, Chris, you came through again. It was a very simple ceremony that both of us were happy with. We didn't have a honeymoon per se, but I would assume I took a few days leave for some time with her. The scare we had on the road was put aside and just became a story told once in awhile. After all was said and done, there I was married again at, I think, twenty-three years old.

For those of you that haven't had the pleasure of barely surviving financially, I'll go into daily life for just a moment. This is not a pity party, just a story for you readers. It was my life. Because of that vicious cycle we all get into we had approximately $2,500 in bills and made $2,000 a month. This obviously doesn't compute. Now I will say we had some good moments where we got long stints of from work but typically it was fifty to seventy hours a week at times. PT was around four thirty to five each morning, and we got off around the same time twelve hours later. That does not include the driving time for living in the cities. So Dina and I had some stress times on a daily basis. Her stress was taking care of a baby and raising two young girls. When you take our day-to-day struggles and add to that our struggle to just pay bills, it wasn't fun. Yes, you're right; we did acquire the debt ourselves and gave into that cycle we talked about. That's our faults obviously. You can't change the past, and it was too late to worry about what we did, we just wanted to raise our family now.

I guess one of the nice things about it all was the time that Dina got to spend with the kids. She did a wonderful job just being a good mom. One thing that I do remember that was nice was our trip to Taco Bell each weekend. We were very poor, but once a week, we loved to take the kids to Taco Bell. I think the bean burritos were only .49¢ or .59¢ at the time. Chris and the girls loved their pintos and cheese. Then we would go see Grandma or Grandpa or maybe even Uncle Kenny. Dinners, as I'm sure you know, were always a big deal in the Kelley family. Having dinner at the table was always the perfect way to end my day no matter how stressful the day was. In my eyes, it is like reaping what you've sown. When I sit at he table watching my family eat and talk about the day's happenings, it makes it all worth every moment in my day. Doesn't matter how bad your day is, that moment would wash the whole day away so I could tackle another day tomorrow.

We was still paying on the 280 ZX, two maxed-out credit cards, a personal loan, a fairly new pickup, and plenty of mouths to feed. The rent in Romana was holding us back a lot too. Through many hours of discussion, Dina and I decided that maybe bankruptcy was our only options. Chapter 11 seemed to be the wise choice for us, which would take that cool-looking truck of ours. The one glitch in all this was the $750 we had to pay the lawyers just to go bankrupt and the car that started our relationship was banged up by Uncle Kenny when he needed it for a little while. He ripped up the whole driver's side when he sideswiped a semi at ninety miles an hour. That car still ran good and was the only thing to hold on to because we only owed a small amount to pay her off. This was a good decision for us and helped us fix a lot of real bad decisions. It was a big step that gave us a little breathing room for a little while.

We also had to move again to a smaller rent payment. I may be wrong, but I'm pretty sure it was her mother's small trailer at Lake Henshaw. I have to say from my background that you already know I loved living out there by the lake. It was very peaceful. The trailer was only a little one-bedroom camper of sorts. There was an add-on which had been made into the living room and now was the kids bedroom. The so-called bedroom was completely taken up by the queen-size bed. The kitchen/dining room was ridiculous, but this became our very cheap home to help us catch up and finish paying for the car. The trailer park was a dirt road with very few full-time residents, so it was very quiet indeed. As you can imagine though, the weekends were packed to the gills. If my memory serves me right, Dina worked at the café on the weekends to pay the lot fee while we were there. Dina's mother had moved in with her new boyfriend who owned the lake or maybe just the trailer park. Bottom line was it was very cheap for us to live there.

A little story, I'm sure Chris has heard, was a little incident with a pan of grease. I couldn't tell you if anyone still cooks fresh food anymore, but we, I should say Dina, was cooking some homemade French fries for all of us one day, which we all loved. That was especially true for Christopher and I, like father like son; and I still love making fresh food. Well, he was walking now and talking a little, and he took it upon himself to grab some more French fries while Dina and I weren't looking. He knew that pan was where the fries come from so he reached over his head and grabbed the pan from the stove and spilled hot grease which burned his hand and his foot. As you can imagine, he was screaming bloody murder now and came running towards us in the living room where the rest of us were. The ultimate fear and pain I saw in Chris's eyes could now be seen in Dina's. A quick assessment of the situation led us to the conclusion of an emergency visit to the closest hospital. After a very brief call to her mother so she could watch the girls, we took off at high speeds to, I think, Lakeside to take care of our son.

The initial burn screams were nothing to the trip to the hospital. I hope none of you will ever see the pain in a child's eyes with burns like that. Dina, I think, was even in more pain than Chris from the tearful concern of her little boy. Her pain and fear were deep seated in her heart. Looking into her tearful eyes was enough to make anyone see the love Dina had for her children. She could be a fairly mean mother, strict, and fierce but caring. As I sped through the country roads, we both were saying over and over how sorry we were to Chris, but the words didn't even faze him in his agony. The only solace that he had was holding on to his mother. As we pulled into the emergency room, it was almost impossible for them to take her baby away from her arms, but she finally gave in as they set him in the bed to investigate his wounds. They had instructed us to put a cold cloth on him, and when they removed it you could see for the first time how serious the injury was. The skin was starting to peel off and they told us he needed a sedative.

Then for the first time we could see him relax, and he finally feel asleep, giving Dina time to let this all sink in.

We stayed the night there with Chris and the next day found that his burn on his hand was not that bad but his foot would need a skin graph. They instructed us of the procedure and told use they would use part of his leg for the skin. Recovery would be time consuming because of his age, and the scare would be like a birthmark to him. We consented, and everything went very smooth with the surgery. They weren't kidding about the recovery. Since he was just a baby who just learned to walk, it would be like keeping a black lab locked in a cage. The bandage was sort of funny looking with it being so big due to his age. He wore a real tight like sock for a long time after to keep the graph on as it healed. Still to this day, Chris, we're sorry we didn't see you in the kitchen doing what you did. Luckily, you were young enough to get through it so easily.

Life got refurbished to an extent after that happened, and we went through some financial woes, but things felt good for us around that time. A decision was going to have to be made about the Marines very soon whether I stay in again or not. This was going to be a big one that will affect the rest of my life. Me personally, I was tired of the Marines and wanted to have more freedom. To Dina, it was a no-brainer, stay in for the security. I just wanted to start living a life of my own away from the daily problems of the military. Don't forget I was a John Denver fan and had thoughts of moving to Colorado. Somewhere in all this, we took a quick vacation out to Colorado and became pregnant again. I was excited about both.

"It was the corner of highway 76 and Poway Road. As dark as it was in the sky, the little window shined bright through the ambulance door even through all the flashing lights."

CHAPTER 40

A Quick Run to Colorado and an Exciting Birth

I don't remember the exact route we took, but I know we ended up in Woodland Park towards the end of our trip. One spot I won't ever forget is a place called the "Three Sisters." I want to say we were on the I-24 when we came around a bend and, **boom**, three mountains all over fourteen thousand feet. Talk about mind blowing. I always loved the thought of seeing what's around the bend. It's been in so many songs, at least songs that I know well. It all ties in to my perspective of things, I guess. I'm sure you can remember some of the thoughts that I've shared with you so far. It's sad to me to think of the people out there that don't just live. There is so much to see in this world, and a lot of it is right there in their hometown but they forget to look. Struggling through life is what society tells us to do, but who cares what society says, I'm going to enjoy everything I can, I want to know what's on the other side.

Why do we stomp on other people's journeys through life? Isn't it enough to just enjoy your life and make friends along the way? "Jim, that's just too easy to do. I don't owe anybody anything." Sounds kind of selfish, doesn't it? "Life is supposed to be hard, if we were all friends, that would make things too easy." I rest my case.

The trip to Colorado was very inspirational to my whole family, and now we couldn't wait to get out of the corps. First things first, we had another life to bring into this world. Living at the trailer park put us into a position that this child wouldn't be born in Fallbrook but in Lakeside or El Cajon. One other thing, with this child, we decided to wait till we found out the sex of the child. We were pretty excited about having another baby, and Dina would have a child born in her hometown. As you can imagine Dina, after three children, was becoming a pro at this birth thing. They told us because of this it could be fast when the time comes. Boy, they weren't kidding.

I remember Dina waking me very quietly and, with all the calm you can think of, said, "It's time to get going. Call Mom quick so we can leave right away." We had everything set up with her mother for the other kids and we took off. Something I forgot to mention to you. We had gotten rid of that famous car that brought me and Dina together. The 280 was gone, and we ended up with a Toyota Tercel. Great for gas, but very small compared to the truck. In actuality, the Toyota had a lot more room then the 280. Anyway, we hopped in the new Tercel and drove off in the night. "Jim, I think we need to hurry now, the contractions our only a few minutes apart." Oh great, I'm thinking, "Child born on highway 76 on there way to hospital in there Toyota." That was going to be the headlines, I was sure of it. "We have to stop in Ramona at the fire department. I don't think I'm going to make it to the hospital," Dina said as another contraction started.

We pulled into a dark firehouse late at night with only a doorbell by the bay doors. As Dina lay in the car in more and more pain, I'm ringing the door and pounding in frustration of the moment. It seemed like forever when the door finally swung open with a fireman half-asleep, standing in the doorway. "Where's the fire?" he says. "My wife is having her baby and was afraid we can't make it all the way to the hospital before she has the baby." "OK, calm down and will get the EMPs out here to look at your wife." Why in that kind of excitement do they always say "calm down"? I was becoming more and more hysterical at every minute we wasted just standing at the firehouse. I was beginning to think I would've been better off getting there on my own. I was obviously wrong as you'll see.

After what seemed like a lifetime, they decided not to risk anything and took her in the ambulance and said to follow them to the hospital. "Love you, honey," I said as they shut the doors and drove off. I was really excited and put my Elton John tape on and cranked up as much as possible listening to our baby's song, "Harmony." That was going to be her name for sure. We did tell them not to give the sex but during one of her ultrasounds, we speculated that it was a girl from the view that we had from the picture they gave us. Man I loved that song. It had a lot of energy in it. Of course Elton was known for that. I was singing as loud as I could racing down the highway with my little Tercel at 75 mph. What a great memory that was for me. The music was so resounding in the moment.

So there I was, singing along when we pulled up next to a stop sign at the side of the road. It was the corner of highway 76 and Poway Road. As dark as it was in the sky, the little window shined bright through the ambulance door even through all the flashing lights. It was as if God was lighting that corner for your arrival, Zach. I instinctively jumped from my car and ran to the window to see Dina's face struggling through another contraction as she held herself up with her elbows on the gurney. Doufus, the medic, seemed to be looking at his computer talking to the hospital on the phone about Dina's vitals, I assumed. Later Dina told me she kept telling him the baby was coming now and his reply never changed from saying, "We have plenty of time, just relax and stay steady with you're breathing, ma'am." This was driving her nuts to say the least. Dina never got along with so-called stupid people, as she would say, and this guy was nuts.

Around this time the driver comes running to the back of the ambulance, saying, "Sir you can't follow me that fast down these roads. My sirens don't give you the right to break the law." "Are you kidding? You're only going 75, I go faster than that on my way to work. Not to mention its three o'clock in the morning and we haven't seen a car the whole way. Also, that's my wife and to-be daughter in there, so don't try to tell me what I can and can't do!" Just about the time I finished my statement to him and was pointing to Dina who had her gritted teeth, like she was pushing, it happened. The guy with her seemed to be nodding no to her when out popped the baby on the gurney. I don't read lips, but I could tell just then that she said, "I told you."

My conversation with the driver changed instantly as he went back up front to talk to the guy inside with Dina. My attention was back inside as the man with Dina franticly helped for a few moments, and then he was back on the phone that he had dropped just minutes ago with the baby's surprising beginning into this world. A few minutes later, the driver rolled his window down and instructed me to go ahead and follow him now since the emergency was over. Because it was much closer, we headed to Poway Hospital, which was a beautiful hospital but not our hospital. The military insurance was not accepted there. Poway was one of the many ritzy areas around San Diego.

Now during all this I didn't see any equipment, so I still had the idea that this child was a girl. So the music blared again as we drove down the hill to the hospital. Y'all know how I feel about being there for the birth, if anything, so the mother has me there for her support, but more importantly to be there for the child's first time out of the womb. Again, I sort of missed this one, but if the glass is half-full I watched the birth with my own two eyes by the miracle of me speeding. I parked the car after seeing Dina and giving here a huge kiss real quick and followed her into her room.

As I stepped in, they said, "Congratulations on your new *boy*." Boy . . . , this was no doubt a good thing, but I was a little shocked as you can probably imagine. During that whole time driving, I was thinking about having a girl the whole way, and there you were, Zach. To say the least, I was pleasantly surprised. Obviously we didn't name you Harmony though. The hospital had to keep you in an incubator while you were there, which was really kind of sad when you saw all the other babies in their crib. Mom made them leave you in her room while you slept so you wouldn't stick out in the maternity room. It was the beginning of an exciting life for you Zachery. Why **Zachery**, you might ask? Zachery was John Denver's first child that he had adopted, and yes there is a beautiful song called "Zachery and Jennifer" that he wrote. Chris was my namesake. Christopher James. Dina picked out Christopher and Zach's middle name, Allen. Don't remember if there were any details. I think Allen was a relative though. It was actually Dina's idea for James.

We had become a big family indeed. I still can see them playing ring around the posse in my head. I was blessed with a loving and fun family for sure. Our home was very small, but we were very content. Living out there by the lake was very nice, but we wanted to try something new. See, the military is very proficient at getting you to a final place when you get out, so we chose Colorado. Dina knew how much I loved John Denver and how cool it would be to live there in the Rockies. I have to give her credit for letting me live out my dream. She thought Colorado was beautiful too, so it wasn't just my idea either. We knew where we were going to go.

My last short period was spent in the main chow hall for supply battalion with a colonel named Kelley for a CO. He was very hands-on, so he would come in the chow hall a few times each week to check on things and have some of my creamed beef. I can't remember what it was in particular that I put in it, but he would always ask if it was my creamed beef. It was either Worcestershire or garlic salt that wasn't on the recipe card but he made the head cook right it on the card so his troops could have some every day. He and the first sergeant tried all the time to get me to reenlist but "Rocky Mountain High" seemed to always be on my mind.

Remember the sword that I talked to you about at the beginning of the Marine Corps? I still didn't have one, but my priority changed to something much bigger for me while I was in. I wanted to be able to say I was a sergeant in the Marines. That was all I wanted from them at this point. Finally, it came through just before I got out of the Marines. One of the last things I did in the Marines was getting pinned as Sergeant Kelley. Oh rah!

"I guess, in a way, being naïve when I was young and joining the Marines kept me from being too corrupted."

CHAPTER 41

A Short-Lived Trip to Colorado

Got the stripe but didn't buy the sword. The U-Haul was scaled of, the Tercel was loaded, and it was time to leave that life of the Marines. We were headed to a whole new world for me. I was a civilian now and had no clue what I was going to do to support my family. The only background was in the cooking and baking field. I also had that experience in the Sizzler and Taco Bell. At Taco Bell, I can say I was a supervisor when I left, and at Sizzler I started waiting tables before I left. The Marines gave me two little certificates for going to backing school which came in handy during this time of my life. I loved the Marines, but at the time it didn't seem too appealing to get stuck there for twelve more years. Trust me, in retrospect, I would have been retired now for close to eight years, but no sense in the "would've, could've," is there?

For those of you that don't know, Woodland Park is up the hill from Colorado Springs. If you were in Colorado Springs and looked toward Pikes Peak, it was just to the right of it up in the mountains. It was a very small town with a beautiful view. We found a very small but beautiful home in a very nice neighborhood. It looked like a suburb neighborhood to a certain extent, but it was very nice and fairly new to boot. I have a memory of us driving around the neighborhoods, sort of dreaming about these beautiful homes in the hills and all around. Some of our drives would take us on day trips to places like Cripple Creek, Manito Springs, and of course a run down the hill to Colorado Springs ever so often.

One thing I find interesting, as I write my thoughts to you, I reminisce about things from my past and feel very good about things. It makes me feel relaxed about things. As you know, I truly believe in the thoughts of your life as the "memories that save." As far as I can see and from my perspective, the experiences of our lives are the answer to each individual's quest for the reason to live. A lot of times we forget to just live as we contemplate this and many other questions. Looking back at my life, I think, makes me wonder why we even try to answer that question. Should we even care about what is wisdom and intelligence? Is there really some awe-inspiring reason to be here? Everyone has their own experience and thought about this, but it's on an individual basis. I know that as you go through life, you truly make it what you will.

There are many evil people that will try to manipulate the answers for you and take away the wonderful parts of reminiscing. As we all know, some people go so far as kidnapping, murder, and many other unspeakable things. One thing people don't realize is through manipulation, they are killing the souls of millions of people. Be cautious and vigilant, but enjoy the things that you have in a responsible way. Sometimes it's tough to stay away from people like that, but keep your head about you and know right from wrong. You have to know that morals and ethics are what make us human and don't forget about them. It goes back to the thought that you treat people the way you'd have them treat you. Basically have the decency to just stay away from being like the people that hurt you. Remember the tree and the bug? Remember, the soul is an individual thing but can be hurt and scarred for life. Don't be the one that stomps the bug out.

Sorry, don't know where that came from. I guess it's the memory of being back in society for the first time and starting to see things through completely different eyes. The Marine Corps was gone, and it was all up to me now; they weren't there to hold my hand anymore, and the security blanket was gone. I obviously saw life around me, but it was through the shield of the Marines that I saw it through. Were my morals and ethics strong? Did I even know what they were? I would like to think so. I guess, in a way, being naïve when I was young and joining the Marines kept me from being too corrupted. It didn't matter at this point. There I was in a dream home and a great family.

The Marines gave me plenty of money so we could set up this new home, and I ended up being a baker at the City Market. (City Market being the name of the grocery stores in the area around Colorado.) For those of you reading that haven't traveled much, different areas around the States have different big company stores. Safeway, Albertsons, Cub Foods, Piggly Wiggly, and many others I don't know I'm sure.

I never even noticed the stairs going up to nowhere when I used to go in stores. Now I know where those stairs go. I know, kind of naïve, huh? It's the little things in life that make it fun I guess. I would start real early in the morning, like 1:00 AM or so and go home at eight to ten. During my lunch, I could look through the window in the lounge and watch the people as they shopped. The interesting things that we all do when we think no one is watching. Sometimes they were bad things like a father beating their little kid for just being curious. There were a lot of funny things too though. You know, picking their nose, readjusting their underwear, and or testing products—that was always a good one. It was always fun to watch. During my short time there, I also found a love for French bread. We had a bread machine that rolled them out, and the only work was making the dough and placing them in a pan. A lot of people would come in every morning to get fresh bread. Just like before, we did a lot of things from scratch there. All different kinds of cinnamon rolls, pecan rolls, twisted cinnamon, and so much more; but of course, now it all comes in a box. It's cheaper for the companies not to have the labor of fresh bakers on payroll.

At first everything seemed like it was going OK but as that first month went by, the honeymoon was over and the arguing began, and it wasn't working out the way I wished it would. Dina was a California girl through and through. She loved the sun, beaches, big malls, smog, and I don't know what else. See, I never understood the draw to the big cities. I'm just too laid back, I guess, to get excited about the traffic and all the hoopla that goes on. It was becoming obvious that Dina was homesick. She agreed to give it a little more time. Then something totally off the wall caught Dina by surprise—a snowstorm in October. Complete whiteout hit us for two days. I was in heaven; after so many years in the Marines, I was back in my element. Being in a snowstorm and having to work real early gave me some fun on my way to work. For those of you that have never experienced fresh snow early in the morning with no one around trust me it's a blast. It's so peaceful in a snowstorm. This was a dump, but not a blizzard. It was beautiful.

This was not a good thing for Dina though. The kids had a field day with all the snow, but after the initial fun was over, Dina was in shock. She hated the snow, she mainly saw it on TV or up at Big Bear outside of LA, but only when she wanted to. This isn't going to fly for her so I agreed to move back to San Diego. This was going to be a bit different without the Marines to help. Renting a U-Haul can get very expensive.

I probably hid the fact that I was in love with Colorado because I didn't want this to turn into a huge battle. She was uncomfortable, and I think there was a hint of her wishing we had stayed in the Marines. I was very happy to have the freedom of life, now that I was out. You know as well as I do, looking back, I had found my home in Colorado. It suited me and who I was inside. I had that feeling that little time while I was there but didn't react to it yet. My other influence was my love for Dina and the kids. Our relationship was rocky, but we still had a bond at this point that held us together. It was time to move back to California . . . again. "California, here we come, right back where we started from." I remember thinking about that song on our way back. Music has a way of bringing back memories, doesn't it?

"At that point, my whole body turned beat red. I was like one big rash all over. Moving was starting to hurt, like pins sticking in me."

CHAPTER 42

Working at a Resort
A Trip to Texas

It was back to our little trailer again. We had no idea what to do, but living at the trailer obviously helped us financially. Dina could always go back with her mom, but I looked around for something more. After looking around, all I could find was a wait staff position at a resort out there in the country by Lake Henshaw. It was a privately owned resort so not a lot of tips but enough to get Dina and me afloat then. I do remember small bits and pieces of that restaurant. Some parts were very old and supposed to be haunted. The lounge area especially was thought to be haunted. I don't recall exactly what the building used to be, but I know it was from the 1800s. The many late nights I spent there I can't say anything happened while I was there. "Do I believe they exist?" Well, it's never been proven wrong to me, so I don't really know. I think anything is possible unless it can be proven that it's not. I believe the human mind has many questions, and anything is possible.

It's all way too big of a subject for me to be putting it in this book; that would be another book entirely. I will say that the paranormal is interesting to me, big time. Like religion and politics though, some views are better left unsaid. They are too much of an opinion-based thing to be forcing people to listen to your own views. I think that they should be left for each individual to decide what's right for them. I personally have had the gut-wrenching feeling that something was present, but that neither proves nor disproves anything to me yet. One of the nights I closed the bar just got a little spooky. After a while obviously, I was learning the bartender thing. I had some fun working there but it was also a bad influence.

Y'all have been with me for a while in this book thus far and have never heard me say anything on the subject of drugs. I knew about my sister but stayed away from that subject the few times I saw her. There is a good reason for that at this point. I had never touched them. Till now. In conversation, I knew that Dina's ex was into drugs, and she had admitted to trying them too. It was at this resort bar that I learned even more about Dina and drugs. I personally hate drugs at this point in my life. They make people lose reality, and in the long run, when they think it helps them cope, they get so far into staying high, and then they don't realize that it just makes it even harder to cope. See, at that point, they can't afford it, and they end up doing stupid things.

Now Dina and I, to a certain extent, don't have addictive personalities. We were social drinkers, meaning only on occasion. We weren't smokers, so other than the pot of coffee each day, we were pretty clean. Our lives got very complacent during this time. We had a lot of fun spending time with the kids and worked to save money. We couldn't spend a lot of money so we stayed at home most of the time. We did get a hold of a Nintendo, which helped to break the monotony.

Before I finish that thought, I have to break some news to people. There are way too many families out there that just survive. We could sit here for hours laying blame on why this happens. There are some of you though that make it very difficult to raise their children in this world. The generations, in time, have gotten lazy. I feel into it also at times in my life. What people need to see is that some of these families are hardworking and struggling families. Turning our backs on them is just the wrong thing to do. Looking down at them also is majorly wrong. Our society has built a hole for them, and sometimes I wonder if they can ever get out. It's very sad to think of how this poverty is working on Americans like the plague. Now I don't have the answers to this dilemma, but I do know how difficult it is to see people looking down at them because of their status in society. There is another part of our society that is very hypocritical.

People that have seen poverty firsthand won't so bad to help them, but they can't afford to help out the needy, and then there is the people that have the money to help out and they look down on them so they don't help. I don't mean to sound like they should all have handouts, but some of them are trying real hard and there isn't enough good jobs for them to raise a family. I know from firsthand experience that there is more than enough help out there to take care of the people that need it, but there are many lazy and complacent ones out there that ruined it for the people that just need a helping hand once in a while. There are problems on both sides of this picture. You have lazy people that think they should get whatever they want, and on the other side you have the very greedy people who have no morals, won't lend a hand. Things like these really upset me when I think about it. "Can't we all just get along?" Teach your children morals and ethics, and it would all work out.

"That's great, say stuff like that and here I go with my chapter on drugs." Well it wasn't a huge thing for Dina and I, but you just deserve to know about it since you're my kids. I would never glorify my experience especially since I'm so against it. One day at that resort job, one of the cooks asked me if I wanted some meth. I had never done it and told him I didn't have the money, but I might take some on payday. When I told Dina, she got excited and said, "Why not?" Well, there was a sense of excitement for me due to the Marines keeping me out of drugs, and now I didn't have them holding my hand. "OK I'll pick some up on payday." I could see the anticipation in her eyes. By this time you have to understand that my sister, we knew, had gone down this path already and had become a menace to her own life. In the Marines they do drug screens all the time, so I didn't have much choice. If I hadn't been there, I may have turned out like my sister. You never know.

The time came and I took it home and really enjoyed it. We had **Mario Brothers**, and played for a few days straight. I was thinking, "This is a great feeling," but saw how distracted from the kids we got. Alcohol would do the same thing, but we stayed away from that too for that reason. Don't get me wrong, it felt great but getting myself to the point that it became an obsession just to get more made it really bad. At one point, we couldn't get it from the regular guy and had to go elsewhere to find it. That was all it took to get me out of it for good. The situation I put myself in was the first experience with so-called crime. Buying it from my so-called friend wasn't that big of a deal because I knew him, and he wasn't some big dealer. For y'all that have not had the experience, thank God, and stay away. But he only sold a small amount to support his own habit. Not that that's OK, but this guy I'm about to talk about was a big dealer, and that was the difference.

Dina had a friend that had a friend that sold what we wanted. I was still very clean-cut looking and to him I'm sure I look like a cop. At one point, that came up and he made me use in front of him. That's where things got a little interesting. This location was somewhere on the outskirts of downtown San Diego. The houses were very close together, and when we got there we went to the back alley by his garage. There were parts and even an engine block sitting on a table that he was working on. The garage's look was totally unorganized and dirty everywhere, and he was a rough-looking guy with a greasy T-shirt and a baseball cap to boot. His face was rough and greasy with a very nonchalant look on his face. He seemed very unenthusiastic and distant, as if he was ignoring me my wife and her friend. You would think he was ignoring us except when he said, "I really don't trust you and that clean-cut look about you," he said then finally turned to me with his hand on a rag that I'm sure only I could see and say without missing a beat, "Are you a cop?" My thoughts at the time were very naive because I couldn't see his point at that moment. I hadn't been around drugs long enough to know how paranoid they are around people they don't know. So of course I chuckled a bit and said, "Are you kidding, I just got out of the Marines and wanted to try something different, and our guy can't get any right now so here we are."

He went with that and relaxed his hand on the rag and said, "We will make sure and we can try a doggy bag each." What the heck is that I'm thinking, and at that moment I caught Dina's eyes looking at me and growing in size about this so-called doggy bag. I kept my cool and just nodded in acceptance. After digging through a drawer and pulling out this bag, he then pushed the rag across the table with a metallic heavy sound on the table. Then he reached back in the drawer and pulled a small mirror and this funny-looking straw like piece of brass.

The so called doggy bag was huge in comparison to what we would do in a weekend. After struggling with the brass straw, I admit that I was feeling great, and it was all Dina could do to get me back in the car. I was flying as people would say. We ended our transaction with four times what we normally would buy on payday and then drove home to start what was the worst days of my life, or at least top ten worst days.

It started off innocent enough. We spent a lot of time playing with the kids outside and having fun with them. If you can imagine, they slept real good that night. We kept them going pretty good there. Then Dina and I would try to beat **Mario Brothers**. It was pretty silly at first. After two days of this and having all that extra meth, we got pretty strung out. Sometime that second evening, I started feeling very strange. We ran out and it was time to crash the plane. I hope none of you have to go through that feeling. I couldn't stop fidgeting in my whole body. For y'all that don't know, they call this "Jones zing." At that point, my whole body turned beat red. I was like one big rash all over. Moving was starting to hurt, like pins sticking in me. Dina and I were both really scared.

I have to tell you that during the course of the few months that I had been doing this, I learned that the easiest way to get rid of symptoms of crystal all you did was drink liquor. So to fight these bad feelings and feeling very sick, we decided to drink a bottle of vodka. Yes, the whole bottle. I can't remember how long it took to get rid of this, but I can tell you that I've never felt that sick ever since that day. That feeling of losing it will stick with me for a long time to come. I truly can't tell you how much that mistake made me feel like a complete idiot. I knew better than to let this happen to me, at that time I had never actually been around that life, so I didn't no how to deal with the temptation. People, just open your eyes and look around you, it's everywhere. Some people glorify it, but they do so to either sell to you or hide their own problems and justify their own use. I can justify by saying that it felt great, but that was only true in the beginning. Drugs and alcohol can destroy you and your family. There are plenty of other ways to help you through life that doesn't include making it worse by using.

My scare was enough to cure me of using. We had our scare, and then we moved on. I'm not sure how we decided to go to Texas, but I'm sure it was a mix of a lot of things. I know one was the idea of how expensive it was to live in California. Now, granted there is a lot more money to be had, but neither one of us had the education to put us in the right place in the job market. We had to find someplace that had good work but more importantly affordable housing. Remember when I talked about living in your means and not what the media made you think you needed? Well, we wanted more for the kids so we took drastic measures to have more money for the kids' plate. We also were using a small helping hand from the government food stamp program. Dina's ex wasn't paying any child support, but we didn't think that was a big deal. It would've been nice, but that in our eyes was something he would have to deal with on his own. Bottom line was we were struggling and needed to find something else quick.

We left California with practically nothing. What we did have was sold off or lost in the traveling we did to Colorado. In a sense we left with the clothes on our backs. If you can imagine traveling with four kids, one being a new baby, in that little Tercel, it was a very long and tough road to take. But we did it with a smile on our faces and the dream of making an easier life for the kids. It was a means to an end of our plight. In retrospect, I'm not sure where Dina stood in how she felt about our predicament, but I know she wanted more stability. We truly thought this was going to work out, meaning running off to Texas. But neither one of us had ever lived in Texas, as adults I mean, and even though I had lived there, you know how much I remember from that time. Not to mention how bad Colorado turned out for us. Of course, I think we would've done great there, had we stayed, but it snowed there.

"The restaurant business, like many other things you kids will deal with in life, can be a lot less stressful if you deal with the problems of now and don't worry about later so much."

CHAPTER 43

My First Civilian Management IHOP

My family was living in Waco, Texas, at the time and as far as cities go, I loved it. Great food, nice people, a beautiful lake, and then there was the weather. Oh my God, I don't know how people can take that weather. You take a shower, and ten seconds later you're sweating to death. In Minnesota, we close the windows and heavy curtains during winter to cut the heat bill, and there you put the big curtains to keep the heat out. This is crazy to me. "Man, I love Minnesota." Anyway, it was truly hot down there, but I did love the city of Waco. It was just a bit of a shock to me at first, but I admit you do learn to tolerate it better. Notice I didn't use the words "get used to it." It isn't worth it for me. Some of you love it though. "Different strokes," right? One of the beauties of knowing yourself is realizing that everyone has their own opinions, and that their opinions are not targets to pick on other people. Keep a relaxed mind towards other people. Their beliefs are not going to change your beliefs with strong roots under you, and there is no need to bother someone about there beliefs.

After some help and a lot of searching, we found that just like California, you have to live outside the box to keep the price down for living. We found a slightly dumpy and very small trailer that was real cheap but seemed to be in a fairly decent neighborhood for the kids. This was in a suburb town called Bellmead. After a little cleanup, it turned out pretty nice.

Zach, that picture you have with the mirrors in back of us was that trailer. So y'all know what I'm talking about, the living room was right out of the '70s. It had the fake paneling all around the house and two or four tall mirrors against the living room wall. If you could see the picture, there is no furniture yet, and it was bedtime or morning when it was taken. I don't know what it was about, but for you young ones, there was a big to-do about mirrors everywhere in the '70s. In retrospect, I think I lived in a few trailers that were like that one.

Now it was time to find a job. It didn't take me long to find work in the restaurant field with my background as extensive as it was. They were looking for a new night manager at the IHOP. The GM quickly snatched me up and gave me a decent salary, or so I thought at the time. I don't recall exact numbers, but it was in the three-hundred-dollar range per week. Where you get killed is in how many shifts you got. My training for this place was very extensive to say the least. It started out with six weeks on the cook side of things. Cooking at this place, as busy as it was, could drive the average person insane. I know there are a lot of people that have never been behind the scenes of a restaurant, and all of you that have will enjoy the next few pages. For my kids out there, I hope you go to school and get an education so you don't get stuck in the food service industry. With that said, this industry suites me very well. It just seems to fit some people. We kind of like all the stress. "Well, that's just silly, Jim, no one enjoys stress." That's what y'all might be thinking, but for you guys that have been in the industries, you know exactly what I'm saying.

As you all well know by now, I really do enjoy working in the field. If you can recall, it started back in the Marines in the chow halls on mess duty. The IHOP was a training ground to make me the manager I am today. My first few days there were during the week, so it gave me time to get familiar with the setup. Then that first weekend, as you can imagine, the stuff hit the fan. Now look back and you'll remember Sizzler that I worked part-time at. That was a very busy place also but that was a cake walk compared to a Sunday at IHOP. That place was nuts. See, we were right next to Baylor University and right on

I-35 there in Waco, Texas. Not to mention we had great food. Talk about stressful jobs. It sure was a lot of fun though.

I think there is a pretty decent-size chunk of people in the US that have worked for a little while in restaurants. Down on their luck and no jobs, first job as a teenager, or someone working there way through college. I was a lifer, or so it would seem. I just liked the work. It's a job were I have the ability to make people smile. Oh, I can think of so many times and situations where I helped people just smile working in the business. I have this image of thousands of faces running in my mind, thousands of conversations about so many different things. People that you think are so introverted; just give me a couple of minutes and a great meal in front of them, and they'll drop all there inhibitions for just a few moments. It's a wonderful feeling to me to see someone enjoying the simple things in life like a good cup of coffee. Remember me talking about that beer in Belgium, the spaghetti at the airport, and especially that bottle of milk that I shared with the milk man in England? Maybe . . . just maybe, some of them people I took care of will remember that moment at the restaurants that I've worked at. That kind of makes me feel real good just thinking about it.

IHOP was not all roses, to be sure. The GM that I had there was very good at running a restaurant, but his personal life tended to interfere with things that happened at the restaurant on an almost a daily basis. I won't go into detail about that because the book isn't about him. I will talk about how the restaurant business has a tendency to be a big soap opera. All of you that have worked at a restaurant for any length of time know what I'm talking about. I can say that this first time around at IHOP I was to busy trying to keep my shift going to really get involved in the soap this time. Once I finished my training I'd like to think I exhaled there at IHOP and in a short period was being noticed by the corporate office to be a GM. Or like a lot of business, they use carrots like that to motivate you to work above and beyond you're ability.

I started off with that small salary and quickly got into the five-hundred range. That sounds great until you hear how many hours you end up working. I was a slave there for seventy to eighty hours a week. Their thoughts are we can always get someone else if you don't like it. See, in the restaurant business, all of us are very expendable. For every one employee at a restaurant there are twenty more applications to replace you. I know this 'cause I've been a manager, of and on, in the business for a long time. I've seen it many times. Now don't get that media thought that it's a big thing that we need to fix in are system, it is just a fact of life for millions of Americans, and it's not always exploited, but there are some mangers that use the tactics. If the shoe fits, they know what I'm talking about. We all know it isn't just the restaurant business. There is also the other element of the wacko employee too. So as I said before, it's an ongoing soap in every restaurant across America.

The IHOP I worked at was a very good location and had a line out the door every weekend and at bar rush every night it seemed. Things would get so bad on Friday and Saturday night that we had two off-duty policemen that worked for us from 11:00 PM to 3:00 AM. I think that was one of the reasons people came there so they could stay away from trouble spots around town. I'm sure most of you out there at one time or another has visited a twenty-four-hour place in your lifetime. Now from my perspective, I have to laugh out loud because I've seen some very interesting things in my life and a lot were from IHOP. There is some good reasons people don't remember what happens; they don't want to remember how much of a fool they were at IHOP. It's all in fun until things get to serious. If you think that kids in school fight over stupid things, you need to remember what happens at them twenty-four-hour places. I've seen men throwing food at each other; I heard the "he said, she said" time and time again. "He was looking at my wife funny" was always a good one, and some things that I can't talk about in a G rated book. That is just a few of the customer's situations, how about the staff on a busy night under pressure?

I could go on and on about staff. One time all of my cooks came up to me on a Friday night just before the bar rush and told me if I didn't give them all a two-dollar raise across the board, they would all walk. I just looked at them and said,

"Then it's going to be a long night for me, isn't it?" They all gave me a dirty look and walked away. Yes, it all worked out. I called the GM and a few cooks and we toughed it out. I've had servers come up to me crying, managers walk out in the middle of the rush, cooks screaming at the servers for batching tickets, cooks screaming at each other because they put mayo on the wrong sandwich, servers yelling at her boyfriend who is a cook, dishwasher dropping a tray of dishes in the middle of a rush, and in the middle of all that have a fight break out in the lobby because they had too much time waiting in line standing next to someone talking trash to them, and the stories' go on and on. It was a wonderful life back then. I can't tell you why that never got to me as much as others, maybe it was boot camp, I couldn't say.

Management has changed a lot since that time frame. I can't say if it's gotten better or worse, but I still get a kick out of what I do. IHOP was I think the first time I could use my sense of urgency that I got from the Marines and turn it into a very productive thing. The restaurant business, like many other things you kids will deal with in life, can be a lot less stressful if you deal with the problems of now and don't worry about later so much. When you have a slow moment in a restaurant, you can prepare for whatever comes, but when you start thinking too much, you'll overlook something that is so simple that you'll kick yourself later for. The one little thing, if you let it, will blow up the rest of it and snowball everything else. For me, the one-big-picture thing that helps me get through the problems is to have fun. I have my moments of frustration, but I try to keep them to myself. That's probably something I wished, in hindsight, I knew then for my relationship with Dina, if it could only be a perfect world.

One of my fondest memories of there was that little bit of time that I did the paperwork of the day each night between three and five. We didn't have a punch screen, it was handwritten tickets. The servers were responsible for their own tickets, and I checked there corresponding numbers, legibility, and math for all the orders of the day. The GM was overly strict about all those things. Anyway, I usually had the pancakes or a club sandwich and would watch a server talk to the customer to make sure they did their steps of service. The restaurant was very nice and very cozy, and I think it gave me the old sense from watching my mom work at her restaurant many years ago. It was a very good time for me to reflect on the busy night and gave the employees a chance to clean up for there relief. Then the onslaught of coffee drinkers started. That was my cue to go home, see the family, try to sleep a little, and get ready for another fun night.

CHAPTER 44

California, Here We Come AGAIN

I was so close to getting my own store. They were talking about moving me to Collage Station, but the stress at home was too much to bear. I was basically never home, and when I was, I needed to sleep as much as I could for the next fourteen-hour day. The kids were so young that Dina couldn't work, and we did the food stamp thing to make sure there was food on the table, even if it was just goulash. Dina and I, at times, were at each other's throats. She was essentially raising the kids on her own. "Oh . . . what a sad story, Jim." Yes, it sounds like I'm whining, but that is just the way things are for a lot of people out there. The folks out there that have never been there can look down on that if they wish too but the ones that have been there know what that life is like. In general, we are all happy and have way too much pride to let anyone see you that way. That's where that wisdom and intelligence thing kicks in again, with people judging others with no understanding of the background or reasoning behind what got people in such a predicament, how can they know there story to judge at all? "Oh, you could've went to college or got a small education somewhere in all that time, Jim." That may be so, but I didn't, and don't regret or feel bad about it. Life has a way of controlling your moves when you're in the situations I was in. It doesn't make me smarter than some, but it does give me the ability to understand more.

There was a little more to this story that I didn't speak of because it is a very soft spot in the family. Dina and I had a big run in with my niece a few years before this all happened that I won't get into for this book. She was very young at the time, and we made a big mistake with social services that turned out OK in the end because of my dad's tenacity. Our relationship with them grew back overtime, but us living there made it difficult to boil over. Those scars were still with all of us. We did heal very well while we were in Waco, but Dina was very home sick, and the decision had to be made to go back to California where we had a trailer we could fall back on. To y'all that are reading my book and are not part of the family, I apologize to you for leaving you in the dark about this one. Please don't get the wrong idea about what the secret is. I assure you that it was strictly just something to do with family problems, nothing more. For the ones involved, I'm sorry I was so naïve and didn't stop things before they got bad. I hope everyone can forgive me for what happened. Speaking of my niece, I just heard today that she will be having her first child. Congratulations to you and you're family-to-be.

To move along, I have what I thought was a funny story. Chris and Zach, you two were playing one day at your grandma's, and Chris started getting too rough with you, so I had to get Chris to stop. That obviously isn't the fun part, no big deal, right? Well, little Robert, my sister's boy, was playing close by and was around the same age as Zach. He was a much calmer child per se than my kids were. I was a Marine, remember? So things were a lot louder in our home too. Well, instead of being calm, I hollered "CHRISTOPHER!" That was a bit of a mistake because as soon as I did that, Robert, you slammed your head to the floor and started screaming bloody murder. You would've thought someone shot you or something. "What did Chris do?" you say. He slowly just turned towards me and said, "What?" You were totally calm with a look of irritation on your face since I interrupted you from hitting your brother. I felt so bad for yelling so loud, but knowing Chris, that was one of the few ways to get his attention. See I was the typical Marine father that liked to wake my kids with loud noises all the time. Not to mention I have a tendency to be loud anyway. With that scream, I definitely felt bad for shocking you, Robert, but you're not the quiet type now like you were back then.

Well, the few times we did get to spend with Mom and Dad were good, like I said. After a while, our little situation sort off disappeared and was never mentioned in conversation. All that set aside, I was happy to get away from a job that paid so little and expected so much. My GM wasn't very happy, but I did give him a two weeks' notice, which comes in handy later on in life.

We hadn't built up much stuff, so it was fairly easy to pack up and drive back to California. Each time I did this drive, including the trip that Dina came to surprise me, I did it without stopping, other than food and gas of course. My enjoyment of the open road just continued to grow more and more every time I did this. I'm sure you remember the maps and all the other times from before. I sometimes wonder if the trip we took from Texas to Minnesota in our brand-new Cherokee was the start of this passion for the open road or maybe the song about what's around the bend. Come to think about it, I wonder if it was the trip from Barstow to 29 Palms. I'm sure you remember the tree and the bug analogy of our souls.

"We were about to go into Iraq, and they needed more troops in our military so they offered a two-year hitch to go and help. I'm sure you know I didn't get to do my real job in the Marines, i.e., "going to war," so I was more than willing to sign up."

CHAPTER 45

Where Were You When We Went to Iraq?

I was down and out of money with nowhere to go. I did have a job though. I want to say this is the time I worked at Dunkin Donuts. Yes, I worked there too. That's were I probably picked up the largest amount of weight in my life. Boy, those doughnuts were good though. As you can imagine, this wasn't a lot of money, but I think we did manage to get a place closer to town. Not sure where, I can't seem to remember. No matter, it was much better than being way out there trying to survive in that dinky trailer. We had grown fond of that dinky trailer, but with four kids, it wasn't right for us. Fighting was becoming more and more commonplace for us by this time. I think I still had some growing up to do and didn't seem to do good with anything but food service. It was getting to me that I had no real skill either. My brother-in-law and his father were both in construction, and except for down season, they did real well. My brother had finished his school and was a teacher, and other than my sister, everyone around me was getting somewhere.

I spent almost eight years in the Marine Corps but had no real training and had become stale in my job but found that I was good in the restaurants. Something I did forget to think about is going to a college in '88 and getting my diploma. By the way, I did ace every class for some reason. I guess it may have been maturity and a relaxed mind that made education easy at that point, but it didn't give me the time I needed to go to college. We had to have food on the table, and for that matter, a table to put the food on. Having four kids and needing help to survive didn't leave enough time to go then. I don't know, maybe I could have, but that was then, this is now. Trust me I've looked at my life from many different angles, but I refuse to feel bad about my decisions at this point.

I can say I don't think I had any self-confidence when all this was going on. I just think I faked it real well. Don't get me wrong, there was things I was good at, but I didn't have the confidence to make something more of myself back then for the kids. I would've never written this book without the push from my fiancé now. She made this happen. I was not the man that Dina had married. I was a confident Marine when she found me at that restaurant years before. If you can see one of the many reasons I've written this book was to help people see themselves and give them that little nudge that I could have used so many years ago. Showing the average Joe the sense of pride in them selves will help a whole lot. I could've used it for sure.

There we were, struggling with life, when we were given a little help from the Marines again. We were about to go into Iraq, and they needed more troops in our military so they offered a two-year hitch to go and help. I'm sure you know I didn't get to do my real job in the Marines, i.e., "going to war," so I was more than willing to sign up. Plus it would get me back in and give us that stability that we had back. This was going to be my opportunity to answer them questions I had when I was in that bunker in Egypt. There was a catch though. I had been at Dunkin Donuts, so I weighed around 235 pounds, so I wasn't eligible to get in. That was made worse by the fact that in four days, I was due at MEPS center for my physical. Not good at all. But this was very important to me and my family. I'm not going into detail about how I did this because I don't want someone to try the same thing and get as sick as I was those four days. I had to be 207 or less to get in, and I made it by weighing in at 207 exactly. You know it wasn't drugs that I could take because of the drug screen to get in, but we will just say I made it in. When I went home, I ate like a pig to celebrate our victory. That was the way it felt for us at least.

We had to wait a few days to get my orders on where we were going, but we assumed it would be Pendleton right there in California, but to our big surprise, it was back to North Carolina with the Tenth Marines I think. I was heading to a grunt platoon for the first time. Here is the kicker though. The day I signed, in they put me on thirty days' leave to travel. That was the stupidest thing I had ever heard, but who was I to argue with the government? The decision was made, and they gave us plenty of money to get to Lejuene. They told me when I get there to get my chits for brand-new uniforms, which now included the blues uniform. That was a little exciting for me I guess. I thought maybe this time I could get my sword.

There we were back in the car again heading for North Carolina and made a quick stop right back there in Texas. This was a lot less stressful traveling with a little money in our pockets and our future was back on track. Now mind you, the so called-war had already begun and we watched intently on what was happening over there. It sure was happening fast though. By the time we got to Lejuene, the war was already over and we, as a country, was already celebrating, and I got to my new duty station, and they were already over there and were slated to come back soon so they kept me back for the embarkation side of things, which I had trained for from earlier. So I was feeling kind of left out now but things were looking up for Dina and the kids.

"Bush Sr., or President Bush cut our military in half and my reenlistment package came back denied."

CHAPTER 46

The Beginning of the End
Training in Norfolk

We had found a very nice and big trailer that was right by a small river or bay that led to an opening a ways away from where we were. We had a very nice, big yard and were already looking at a dog for the kids since we knew we'd be here awhile. The first few months in our new home were paradise. I remember one weekend; me and Dina were celebrating with some kamikazes and were playing with the kids outside like I was real drunk and acting silly with the kids who were trying to help me get back in the house. I kept intentionally falling in the bushes, and they would just laugh out loud the whole time. They had so much fun that day that later in life I asked Tiffani what her favorite memory was, and that day is what she remembers most. It was a very big moment for me to hear my children's memories as they remember things. I see now that this will probably be an interesting book for my mom to read. Well . . . that thought caught me off guard.

Everybody that's reading this that has kids that are grown-up should call them right now and see what their fondest memory is and tell them one of your fondest memories of your child growing up. Think back and remember that I said that the best memories of the little things in life are what can save us? "The memories that save," obviously our children should be the

303

best of the best. I think little by little you're seeing that you are the one that can help yourself more then anyone else. When I think about that place, I feel warm inside about the life I had with Dina; I'm sorry to say that that was one of the last good memories of our relationship.

After a little while we decided to get a bigger place out in the country with a fence for many obvious reasons. The trailer was beautiful, but the place we found was great. Other than a few neighbors, this was a very secluded and cozy place. One side, which was actually close compared to the other side, was a corporal in the Marines living next door. We had some nice trails by the house, which made for nice walks with the dogs and kids. The inside was huge and almost brand new as far as I can remember. Things were feeling better as far as I could see. Watching the kids playing ring around the posse in that big living room, hearing Zach say the words wrong is a big memory for me about the kids. (I think I mentioned this before but it's a good memory so I'm leaving it again.) I might be wrong, but I think we had also finally found a bigger car for the family too. If I'm not mistaken it was an Oldsmobile station wagon.

We also tried to secure me a good job for my time here at Lejuene by becoming a career planner. This was what they called a B-billet in the Marines. All Marines did one of the three as parts of there rank as E-5 or above. The choices were career planner, drill instructor, or recruiter. Well, there were no openings for recruiter, and I was definitely not hard-core enough to be a drill instructor, so I signed up for career planner. This was supposed to be a three-year thing by the way. But there was speculation that because of what happened in Iraq, so quickly, they may cut the military, and we wanted to stay in. She especially wanted to stay in. We did have this discussion, and she knew I would just rather be a civilian than back in the Marines. She obviously won the discussion, and I was willing to go along with it to take care of them. Not to mention I really wanted to go to Iraq.

It was off to school then, time to learn how to be a salesman. I don't really remember a whole lot of details about Norfolk.

I do remember docking there for my trip to Norway years before. I spent that time by the docks mainly. I do remember it being a huge base and going to the NCO club a few times. There was nothing much to talk about, except maybe some good fried chicken. Most of the school was there, but we did go to Quantico, Virginia, to learn more about the control system in the Marines. That had a few interesting moments I guess. The one that sticks out was that second lieutenant, or butter ball I should say, we ran into walking from the barracks. Butter ball is obviously slanged for second lieutenant.

A little lesson for you civilians out there, Quantico is our OCS training for officers in the Marines. Their training is very rigorous, and they have a lot of self-pride and can't wait to get to the fleet so everyone will cower at their feet, or so they think. Please understand that that is just a comical way of putting things to y'all that haven't been in the military. We all respected them, but some had a hard time respecting the little guys out there. They learned real fast in the real world. We all would like to have respect, but there is a time and place to push your rank around, and it's not on a couple of sergeants just walking to school after eating chow. For all you manager-types out there, treat your people with respect also, and you'll be surprised how much work you can get out of an average Joe.

As I said, a few people from the class and I were walking back to class when a car came at us. In the Marines, we salute officers while walking down the road no matter what. No, we don't have to stop and come to attention unless they stop to talk to us. There are little red or blue stickers on military personnel's cars. Blue is the one for the officer. Sometimes, when you're deep in conversation, you forget to look for the blue sticker on cars, not to mention you could tap your hand in a salute position on a base with mostly officers. That's what happened to us; we didn't salute one of these young kids, and he slammed on his breaks, got out of his car, locked us at attention and commenced screaming at us for not saluting him. "He deserved our respect." He screamed over and over. Man did I want to hit this kid. He was probably twenty-one years old and just out of college, and he loved to cause out a small group of salty Marines to prove that he was bigger than us. In all actuality, he made himself look like a total idiot. At least until a colonel pulled him aside and told us to leave. He made sure we could hear him teaching that lieutenant a little bit about respect. I had never hit someone in anger, but man I wanted to hit him. Wait a minute, that's a lie.

I wonder if you can remember this one, Scot, It takes me back a bit in time, but it's relevant. I can't even remember what the fight was about, but I remember being in the driveway on Hemlock and I got so upset about something I just hit you across the face, full force. When you looked back at me, I felt terrible about what I had done, and you walked away with your hands on your face and didn't shed a tear. It kind of looked like you were shocked and disappointed that I hit you so hard, almost a humiliated look on your face. There was also a sense of "how dare you hit your brother like that?" It was uncalled for. Sorry about that Scot, it was a long time ago, and I know we fought before, but that one sticks out for me. I also remember all the times I ticked you off and you would start wailing on me, and I would just laugh the whole time. Man that used to get you so upset. The day in front of the house probably really hurt your feelings. You never even told Dad about it. Looking back though, you were so much more mature than I. I always did look up to you as we grew up. It was as if you were the older of the two. You had a lot more strength than I did. You're a good man, Scot, and I couldn't be happier with the relationship we have.

School finished, and I headed back to the nice home that we had finally found in our life. The kids welcomed me with open arms, but things seemed a little different when it came to Dina and me. She seemed distant for some reason. I remember going for a walk with her and talking about things, and she made me feel a little more comfortable for the time being. Our dog also had just had puppies, and Dina spent a lot of time at night outside with them. Work was fairly boring due to the fact that all the troops I was supposed to be working with were still in Iraq. Dina and I were trying to fix a troubled relationship, and the word on the career planner news was I might not be able to reenlist for retirement. I had a feeling this was going to be devastating for Dina. So I automatically put in for my own reenlistment to try and secure things before the government pulled the wrung off me later in life. It was too late.

Bush Sr., or President Bush cut our military in half and my reenlistment package came back denied. Once I got it back, the first thing I did was get a hold of my monitor and asked him personally why he denied a perfectly good application. (Monitor in the Marines handled the sergeant's and above careers. He worked with the Marine Corps to decide who was needed and were they were needed.) The gunny that handled the cook field apologized to me personally and gave me the option of getting out now or finishing my last year in the corps. As I contemplated this, my thoughts were about my age and what to do next. I wasn't getting any younger, and another year wouldn't make a difference. So to me it seemed logical to just leave now and try the civilian thing again. Not that I had a choice. When Dina and I talked, we decided to run back to California. At least at the time I thought that was what she wanted to do. Boy was I wrong about that.

Well, we set everything up for the trip, and I was in the beginning stages of checking out of the Marine Corps for good. The plan was to rent a U-Haul and drive with all our stuff back to California. The Marines, like before, took care of everything. We had everything set up, and we were waiting for that day when the ground beneath me just dropped out. Dina didn't want to go to California with me; she was staying and didn't want to be with me anymore. Now when I lost Susan, that seemed hard, but this was devastating to me. I felt my heart break in two. I can't begin to explain the pain at that moment. There is much more to the situation, but as I said before, you kids don't need to hear all the gory details of your parents' demise. In retrospect, I sort of understand more now and think I've given plenty of reasons to all of you, as you've read the story of my relationship with Dina, to give an understanding of our breakup. But for me at the time, I couldn't understand why she would do this to me. I was confused, devastated, and understanding at the same time. I didn't want to make things worse by screaming at each other.

That said, the ball was already rolling on our so-called move to California, and we had to be civil for the kids' sake and our own sanity, or at least mine. This all happened so fast that I didn't have time to let it sink in and I was trying, even after what happened, to salvage this relationship. I think I felt a false sense that maybe we could work things out; boy, I was so wrong. It would take a trip across the United States to figure this out.

"After a while the time between the "pressures of thought,"
lengthened, and I was able to reflect and enjoy some of the
things around me."
"In all that, I used the simple things in life to get through it
all. "The little things that can help us all."

CHAPTER 47

What a State of Mind for Hitchhiking

I finished checking out of the Marines, again, and had
the U-Haul ready to go, and Dina said she couldn't stay in
the expensive house since I was getting out. She had found
a trailer, and we used the U-Haul to get her situated in her
new home. The money we got for my travel to California was
all but gone to pay the down payment on her new place, so I
didn't have all the money for gas that I needed to get to San
Diego to turn in the U-Haul, but I had a last check being sent
to where Dina was, and she was going to wire more to me,
wherever I was at the time. I only had so many days to get to
California, so I had to leave right away. Being very rushed at
the moment was probably a good thing. It was enough that I
was leaving my life behind, but then to make the good-byes
even longer would have been even more damaging for me.
Once I got Dina and the kids settled, I gave the kids some
tearful good-byes, and when I talked to Dina it was more gut
wrenching stuff, like "If you want to come back, you'll have to
get your own place. When you do come back, it will be better
for you in a motel than here."

It was time to hit the road again for me. Normally, I would've
loved this trip; but under the circumstance, I couldn't stop
tearing up as I drove away. As I pulled into Little Rock, I was at
the last of the money and decided to wait there for the money
to be wired. I found a decent place to park by a Western Union

and made the call. "Dina, I'm here in Little Rock, has the check arrived like they said?" She said no and very quickly hung up after I tried to work on things. "Well, now what" I thought as I stood by the pay phone. I still had a bit of money, so I got a decent dinner and climbed in the big cab and used my old sea bag with a small amount of clothes for a pillow and went to sleep.

The next day was more of the same, and we talked a little about what to do when I got to San Diego. She said her sister had a spare room I could use while I waited for the settlement with the Marines. The checks still hadn't come yet, but I kept checking in at the Western Union as she says she will send it as soon as she got it. Well that day went by and nothing happened, and the next day is when she dropped the bomb. "Jim, I got the money, but I need it for me and the kids, you'll have to do what you have to do." "What am I supposed to do, hitchhike to California?" I said with some anger I'm sure. "It's not my problem anymore. You're on your own." Click! My mind was lost in fear. I had no idea what to do. After all the things that we had been through, what did I do to deserve this? I guess a part of me later thought maybe the people around her had made her think I was going to do something evil because of all this stress. Some people out there would say other than killing someone she might have deserved something, but by now, y'all know me enough that I would never do anything like that to anyone. I had something more important to deal with right now. I'm stuck right here in the middle of nowhere.

After many hours of contemplation, I decided that I could turn in the U-Haul and just hold out the thumb. I didn't get enough back to hop on a bus, so hitching was really the only option. The problem now was which way to go, east to the life that I had lost, or west to the unknown. I did need to turn in the U-Haul in San Diego though so that, I guess, was the deciding factor. West it is I guess. I never really liked San Diego, then again, I hated big cities period. I wasn't sure of my decision at the time and, to this day, wonder what would have happened if I went east. That won't change anything now and as tough as the decision was, it makes it hard to think back on it even in retrospect. Writing this today has it's moments of pain. I would assume most of you have never had to hitchhike across the United States or at least I hope not.

There I was standing on the highway after losing my heart and my family. There was truly a lot of anger in me too, but not for what you might think. I was taking it out on myself. "What did you do to her and the kids? What did you say to make her go away? Did you do enough for her? Were you making enough to support you're family? Why did you get out of the Marines in the first place, you could have retired there? Were you a terrible lover to her? Did you spend enough time with her? Should you have not argued with her at all?" All of this was like a tornado in my head. I couldn't stop spinning around and knew that this was the end. I felt like just letting the tornado take me away from all the pain of this. It was hitting me like a rush of pain and suffering for what I did or didn't do. My life was over, and it was very clear I thought after she left me with no money, no family, and only the clothes on my back.

Somewhere in all this wondering my mind came back like a flash to my predicament now. I was standing on the side of the highway with cars whipping by on a beautiful day, and I needed to go that way, as I faced west. For that moment, I caught myself looking through the windows of the cars as they went by to see the many faces as they would drive by. Then it struck me funny, they were doing everything in their power to ignore me completely. Some would just give you that dead stare, but it was like I didn't seem real to them. Mainly though the majority of people just drove by ignoring the man in need on the side of the road. I was clean-cut, well groomed, with clean clothes, and a smile at first. It was just not working. Then a thought hit me. I must look lazy to all these people just standing there for a handout. So I started walking.

Believe it or not, about five minutes or so later, someone stopped and gave me a ride out of the main part of Little Rock and said, "You'll get more rides out here, and they're probably not just heading for work and don't want to stop." "Thank you very much," I said as I put my seat belt on. "You should get a sign and carry it so people know where you're going, then if you do, put 'Coming home from the storm' on it too." See, we had talked a bit, and he knew I was a Marine. "Here is a black marker you can have, but I don't have any cardboard in the vehicle, sorry." "Thank you again, sir, I do appreciate it very much."

As we pulled through town, we talked of small talk, and things sort of cleared out of my mind for a little while, and I felt a little better; but then his ride was over, and I stepped back on the concrete again. Then the thoughts came back rolling in. So I tried to focus on the task at hand. I began my walking towards the west. The goal in my head was so far of that it didn't seem real to me. California was a very long way from Arkansas, but I continued to walk. In the Marines, that was the way we trained. Just do what it is that you need to do no matter what is going on, you trudged through whatever problem you had to solve. Don't mess you're mind up with the "pressures of thought." Yes, the Marines teach you to be numb of everything around you and just take care of what's in front of you. Under the extreme situation I was in, this was keeping me going. I walked the whole time I had my thumb out. Obviously my mind tended to wander down the path of my destruction many times while I was doing this whole thing. After a while the time between the "pressures of thought," lengthened, and I was able to reflect and enjoy some of the things around me. It always seemed like the times when I was thinking about Dina, things never got good. I was constantly picking on myself about what I did or didn't do. It was hard to think of anything else.

There was a constant that kept me moving, San Diego. It wasn't going to come to me, so I kept marching each day, ride here, a ride there. I was going to make it no matter what. Time obviously was not an issue at this point. I had already turned in the U-Haul so all I had to do was get there.

In case anyone is wondering about food and sleep, it was not as big a deal as you might think. I'm not going to stretch the truth about the difficulties with my travels. Remember, I turned in the U-Haul and had I think $75 when I started this. Every so often I would get a real nice person that would offer me a twenty-dollar bill or a ten to just be nice. I never, the whole time, asked for money. A few times my feet hurt so bad I rented a room for the night to rest. At one point, I remember stopping at a Wal-Mart to buy some tennis shoes because the ones I had had wore out from walking every day. You remember how cool it was to get a new pair of shoes when you were a kid? This was a hundred times more exciting than that. So far the walking was tough on me, and finding a good pair of shoes was more rewarding than I can even begin to tell you. I can still see the blue with silver streaks down the side of the shoes. That was a little thing that moved a mountain.

That thinking is what got me through things while I was out there watching the world go by. Watching the thousands of faces as they rolled past me, it was like thousands of memories flashing by. I found myself talking out loud and trying to decide what type of person was driving by me. "I bet you he is in construction, with that big old F-250 rolling by. I wonder what that woman is yelling about to the man sitting to her side. Why is that woman staring off into space thinking about?" In retrospect, we have all done that at the mall or sitting in a restaurant, but now I was a distraction in their thought as they drove by. Driving down the road seeing me there must have made them wonder about me. Were they looking at me in disgust, in fear, in a sad way? Or maybe they were thinking "that guy's crazy." I guess I'll never know, but sometimes I remember it like it was yesterday.

One day was probably the worst of all. A sheriff in a small county before Oklahoma City had picked me up and instructed me that what I was doing was illegal, and if I get stopped inside Oklahoma City hitching, they would lock me up for thirty days. He suggested that I go around the city. He also told me the reason he gave me a ride was he didn't want to do the paperwork on a hitchhiker if he got killed in his county then dropped me of outside his jurisdiction. He was very polite about it though, and I took his advice and took a route outside Oklahoma City. Little did I know how bad this would be. All things said and done, I would've been better off in jail.

I had been walking the whole day with not one person stopping to give me a ride. Dusk was coming on, and it was at least a beautiful evening, but I was discouraged from not having a ride that day. There was a long time I didn't even see a car coming. Then they started rolling in. It was like an answer to a prayer, but one by one they just ignored me. I did have teasers, which was just a bunch of teenagers, but that was it. Then as time went on, I started seeing paint and signs on the cars and trucks: "Go Tigers." It was easy to decipher things now, a big football game somewhere up ahead. "Come on what's the problem, I'm' not asking for a ride to San Diego, just down the road a bit!" I was starting to get frustrated more and more. I was getting really tired that day and was thinking about renting a room for the night, but this was a rural area with no businesses to speak of. I hadn't even seen a convenience store in a long while. Mind you, I had walked the whole day and hadn't covered much ground that day, but I kept my head up high.

It was getting dark, and I hadn't seen any cars for a long time, but I was still walking. The walking thing, by the way, had become an obsession thing of sorts. I was telling myself I didn't deserve a ride if I wasn't at least trying of my own free will. It seemed to work or at least that's what a few people had said in my travels. About what people said while I was out there, I didn't have a recorder with me, but the people that picked me up in general were very talkative people. Obviously they were all friendly, or they wouldn't have stopped at all. I could probably write a whole book about America when it comes to what kinds of conversations I had. Back to the story, don't want to get sidetracked.

Like I was saying, it was getting dark out and quiet, but off in the distance, I could see the lights of a big area. Not a town, but maybe a football field lit up. Anger kind of crept up a little at this point and then like a rush, "Here they come." One after the other F-250, the woman was being nice to her husband now, and their football son in between them. He had a great game but didn't get a touchdown because he likes tackling. He did get a sack though, and Dad got some pats on the back. "Your boy played well." He was so proud of his son it almost brought tears to his eyes. And they all drove by the guy that they left on the road who just needed a lift, even if it was only five miles. All this was going through my head while I walked towards the lights that could've really helped me, for just a moment of their time.

Now I have to say before anyone goes and picks up a hitchhiker thinking it is all romantic and such. This is not something anyone should do. If you're not big enough to protect yourself, then you shouldn't be even thinking about it. There are some strange people out there that I wouldn't be letting in your car. On the same note, some just need a hand for a moment.

As I walked by the school, I had enough time to calm myself before I got there. It was a very nice small community school, and from the distance I saw the home team had won the game and they were doing cleanup around the stadium. When I saw the guy in the background, I felt bad for him and myself. All those people just ignored me, and that man cleaning the stadium was ignored. People just think the cleanup gremlins clean it late at night while they're all asleep. Then when they saw me, they figured someone else will pick him up. It was all kind of difficult to swallow. I finally moved slowly away from the school and headed out in the fields and came up on the last turn before I got back to the main road, I needed to get back on the highway. I was so tired that I found a place under the overpass that was way up in the corner that I knew no one would see me. I always felt weird sleeping on the side of the road, so I would find a place where no one would see me. I felt embarrassed to be like a hobo.

A lot of people would say, "How could you sleep out there in the fields or under bridges?" "Walk for twelve to fifteen hours and you could sleep anywhere. Not to mention being able to sleep through anything." That night actually ended up a little different. Sometime in the middle of the night I woke up with a sharp pain in my left hand. As I opened my eyes I felt something biting me and trying to pull on my arm with two of my fingers in its mouth. I think it was a possum, but I really couldn't see the animal in the dark under the bridge. I ended up using one of my old T-shirts to stop the bleeding. At this point, I was completely stressed again, and even though I was tired my only thought was to find a motel and catch up with some rest and maybe watch some TV to get my mind off my predicament. My body was just overly exhausted, and my mind was even worse.

I got back on the road and used my own medicine to clear my head. The one thing I haven't mentioned is the little things that made me feel so much better as I dealt with my surroundings. "The little things that can save us" were all around me. You know what I'm talking about, "Seeing the forest for the trees." My whole life had shattered all around me. I was hitching my way to an uncertain future. I walked in the neighborhood of twenty to twenty-five miles a day for ten days or so. If you think back, this was the second time in my life I gave up everything to an ex that I lost. And not to mention my cool blue sneakers had a flat tire already. In all that, I used the simple things in life to get through it all. "The little things that can help us all." "What exactly does that mean, Jim?" Funny you should ask.

Over all this time, each day I would see things that I would never notice about everyday life. When we all drive down the highway, were going sixty to eighty miles an hour, and we may see things off in the distance, like when I was on the bus headed to 29 Palms, but we don't really see it. It's like the people we see in our everyday life; we don't see them for real. We walk right by each other with maybe a weak hello or a smile, but that is all it ever is. It has gotten so bad each and every day. While I was walking, I saw the world for the first time. Or at least it seemed that way. Life was so much more detailed as I walked on the side of the road. Sometimes I would find myself off the road a bit, looking at things that caught my eye in the distance. Sometimes even looking for a bit of shelter under a tree and seeing an anthill by a tree. Another interesting thing is the overpasses. The graffiti of someone's initials from the '70s, or it sometimes would be a small panting that was actually really good. Yes, I did see the evil stuff there too. It was all incredible and made that day-to-day trudge that much easier. And I haven't even mentioned the animals and flowers in the strangest locations.

I have to admit that even the towns and cities were mind-boggling as you saw them for real. Watching a small neighborhood or seeing a busy section of the highway with all the faces as they passed you by. Sometimes you could see interesting cracks or problems with the construction of the highway. I can't believe they wouldn't notice some of the things I saw. One thing you notice a lot more is the temperature around you changes drastically in the cities. The smells are also very apparent wherever you are. All of your senses work so much better when you are aware of your surroundings. You probably wouldn't live next to the power plant if you sensed how it really smells. Everything around you is much more relevant.

That relaxed feeling also gave me plenty of time to reflect on what was going on with Dina and the kids. When I let that control my thoughts, it was hard to do anything at all. But all of this time, even though it waged heavily on my heart, it did help me from just losing it. No one should ever have to go through what I went through, but no regrets for me. Kids, let the little things heal your heart whenever you need it and always keep your eyes open.

The next day was here, and it was time to step back on that pavement. Like I said before, I was looking forward to getting to a small town to get some rest after the longest night of my trip so far. Right then, a van pulled up. If I'm not mistaken, it was a Volkswagen, and yes it seemed kind of unreal with the peace sign and all. I don't remember his name, but I do remember where he was headed. You guessed it, San Diego. This had to be a miracle or something. He was a very nice guy headed to see, I think, relatives. Once we got through a few hours of getting to know each other, he told me to try and relax and sleep for a while so I could keep him up at night as he drove. This was obviously a huge relief to say the least. I wondered sometimes if I would ever make it, and now it was going to be no problem at all. All the stress of wondering where to sleep, how far to walk that day, watching your food intake, and of course making sure you carried plenty of water. It was definitely a big moment in my life.

"Looking back now, I was a product of my surroundings. But I had blinders on and just went with the flow of everything I experienced, and the people around me pushed me the way they wanted to, especially the Marines."

CHAPTER 48

My First View of a Pistol in the Civilian World Back to the Trailer

Well, after my life-changing experience on the road, pulling in to San Diego was a relief of a lifetime. I had to go to his house for a little while then he took me to Dina's sister's, which is what we had set up from earlier. She wasn't there, but the nanny was. She let me in, and I asked to use the laundry room to get my close cleaned up. I started a load and took a quick shower to get cleaned up before her sister got off work. I had been in that van for a long time. I had a robe the nanny gave me and proceeded to the laundry room to put the clothes in the dryer. When I came out of the restroom this was where he confronted me.

You may not remember him very well because I just mentioned that her sister's ex was a cop. This guy was fairly small compared to my average size of six feet, two hundred pounds. He was a little skinny and probably 150 to 160 pounds. But the pistol he pointed at me made him ten feet tall. "You need to get out of this house now before I forget you're Dina's husband and kill you for trespassing." "But I was told . . ." "Get out now," he said, as he lifted the gun to my face. I mentioned the laundry, and he made me change in front of him into my wet but clean clothes. Trying to hold back my tears, I headed to the door with a duffle bag full of wet clothes, and before I could even turn my head back to look at him as I went out the door, it slammed.

"What just happened?" Standing there in the suburbs of San Diego with people either standing out side watching or looking out their windows to see what was going on, I was standing there in complete and utter humiliation with wet clothes and tears welling up inside me. I would bet that was the most humiliating thing that ever happened to me. I was so lost right then that I just tucked my tail between my legs and headed for the pay phone I saw a mile or so back as we drove in. We had stopped to get a soda there. The time it took me to walk there calmed me down a bit and gave me a moment to gain my composure. Not to mention air-dry my wet clothes.

Well, after my walk, I decided to call Dina's mother. She was literally the only person I knew in this big metropolis. She answered and it took her a minute to calm me down and she said I could stay in the trailer until I got my papers and money back from the Marines. I mentioned I had no money left, and she offered to stop by the grocery store on our way back to the trailer. She did mention she didn't have much money, but she could squeeze out fifty dollars for some groceries. That wasn't much for a month of groceries, but I stretched it with rice, beans, top ramen, and a bag of potatoes. Yes, I got some coffee too. She saved me that day from what could have been a much worse situation. I'm very thankful to you for that day, and I hope you enjoy the book.

A few hours later, I was back in the same trailer that Chris had burnt his foot, with no TV. I did have a couple radio channels on a cheap radio that was still there. I'm sure you know being in the same trailer with all them memories flashing through my head was very tough. Not to mention Dina had told me she was dating our old next-door neighbor. That was like putting salt on a wound. By the way, she never really did explain what happened at her sister's house, and when I told her the story, she just laughed. Looking back now I can make it sound funny, but I assure you at that moment, it was not something for me to laugh at. Having a cop holding a gun in your face was not what I think or as funny. That day is long gone now, and I do my best not to think of it.

Other then a mean letter I sent to Dina in anger, my two months there were hermitlike. There was a guy that lived right next door that helped me keep Dina off my mind each day. Not by great conversation but by getting me drunk enough each night to fall asleep. I would clean up the docks each day which only took an hour or so, and in return I got a twelve pack of cheap beer each day. We did sit by a fire each night and drink and talk, but it was mainly the alcohol that helped me keep her away for the time being. It really didn't help to be in the same home that we spent so much time in. Going down to the lake and taking walks helped a lot during the day. As you may recall, I ate a lot of beans and rice too. It was food, I guess. I got too really like that a lot while I was there. Of course, that's all I had to fill my belly.

It was very hard for me to just give up on my relationship with Dina. I did try many times to get her to come to California with me but failed. She was falling for the guy she told me about and always seemed to try to push me towards going to Texas, and that in the long run, was the decision that I made on my own accord. Frankly I didn't know what to do in this situation. I had grown up a little on my hitchhiking trip but I was still a bit naïve. Remember I still haven't been on my own yet, and I was around twenty-six now. This was going to be like time warping back to being eighteen again, and I was going to have to live with my parents for awhile. Essentially, I lost nine years and still had the mentality of an eighteen-year-old. I was married to the Marines, Susan, Dina, and I had no idea who I was yet. Was I the hard-core Military type, "the Marine"; the country-boy type with the spotless personality, "Susan's husband"; the hip-hop, rowdy, rocking roller, "Dina's husband"; or was I a little bit of the "John Denver type," fun-loving, forest-for-the tree type. Heck, I sure as the stars above didn't know.

Looking back now, I was a product of my surroundings. But I had blinders on and just went with the flow of everything I experienced, and the people around me pushed me the way they wanted to, especially the Marines. Don't take that wrong though, I loved the Marine Corps. Dina had let me grow a little and made me a better man as they might say. This time I had to start over again without anything to help but some time with my parents. It was going to be like starting over again in life. I couldn't wait to get to Texas and begin again. I would do my best to find out what I did wrong with Dina and make my next relationship work for sure. Or so I thought.

Once I got the money, I spent a little on having a party for the people who stood by me those many nights sitting by the campfire, getting drunk and keeping things numb for me. I had everything all set and got my friend to give me a ride to the Greyhound to save some money. They all thought I was crazy because even after all that happened, I sent Dina and the kids half of the money. I had enough left to get me to Texas and get me a car.

"I guess my point is as a server, you set your pay by how good you are. There's no set amount of what you can make, and I definitely hate people charging automatic gratuity."

CHAPTER 49

Back to Waco

Alone

Time lines are a little sketchy there in Waco. There is some basic information like going back to IHOP for awhile. The GM that was there before bought the store I was supposed to go to as a GM. This guy really new his work, but he had a bit of an anger issue. I dated a few girls while I worked there. Nothing serious ever happened with them. One was a nineteen-year-old that had family who was friends with Willie Nelson, but I only met a few of his band members. That was kind of a neat memory. Two of the girls I dated were divorced with a few kids. I became good friends with one of the students from Baylor for a short time. Work was the same, long hours and no pay. Pam Tillis came out with "Maybe It Was Memphis" right about this time, and I loved that song. I got my first apartment then, which was really fun. I used one of them RAC places to furnish it. It was a little crazy.

After a short period there, I started at Olive Garden by the mall. Then the fun began for me. I had fallen back into something I really enjoyed doing. This wasn't a part-time job like before. I essentially could work as much as I wanted to, or as little. Tips were really good, if you were good. We only made $2.13 an hour but that wasn't the point. You made what you deserved back then in the service field. Now in some places they automatically charge a gratuity and they have to pay a minimum wage so they make $7 or so an hour. Then there are some that complain anyway. In some cases they're making $20 to $25 an hour. But the one true statement is they don't get a lot of hours.

Don't take this wrong at all, please don't mistake the fact that they work very hard for what they do. Not to mention they're raising a family or going to school all week. There are also a lot of us, especially in Middle America, that work very hard for what little we do get. It is definitely the "working man's dollar," as Chris Ledoux would put it. I guess my point is as a server, you set your pay by how good you are. There's no set amount of what you can make, and I definitely hate people charging automatic gratuity. They wouldn't have to do that in the certain states that do if everyone tipped out right. Like I said before, the best tippers are the ones that can't afford to. The rich greedy ones won't to get by with the least amount of money they can, for services. They don't care how hard you work, they just want it cheap. Again, I'm not generalizing the wealthy but if the shoe fits, quit being so greedy. It's not like you can't afford it. There are a lot of struggling people in the restaurant business, and we shouldn't rush to judge them either. I apologize for making it seem like a judgment to some people. I know as well as the next guy that it's hard on everyone, but "the little things."

To some extent, while I was in Texas, it seemed as if I always worked. All of my memory there is of the workplace. Is that what it was like for all of you that didn't join the military? It was like being on a constant roller-coaster ride thinking about when you could wind down and go party or try to find relationships? There seems to be some interesting concepts in what I saw in the civilian world. What else do people do? See, I'm thinking about that song I told you about. I'm thinking about "Eclipse," the man in the distance who sees the little things in life as he watches life from the outside. When people get caught up in that ongoing frenzy, they don't look at life from the outside anymore. Media, TV, music, and other things make you feel like you need to go out socializing and drinking when there is so much more to life. I do apologize for it sounding like generalizing, I don't mean to. It is the old saying of "if the shoe fits." It is sad to see people around me that get caught in that terrible cycle. It truly is sad, like the old man says in the song.

One thing I have noticed over the years is that all the things that I talk about when it comes to seeing the outdoors is now coming with a price tag. When I first got to Texas, I remember going to the lake a few times, and as the years passed, it started costing money to even park anywhere by the lake. This problem and reasoning behind it was twofold. The first part is the cost of taking care of the grounds. That is totally understandable. The part that bothers me is the people that ruin it for everyone else. This is the people I talked about when we discussed the bug and the tree. They trash things around them with no respect for the next person that uses it. This really chaps my hide, and I know it does the same for a lot of you reading this. In a way it's sad to think that the people I wish I could talk to about this probably wouldn't read my book anyway. I hope you kids don't turn out this way. I saw a lot of the aftermath of these people a lot out there at the lake. Take care of your surroundings, people. It doesn't hurt to bring a trash bag along with you.

The time I spent in Waco doesn't hold a lot of water when it comes down to it. IHOP was extremely frantic and very draining. I had two short-lived relationships and almost met Willie Nelson, but that is really all I can say. Olive Garden was very close to the same but really only one volatile relationship with a very nice French girl with bipolar disorder. She even got me into some fights at the Continental Cowboy (same place I mentioned earlier that I called Dad "Bob"). At one time she talked me into my two-week stint of college. In fact one morning, on my way to school with her next to me, I saw a plume of smoke off to the east and turned the radio on to hear about the David Koresh compound going up in flames. "Where were you when that happened?" I don't remember all the circumstance around the reasoning to stop school, so I can only speculate it had something to do with my girlfriend at the time. I don't mean it was her fault, but it was tough to go to school where she was after we split. I don't think I was made for college anyway.

At one time or another I ended up in Temple, Texas, at the Olive Garden there. That is also where my family ended up after a while. I wasn't around much before now, and my father and I were getting along just fine there. Scot was doing great, as usual; he was a teacher, I think, by this time. I couldn't tell you much about my sister. To be honest, she was always a shooting star in my life. I'd talk or see her very briefly through the course of the years. Jason was fairly hidden from me. I always had his grandma's number and would call from time to time to see how he was and possibly talk to Susan and see what was going on. Chris and Zach were still in North Carolina with Dina's new boyfriend, but for some reason or another, we were still married, and that was about it for Texas. There were some small happenings here and there but nothing so important that they should make this book even longer than it is. Then something happened that would change the flow of my life completely.

I started training a bit for manager at the OG. Now that in it's self didn't change things, but the idea it gave me did. One thing I didn't mention, which will be relevant in a moment, was the new Datsun 810 station wagon I was driving. She was in real nice shape but overheated around fifty to seventy-five miles. I personally had never been the mechanical type, so I didn't realize all I needed to do was put a thermostat on her or maybe a new radiator. I know that now, but it sure would have been nice to know back then. That is another thing I never got the opportunity to teach all of you kids about. Make sure you learn as much as you can about cars as you grow up. It's like having an insurance policy on your vehicles. It's the generation of taking your car to a shop for something simple like changing the oil. Trust me and others around you that know; it only takes a half hour of your time to change it yourself, and it's a great way to bond with your kids.

"Yes, we lived in a tent with two dogs' right next to the Colorado River."

CHAPTER 50

Going Back to the "Rockies"

While I was in training, I learned that with the Olive Garden, they had a policy that gave employees the benefit of transferring, wherever they wanted to, as long as that store had an opening. My life seemed to be going nowhere there in Texas, not to mention hating the weather there. Something felt like it was missing for me. Later on though I learned that I had a thing for traveling; remember the maps, the bus rides, and most of all, waiting to see what's around the bend? The passion I felt for the Rockies was built on a daily basis of listening to John Denver for so long. The little hint of it when I was with Dina was also coming back in memories on a daily basis. Then they told me I had a free pass to go back, so what the heck, right? It was a quick decision, but in a roundabout way, I had been building towards it for a while.

I saved my tips for two weeks and had close to five hundred dollars, and it was time to move on. All my friends and family thought I was crazy dropping everything and just taking off, but I felt that this was the right thing to do for me. In retrospect, I'm glad I did. Texas was not the kind of place for me. As I told you before, the heat was killing me. I never could get used to it. I could tolerate it, but that was all. The scenery was very nice with the open country and beautiful trees, but just too flat for me. One thing I do owe to Texas is what it had made me while I was there.

Before I got to Texas, I still wasn't sure who I was. I couldn't tell you what kind of music suits me most. We all know that John Denver was a big influence, but I knew there had to be something more for me. It was also apparent that I had no style per se. I wore what everyone liked to see me in or a uniform. What was my favorite décor? I had no idea. I was in an identity crisis. This started to cross my mind when I got the money from the Marines and went to buy clothes for myself for the first time without having someone there to hold my hand. It continued to grow while I was there in Texas. Some of you will jokingly say how sad it is that I had such an influence from Texas on the country boy side of things. I had become a "redneck." If you think back though, I was always a "redneck" anyway. I was just like my "Calderwood" background from so many years ago.

My first clothes I got for myself were Dockers utility pants. That was from when I did my bus ride from California. I remember there being a Western-wear shop across the street from my parents' house, and as time went by; I switched to jeans and button-up shirts. Popular Wranglers were my favorite. I think I bought my first pair of boots there with the hat to boot. My favorite singer quickly became Tim McGraw. This was all around the time of his first album. I also listened to a lot of Dwight Yoakum. Don't get me wrong, rock and roll was still a part of me. Van Halen was a favorite. I also have to say the movie *Pure Country* had an influence on my style. This will all come out a little later in the story too, but this is where it started.

So here I go again, back on the road to an uncertain future. I set up a transfer to Colorado Springs and had a little money with me, and everything I owned was in the back of my 810. This was going to take me through some famous places like Wichita Falls, Amarillo, Raton, and winding up at Pikes Peak. They told me the main dining room at the OG looked up at Pikes Peak. I can't tell you how excited I was. I was on top of the world and headed up. My anxiety was through the roof. A mechanic had looked at my car and put this stuff in the radiator and that got me almost to Amarillo before she started up again. In some ways, having to stop every 100 to 150 miles was a good thing, but I didn't feel that way at the time.

Usually, you are heading down the road just cruising along and missing everything. That day I learned where every rest area or each pull off was, from Amarillo to Colorado Springs. I had more than enough time to see "the forest for the trees." Every time I stopped, the longer I let it cool off, the farther I could get when I pulled away again. I didn't have enough money to fix the car and had no credit cards. (Remember, the bankruptcy kept me from having one.) It was a lot faster then hitchhiking, I tell you. Not to mention I had nothing but time on my hands to get there. My new boss said he would put me on the schedule when I arrived. All of you remember how much I enjoyed a long drive. So much to see on this drive; some of it was new and some parts I had seen before like Amarillo and Colorado Springs. The most interesting part was coming into Raton for the first time. Raton is in the northeastern part of New Mexico.

The reason this was so big, for y'all that haven't seen it, is after driving in the desert from Amarillo for so long, it's really nice coming up over a small hill and seeing the Rockies for the first time; it's awesome. Then again, maybe some of you have driven through there and don't recall seeing it. That's not to mention listening to "Rocky Mountain High" as I came upon Raton. If you pay attention, you see a lot of very beautiful things in this world. As life moved on, I went through Raton many times, and each time it got prettier. It became a regular stop for a meal. On the road going to Amarillo there was a great café on the north side of the road. It was an old truck stop there in Raton.

After a long wait at the café, I jogged up the hill towards Colorado Springs. When I got there, it was dusk and you could just make out the view of Pikes Peak through the Olive Garden windowsill. I had introduced myself and sat down for dinner and the classifieds to find a place to live. Out of the $500 I started with, I had $325 left. As luck would have it, I found a roommate add for $300. I called this older lady up, we talked for awhile and there I was, all set to start my new life, *again.*

This store wasn't as busy as where I came from but still made decent money all the same. The view was breathtaking to say the least. After my messed-up past with women, I tried to stay away from relationships but ended up dating an older woman for the first time. I can't recall her age, but it was close to thirty-five or so. She had kids who were all teenagers; one was even living with her eighteen-year-old boyfriend. Glad she wasn't my flesh and blood or that boy would've hated me and my shotgun. Things were as civil as they could be, I guess. At one point during this, I decided I wanted to smoke a pipe like Frank did when I was around him. I'm sure you remember him. The tobacco I found was a great smell. It was better than the cigarettes' smell from my new girlfriend and her kids. I can honestly say I rarely ever inhaled the pipe smoke though. That was probably a good thing because the pipe thing only happened for like a year. I kept my collection of pipes for a little while though.

On a few occasions, we had two or three consecutive days off and would go for little excursions to different places. One was an outskirt town between Colorado Springs and Woodland Park called "Manitou Springs." I mentioned this particular day because of a change in music, or should I say I added to my already extensive music taste. We were in an Indian store, I think, and heard this music with wolves howling in the background, and I had to have it. This was my introduction into "New Age" music. I have to think back a little first to tell you about my first experience with music like this. It happened with Bob one night when I stayed over at his place. I'm not sure, but I don't think they called it "New Age" back then.

Bob got the album originally for the cover, but we both got into the music. It was a bit of techno with a lot of synthesizers and rhythmic computers that made up the sounds. At one point in the music there is a large laser beam-like sound. Not that any of us know what that would sound like, at the time all we had was *Star Wars*, but it was very cool. The beginning of the album was a little creepy but great music nonetheless. The cover was earth with the outside layers, or land, was like skin, which was being peeled of to uncover a skull. Trust me, for a teenager, it was very cool looking. I still have that album in my collection, among many other New Age artists.

We also made it to Woodland Park and up in the neighborhood of Cripple Creek. After a while we started venturing farther away. One weekend she wanted to show me where she grew up, in Glenwood Springs. This is where they buried Doc Holliday, the friend of Wyatt Earp. This is also the town you go through to get to "Snowmass and Aspen." Glenwood is right there on I-70 past Vail, and fairly quiet for the most part, as far as I could see. We were having lunch at the Kettle and got in a conversation with the owner. I couldn't get over how peaceful it was there in the mountains. To his credit, he picked up on that and gave us a job if we wanted it. On the drive back, it didn't take long with the scenery we were seeing to decide to move up there right away. Her kids were keeping the house we lived in, and we got all are camping gear ready and headed back up to Glenwood. We had a friend from the Olive Garden that decided to come with us and will just call him Tim. Tim was a pothead real bad, but he was very shy and quiet. He had been a real good friend to my girlfriend a long time. I also learned the term "wake and baker." That was Tim for sure. He was a good person and a great waiter.

When we arrived, Tim found a room at a motel right away, and we only saw him from time to time. We were living at the "No Name" campgrounds just outside of town. Yes, we lived in a tent with two dogs' right next to the Colorado River. I would later learn the term *transient* from personal experience but didn't consider myself in that category at first. I had lost my car (the 810 Datsun) a short time ago in a bad deal for one of them blue Cherokees that was just like the one from my childhood. I guess I have an omen with them now. There was a path though to town, and I would walk it at times when my girlfriend needed the truck. We had a little white Toyota pickup. We typically worked different shifts so it worked out just fine. We did drift apart kind of quickly after that. It was truly sad how it happened, and I also would miss Fritz, our black lab.

Fritz had gotten very attached to me out at that campsite. He spent a lot of time sitting with me at the many campfires we had. One thing you may have forgotten at this point was that I did teach myself how to play guitar. Out there at No Name, it's seemed like I learned to play for that six months or so at the campgrounds. What seemed like every night I would end up having a mini concert of sorts, right there at the campfires around the campground. It was like a dream come true to have all them people enjoying my songs (John Denver's songs of course) on their vacation. I spent a lot of late nights playing for all those different people.

Something I have to share about Fritz was how much he loved playing ball. I mean *loved* playing with that tennis ball. This dog was nuts over that ball. Remember that we were right next to the Colorado River? I could throw the ball to the other side, and Fritz would jump in that freezing water, the current was strong enough to float him down close to a half of a mile before he made it to the other side. He would run back and find the ball then he jumped right back in again to give it back. Another half mile later, he dropped it right at my feet. "Do it again, Dad." You could see the excitement in his eyes. Talk about a fun and loveable dog. Fritz was all that and more.

Things were looking up at work also. I had been the night cook for a little while, and she was a server during the day. One day between shifts, like always, we ate together then she would go home; this day, the owner came up and asked if one of us wanted to be the new manager. We both said yes, but he only needed one. At first he left the decision up to us, and my girlfriend said flat out, "If you take this job, then we are over." That was a bit of a shock. In time I did end up with the job, and she moved in with someone else in town and left me the tent till I found something else. Shortly thereafter, I ended up sharing a room with Tim for a little while. This didn't last long but worked out for the time being.

I finally found me a small trailer again, just down the street. Things got very intense very quickly at the restaurant though. Being a little naïve hurt me here for the first time in my life in a scary way. I slowly found out that there were tons of drugs moving through this area to all the ski resorts in the area. Glenwood was like a distributor of drugs going all over.

It was the perfect geographical location for all the resorts. Some of my night cooks were part of all of this, and when I found out I decided that I should probably get out of here as soon as possible. The only problem was that one of these guys helped me get set up with a house and a mountain bike for coming and going. Don't ever borrow money from a guy that doesn't make very much money in the first place. I was so naïve at the time. I got the loan down to three hundred more that I owed but had arrangements to sneak out of town on a Greyhound the next week. I also didn't know those guys have ears everywhere. He found out, and I didn't know what to do at this point. It was becoming apparent that I needed to find another way out of this.

"My thought would be which came first, the violence you see on the streets now or the movies depicting the violence in the way it is now?"

CHAPTER 51

Accidentally Finding Paradise
Steamboat Springs

One of the waitresses that I sort of dated since my last girlfriend said, "Jim, you need to pay him or just leave tonight." That was going to be pretty difficult since I had no car. Then my savior spoke out, "Jim, you can move to Meeker with me till you find a place." This lady was one of my best customers. She came in and flirted with me all the time. We became good friends after she broke up with her husband who worked at a gas station nearby. "What about your husband?" After giving me that deer in the headlight look, she said with a bit of anger in her voice, "He isn't going to be married to me much longer, and he moved in with some girl here in town." "Well, if you don't mind being sneaky about things when you come, could you get me tonight?" She agreed to meet me later after my shift that night.

This was one of them moments that could've changed the course of my whole life after that time. Worrying or wondering whether we make the right decision in the past I think is more detrimental than it's worth. Y'all keep that in your head. It is something that you can't change, so what's the point in thinking about it? Doesn't mean you can't think back in retrospect; just don't beat yourself up about something you can't change. I personally would probably go insane if I even began to think about my mistakes. At this point, it was back to Texas or another new bend in the road.

It was off to a little town called Meeker. It was a very serene place, to say the least, basically just ranches, hunting, and a few small businesses with one road in and one road out. She helped me get set up at another weekly rental place that, by the way, was very south west looking. I loved my new place. The sad part was that I started spending most of my days with her and her son. I spent a lot of my days looking for work also, which it didn't take long to realize there was no work at all. Remember, small town and all. She then told me about a town called Steamboat Springs and that there would be plenty of work there. Only problem was it took two or three hours to get there from Meeker. So then I had to have a vehicle and we started tinkering with an old utility truck she had in the backyard. After we got that running, she got a hold of her friend in Steamboat to work out some lodging while I was there. We felt I could go out and work for four days and come to see her on my three days' off. It sounded good at first.

Before all that started, I did some minor things with the house to help out. It was kind of a payment for helping me get set up there on the western slope. One thing she needed from me was some shelves on her porch. I lied and said I knew a little carpentry but didn't have any tools. As you can imagine, it didn't take her long to get a hold of a skill saw, sander, jigsaw, and a few other things. The shelves were going to have bottles of bleach, cleaning supplies, and some other pantry items, so it needed to be sturdy. I sat down with a pencil and paper and started to design shelves, which I decided to make from two-by-fours. One weekend later, she had some nice white sturdy shelves. She was more impressed then I was but this would spark one of my favorite hobbies, woodwork. It became a passion later on.

The relationship started really well, but I think she was talking with her ex at the same time we were arranging our set up in Steamboat. That was not apparent the first few weeks we did this. The lady I stayed with was a very interesting character. She took the whole "saving money" to the extreme.

The first few days I was there, I got really sick and didn't come out of my room except when my friend from Meeker came to visit me and helped me get better. She brought me soup, cold medicines, and basically came to help me with simple things while I healed. After that one day, I was going to do some dishes and clean up a disgusting sink, and a bit later my landlady came out screaming at me for running water to do dishes. She said, "That water was still good for a few more days, why did you drain it? You're wasting a lot of water and money." The water she spoke of was from when I cooked the first day I was there a week earlier. Yes, a week earlier. She also told me I should go to the YMCA if I wanted to shower each day. Needles to say, this was not going to work. I think I was there for three weeks.

I told my girlfriend about it, and she told me a story of her being in a coma from falling of the "clock tower" building, which was three stories high. This building used to be a club in the '80s on the mountain, or should I say by the ski area. My friend from Meeker grew up with her and knew her before she got the way she is. She had four cars but hitchhiked everywhere because she wanted to save gas. She would go to all the places that had free coffee before she would waste the water at home so she wouldn't have to pay for the water she used to make the coffee at home. By the way, her family was the richest in Steamboat, so everyone left her alone. I stopped telling people I lived with her for a while because everyone knew her in Steamboat and would look at me funny. Later I found we had a guy that was a little strange there in Steamboat too. You could find him walking barefoot in the winter in the middle of the street. He also came from a wealthy family.

I'm glad I'm poor, huh? If this is what money and greed do to you, I'd rather starve to death. *Greed*, I hate that word and everything that comes with it. "The simple things in life are free." I guess it all goes back to that saying that "money can't buy us happiness." That is so true in a lot of ways, but having enough to get by is nice too. Part of that to me is just getting up knowing I have to go to work to survive. It doesn't matter to me what I do or how much I make, but the sense of accomplishment in doing my part to society. Greedy people have a false sense of pride. How much they have and how little they have to do to get it is what makes them happy. That's not to mention they don't care who they hurt on the way up. I'm being very careful not to show my political side on this so maybe I should leave this thought to my personal conversations with people. The point of all this is to look at the simple things and see how much more powerful they are compared to money or materials. Also think back to when we talked about "basic reality," I don't think *greed* is one of them. As I said many times already, "it started somewhere."

My first job there in Steamboat was perfect for me. It was also close to the west side of town where I was staying. It also was an area where you couldn't see the ski area which was kind of funny later on when I started working at Alpine Taxi. It was a little café called Sharon's. It was the local hangout for the working class of Steamboat. Incredible portions and incredible taste, there was never a better deal in Steamboat. The green chili was to die for, and all the bread products were freshly baked daily by Sharon. She made everyone feel at home there. It was filled with booths and some big tables in the middle. When you ate there, it was like the perfect stop before work for hundreds of people, and each morning you could be eating with a perfect stranger. It was never being sat at a table, you were sat in a chair. The tables were there for anyone like a cafeteria. Lots of regulars came in, and we knew what they wanted without them even saying. Some of them I would just start their food before they even sat down. It was a great experience for me.

Talk about busy, we were swamped every weekend. We would do like 1,200 just for breakfast. "How did you know that, Jim?" you say. I made a bet one day with Sharon, and if I won she'd give me a big raise. She said, very clearly with a weird smile that said, "There's no way," "Jim, if you can do 1,200 breakfasts by yourself, I'll give you that big raise." She lived up to her promise after that weekend. Sharon took good care of the few employees she had there. It was also were I meet a lot of the drivers from Alpine Taxi.

Alpine was a very reputable company that took good care of all the locals. They were always there when you needed them most, even at two in the morning. Not to mention they were the first person the tourist saw and the last. They had a lot of pull in the community. All the drivers that worked there were the back bone of Steamboat Springs, meaning, the construction guys, the ranchers, in general the ones that built the town with their own two hands. If you want to know anything about Steamboat, ask the drivers.

When the first season was almost over in Steamboat, my relationship with the Meeker girl had died. I knew I couldn't stay in Meeker due to the fact that there was no work; Steamboat was to expensive to live, so the only thing I could think of was a country town called "Craig." Craig was actually in between Steamboat and Meeker. It had around ten thousand people, just like Steamboat when you count only locals there in Ski Town. Craig was a "cowboy" town in a real sense of the word, lots of cows. We also had lots of "coal." The biggest power plant and mine was in Craig. There is a smaller one in a town between Steamboat and Craig called "Hayden." Steamboat, by far was the prettiest of the three. It even had a valley, south of Steamboat called "Paradise or Pleasant" valley. If you kept going south out of Steamboat you hit "Oak Creek" and "Yampa." This whole area was called "Yampa Valley," after the river that runs through it.

Now that we got that straight, Craig became my new home now. I even remember my first apartment was on Seventh Street. I think it was the spring now and I got a job at the local "village inn" as a cook. I still had no car so I walked about ten blocks each day for work. There was a grocery store right by work so I could do that on my way home if needed. My job, as far as I was concerned was great. I was trained in by a guy who became a good friend. He kind of reminds me of Larry the Cable Guy. He was as redneck as they came. We were both in jeans, cutoff T-shirt and a baseball cap that said "John Deere" on them. We were known as the singing cooks. We both had the happy-go-lucky attitude towards everything, even when we were in the weeds, we still made fun of it. In the weeds, for some of you that have never been in food service, is when you're so busy you can't ever seem to catch up or get a breath. So, it's like trudging through the swamp "in the weeds," trying to get out. I can't remember ever hearing it except in the restaurant business.

This cook and I were great together, and there was always drama in the background of the restaurant. At one point, guess who shows up one night? Remember the girl I dated a little after the one from Colorado Springs? They came back and said someone was asking for me. As I stepped into the dining room, at first I was excited to see this girl I liked, and then it happened. The guy from the drug group sat next to me with a hint of the friendship we shared before things got edged. "How have you been, Jim, I can't help but feel like you are neglecting our friendship." The girl spoke in just after he said that and said, "I knew we'd find you, it's not like he left the state or something." He spoke back with a laugh and asked me if I could step out to the car after they ate, and of course, tons of stuff raced through my head as I watched them eat without them seeing me.

The waitress informed me of their departure, and I headed out the back to see them. He was standing at the car now with a serious look now as he spoke sternly. "Jim, I'm disappointed that you left without paying your debt. It's only three hundred more, and it will be all over. Call me later when you get it settled, and I'll come back to see you." He finished his sentence, turned away from me to open his door to climb in his nice sports car. As he settled in his seat, he pulled a pistol from his jacket pocket where his hands were keeping warm as we spoke. He set it down between them on the seat and raised his hand to shake mine. "Please don't disappoint me again, it's nice up here, but I don't like visiting you for this reason. Take care, Jim, and I'll see you soon."

As I stood there, shivering in the cold, I couldn't wait for them to drive away. It was scary in a way I can't explain. Maybe the unknown was the fear I felt. Would he actually use the gun to intimidate me or was it all for show? These were small community people that seemed very down home to you. Not the stuff you see in the movies. Actually, I would think that the movies just gave them a tool to use to get what they wanted. The people I did meet in this world were just everyday people. Their life is not the drama they portray on the screen. In some cases, I'm sure that in some cities they have some serious issues. My thought would be which came first, the violence you see on the streets now or the movies depicting the violence in the way it is now? What I mean is if you listened to the old-timers, there was violence before, but it wasn't pistols and guns. It had a sense of pride back then. I don't mean to sound like I'm condoning any of it at all. It just seems like the media has a part in making it as bad as it is now on the streets of America. "What came first the chicken or the egg?" Will we ever know?

To remind all of you, this was still in my "finding out who I was" stage. I had already been to the pawnshop to buy an old skill saw and some other hand tools for starting my new hobby. If I remember correctly, the first thing I made was an end table. It was small, but for someone with no background in construction or a memory of shop class in school, I did just fine. I had the bug really bad after that. All I wanted to do was build stuff. It always feels good to create things. Even back in Texas, I had made a bunch of beaded key chains with that Southwest art look to it. As some of you know that became a big thing for a while. A lot of it had to do with *Dances with Wolves*. It became a big deal for me. I had been slowly tinkering with the whole Southwest art look. Dream catchers, beads, wolves, Indian art, turquoise, and I fell in love with the Indian music too. I had the movie memorized word for word after a while. Needless to say, building furniture was becoming my favorite way to express myself, and I started mixing Southwest art with it.

I kept fairly quiet for a little while just tinkering with craft stuff and then decided to get a second job working at another café in the downtown area of Craig. It was a little closer to where I lived. I would catch a movie from time to time. Y'all know me. All in all, I guess I was at a stalemate.

"Just watch how people react to each other. I assure you most of the people you see will walk around without even noticing the people around them."

CHAPTER 52

My One and Only Girl
Mattie

As I said, things were very quiet, but then this young girl I met working at the downtown café struck my eye. It took all I could to ask her to go to a movie, but surprisingly she said yes. We all know I'm ADHD and pretty hyper, but Connie is just the opposite. She always had this calm look about her, and if I walked 100 mph, she went ten. She was never in a hurry, but she showed an interest in me and I didn't have a lot of luck over the past few years. She was very dainty but friendly to me. Over a short period, we decided to make a go at it. Not to mention Anthony was having fun with me around, obviously her son. Don't worry, she was around nineteen at the time we started dating. I guess my happy-go-lucky attitude made her feel good; she always seemed upset, to some extent. I saw past that very easily and quickly.

She was originally from Kansas, and her mother and father were separated but living in Craig. She was living in what some people in Craig called the projects. It was government housing and was very helpful to young single mothers. It was also where a lot of drugs changed hands to. She and her mother lived out there, and I think her rent was like twenty-six dollars a month. Now I was no Casanova and barely had a pot to piss in, but we were happy together. We decided to make a go at it. For the time being, we also believed it would be easier to just have me move in with her. That ended up only lasting a short time, and I talked her into moving out to Texas so I could maybe get a steadier job. There just wasn't a whole lot going on in Craig at this time, and she didn't want to be around the soap operas concerning her family, so I thought this would be a good thing for her. We weren't sure how this was going to go, so to be safe, we put all of our stuff in storage and then went to Texas, "shooting from the hip," as it were.

I have to mention again, like a broken record, that the time frames may be messed up. Connie, I hope you don't worry about the time thing. It isn't relevant in an autobiography in a lot of ways as far as I'm concerned. There was a time that I either went to Texas early without Connie or when she went back to Colorado. I'm pretty sure we went to Texas together.

We initially lived in a very small apartment by the mall, and I remember there was a good Chinese restaurant across the highway, and the OG gave me a job right away since some of the people I worked with were still there. In time I was talking to them about management again, but then in the middle of that conversation, I was offered a job managing the Case Ole in the mall. I actually liked that better than the OG; due to the major company policies at the Olive Garden, I wanted something a little more laid back. In time I really did enjoy Case Ole. It was also the second time I learned a little more Spanish. The first time, which wasn't much, was at IHOP training with the cooks.

The United Sates and her thousands of malls are grounds for some interesting perspectives. I am back in my home state of Minnesota, and our mall is actually called the Mall of America which is in the twin cities. As a child, the mall in Duluth was quite small but very homey. A very fond memory was the few times my parents brought us kids there to shop, which really meant playing video games for me. Scot always either saved his money or bought a new Beatles album or tackle. Pam basically just got new girly stuff or candy. My parents had it the best. The Walgreens back then had a small café in the mall before they had big food courts, and the booths were open to the mall. My parents would meet us there at a particular time and got there before us and just sat drinking coffee and people watching. Sometimes I'd get there early and just sit with them; a lot of interesting people walking by. Most of the time they would always find me at the arcade; yes, kids, when we wanted to play games, all we had was the arcade. But at least it was so much more involvement than the video games at home or on line games. Don't take it wrong, kids, I get it, I really enjoy a good game of Halo or racing games. What I'm saying is how much interaction do you get from a controller?

The reason I'm bringing it up is my time at Case Ole was very interactive, so many people walking by or eating at the restaurant just like sitting with my parents years before. As you will see soon I went on a hiatus from the restaurant thing, but it was for stability reasons. I also would like all of you who are reading this to go and try something; it's not a test but something to help you guess to see yourself through the eyes of others. Another thing I want all of you to remember is the conversation about being caught in traffic. For you, that are in your forties or older, remember how much fun hanging out at the mall was? We didn't have the same kind of distractions that these kids have, and it was just fun to go and see your friends instead of texting them. All of you, watch the distractions around you. I hate to even imagine how many people you will see talking or texting while there at the mall. Just watch how people react to each other. I assure you most of the people you see will walk around without even noticing the people around them. I'll hold my tongue about some of the clothes people wear. I would bet if you've been paying attention to my book, you'll be able to see a lot of the situations going on all around you. Make sure to see the "forest for the trees" while you watch them scurry all around.

After some time in that box we lived in, we finally ended up in a nice apartment in Troy, which is just north of Temple. I had started my so-called "hobby" and was going to town with lots of stuff for the house. Somewhere during all this, we got pregnant too, and for the first time my mother would get to be there when the child was born. She was so excited to see a grandchild born. Scot was also getting into the whole woodworking thing. He had better access to the right kinds of tools. At one point, he helped me build a really nice bookshelf that lasted me for many years made out of red oak. Also at that time I made a beautiful maple bookshelf. Things were going good, except the heat. We were pretty excited about the new child too and couldn't wait.

Another thing before Mattie came in was a hobby for Connie. Ceramics became another passion for us that grew onto some nice things for the house. Painting ceramics for me was very rewarding and fun for Anthony too. It took up a lot of downtime around the house while she carried Mattie. As I sit here in retrospect of my life, I realize how much time is lost in too much TV. Looking back, I remember as a kid really only watching intently on the weekend to watch are favorite cartoons. See, for you young ones that weren't there, we only had a small amount of channels to keep us company, and on the weekend, they devoted those mornings for cartoons only for the kids. In general though, I never really got into the whole TV thing but only because I had better things to do. Same thing there in Troy, don't get me wrong; I watched plenty of TV at times, but my memories of watching a lot of TV are of *Three's Company*, *Taxi*, Laverne & Shirley, *Happy Days*, and can't forget my persona favorite, *Mork & Mindy*. There were others, but you're getting the time period.

I think as I grew up, I liked good movies instead. *Midway*, as a child, was my first theater movie. I liked setting aside a particular time and place to just explore through the magic of movies. No interruption, just a complete escape from reality for just a spell. I also can't stand commercials. I literally won't watch TV because of commercials. Whose stupid idea was it to have commercials? I guess they feel when people's brains are messed up enough with propaganda, that it brainwashes people into buying their products. It's sad to think that this brainwashing actually may work. Says a lot for the human race, doesn't it. Oh boy, is my mind racing now.

Does anybody else see the stupidity in all this? People buy airtime to sell their product. In a way, the consumer pays for that because part of that product price pays for commercial airtime or advertising. Would any of you like your favorite products to be cheaper? Stop running commercials so people that don't watch TV are also paying for something they don't use. What if you just paid for the channel and that's how they make their money? *Oh yea*, that's how cable started, with no commercials. But don't they all have commercials now too? Whoever *they* are, knows that they can subconsciously control the things you think about or buy through their propaganda, can't they? At the beginning of my book, I talked about "apathy" and how that gives *them* the ability to control how you think.

Are you going to go buy that beautiful jacket and pay five hundred dollars for it because they make it sound so wonderful? You could probably buy it for one fifth the price at another store that isn't trying to control your thoughts, but they are slowly taking that away because they're getting rid of the little store that makes the same quality at half the price. Now even the big stores are having problems because you can buy on line. Why should you get of you're you know what and go shopping? At some point, they're going to take away the "little things in life" and will be sitting back, on our computers wondering why things are so tough. But that's OK, you just got your new big screen with the new video game and that cool new Twitter phone from E-bay. All is well.

Sorry, a little exaggerated, but I think you see where I'm going with this. Doesn't it seem to be that way a little *now*? I don't know, it's your life, I hope you have the mind to see the forest for the trees. Just try your best to hold on to "the little things in life that make you whole." I see a lot of money that gets spent in weird ways on TV.

Back to the story at hand, Madison, she is just the most wonderful thing. I hope you're brothers look after her when I'm gone. I hope that this book will bring all of you together to watch over each other. Madison, you were a very proud moment for me. Having you born there around your grandparents was very special to them. Your mother was very strong during your delivery, and while she rested Grandma was holding you and going on and on about her little granddaughter. Grandma was the first to change you. By the way, you had a little accident while she changed you too. Your mother picked the perfect name for you. I can't imagine anything else sounding sweeter. Madison, you will always be my perfect flower.

Other than you, Mattie, things weren't perfect; they were weighing heavily on me that I still worked in the restaurant business. I wanted to give a nine-to-five job a try, but no one was hiring. It was bothering me more and more. I'm not remembering exactly what happened, but Connie was going to take the kids back to Craig to make things a bit easier on her. I don't remember, but driving a truck may be the reason.

"To some extent, I regret that day, but I'm sure that chew saved my life many times while I was in my driving career."

CHAPTER 53

I Finally Had a Reason to Have Lots of Maps
Truck Driving

Before I get into this, I need to explain the last few chapters to you. The last fourteen years of this book are going to have to be split up into different sections. It's not possible to go chronologically like before. I was a truck diver seasonally. I was a shuttle driver in the winter. I didn't only truck drive in the summer. I did a few things during this time. Trenton, you were born during this time, and I got to spend some precious time with all of you at one point or another. I know y'all hate to hear this, but I'm getting close to the end of my book. I could get into a ton of details about these past few years, but that really is another story. This book is a little story of trying to keep my sanity and find the serenity in life that a lot of us never had. I have found that serenity in life over the past two years, and the book is kind of like a closing chapter to start my new life. So for the remainder of the book, I will talk about particular things and get to where I am now.

I always had a thing about traveling as you all know, very well. One day while I was sitting, looking at the employment section of the classifieds, I noticed a statement about seeing the United States and getting paid to do it (which is kind of ironic when you think about my last chapter and the part about the commercials). Traveling for free sounded good to me. All I had to do was go to the Holiday Inn and listen to a speech, no strings attached. What the heck, right? I went down there, listened to their presentation, and I couldn't wait to sign up. A reputable company pre-hired me, and they would pay for the school. This was going to be fun. Actually, I think this is why Connie went to Colorado. I could live there as a home address, and during leave time, I could come visit them and not to mention get out of the restaurant business. I put in a six week's notice at work, and I think that's when Connie went back to Texas. It may have been after school though, I'm not sure.

School was in a small town south of Dallas called Palmer Texas. As the students, we stayed in a motel which was primarily students from the school. A lot of the school was training in their field facility, and we did some paperwork and lectures. I remember one of the instructors, who was close to his sixties, had told us in his gravely voice, "Life is all about attitude." Another one of his sayings was "Just work hard every day and someday it will pay itself off." I haven't seen it yet, but I think it depends on how you look at it.

I think his general perspective is obvious. You work hard all your life and you will have all the money you need. My Statement after I wrote "I haven't seen it yet" is typically what you are going to hear from my readers. Looking back, I totally disagree with that because it truly is how you look at it. I think it was a wise way to say, "Work hard all your life, and you will be paid back tenfold with your experiences and a strong background for your kids to grow up with. It will give you a strong sense of self-accomplishment knowing you worked hard for your life." Those ethics will keep you strong, and people around you will look up to you for it. If money is all you hope for, then I pity you. "Jim, you just say that because you never had much to survive with." If that is the way someone views life, then I rest my case.

I had a terrible time in high school because of my environment. Out here in the real world, I excelled there while I was at the school. I guess I should have gone to college, huh?

Can't change the past; truck driving will have to do. I like to think that the school I attended was one of the better ones that are out there. The old man also said, "There is no such thing as an uncontrolled accident." The one thing that we did the most in school was backing, which is so critical in the trucking industries. While I was at school learning the fine art of backing, I remembered my years running a forklift back at twenty-two area at Camp Pendleton with the "Rat Pac." I always had a lot of respect for them drivers when they were backing up. We had a few that were incredible, and you had the ones that couldn't hit the side of a barn. So I paid a lot of attention at school so I hoped to be one of the best at it.

The day the driver test came up, and my test scores were in the high 90s, I know it's no big deal to some of you, but I was happy about that. I found something other than cooking that I really enjoyed. It's kind of a neat feeling to be at the wheel of a semi. I know a lot of people think that the truckers act like they own the road, but in that defense, there is always going to be that small percentage that ruins it for everyone.

I remember stopping at a rest area during the day just outside of a city when this lady in her forties came over to me, screaming at me, "Are you a truck driver?" "Yes, I just pulled in. Did I do something to you?" "Oh no," she said. "This guy kept going, why in the hell do you guys keep running up on me like you're trying to scare me? I was in the middle lane doing five miles over the speed limit. I wasn't hurting anyone, what the hell is y'alls problem?" "Well, I'm sorry they tried to push you around, but you where in their fast lane. In some states, it's illegal for a semi to be in the outside lane, especially in some cities. Some of them are very pushy, and some are just giving you a sign that they would like to pass." That got her quiet in a heartbeat. "I'm sorry, but the ones that are bad can be very intimidating with them big trucks."

There in lies a big problem. Most of you truck drivers, I hope, will concur with me when I say, "It's like giving an a-hole a gun. They get stupid and try to act all big around other vehicles, but when they're sitting in the truck stop, they're the strange one sitting in the corner that won't talk to anyone in

the TV lounge. Without that truck, they're just an average Joe."
Just because they have a "big truck" doesn't make them a "big
man." For all of you that have never been in a truck before
trust me. After you spend a lot of time on that radio and on
the road, the drivers do their best to police the ones that ruin
it for everybody. You know who's who on the radio just by the
way they talk on it.

It's a very interesting world out there that only a few ever
see. Someone said to me once it's "seeing the United States
from the back door." "Pull around back and leave your radio
on till we need you." I can't tell you how many times people
say that to you, that is when the drivers usually say, "But my
appointment is for so and so time?" "Yep, and you're on time,
we will get to you when we can." Any of you drivers out there
getting some memories back? I can't mention companies, but
how many of you sat at the truck stop there in Denver, and how
about rewashing a trailer two times there before you can check
in? I also recall a town around either Cleveland or Cincinnati
where it always took forever to get your load. Do any of you
drivers remember how bad things were on the radio in West
Memphis? For all of you who aren't drivers, none of that will
make sense to you, but trust me, the ones that do will respect
me as much as I respect them. Trucks aren't so bad, it's the
people driving it and driving around it. Kind of like the saying,
"The gun doesn't kill people, but people do." Truck drivers,
know I could almost write a whole book dedicated to just
driving a truck, but this book is getting long as it is, and I just
need to leave it at that.

Something that is relevant right now is when I was with
the fleet I would drive for with my trainer. He was basically a
clean-cut, relaxed type, who was a bit of a country boy. He was
also a chewer. For y'all that don't drive, we have a logbook with
us at all times. You've heard in movies and songs that you can
cheat that log or carry two. Well, I assure you that laws keep a
tight grip on that, but just like anything in life you can stretch
the truth. The formula for stretching the truth will only let you
go so far. The days of traveling for days are gone. Everything
is based on your speed limit, the first part of the formula. The

second part is your fuel stops. Last part deals with where the scales are located. That was what I was learning on the day that is relevant.

It was late one night towards the end of training, and I had 120 miles before I could stop at a fuel station. (Truck stop our company dealt with.) I had already driven for twelve hours and was struggling real hard to stay awake. To his credit, my trainer was staying quiet to give the full effect, which was necessary to keep my mind on the task at hand. Without missing a beat, he threw his can of chew on the dog house with a plastic cup and napkin. "This will fix it," he said as the chew settled to my right. (Doghouse was like a housing unit between the driver's side and passenger side, kind of like two bucket seats with a box in the middle.) "Don't swallow and don't take too much the first time." So what the heck, I would give anything a try at that point.

Man did I wake up in a hurry. I could have driven for another ten hours. This was great, and boy did this help my job as a truck driver. To some extent, I regret that day, but I'm sure that chew saved my life many times while I was in my driving career. I admit that it's a nasty habit, but at least I wasn't blowing smoke in the room. In time I did quit, but I chewed for many years to come.

I hope all of you can remember my thoughts on driving from earlier, and if so, I'm sure you know I was in paradise in this field. Being on the open road driving around all of America, listening to music, watching movies on the weekend at some mall, talking on the CB with complete strangers with a camaraderie that makes you friends instantly, not knowing where you'd be heading the next day, sleeping in the strangest places in America, watching people in traffic jams, listening to a books on tape in the wee hours of the morning in the middle of the desert, and not to forget the few convoys I hooked up with in Ohio late at night.

I swear I could write a whole book just on those few years as a truck driver. You have so much time to contemplate life while you're out there with the right state of mind. It is nice being in control of your life out there. I understand you had to take loads off your computer, but the time frame they gave you for each load had plenty of time so you could work at your own pace. Would I do it again? If the right circumstances ever arose, maybe. But I don't think so. That was a wonderful experience and has taught me more then you'll ever know.

"At one point I looked out the passenger window and my trailer was there in the window. That's something I never want to see again."

CHAPTER 54

A Few Other Jobs I Tried

Like I've said before, the chronological order may not match, but these are things I did. If you think back just a little; I was trying to find something outside of food service. I lasted awhile the first year in trucking but felt the need to be home with my new daughter. You were so precious and grew so fast it seemed. I can't tell you how tough it was the past few years when I couldn't find you. I got so caught up in each relationship that it ruined my life with you and all the boys. I don't think I'll ever be able to apologize enough to each of you, but I'm sure going to try.

I actually can say I helped build a house or two in Steamboat. I got hired as a framer one year and it didn't really go great, but I learned a lot with the people I worked with. The main reason I didn't make it in the field was anger. At this point in my life, I had seen plenty of anger towards me but nothing like this. The foreman obviously wasn't there all the time, and the two guys that I worked with were fairly lazy compared to the foreman. When he wasn't around, we were on a completely different pace. We were working but not the way he wanted. A lot of times, I got the brunt of the anger because I was the new guy. I think later he realized it all wasn't me because he had sent me to other jobsite with some other people, and they were happy with my work.

Guys, don't get discouraged by this type. Some people tend to show their frustrations in bad ways. He was actually very good at what he did, and when he was there, things went smooth and quiet. When you let their anger feed into you, then the stuff hits the fan as they would say. I guess in a way I'm telling all of you not to take things so personal. I hate the excuse that that's just the way there are, so do the best you can to fix or help the guy that's having problems. Remember I think I told y'all to not jump the gun in the moment, just take care of the task at hand and then go back and say what the problem is. Relax the situation first and then go in and don't let it start up again. Not only will this help at work, but it can keep a relationships strong.

If you're wondering why I went to construction, I have an answer for that. When I was managing the IHOP, I remember seeing these guys in the morning with tattered old clothes, rough-looking beard, rough old work boots, and a greasy old baseball cap. I thought to myself at first why would somebody dress like that? In conversation, they were great, friendly, happy-go-lucky, and no care in the world. They were always talking about their situations with their equipment or a problem with a wall on a house. These guys were the "heartbeat of America" or some would say the "backbone" of our country. Because of people like this, we have a home to rest our heads, and they built our world, in a sense. My respect grew for them while I worked there at the IHOP and I wanted to be like them.

That didn't work very well, but I found a way to stay around the field for a while and was driving flatbeds for a lumber company. "At least I was working with wood," I thought. It was actually a lot of fun and sometimes very interesting. Some of the places you would take loads was insane to say the least. I remember one place they were building was at they end of this winding road up over a mountain that they had built just for this house. It was a six-mile driveway of sorts. It had to go over this two-thousand-foot hill so there was a lot of switchbacks that made me do three-point turns with the vehicle I drove out there. Like I said, it could be interesting at times. I think what scared me away from doing this was driving them rigs in the winter. I had a good scare in a semi driving in a snowstorm on Route 66 around Utah, I think it was. At one point I looked out the passenger window and my trailer was there in the window. That's something I never want to see again.

Another job that I really did like but the pay was terrible was being a ranch hand. Yes, I got the opportunity to be a cowboy. It was short-lived, but it was great. You want to try some hard work, then become a cowboy. I probably would have kept doing it, but raising a family on them wages didn't work very well. I was working for a lawyer there in Steamboat for one spring during all this. It started off learning the irrigation ditches. Just a shovel and some tarp to start of; in the morning, I walked the fields, moving the tarps for the next day's saturation. Then you did chores like checking the cows, graining them, setting up trailers for the next days, supplement hay for the cows, feeding the horses, checking the fence, and once you got that done, we did special things for each week and would work on that. Before the end of the day, you went back and checked the tarps again. All in a day's work right? Somebody has to feed the country.

We also did a few branding parties and built my first fence for the boss. I've built a few fences since then. Got the experience of loading semis with hay bound for Kentucky; it all kept me really busy. I don't regret working there because of the experience that helped me later with other jobs, but I wished I could've made enough to keep me doing the work.

All of them were fun for me and gave me more then enough experience for what was to come. As I said, it wasn't chronological, and a lot of other things went on at the same time.

"It was like getting a ten-year education. These were scientist, doctors, lawyers, and some famous people, your average Joes that saved for years for a vacation, archeologists, and even an occasional paranormals."

CHAPTER 55

My Main Work for Ten Years or So

We will start of with my winter job. With truck driving "over the road" for a few summers and some work on locations in Steamboat from hauling wood, I landed a spot with Alpine Taxi. This was the starting ground for a lot of people in Steamboat. They were a very prestigious company all around the western slope. There vehicles can be seen at all the resort towns from Steamboat to Denver. They have one of the most outstanding records around the business for safety. They are highly respected all over the western slope. The people that work there are a handpicked wonderful group of very professional people, with just a hint of down home in them. The owner, back when I started was at the top of my list of people that I have come to know and call my friends. They saved me so many times with their friendship and financially. I will always remember the time I spent with them. Looking back, I'm surprised they put up with me as much as they did. At one time ownership switched hands and she was just as much a friend as the first.

Through them I also met the other boss that I feel the same way towards. Adam's Fencing, my home for I think eight years. I probably owe my health to Steve, the owner. Don't take that in the literal sense. I'll explain as I go here. Fencing is a very physically demanding job, as I'm sure you can imagine. I would still be working there if he hadn't moved to Texas for the water-skiing. I think in some ways he gave me a lot of self-confidence and helped me turn the pages in my life. As you have seen throughout the book, I had none for the longest time. I was never sure of myself or my abilities as a person. The scars of my past became just that, my past. Fencing gave me a sense of pride. I was that guy in the beat-up jeans and baseball cap now.

I'll tell a little bit about both jobs, will start with Alpine Taxi. Driving for them was an experience in itself. One of the great things about Steamboat is our own airport there in Hayden, Colorado. It's about forty-five miles from there to Steamboat, and we handled a big chunk of the shuttle service from the airport. We also were the cab company in town. The bus system was free, but if you wanted your own ride, you called us. We all had driver numbers for the radio and paperwork, and I was 84 the whole time I was there. They sent me for my passenger endorsement right away since I already had the CDL. That put me with the big shuttle fleet right away, which was nice. My first year there just happened to big a huge year for snow, I think we hit four hundred inches that year. I know earlier I mentioned a fear of driving in the snow, but up here everything was studded tires and the best equipment you could ask for. Those vehicles, especially when they were loaded, were as safe as you can get.

On a daily basis, I would meet a hundred people a day. I would spend, on average, one hour with each group. The conversations would run wild at times. Speaking to those people gave me a sense of pride that I can't explain. This was my home, and they came thousands of miles to visit. I guess that's about as close as I can get to explain things. As long as I gave them respect, they respected me in return. I could've just driven and dropped them off, but that wasn't in my nature. I gave them a tour of sorts and did quite well with gratuity. As far as I was concerned, I had to earn it. I kept them company and helped in every way I could.

I know there were a few times that I messed up, maybe missed a stop or didn't get the right paperwork, and in some cases, talked too much, I'm sure; but I did the best I could every day for the ten years I drove for them. This was the perfect job for me. I got to meet lots of people and talk to them, plus I got to be outside and drive. The conversations were endless. They would talk of thousands of different things. Talk about a plethora of information. It was like getting a ten-year education. These were scientist, doctors, lawyers, and some famous people, your average Joes that saved for years for a vacation, archeologists, and even an occasional paranormals. One even was able to see the two times I almost died. Remember the red truck with Dina and the kids on our way to get married and also when my dad got something on his arm and for a moment forgot me in the Gulf of Mexico? That was an interesting conversation. Bottom line, I hope you can see my point. I met thousands of people, in that people mover, and got a free education.

I definitely learned how to drive in the winter. I can't even begin to count the amount of times I went over Rabbit Ears Pass in a complete whiteout. Not to mention Eisenhower Tunnel. I had very few incidents, but I did have my share. One time I got a flat at forty-five miles an hour coming down from Eisenhower tunnel on a 6 percent grade. Man did that steering wheel jerk when it blew. One day Rabbit Ears was closed, and I took another path which had no cell service and a passenger went into convulsions. All the drivers had to have first aid and I got him and his family calm and raced carefully down the hill to Kremling emergency. That was a fun day, *not*. Remember I said the old man in training said there was no such thing as an unavoidable accident? That happened at an intersection and was the only accident I've ever had. Knock on wood. The only person that got hurt was me from the air bag deployment. Everyone, including the small pickup driver, was just fine. I got scrapes from my watch when the bag went of.

The people I worked with there at Alpine were family in a way. I won't mention their names since a lot of them still work there. There were a few I didn't get along with at first, but as I got to know them for years, we learned to either tolerate each other or a few cases became pretty good friends. One driver, whom all the people that work there will know who

I'm talking about, was just mean, I thought at first. His humor was very harsh, it seemed. He also had a thing against people who just thought the world of themselves. But as time went on, we became decent friends. That, for me, was a lesson in not judging people. Admittedly, he could be abrupt, but he basically didn't take any crap from anyone, especially when people got in his face. Hell, I was afraid of him at first and later told him so. He was good person.

Just like any workplace, there was drama at times, but we all had a lot of good times there. I had never known anyone for any length of time, but I knew them for ten years. It is strange for me but nice to be able to call there and say hi to old friends. Writing this book actually gave me a bit of that just recently when I talked to the owner about putting the company name in the book. It was very cool to be able to talk of old times for a moment. Through here, Steve's family still working there, so I was able to contact him also. That was also a nice look back in time and a little catching up. It was almost like looking back in time to the way it was. Lisa and Steve haven't changed much, and I still look up to them in high regard.

Me on the other hand, I don't seem to stop changing. I will say that now, as I write these words, I have finally found where I wanted to be. As I look through the sands of time, I have finally found what I didn't even know was there. It was hidden from me in the eclipse of life itself, stopping me from being myself. Soon I'll be explaining that a little more in detail. It is just the idea of being able to talk with these people who helped me be who I am today. Remember, the little things in life make you grow. In a sense your experience is your life. I've known them now for some fifteen to eighteen years or so.

When it comes to Steve, I think a lot of my work ethics came from him. Not all, the Marines played a key role in that also. The Marines gave me the boast I needed before I met Steve. His old foreman was not going to be with him in the coming fence season, and he needed to replace him. We talked at length at the airport while in downtime with Alpine Taxi, and he agreed to give it a try and see if it could work for both of us. I think my first job was in Hayden next to the Yampa River. It was a barbed wire fence. I could be wrong, but almost anywhere we worked the scenery itself was awesome. Getting paid to enjoy someone else's paradise was kind of neat. Everything was really basic when it came to the fencing, but learning the ins and outs of everything has been the interesting part. How to do simple things seemed silly at first but making a mistake would take hours to fix. There are also the simple things, like choking up on your hammer at first or wearing gloves to keep from getting blisters. I know it sounds simple, but a lot more people than you think don't have the basic mechanical skills. Doesn't make me or Steve better than someone else, but as you know the way things are today, a lot of people can't even swing a hammer. It's kind of sad when you think about it.

Being in fencing made me learn a lot of survival skills that I was never taught as I grew up. Learning basic mechanics like changing oil, changing a starter, fixing the brake line, just simple things that we needed to know when you were out in the middle of nowhere with no brakes. It's hard for me to explain a lot of things I know or learned because doing things like this is the only way I know to teach someone. Like how do you keep a line straight over the crest of a hill, how high can an Elk or deer jump, and what height should you make the fence, how deep should a chain link post be for a six-foot chain length fence, and things as simple as how many feet are there in a roll of barbwire. I can answer all of them easily, but it's best to show you how to do something than it is to read about it.

There are thousands of fun stories about me and the guys that maybe I'll write about or even talk to you personally about some of the neat things that happened out there on the fence line. Things like being stung over thirty times from hornets. The day we couldn't move a buffalo off the path, getting stuck on the side of a cliff, spending a day in the hospital after looking while Steve welded, and this is just a few of the stories I could tell. Hopefully the book will do well enough to write a book of silly life stories, or I'll tell you some in person. I'm sure Steve can remember a few.

"My roots weren't strong enough to hold me in one place at the time. If I didn't like something, I just moved on.'

CHAPTER 56

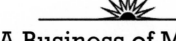

A Business of My Own
Losing another Family

I think I had worked my first year at Alpine at the point when I started a small furniture business. I called it Jim's Woodwork: You Design It, I Build It. I personally didn't have the money to start this business, but I had met someone out at the projects that had an inheritance or something that I wasn't aware of and he gave a slight loan to buy the equipment like table saw, router, and such to make the furniture. The business started very slowly but built up fairly well. I was cooking at night at the time to supplement the income and loving the furniture deal. I got to make some interesting things. I even did shelves for CDs for a new music store. At one point, we did a craft show that did me really well too.

All of this was short-lived because of my new partner of sorts. He spent all of the money he had after loaning it to me, and I had to sell most of the equipment to settle with him. From that point, I didn't have the ability to sustain a business on my own and had to close shop. This as you can imagine started a roll into depression for me. We were still struggling that summer because all I could get, so it seemed, was restaurant work. Connie had gotten complacent about us and in some ways demanding and angry with me. I couldn't seem to do anything right. She had every right to feel that way though.

She was with me during a time of indecision. I had a solid job finally but only during the winter. I hadn't started with Steve yet. Some of them other jobs I mentioned were during this time, not to mention trucking also before we came back to Colorado. She was struggling with me, and I think it rained heavily on her. I guess I could say it stressed her out. The time I spent working the ranch was probably the worst. The stresses of child support were always there also. Now looking back as I write this, I have to apologize to Connie and you, Mattie. My brother had even told me, "Jim, you need to stay in one place and one job so you can stabilize." You were right, Scot. Mattie, it was a time that I just ran from trouble. If there was something I didn't like about the boss or the work I did, I would just go somewhere else to work.

Anyone of them things I did would've turned into something I could enjoy, but I didn't have the patience at the time. It had become a destructive thing that I couldn't change for some reason. Mattie, please don't be angry with me. I was caught in that "I want more" stage that I'm sure everyone goes through. My roots weren't strong enough to hold me in one place at the time. If I didn't like something, I just moved on. None of this was because of you, Mattie.

Around the end of things with Connie is when I met Steve or should I say when we had the conversation that got me hired. Me and Connie had both grown cold with each other and sometimes it would break us into fighting, even at this time though, we had our moments. One was when we could finally move into our own place instead of the government housing. It actually ended up being a small trailer. Things calmed down for a time once I started working with Steve. The only thing that got to me at the time was Connie had a very independent life before me, and I had the same feeling of inadequacy that I felt with Susan and Dina. I couldn't finger what it was then but it was like I couldn't do anything right. I couldn't see past it at that age. Independent people aren't doing it to be mean.

I have found at this point that I have those tendencies. But because I see both sides now, I try to control it.

I feel terrible now about things from my past, but I can't change what happened. I never took the time, like I said to you kids towards the beginning of the book that you should grow up first before you get too involved. The terrible thing is the fact that once you make that leap, if it was too early, you'll always have that problem. Trust me, it will happen over and over again. It is a vicious cycle to get in, but there are a lot of single mothers out there because of it. Kids, getting married don't make you an adult. Learning about morals and ethics does make you an adult. Learning about yourself and what you want in life does. Working or going to school and finding something you're good at makes you an adult. Enjoy being young before you think of the rest of your life. Date and get a feel for the type of person who shares the same wants and needs. Don't do what I've done.

Mattie, in short, because of my immaturity, your mom and I broke up. I instigated the break up because I couldn't take the things I mentioned. I wanted to try something else. I never cheated though. I was always faithful to your mother. I just didn't want someone pointing out my downfalls. All I had to do was listen and fix whatever the problem at that moment was. This is a huge problem all over the US. I wish I could have worked things out, but you can't change things, as I said. I guess maybe we should all listen to our parents more. "Why would you do that if you can just go online and get all the counseling you need right there?" I hope there's none of you out there that feel that way. Learn who you are first and then enjoy life.

"As far as I'm concerned the military, police, and fire department are the best part of our government. "To protect and to serve"; keep it up y'all."

CHAPTER 57

A Christmas Gift

I don't remember the exact time frame of my break with Connie, but I do remember moving to Steamboat after. I would assume it was in the fall. I do recall the apartment, or should I say the room, I moved into. There was a restaurant just outside of town, and it had some rooms upstairs for renting out. Compared to most of the rooms, I had the nicest of them but it was the one above the bar. With a little effort though, it was real nice for one guy. I had a small shower, got a queen-sized bed, and had a table and two chairs with an electric burner for cooking. There was a small refrigerator and a Lounge type chair, and I was all set.

At first I didn't have a car, but living in Steamboat, I had the luxury of using Alpine to get me back and forth to work. I did end up buying a Toyota pickup for three hundred dollars; it was a '70-something. It ran great though. Not to mention it had a cab shell on it. "Remember the Toyota Dina and I lost in the bankruptcy?" This one was blue though. Other than thinking about you, Mattie, I was OK with where I ended up. I worked all the time while I was living there. I did date a new driver for a few weeks, which didn't work out. And then she quit. Not because of me though. The driver manager that had her train with me said he'd never let me train a girl again, which became an inside joke with us. Yes, I had become one of the people they used to train drivers for Hayden runs. But they were happy; I worked a lot when people called in.

I'm sure you have figured out that I wasn't exactly the party kind of guy. I did the movie thing time and again and did go play pool a few times at the local pool hall and sometimes the VFW, but in general I didn't run around much. I was, however, finally getting into a bit of a relaxed state of mind about things. I think this is also the time frame that I bought my first PlayStation. I was into the car games mostly. I did the Lara Croft thing when it first started. *Tomb Raiders* was a lot of fun back then. I also got a kick out of GTA, *Gran Turismo* 1. I know, it's childish, and all I have done is talk against it. I still am in a way. The problem is the fact that for some kids, all they do is play video games. When I was a kid, we got in trouble for playing records to much. The problem is, the parents don't put limits on them, and that's not to even mention the content of the games. There are some healthy fun alternatives to some of the trash they have out there. Including music, movies, and now even TV shows. Parents need to be parents. Don't use games and videos as babysitters. Get the kids outside and teach them some people skills. These things can be used as rewards for being good.

Things were going pretty good for me at this time. I was starting to get some self-confidence back and was enjoying work tremendously. We stayed pretty busy that year for such a late start with snow. We were the taxi company, but there were also human taxis, "Sky Cabs." One in particular that year I was kind of crushing on. Brenda became a regular conversation each day. She was married though, so it never went further than that. During Christmas time, she seemed very distant and non talkative, and as a friend, I got concerned. One day while I was sitting at the Wal-Mart parking lot, which by the way became a normal spot for me to hide as time went on, I decided on a whim to get Brenda something simple for Christmas. I found a very nice-looking scarf that had one of my favorite colors, turquoise. I went ahead and paid the two bucks or whatever it was and gift wrapped it. It wasn't supposed to be a big deal, just a friendly thought.

It was a few days after Christmas that I got to give her the gift; little did I know, at the time, this was the only thing she got for Christmas other than from her immediate family. I don't know the whole story to this day, but my little gift meant more to her than anything else from that Christmas. She had broken up with him at that point or soon after. Our friendship was growing in leaps and bounds by this time. Little did I know what kind of effect this would have on her. It was just such a simple thing as a scarf that changed everything for Brenda and me. It was the spark that made her feel good about herself and it made me feel good to see the joy in her face over such a simple thing in life.

Before that winter would end, Brenda started showing up in Steamboat to spend a lot of time with me. At one point, I came to visit her and her two kids in Craig, Colorado. You want to talk about hick town. The mall there took around five minutes to walk through, and that was taking your time. At the time she and the kids were living in a motel day to day. We had a lot of very nice times together, but I was the reluctant one of the two of us. See, it hadn't been that long since Connie and I split, and I wasn't that sure what I wanted to do yet with myself, not to mention starting a relationship with someone too. In my reluctance, I decided to get back over the road again. I really enjoyed driving and needed some time to think things through still. Brenda and I decided to keep in touch but slow things for now.

A few months went by, and I got a message to call Brenda as soon as possible. "Jim, I'm pregnant with you and I'm scared." There was a shock for me. After some conversations with Brenda, we thought it would be a good way to work things a bit if she could come over the road with me for a little while. Soon after that she got to see a bit of the world with me, starting with Salt Lake. It was enough of a distraction to make her feel better about what was happening between us. I made her feel safe, she said. Brenda was a great person and beautiful, but I don't think at the time she could handle being alone. During the course of our time together, she grew to be strong and independent.

My time in a semi went short, but I did get a chance to become a trainer before I quit. I got to train three guys while I did this, and during this time Brenda and her family made arrangements for us to move into her grandmother's old house, which was right next to her trailer on her small bit of property. The first guy I worked with was a great driver, but he had an interesting problem. For a while I didn't realize it, but the first time it became an issue, I was shocked. One day I was really tired so I got comfortable in the passenger seat and was dowsing off while he drove. "Make sure you take the, whatever the street was, exit so we can drop this load and get some sleep." He gave me a nod of compliance, and I was out.

When I said that to him, we were only sixty miles or so out from where we needed to be. Three hours later, he woke me up and said, "I think I missed the exit." After turning around and a few hours later, the sign was clear as day and he still didn't see it. He didn't know how to read. If I remember correctly, I handled it very delicately so not to upset him, and after a short while, we ended up putting him with a trainer that was a teacher before a truck driver. Like I said, he was a great driver, he just needed help I couldn't give him.

Since the time I spent having to train people, I now have a phobia of being in a vehicle of any kind with someone else driving. That does include planes. I haven't flown since then. Let's just say I had some really close calls with trainees that I had. A quick for instance was in the hills of Tennessee. I had a younger kid with me, and I had told him time and again to never try to shift going down hill. Well, he was a bit cocky and thought he hadn't picked the right gear for a hill we had and decided I didn't know what I was talking about. As he pulled it out, all you could hear was a loud "thunk!"

For any of you that don't understand, a semi has a different kind of transmission. When you push in the clutch, it doesn't completely disengage so you can shift. The RPMs have to match the gear speed before you can put it back in. Learning to drive a semi teaches you how to double clutch and in some sense shift without the clutch, "except on a grade." The truck's weight pushes it faster than you can keep up with. Now there

I was screaming at him to rev the engine while I was standing in the middle using all my weight to put the truck back in a gear before we have a runaway truck. "Rev the engine and use your left foot to brake at exactly the same time or we are both dead!" *BAM!* It went in with a very load clank underneath us. As it did, it was like slamming on the breaks at 40 mph. That brings me back to where I was at, "standing there with no restraints." I hit the windshield so hard it cracked the glass. I assume just a little faster and I could've fallen in front of the truck. Mind you, that was an afterthought.

Ever since that day and a few other incidents, I just don't like riding anywhere. The best way to explain it is "not having control of my own life." Another quick note is not being able to tell you how many times I was the first on the scene of an accident and yes, a few had fatalities. As a truck driver, with all the miles we drove, the odds of seeing at least one bad accident a week was normal. For all you highway department and rescue service people, I salute you and what you do, and I didn't just watch it on TV, I saw what you do. Thank you so much for what you do for all of us. I hope that other people reading this will say something to one of them next time you see them.

Before I became a truck driver, I hated the traffic cops, then I learned to understand them for what I saw. Every time people get a ticket, their minds wonder to "its politics, they're trying to steal our money when they should be out chasing bad guys." Or it could be the guy that doesn't understand why he got a reckless driving ticket. When all they need to do was see the accident that traffic cop was just at where a mother lost her baby because some guy was complacent about the rules of the road and sideswiped the lady and her child. That's what the cop is doing. They see the aftermath of a complacent driver who thinks the rules are a political way to make more money. As far as I'm concerned the military, police, and fire department are the best part of our government. "To protect and to serve"; keep it up y'all.

When I finally got out of the truck, Brenda and I had our work cut out for us. This house I told you about was built originally in 1892. It was part of an original homestead, which meant it had thirty-six acres when they first built it. It was a log cabin that I also had seen pictures of it from the 1800s. Brenda's father grew up in this house as a child; he was close to sixty I think, maybe his late fifties. Brenda also spent some time in that house as a child, and now her children would spend time there.

The floor was caving in, and the pluming was trashed, so if we wanted this, I had to go to work. The person that helped me do all this was her grandpa who was in his eighties. Every morning he would knock on the door with his cup for some coffee and say, "What are we doing today?" I don't remember the details of the conversations, but they kept me intrigued the whole time. We did a great job with the house. The big thing I remember the most about that was turning on the water for the first time. Seeing that there were no leaks for the first time was a good accomplishment. I was pretty proud of myself that day.

As I was remodeling the house, there was a porch, of sorts, in the back; and as I got down to the core of the house, we could see the original log walls. Because of its location, we decided to leave it open as a conversational piece of the house. Sitting there thinking about who had built that wall and lived in the home was a good but eerie feeling. I have always had a thing for history, but I think of it in a different perspective. I'm more into the everyday life of things. When I look back in time, I feel a sense of jealousy. It's no secret how I feel about technology, I feel that they, in some ways had it worse, but in most ways they didn't have the same worries as us. There would've been much more serenity in their time. People saw things the way they are and not through a computer screen. I always jokingly say that "I was born in the wrong century." Listening to Grandpa speak of old times made me weep.

Once I finished remodeling the house, it became a very cozy place to live in. It had a nice-size yard and beautiful scenery in front of the house. It made for a very serene life there for some time. Brenda's family was into traditions of hunting and camping as much as humanly possible, so we got ourselves a really nice 1976 F-150 extended cab and tried to camp as often as we could. I have very fond memories of that truck. I hope you kids can remember all the fun we had in it. Y'all used to go nuts when we went out in the country playing around in that thing. I would swerve back and forth, and you kids would slide side to side in an eccentric way and laugh out loud all the way down them old dirt roads. Then all of you would get so excited when we'd hit bumps and you'd bounce around. It was so much fun watching all of you as you grew up. While we were camping, we'd go on long walks along the river, and the food tasted so much better when you were camping. Told you, camping came back later on in life for me."

We also had to adjust our time camping for the rodeo. Brenda's sister's boyfriend worked at the rodeo in Steamboat, so we spent a lot of time with them sometimes. Her boyfriend's father was a brain surgeon or something like that, so we spent time after rodeos at their place with some of the cowboy's from the rodeo. This would become a huge influence on your kids as you grew especially you Trenton. Rodeos and fairs are small town USA's life blood. Songs, movies, and many love stories come from the fairs and rodeos. People in cities go to clubs and big parties while small town people eat corn with the stalks, turkey legs, funnel cakes, barbeque, and end up at the hoe down dance later on with the whole family in tow, speaking of Trenton

"I know that, knowing that doesn't change things much, but I wanted you to know that I saw the terrible father in me before that time and don't know if y'all will ever forgive me. I hope in this book I can change that."

CHAPTER 58

Trenton Denver
First-Time Homeowners
Then Alone Again

John Denver was a big influence on my life as you all know, and I had Zachery, which was John's son's name but not namesake. Trenton, when you were born, we thought your name was cool, but I wanted your middle name after John Denver. Your mother graciously let me name you Denver instead of John. We thought that sounded better then Trenton John. I can't tell you a story like Zach being born in an ambulance, but it was a wonderful day just the same. The coziness of our small place was very serene when you arrived. In time we realized the need to find our own place.

Work in a sense had settled down to a norm for the first time, other than eight years in the Marines, so we did OK with what money we had. If you remember correctly, I wasn't exactly someone you gave a loan to, but this was a small town, and we befriended one of the locale real estate people, and she had a trailer for sale that she owned personally. Brenda's family was raised here, so she gave us a loan of her own so we could buy. Before we moved in, there something terrible happened.

Brenda's grandmother lived on the same lot as us and called in a frantic state. Something was wrong with Grandpa.

When I arrived there, he had just fallen by his bed, and I slowly and delicately put him back on the bed. He was tiny compared to me, so it wasn't a struggle for me. He wasn't breathing, and I couldn't feel his heartbeat. Brenda got on the phone right away, and there were emergency services on their way. While this was happening, all I could remember was seeing Brenda in tears, trying to comfort her grandmother and seeing fear in both of their eyes as they watched me began to do CPR on the man I spent so many mornings drinking coffee with as I rebuilt the house he raised his children in.

In a very short period of doing CPR as best as I could, trying to remember from training that I had to have to drive a shuttle for Alpine, a policeman showed up and said to continue with the CPR while he used a piece of plastic to do the mouth-to-mouth that I had been doing. Moments later, when it seemed so quiet as we did CPR, he said "There he is." For the first time during all of this, I took a deep breath just to collect my thoughts as the EMPs showed up and asked me to leave the room so they could take care of him. It was at this time that I finally was able to comfort Brenda and her grandmother.

The policeman came over to us as they took Grandpa away and held out his hand to me and said, "You did a wonderful thing saving your grandpa like that." As I shook his hand, I finally started to cry even more about what happened just then. Sadly though, he had problems with whatever it was that killed him in the first place, and his brain didn't survive, so Brenda's father had to make the decision to stop his life support. The thing that made it easier on Brenda's whole family was the fact that because of what the policeman and I did, now they all got to say good-bye to him. Grandma thanked me because she worried about having to be in the room where he passed, but now he died in peace with the family in the hospital.

Something very simple but very resounding was given to me by her family. They gave me Grandpa's coffee cup that he had with him every morning when he came over. I cherished that cup, but sadly it got broken later on. It hurt me, but I know the spirit he had was still with me. Sadly my whole life, I've had trouble holding on to things. Building up homes and family and then losing everything each time, so the woman in my life had what she needs to move on became a norm for me. I started over way to many times. Little things like Grandpa's cup never seemed to last for me.

It's time to get back to the story at hand. Around then, Brenda and I were starting to feel a little different. I don't remember if Grandpa had any thing to do with it or not, but our age difference was causing a bit of friction. Y'all know I wasn't much of the parting type, but we went out a few times and things would go bad each time. I never went through the dancing and clubbing phase, as you know, but I did my best to get into it for her sake, but it wasn't going too well. There also became a sort of jealousy between us that wasn't there at first. I can honestly say that I never cheated on anyone, but from what people talk about, it happens way too much. Brenda would call and ask when I was coming home and I would have to answer, "I don't know, it depends on when I get this brace done." She would shoot back right away, "That isn't an answer, when will you be home?" I couldn't give an answer when I didn't know myself. It became more than it should have a few times.

All things aside though, we couldn't wait to have our own place. Our new home was in a sad state, but with the experience I had with a little construction and some of the furniture I had made, I started a long-drawn-out job of refurbishing the interior. The walls were paneling, so I trimmed it out with one-by-four and put kilze on it so I could paint it. Floors also needed a lot of work, and we needed a fence in the yard for the kids. I also took some extra poles we had on jobsites to build a homemade shed out back. All of this and I worked forty-five to fifty hours a week. I had become a workaholic like Steve. The work-related friendship we had and the New Mexican crew was making a great team and a good company for Steve, but it was hurting my relationship with Brenda.

The first year or two that I was with Steve, he hired some younger kids for the summer, but they became more problems than they were worth. One day two Mexicans came up and the one spoke English and said the other was looking for work. Steve said it depended on whether he had papers or not, and he did, so that first week we tried him out like we promised. Steve usually sent Isaro with me each day, but the communication gap made things a little difficult at times. He did do a great job and seemed very handy with all the tools we dealt with, so Friday we decided he was good person, so we told him "See you Monday." When Monday came around, I decided I need to learn some Spanish to make things easier, so I started asking him what things were in Spanish. It wasn't as hard as I thought it would be, and we became best friends in time and we still talk to this day. We spent a lot of time out there on that fence line, and he probably knows me better then any man I know.

Trenton, do you and Mattie remember the trip to see my parents? I had lost contact with your mother, Mattie, for a little while, and when I finally caught up to you, y'all were in Kansas. Getting you together with Trenton and Jason was a big highlight of my life. Jason, if you can remember, that was when you had the ceremonies for ROTC. I still to this day cherish the pictures I have from that trip. Seeing all of you together was like looking into a time capsule. If I would've done anything different in my life no matter how good or bad my life was then, none of you would exist. I apologize to all of you kids, but don't regret a single thing. The one true difficulty I have though is not spending enough time with each of you. That trip was like an eye opening for me. It was around that time that I situated my child support with a wonderful lady in the Steamboat Child Services that helped me straighten up with you kids. I know that, knowing that doesn't change things much, but I wanted you to know that I saw the terrible father in me before that time and don't know if y'all will ever forgive me. I hope in this book I can change that.

Jason, this was the time you came up to see me in Colorado. My chronology is messed up, but it was either before the trip to Texas or after. I think after. You were twelve or thirteen I think. I was so excited to see you that I forgot to pay you while you worked with me. Steve let you go to the jobsites with me. I hope you remember driving my blue F-150. Of course you never got past first gear. You hadn't learned to drive a stick yet. You may not recall where we were working, but it was doing top rail repairs at Wolf Mountain ranch. After a few days of listening to the elk bugling in the background, spending all that time by the mountain stream for lunch and seeing the Aspen glow, you still liked Texas better. I said, "What do you think of Colorado?" Then after a slight pause, you said, "Not as nice as Texas, but it's nice." I couldn't help but laugh about that. You did seem to like it there a bit. Thank you so much for letting me enjoy that time with you, Jason. The memory will always be with me, and I'll always have the picture in my head on the mountainside with you.

Trenton, I'm sorry your mom and I didn't work out, but before I get to that, I have to tell them about our big scare. I think it was Patrick's birthday and we were going to the bowling alley for a party when it happened. At the entrance, there was a metal grate for getting the snow or mud of your shoes before you went in. As we came to it, we were holding Trenton's hand, and he didn't notice the grate and tripped on it. I think his other hand was in his pocket so when he tripped, he went straight down. BOOM. He hit squarely on his head to the grate. He was crying so bad and had a golf-ball-sized bump on his head, so we got the kids settled, and Brenda and I took him to the emergency. They did a brief check on him, and Trenton's spirits seemed fine, so they told us to go ahead and head home and let him rest. We were also instructed to keep ice on it and if he became sick the next day to bring him in so they could run more tests. That night, things seemed fine.

The next day, it started slowly, but he progressively started getting sick, so with fear in our hearts, we went back to the hospital. After a few hours of testing and the nurses getting to know Trenton, everyone got real quiet. It felt strange that everyone sort of got quiet. Then the doctor came out to give us the information about the bump. "The fall isn't what's affecting your son, it's what we found in the brain area that we are concerned about. We have sent copies of the MRI to radiology in the Denver Hospital and should know something soon." He had this large area of black on the images that this small-town doctor didn't want to speculate about without consulting a specialist. "All I can tell you is were thinking what we are seeing is amniotic fluid, which hasn't gone into his spine like normal, but I don't believe there is to much concern with the little info we have." This is what he said but why was everyone so quiet all the sudden? This guy was nuts thinking I was going to be calm about this, but he did continually tell us not to worry so much.

To make a long story short, Trenton had what they called an "arachnoids cyst" and they needed to put a shunt over his skull to help drain the fluid where it was suppose to go. I was scared to death; this was brain surgery, but it was the children's hospital in Denver, which made it a little better to deal with this, was a very well-respected hospital all over the world. Trenton, you were a trooper the whole time. You never complained, and you were cheerful the whole time we were there. I think you were two or three when this all happened. I was very proud of you that day and still am. Trenton, for all of you reading this, will always have that shunt, but you would never know unless he told you about it.

Sadly after that, but in no respects because of that, Brenda and I broke up and went through some terrible times because of a misunderstanding between her and me. As I said before, this book is not about telling my kids about certain things that they don't have to hear unless they ask me or Brenda. I'm sorry again to y'all reading this and hope you understand. Some things are better left unsaid. Trenton, I am truly sorry that things went the way they did. I will tell you that my pride got in the way, and it was mainly my fault what happened. You have a good family there, and I'm here if you want me to be. That goes for all of you. Well, all of my kids, that is.

Brenda didn't want to have to take care of that old trailer. I was still working on it so that became mine, and it was still in need of some repairs. A short time before we needed to sell my big old truck, so when we split, she took the car, and I bought a Ford Probe that I actually really liked. It had a great sound system in it. My house became the new headquarters for Steve and me. Before we use to park at the back of a cleaners, but it worked better at my place after that.

This was in some ways a great year, but in the sense of you, Trenton, it was a terrible year. I was finally paying my child support and talking to you kids, but then all the stuff with Brenda put me right back in a bad state. Being alone again was not what I expected.

"I've been terrible to miss so much that you've done that I can never forgive myself for. For now though, I will cherish the memories I do have like rose petals in my mind that I will always have even after I'm gone."

CHAPTER 59

Where Were You for Nine Eleven?
Single Again

In some ways this time being single was a lot more productive then Texas. What I mean is, by becoming me. The country boy came out full force. I think deep down inside I always was a country boy. This was also my peak in a physically sense. I became a better man during this time. I was actually paying my child support, working out as much as I could; I was Steve's foreman on salary. Did most jobs on my own with Steve, and after a while I was feeling pretty good about things. I was finding myself and loving life for everything it gave me. I was actually dating for the first time in my life, meaning I didn't just jump into relationships like before.

One of the ladies I dated had a crush on me who I saw at the gas station each morning. That was short-lived when I found she was dating someone but was curious about me. I went out a few times with a flag girl from a big job site I was on. I think she was still in love with her ex. And yes, I even went to some chat rooms. Other than a girl I enjoyed talking to from the Isle of Man who liked John Denver, I would stay away from them; other than that, I was a simple man that loved his music and movies, with an occasional video game on the weekend. Then life changed as we know it for Americans.

9/11 happened. We were driving out to 131 where the big job I was doing was and stopped by Alpine Taxi to get fuel for Steve's truck and the skid steer. Someone I know was working in the gas station that Alpine owned, and they told us about the attacks they were seeing on the TV. We ran in and watched for just a few moments because we needed to get to the jobsite. I kept the radio on all day long so we could check in from time to time to see what was happening. Just like everyone else, I was dumbfounded. As a Marine, I was pissed off and wanted to go wherever they needed me. Work was difficult, but it was work that we needed to get done. The worst part of it all was that I had no cable now, so I didn't watch any of the broadcasts about the towers. The radio was my news channel at the time. In my anger and frustration, all I could do was cry all night, sitting alone in that trailer, listening to the horror that was now part of Americans' burden, that horror was terrorism.

I thought to go back in but decided that my life was here now, and I had responsibilities that I couldn't ignore. I gave all of you eight and a half years of my life and wasn't sure if a thirty-something running from the bad guys was a good idea. I listened intently to keep up with things especially when they decided to send our boys over there to take care of business so it doesn't come over here. I also knew that meant one of my kids may end up over there someday too. Jason was a good candidate for it with ROTC. God bless you for your patriotism, Jason. After that, the year went by slowly for me. We finished the big job, and now Steve had us a Skid Steer which was a great asset to the fencing company.

The last thing Steve and I did was a pipe job that we needed to tie up for the winter, but winter made it hard on us and came early. A big storm came in and dumped three feet of snow that week, and the day we went there was almost a whiteout. So we sucked it up and put on the bibs and went for it. "Jim, I know you don't usually weld for me, but I just need you to hold them in place till I tack weld them. Whatever you do, don't look at the welder while it's sparking." "No problem," I said with a grin, but little did I know. Well, a few times I saw it by accident and thought he was crazy. "This doesn't hurt at all," I thought to myself. It was a tough day for us, but we got it done and headed home. Didn't think much of it and went to bed, not feeling a thing.

At around midnight or so it hit me. The pain was like someone literally taking a pin and poking my eye over and over again. The pain was so intense that I couldn't open them or see for that matter. Now the only person I know in the area is Brenda, but to her credit, she helped me out that day and took me to the hospital and stayed with me till they sent me home. They gave me some pretty strong drugs and put patches on my eyes and I was to keep them covered for twenty-four hours. I was only blind for twenty-four hours, but it felt so bad having no control and not seeing light. I fumbled my way around and would highly suggest to all of you to listen when they say not to look. As it happens, you will feel nothing but it will come back with a vengeance.

That winter at Alpine went pretty good and I also spent a little time at some of the restaurants on the mountain. Because of my jacket being Alpine, we got a lot of discounts, being the only cab company there. I did go to a view clubs but usually it was the VFW for me. I always used to joke about the fact that they say Steamboat is a cowboy town and the only place for a long time with country music was the VFW. I dated a few people there and also started bowling on leagues for the first time. Love bowling, by the way. My average is around 170 to 180. Then there was Allie.

I was at the Slope Side Grill eating dinner, and these two ladies walked in and sat next to me at the bar. Probably the only seat at the bar I thought at the time. It didn't take long to know they were from England by their accent. I think they were surprised at first that this old cowboy would've been to England, but they knew by the things I said about the area. Yes, there are a lot of people out there that say something and aren't telling the truth. If you've been somewhere, you can usually tell they're lying. Anyway, the one that spent most of her time with me was Allie. She was a cute redhead from Manchester, and she was a "copper" as the English put it, a cop. They had just arrived from England and were on holiday for three weeks. As the conversation was close to ending, I invited her and her friend for some country music at the VFW the next day and they accepted.

That started my only long-distant relationship in my entire life. We spent as much of the three weeks as my job would let us together. Once she went back, we kept in contact over the phone for a whole year I think it was. I could buy phone cards for twenty bucks at 7-Eleven. Steve thought I was nuts, but it probably kept me out of trouble I guess. She was good person, but I know now nothing was ever to come of it at all. I could never see myself not living in the US. Don't get me wrong, she was nice and I did truly love Europe, but I am American through and through. "Life goes on" as they say.

Summer came again, and this was going to be an interesting one. I get a call from Dina, and the boys are coming out for a month to see me. I about wet myself, I was so excited. The last time I saw them was when Zach was two. Now its ten years later, and I have my own place and a good job that gives me the ability to take them to work each day. I couldn't wait to see them. This was to be one of the best summers of my life. I was dating someone at the time, and her daughter was the same age as the boys. Y'all remember her I assume? This was going to be intense. Don't forget about Trenton, guys. I was going to have all three at my house at the same time.

I went down to the Denver airport, nervous, as all get up. Seeing you two again for the first time in ten years was just paradise for me. I hope you two had as much fun as I did. We spent some time playing videos together. Zach, at one of the jobsites, was out running around and caught a baby deer in the bushes, and it was tough to tell him that this is not a good thing due to the fact that the human smell will scare the baby's mother. We spent some time at the riverside, playing, but the memory that sticks out the most for me, boys, was the trip to the falls. Y'all remember that? There in Steamboat and very serene to say the least. The boys and I spent a lot of time wading in the water and picking out pretty rocks. I also got some beautiful pictures of you boys there. I also have found memories of taking y'all to the Slope Side Grill a time or two. It was all overwhelming to me, even seeing them out on the fence line working.

Boys, and all of you reading this, being up there at the falls and everywhere else we went meant more to me then you could've ever known, but now that you're reading this, maybe you can see how much. We have been talking about all these little things in life throughout each chapter. The bottle of milk in England; being out on the ocean at night looking at the stars, the tree, and the bug in the desert; the beautiful scenery all over the US in the semi, Horseshoe Lake on an early morning; the beach on a cloudy dreary day in Belgium; the shores of Norway seen from the ship; the whales' tail breaching the sun on the side of the ship; the Maroon Bells (which I forgot to mention); and so many other things I'm forgetting for now are nothing compared to seeing you kids the few times that I did as you grew up. All six of you are the little things that save me. I've been terrible to miss so much that you've done that I can never forgive myself for. For now though, I will cherish the memories I do have like rose petals in my mind that I will always have even after I'm gone. I love all of you with all my heart.

When I was getting every thing set up for them to go home, something wonderful but a little strange happened. I was talking to Dina on the phone, and she got much quieter just before she asked me this serious question that I'm sure, in some ways, she was still hesitant to ask me. "Jim, I need to know if you can keep Zachery for a while. He tried to run away, and he has problems listening to me. He needs his father right now." And I was speechless. As quickly as I could gather my thoughts, I said, "Of course I can take him, and for letting me do this, I thank you from the bottom of my heart for trusting me with him." Don't take it wrong, Zach, but in the back of my mind, I thought this was nuts. I was a single guy just having fun and didn't know what to do, but I'm here to tell you it was the best thing I ever did. Zach, you and I know this was very difficult for both of us. See, Zach was a little out of hand, but with a little Marine Corps and fatherly love, everything turned around as far as I could see.

I decided I wanted a bigger school for Zach to give him more opportunities and for the sake of him having a great football and basketball club. Nothing against Hayden. I just wanted him to have a bigger school. The competition would be much tougher. So after a little while, I found a decent apartment for the two of us, and we started our life together. It was a rocky start, but we became good friends and had a lot of fun with each other, but now he had a caring father to discipline his actions.

"If you can't share the simple things in life with your children, why should they ever share with anyone else in society?"
"It just fit for me to love NASCAR under my circumstances from the past."

CHAPTER 60

Becoming the Father
I Should Have Been

Zachery had a tough beginning from what I understand. Not from his mother but from the man she was seeing. He had a half sister with him, but he was way too tough on Zach. As you know, I could relate to that real well. Zach started his grounding pretty much right off the bat with me because he lied to me about something I can't remember in Hayden. When we got to Craig, something else got him in trouble. My sunglasses. Every year, I bought a nice pair of sunglasses for both of my jobs. Over the weekend, I didn't wear them much; then Monday came, and no glasses. "Zach, have you seen my glasses anywhere?" "No, did you leave them in the truck?" he said. "No, I put them on my shelf with my wallet all the time." With a hint of fear in him, I heard him say as he walked towards his room, "Sorry, Dad, I didn't see them anywhere." That seemed a little strange, he was avoiding me now. Just before we were both going to head out, I snuck in Zach's room and took a look around and there they were, broken in half.

"Zachery, you sure you didn't see them anywhere at all?" I even said it real slow with eye-to-suspicious-eye contact. He took away the contact and said in a small voice, "No, sorry, Dad." "Zach, you know you're getting off being grounded this week, right?" "Yeah." This time it was said with a hint of fear in his voice again. That's when I pulled out the glasses and said "I think that is going to be extended a bit." He saw them and tried his best to apologize about breaking the glasses and that it was just an accident. To his relief and shock, I didn't freak out and start yelling at him. "Zach, you're grounded again, but not for breaking my glasses, I know they're cool glasses, and you wanted to try wearing them like me, but you lied about it. I could care less about the glasses, but I can't let you keep lying to me. It's got to stop or you'll be grounded your whole life." After, I think it was eight or nine weeks, he finally got the message. I was finally being the father I never was.

A little necessary short story about video games is in order here. I was very found of a racing game called "Gran Turismo." The new one got set back on its release date and I was having withdrawals about racing there for a while. To take the edge of, I rented a NASCAR game to relieve the pain. Now some father and son's love things like football and basketball. I have some personal reasons not to like them but I tried to share that with Zach as much as possible but because of NASCAR we found our thing. We both feel in love with the sport in a hard way. Me, probably more than Zach but it was something we started together. It just fit for me to love NASCAR under my circumstances from the past.

Now when it came to sports, I, as a father, was spoiled to death. Zach, you were incredible. "Boy, your son played a great game" resounded each week most of the time. He has a gift, I tell you. But for some reason, schoolwork was not very good to him. He was so distracted from everything that he did outside of school that he did poorly in school. He was passing, but just barely. We talked about it many times, but sometimes I wondered if I ever got through to him about the importance of school. It was strange to me at first because I knew he was one of the popular kids in school, which was a shift from what I was in school, but his schoolwork was done very lazy like for me. On the field you couldn't stop all the energy, but he had none when it came to school. Maybe all the pressure that I never had from being popular was just hard on you, Zach, I'm not sure. It's funny, Zach looks just like me when I was a kid, and he is the cool kid, and I was the dork that couldn't find a girlfriend.

We had a lot of fun during that time, and Zach even put up with me dating a few girls before I met my next wife. Women were becoming very difficult in my relaxed world. The thing that was so different now was that I understood who I was and knew the type of person I get along with. I talked about this at length before, waiting till you're in your mid—to late twenties, but I can't take what happened to me away now. Some of you I hope will take the time to get to know yourself first.

Zach and I were starting to mesh very well, and for the most part he wasn't lying like he was before. That is not to say he didn't try a few things here and there. In general, Zach, you did great. Remember all the long weekends playing Halo together, Zach? Of course most of the time he beat me, but it was a lot of fun doing stuff together. I would think that some of the best times were out at the lake. We made up this game were we took a volleyball and played a sort of cross between dodge ball and 500. If you caught the ball, you received fifty points, if you were hit by the ball, the other person got fifty points, and if you tried to catch the ball then dropped it, you lost fifty, and he gained fifty—first to 500 wins. The stupidity of it all was that you were wading in the water, and trust me, that ball hurt like hell when you caught it. It was a lot of fun though, wasn't it, Zach? Remember what I told all of you? "Get a stick and go be children with your children, they will always remember it."

Those are just the little things in life that save us all. If you can't share the simple things in life with your children, why should they ever share with anyone else in society? We are enabling the younger generations to have apathy towards the world which shuts them down from ever experiencing all the many things out there in this world. If your parents don't care and just go out and work their self to the ground so they can give you things society says you need, why shouldn't they get everything they need from the government? They don't care; they have a free ticket . . . All you had to do is pick up a stick and give your kids the hunger for life. Share the experience of life with your family. Experience can be considered wisdom as much as any book or computer. There is nothing like being there. Be there for your children. Don't make the same mistakes I made, kids.

"When we got back to the kids, it seemed very surreal seeing all of them playing after what the adults had went through that day."

CHAPTER 61

A Simple Romance and The End of a Good Man

The relationship thing wasn't going real good for me, but Zach and I were. Work also was still doing real well for me too. I was doing a little of both now and had picked up these two guys in Steamboat from the airport who wanted to see a country bar. I let them know about what I told you about Steamboat and the fact that there were no country bars and said they would have to go to the Holiday Inn in Craig for a true country bar. They said, "We're in." "OK, you'll have to set up a ride because I have to work in the morning and can't drive y'all around all night." They decided to rent a car from the local dealer and met me in Craig.

They were from Europe, somewhere that I hadn't been, so we talked a lot the whole night about this and that. I happened to notice a girl giving me that stare we all know, but I wasn't going to be a rude host, so I said nothing to her during the evening. The two gentlemen made their way into a conversation with some of the local girls, and it was time for me to head back to Zach. I think it was early, and decided I wanted to let the girl I had been staring at time and again that I thought she had beautiful eyes and a great smile. After a short pause and a quick thank you, I gave her my number and said my boy was waiting for me and apologized for leaving.

She gave me her smile, but I think she was a little shocked that I left so quickly.

The next morning, she called me bright and early, and we set a lunch date with all of us. (She also had two kids of her own.) Little did I know she saw me plenty of times at her job, which was at the feed mill where Steve bought a lot of our fencing material. Her name was Sabrina, and the children were Alex and Jessie. Alex, her son I spoke of earlier. Jessie, her daughter was a bit younger. We had a lot of the simple things in common like music, movies, and such, so we got along pretty well. Zach got along real well with the kids, and it all just seemed to fit. I was tired of women, she was tired of men. She was a bit younger than me, which was becoming an MO of sorts for me. Most of her family was in Grand Junction, but her father and sister lived here in Craig. She owned a quaint little ranch-style home right by the bike park and city park and had a fenced yard in back. It all just seemed to fit.

We decided after a short time that we should just make things easier and move in together. Obviously, I just moved from my apartment to the house. Steve's business was downsizing, so I started working more with Alpine in the summer going to Denver two or three days a week, and Sabrina was getting a raise and a new title, so it was nice and smooth at first. I was even in contact with Mattie again and was hoping to see her soon. The children took to me in a very short period also. It wasn't long after that they were calling me dad. I was all they've ever known since they had no contact with their father. My life seemed to be coming into place for me. Then the rug was pulled away from me, and I fell right on my face. Something that had never crossed my mind in my life so far in life: my father was dying.

A little catching up is in order now. Over the past few years since my time in Texas and my move to Colorado, I became the son that called once in a while and spoke of simple things with my mother and father for a time and went back to life. They were always there for advice or at least to bounce a stupid idea off periodically, but that was the extent of it. I was a wanderer, as you all know, and wanted to see the other side. Dad understood this and was happy that we had each other in the sense of him and me having the same spirit to fly. I wish or hope some day Scot will write down some of our father's stories because there were just as many as me. We had a kindred spirit, as it were. Think back on the day we spent together in Palm Springs, the swimming lesson in the Gulf, the terrible day at the trailer, the slap on Bob's back, and many more that I haven't the time or paper to tell you. He was a man's man to most people, and even though things were tough as a child, he was still my father. Blood or not was never an issue with me.

He was a smart man, probably a little too smart when you think of some of the things we talked about, but he never did terrible things like killing or beating on people. He was always there for a laugh as we all grew up. He was creative, strong-willed, and in general a kind soul. He quit drinking in time, and that was the only downfall that created the problems with me and other things, but he faced that demon and lived on. In a roundabout way, he gave me the strength I needed for the Marines and other challenges in life, and most of all he was a proud man. Hearing that the time was coming was something I didn't expect until it was too late. I talked with him before things went south, and in conversation, I knew he was proud of me in his own way. He wasn't much the corny type, but he had his moments. Mom and Scot kept telling me that there was nothing I could do and I had a family to look after and they would keep me informed of dad's condition.

They were right that I couldn't do anything, but looking back, I was devastated that I didn't take steps to go down there before something happened. Money was becoming an issue again, and life was becoming more and more difficult for me and my family. Dad was on life support and from what I understood most of the time had no idea where he was or let alone know who anyone was. Lisa at Alpine Taxi again saved me and helped me get down so I could be there for the funeral and to see my family. Mom and Scot somehow knew this was going to affect me worse than anyone else that would be there. I tend to be a little sensitive even though most people that know me don't ever see it. I honestly don't know where Pam was, if anyone is wondering. My mind was a little preoccupied.

Sabrina and I had picked up a great car, which was an Oldsmobile that was very comfortable, even with an extra person with us. Yes, we were able to pick up Mattie again for the sake of saying good-bye to grandpa. So on this sad trip, I had my new fiancé, Zach, Jessie, Alex, and Mattie. Then when we got there, Jason also showed up. My thanks to Connie and Susan for that moment. Losing my father was devastating, but seeing my children there made it a little easier. Everyone except Mattie and Jason had never met Dad, and that waned heavy on me the whole time I was there. Dad would have been so proud to see so many grandchildren that day. Of course knowing Dad, he would've found a place to hide after an hour or two. He loved kids, but that many would've been hard for him to deal with. It was one of the most wonderful things I'd ever seen.

At first I was OK at the funeral, but because of you, Scot, I lost it. I say that jokingly because sooner or later it was going to happen. Scot picked out the music and took care of pretty much everything, but one song in particular blew me away. Y'all know by now music means a great deal to me. The song in question only Scot, Mom, and I would know of its significant effect on all of us. It is an old song from the fifties called "The Old Master Painter." "The old master painter from the faraway hills, painted the desert and the daffodils." Dad loved that song and would sing it all the time. He also put it on that tape I mentioned that Scot sang "Rhinestone Cowboy" in. I did "Crying." Remember? It was quiet as it came on, and I think everyone there heard me say, "That's not fair," when the song started. That's when I lost it. To Sabrina's credit, she did the best she could to comfort me. I hope I told her that. I'm sure I did though.

After that, Dad got a military burial, which I'm proud to say I get one too. The people from the recruit depot did a wonderful job, and it was a tough thing when they gave Mom the flag. I know that will be very tough on my wife when the time comes. It was a wonderful service, and I'm so glad I at least was able to make it down for it. Mom and Scot made it very clear many times that Dad knew my situation and had no bad feelings when I couldn't make it down at first. Remember we did talk for a moment on the phone just before all this happened. I miss you, Dad, may you rest in peace. I'm sure he sees me writing this book also. Love you, Dad.

When we got back to the kids, it seemed very surreal seeing all of them playing after what the adults had went through that day. These were his grandchildren in which some of them he never met. Don't let that happen to your children if at all possible. I think that was the best medicine a person could ever wish for in those times. After saying good-bye to Dad, it was just what I needed. All of you kids at one time or another came to me in private and asked if I was OK. That was the little thing that saved me. Jessie and Mattie were almost in tears when they saw my eyes watering.

Looking at old pictures and talking about old times with all of us sitting at the table was a wonderful time. Some of the stories would bring us all to tears in laughter or silence the room at times. One story that always made me smile was when my dad used a ladder and a hammer to fix part of the roof and found a nest of bees instead. I still see him swinging that stupid hammer all around like fly swatter, thinking in the madness that he might hit them with it. He wasn't exactly happy with us kids for laughing at him, but as I remember, it was a nice family day. I also remember that a few times as we grew up, we would have nice dinners that we would laugh so hard that I would have to take off my belt because it hurt so much when I was laughing. He also did the thumb game, which we would have to catch it before he put it back in his hand. Then later he taught me how to make a kid think I was taking of my bionic finger. All of those things came out that day and eased all our hearts and let us know he would always be with us in spirit.

Luckily, I still have plenty of pictures from that time when five of my children got to share and care for one another in some very resounding ways. How did we keep the kids company for the short period we were gone? Yes, I admit they were playing Halo. I know, I preach about it so much, but sometimes it was a great way to spend time with my kids. Maybe for y'all that don't play games with their kids, try using that to break the ice with your kids. Trust me it will work like a charm. But please learn by doing so it's easier to watch over the amount of time they spend and the type of games they play. That doesn't mean you shouldn't get them motivated to go outside. That is a must in every household. That gave me and the kids some bonding time in an otherwise dreary time for them when we were down there.

"Even though it was all gone, the memories rushed in on me and made me feel whole again. The one thing that was constant there was the sound of nature."

CHAPTER 62

A Downhill Spiral

The trip home was fairly quiet, and dropping Mattie off was another hard thing to do. Oh, how I wish I would've had more time with all of you. We got back into the groove of life that seemed to be getting tougher and tougher. Steve was going to be moving to Texas, I was able to stay during the summer with Alpine, which wasn't much for the area, but was better than nothing. We had to get back on welfare to make ends meet. For a long time, I was doing real well with Steve; he paid me very well. I didn't see very much of it because of child support. At one point I made $3,200 a month and paid $1,900 a month in child support. That went on for a while until Jason was emancipated. The help from the lady I told you about in Steamboat was priceless. She made sure to help me change things to match my income, which was cut at least in half. They can only take 65 percent of my income for child support, but I've been paying it ever since she helped me set it up.

One bright spot in all this was a phone call that I got from an aunt of mine that someone wanted to speak to me. Yes, twenty years later, I heard Nicholas's voice on my phone. I think I was in Denver waiting for my pickup to head back to Steamboat. We spent many hours talking about each other. My mother always kept me informed of how he was doing all through his life, and I had been a grandpa for three years. I had a few pictures, and he sent me some more later. I explained everything that you guys read about towards the beginning and things went pretty well with him. I really wanted to see him though.

Sabrina and I were getting by, but the house was becoming almost every penny we had to keep things going. She had bought the house through all those loans they had set up through the government. One way they did this is they piled the interest on the price and you paid that later. Not to mention through the red tape to qualify, they jacked up the price of the house so you could finance 100 percent, and on top of that, you were paying almost double the interest compared to most loans. Then they charged her insurance through their own friend's insurance companies, which was jacked up also. As you can imagine, I was not happy with what they did to a struggling mother with two kids. Slowly but surely, Sabrina was beginning to see how hard this was going to be for us. One day I told her how bad I wanted to see Nicholas, and she was very supportive of me, so we set it up so I could see my grandkids.

Driving up there was actually quite strange for me. As I drove listening to music, my whole life was beginning to come back to me full circle. Twenty years before, I was heading to boot camp with thoughts of Nick welling up inside me. I was starting my life back then. Now I was headed to see the one person who started my adult life out. Nick had some problems, and everyone around him thought that maybe by getting to know me, which from what I understand was a hidden secret all his life, could maybe set him straight and get him of a destructive path. You also have to remember I hadn't been back to Duluth in some eighteen to twenty years. Little did I know that this would set the course to where I am now in my life. I think though that it was all meant to be.

I spent a week or so with Nick and my grandkids, Emma and Ayden. As I am sure you can imagine, this was a very intense moment for me. These children were here because of a so-called mistake I made twenty years ago. I knew deep down, and so did Sam, that this was never a mistake. We had started a chain reaction to bring Emma and Ayden into this world. Life is never a mistake. Nick, you have a wonderful family, and I hope that maybe this book will be a guide to give you the strength to carry on in a fashion that gives you the experience of life. What is the meaning of life? Life and what you make it out to be, seems a pretty logical answer to that question. I hope that you can take the morals and ethics I've talked about and use them to be the wonderful father I wish I would have been for all of you.

When we, Nick and I, went out to see where he was conceived and where my memories come from, I was shocked to see the old trailer gone. Everything was gone. The garage, chicken coops, the old van, and the old shed. The bent bar I mentioned had also been taken down. Granted they were probably old when we were here, but this was a bit of a shock. There were a few things that I could make out like the foundation for the garage was barely visible, and there was the tree my mother tied wire for clothes line had the indentation of the wire in it. That was about it though, from what I remember. The trail going south had been made into a road, and they built a house a little farther in the woods. I spoke to him for a moment, and I guess the last guy that lived in my old home burned it down, trying to get the insurance he put on it. Bad thing was they caught him in the act so he didn't get anything.

Even though it was all gone, the memories rushed in on me and made me feel whole again. The one thing that was constant there was the sound of nature. Remember me talking about the wind blowing through the trees and the star-filled nights? It was so peaceful being there with Nick, and later I took Zach, Alex, Jessie, and Sabrina out there to show them. I feel a rush every time I go out to Horseshoe Lake. It brings back a lot of memories for me there.

When I returned, I was a changed man. Things that I grew to love about Colorado just didn't seem so exciting to me anymore. I had fallen into a cold state of remorse. Things slowly started to fall apart for me. I was still content and happy; it was just different now. I assume Sabrina felt it but left it alone for the time being. I finally decided to give fencing a try on my own. This would get me back in the field, and it wouldn't take much to get it set up. The only hard part was obtaining a truck. That happened by pure luck when I saw this '82 F-250 that had glass packs, making it sound like the Jake brakes on a semi. It also had a 400 small-block, which gave me plenty of power all for only two thousand dollars. A few other things and I had my own company.

My first jobs gave us enough to at least get some things paid off before It got really stupid. I swore I would never ride a motorcycle, but we were with Sabrina's family out riding in the desert and it looked like a lot of fun. Well, I hopped on for the first time since my dad's Hawk Hondamatic in the late '70s and *bam*, there goes a broken leg for my first ride, and I'm the only employee I have. One kind of neat thing was seeing the fear in Jessie's eyes as she kept calling out, "Are you OK, Dad?" The boys were also very concerned too, but they weren't crying like her. "These people really loved me," I thought as they all tried to help me into the car.

I had ripped my ACL, which I don't think I need to go into much detail about that, but at my age, recovery would take a little while. The worst part was them having to let the swelling down and getting my insurance set up because I, as the father, didn't rate insurance from the government, and a new ACL wasn't at the top of their list of priorities so I was out of work for more than a month. This just added on to our troubles as you can probably imagine.

Long story short, I went through the surgery and due to the laziness of the only two unemployed people, this time of year was digging and tamping within a week of the surgery. Pain or no pain, I had to get money coming in again.

Remember me telling y'all about Alex and the similarities we shared with the kids in school and how he shut down all the time? In time and the fact that I understood the dilemma with Alex and his school, I was able to get him at least calmed down and not shutting down at school. He just needed someone to give him some self-esteem and confidence. Alex, I hope you didn't think I was too harsh or bad to you. I could see the fears in your eyes when we talked about school. I hope that things have worked for you since then.

Jessie, you did real well in school, but we talked a lot about you being stronger and less naïve about things. I was so worried about you growing up and heading out here without that strength. I hope that has come to fruition. She was such a friendly person, and I just wanted to see her build on her strengths and not get her in a bad spot. All of you women out there, I don't think I would have had enough strength to do what y'all do. Being married, we see the things that all of you go through that are better left unsaid. My heart goes out to all of you. To all of you boys out there, hurting a defenseless woman is the lowest thing you could ever do in life. My children, if they didn't know anything, they knew not to touch a woman. It does go both ways though. Don't abuse a gentleman just because you know you can. Showing respect goes a long way in life, especially when it comes to your relationship with your significant other. Take care of each other. If I ever find out about something happening to my girls, you better hope I never find you.

During all these struggles, the kids and I made Halo and other games a good way to have fun together. Then because of Zach, I got into a card game called Magic the Gathering, this became a shared collection I had with the boys. We spent many hours playing, and as things got more difficult, I personally was getting into these kinds of things more and more. It was becoming what I now see as a distraction from the everyday things we have to deal with. Please don't jump to conclusions yet, I still do appreciate a good race game, and I do still like looking at the artwork on magic cards. Remember I was a terrible D and D person. It was my fantasy world of sorts and still is. "Things in moderation," I think someone said that once. With a lot of help and support from my fiancé, I've learned to keep these kinds of things in check. I still love the games, but they're not obsession to me anymore. NASCAR on the other hand has become an obsession. No different than people into football or basketball.

A little later in life, I got a terrible phone call from Nick. He had another child, my grandchild since I had been there, and something happened, and he passed away. While Camden was sleeping, he died of CO_2 poisoning. Doctors said sometimes kids will cover their faces with the covers and breathe their own CO_2. Nickolas sounded fine and hurt, but I feel the calmness in his voice was shock. I obviously got to Duluth as soon as possible, but having to say good-bye to a grandchild you never got to know was devastating to me. During this time, I was starting to feel the urge to move back up here for good to be around my grandkids and live the rest of my days. Seeing Camden in some ways solidified my thoughts.

"Zach, you turned out to be a wonderful kid, and I think you'll be a great man. I'm proud that I was able to have a part in that upbringing and hope that you will pass things on to your brother Chris."

CHAPTER 63

Coming Home

When I got back to Colorado, my family was there with open arms and love. We talked at great length about moving to Minnesota, and I was able to plead with them to go. Sabrina wasn't too excited about selling the house but went through with it after I gave a promise that never came to fruition. My promise that never came to pass was to run back to Colorado in one year if things didn't work out. We put the house on the market, and sometime later, we found a young couple starting a family that took the house. The day we closed, we hit the road, and after a quick call to let people know we left, my heart was set on Duluth, but my aunt talked us into going to Marquette, Michigan, instead. Three things real quick before I go on: aunt Judy had adopted my sister's last born who's name was Sara, so this would be neat to see my niece. If you look back, you'll remember I was born in Ironwood, Michigan, which is just west of Marquette. Also Judy was always my favorite aunt. I'm curious Zach, do you remember listening to Tony winning a road course race and losing my Newman hat as we traveled through Minnesota? We couldn't miss a race, God forbid. I really liked that hat.

We ended up having to stay with her and her husband for a few weeks. which became an issue later on. We never were able to pay them back for their help. Taking this plunge and moving to Michigan first, was not a smart move for us financially.

The only thing we could find was some government housing in a town called Gwinn. The housing was old apartment at an abandoned air force base. The apartments were clean, but the nickname for the place was the Projects. (They were just like were Connie and I lived in Craig.) This wasn't the big part of the problem though. There wasn't hardly any work in the area for someone nonprofessional like me. In a few months when we were close to being evicted, I finally got lucky and found a small truck company who hauled wood chips down to Green Bay. I took the job out of necessity, but that wasn't going to work for me. As you all know, the thought of hauling in the winter gave me the edge to keep looking while I was working there and hopefully find something else before winter. Hauling out of the plant we got the chips from, I met a guy that worked for a separate entity of the plant and got a job before winter hit, using the chips for something else other than the paper mill in Green Bay. You know the wood chips you buy for gerbils and rabbit, making them sacks of chips was my new job?

I actually really enjoyed that job at first but the so-called "foreman" had some serious anger issues, and after a heated discussion on how he treated the two younger guys who we worked with, I lost it, and it came to blows between us. Because of my own morals and ethics, the owner wasn't able to talk me into staying, so I quit. I felt OK about that, but it didn't help our situation because there was no work still. We finally did what we should have done in the first place and moved to Duluth. We had a month paid, so I went ahead of my family to look for work and stayed with my cousin and the aunt that was at my dad's funeral. When Sabrina and the kids arrived, I was still struggling to find work, and Sabrina, in her first week there, landed a job at Wal-Mart, which she loved; and I was still jobless. We joked about it, but very soon after I was offered three jobs and decided to go back in the restaurant field to feel things out on whether I could fence again up here. My job was being a manager at a nice restaurant that I still work at to this day, so I won't say which. It was a bit of a rocky start there with all the soap operas at the restaurant due to a few employees that weren't real happy about me. But before too long, it became a home to me with a whole new set of great friends in which I have a lot of fun with. It's a wonderful family attitude there that matches my personality very well. It gave me a place to settle down at.

The first place we lived here in Duluth was an apartment that had sloping floors and was pretty shot. This was the only place we could afford at the time, in the sense of a down payment. The one great thing was that it was right by the river so I got to take the kids fishing there for a while. It was very peaceful out there in an outskirt of Duluth by a park. Luckily, that didn't last long and we ended up in a nice house by an area called Riverside. The family really liked this place much better, especially the house itself. Sadly, I just fast forwarded through some of the hard times we had sleeping on floors and not having any furniture other than a few items we could fit in a U-Haul trailer from Colorado a year ago. Moving to Duluth marked the year I promised, and we needed some more time to make a decision. Under the circumstances, it seemed that we could make it now, but Colorado was weighing heavy on Sabrina and her kids. This was the start of a stale relationship and a time of separating ideas of what we both wanted in life. I was starting to feel very content with finally being home, and our love faded away, but our devotion seemed to linger.

One of the original ideas about moving here was to give Alex a new start and put Jessie in a bigger school to make her a stronger person than the sheltered person that she had become back in a small town like Craig. They were both scared at first, but it didn't take long for both of them to start adapting with there new surroundings. A suggestion to hang out with some of the Goth kids at school worked perfectly and he made a lot of friends in this type of crowd. We were still heavily into gaming and magic, so the Goths I felt would be a good fit for him. Mind you, I told him there would never be tattooing or piercing until he was old enough to be responsible about it. I told him I didn't mind the clothes too much, but it would be silly to make something permanent at the age of sixteen. What he liked now and what he will like when he is twenty-six will be completely different. I personally have a tattoo if you remember that cross and ribbon I got from Camp Johnson. This many years later, you can barely make out the cross. With strong morals from home, he did real well with the Goth thing.

Jessie, you turned out real good too. Actually, she became a bit of a firecracker, to some extent. Me and you went round and round a bunch of times. She became very independent of herself and the plan which seemed distant to her and Sabrina came to fruition. I'm very proud of you, Jessie; you became a very strong young lady who doesn't take any s—from anyone, including me. Good for you. The only problem I could see before things went south with me and your mother was you two taking advantage of her at times. Respect your parents, people, it isn't supposed to be hard, right or wrong they are your best friend. If your situation is filled with angry parents and abusive, then I understand that different things can put you in a different position. Also realize that grounding or taking your cell phone does not give you the right to treat your parents like dirt. You do something wrong you face up to it.

In the course of a few years, Sabrina and I became roommates of sorts. It started out very simple and ended very simple. Things always were a little tough for us, but we muddled through it each day. I could see the passion for Colorado in her and the kids. Zach also was feeling homesick, and before he got out of school, he wanted to spend some time with his mother. He felt terrible about it, but after we talked with the sadness welling up in his eyes, I knew it was time for him to be with his mother. Zach, you turned out to be a wonderful kid, and I think you'll be a great man. I'm proud that I was able to have a part in that upbringing and hope that you will pass things on to your brother Chris. Chris, I hope you can see a bit of me in your brother, and I hope life will work for you also. This book doesn't replace me, but it's like an apology for all that I missed in your life and all of my children. I hope that in time you will at least know that through a tough life, I did the best that I knew how without too much help. I wish I hadn't been so naive, but as I said before, I wouldn't change anything that would jeopardize the fact that all of you walk this earth. I hope you see me for who I am now.

Sabrina and I discussed the possibilities, but she saw the love I had for Duluth, and I saw the love she had for Colorado and we made a decision together that it was the best for all parties involved. The parting was difficult, but there I was as they all drove off, alone again in the area I grew up in Duluth, Minnesota. Now what do I do?

I lost count of how many times this happened to me. This time it felt different. Somehow through this entire thing called life, I was right back where it started. I was single, homeless in three weeks, and starting a new life. It was like being eighteen all over again. It was as if it all was supposed to happen. I served my country, had all my children, at least started their lives, worked many jobs, got an education in life, and now it was time to start a life for me. I had practically nothing but some old furniture we bought at the goodwill store by the big bridge. Of course I had my Xbox and a pile of games. Not to mention my weekly medicine of NASCAR. I wasn't sure what was going to happen.

Months ago, I had said a prayer to my spiritual entity (I told you I wouldn't speak of religion so I say my spiritual entity) that I wanted stability and happiness. If you can imagine the shock of losing everyone left in my life, I was dumbfounded. Sabrina had taken most of the stuff we had acquired and left me with what she didn't want. The house seemed so empty though. I was left with cleaning up the house and moving on. The last few days there was a little on the depression side, but I struggled through what I had to.

I looked into so many different places; I can't even begin to give you a number. Finally in a very interesting place, I found my new home. It was an apartment on top of a small café. When I found it, I wanted it right away. I didn't care about the neighborhood or anything, I just loved the apartment itself and the fact that I can get up in the morning and go down for breakfast. My thoughts went back to the little café my parents owned when I was a child and how I wanted to be one of the regulars that came in and the owner would know exactly what

I want before I ever sat down. Of course it ended up being lunches that I went down to say hello because my favorite meal to cook was breakfast each day. The owner did make a great hot beef sandwich.

By the way, work had changed a bit after a brief episode at trying to be a car salesman. I won't talk about that because a wise rabbit once said, "If you can't say something nice, then don't say anything at all." That's all I have to say about that. Anyway, after that, I started off just waiting on tables where I am now and after a while became the dayshift bartender and managed Friday nights to give all the managers that day off. Trust me that made all of them very happy indeed. Been on that same schedule for a while now, and I love being a bartender. I still love my Friday nights for sure. With a tough economy, we had to cut down labor a lot in certain areas, but Fridays stayed busy so I have a full crew and get to be a manager instead of a dishwasher because we don't keep one on slow days. Of course after they read this, they'll be trying to get my Fridays I guess. Even though I'm not going to mention the place I work, I really enjoy that place, and the food there is very good, and trust me, when it comes to restaurants, I'm picky.

When I first started, there it was a little rough around the edges, but the place has defiantly grown on me, for sure. To a big extent, we have a very low turnaround compared to the restaurant business in general. As you know, I've done this work a lot in my life, and trust me when I say having a crew that stays isn't your average thing. We have a very nice lady that has worked there since they started the restaurant some thirty years ago. She is from France and tells stories of World War II like it was yesterday. The restaurant also would just not be the same if a certain cook who has been there around twenty-five or more years were to retire. Even in the five years I've been there, I watched employees go through divorces, child birth, deaths in family, marriages, jail time, college students, and I've watched sisters grow up around us. They have seen me through all the things I've went through. I'm sure they're sick of hearing about this book too, but to their credit, they listen to me like the friendly uncle that talks too much and has a tendency to break in to conversations uninvited. Sorry about that guys, I'll try not to do that so much. They do understand that I don't do it intentionally to be rude, it's just my personality and the way I am. One cook said it best when he said, "Jim, you can't stand not getting the last word in, can you?" Sadly, I find that unconsciously true.

I'm sure I get on some people's nerves sometimes, and I apologize to them for that. I'm just a little high-strung I guess. See, the neat thing about family is they understand each other's weaknesses and don't judge you for your misgivings. It is really difficult, especially in the restaurant business to find a situation that makes you feel comfortable but this place does. To everybody's credit there, we make a great team, and I'm proud to be a part of it. We all make our mistakes from time to time there, and it is far from being perfect, but it is a lot of fun for everyone there including the owner. All of us who work there just have to keep complacence at bay while we're there. To all of you who work there, thank you, and I hope we can keep our friendship.

"All the distractions have a tendency to ruin that chance encounter where you meet that one true love. The person that you truly are inside, a lot of times gets hidden underneath and doesn't surface till later on in life."

CHAPTER 64

To the One I Was Looking for
To My Muse
To My Wife

The first few days in my new apartment were filled with freedom. I could play videos all day long if I wanted to. The place Sabrina and I used to rent movies was within walking distance. My boss had helped me with the move because my truck had finally died on the side of the highway earlier while Sabrina was still here. I had me a little black Honda now, which ran great, but now I found myself in a situation where I could walk to whatever I needed. K-Mart was right across the street, and I even had a Laundromat by the video store. This was going to be great.

The honeymoon of freedom only lasted for a short time though. After a while, I found myself staring out the window, contemplating my life and watching the people walk by, wondering if they did better then I did in my life. Now I knew I probably had seen a lot more in my life than most, but was it worth it to live a wonderer's lifestyle. Looking out at the bridge like all Twin Port people do, my thoughts went back to my own childhood and knowing twenty-five or so years ago I was staring at that same view, getting ready to go in the Marines. Somewhere around that time, I realized maybe I missed something more important here.

That got me to start watching more closely to the different lifestyles I saw going into the K-Mart. I could have been like all the other people in my age group that had great jobs, family memories, A house that I had been paying on and only had like ten years left, and was driving one of them nice SUVs in the parking lot there at K-Mart. Then as the moment progressed, I saw a man with a beat-up old Plymouth, A blank look of disgust that he had to be here at the store, a daughter and son who looked a little complacent, with the daughter on her cell phone and the young boy playing a handheld video game, and the mother screaming at her son to turn of the game. The father was ignoring the mother trying to discipline the boy who just looked at his mother in disgust. I wanted to run across the street and talk to that boy, but they'd probably arrest me for disturbing the peace or something. God forbid if that man were to swat his son on the butt, he'd go to jail for child abuse.

While that was going on, I noticed a green peace bumper sticker on the back of an SUV. My attention went to this vehicle, curious to see who gets out of that thing. Moments later in a flash, a younger woman somewhere in her late twenties to early thirties jumped out with a big fancy tote bag practically running for the door as she bent her arm back with her keys to turn on the alarm on her vehicle. Yes, she was also on her cell phone talking to someone and ignoring the couple I mentioned a minute ago. *What's the rush?* I thought as I turned away from the view.

Nope, I didn't miss much I guess. I just wondered which one of them people I would be out there in the parking lot that day. At that point, my mind drifted into all the memories that I have since the time I stared at the bridge as a child. It was a rush of good, bad, and indifferent memories of love, children, places I've seen, the Marines, hitchhiking across this vast country we live in, all the highways I've seen, the ocean, the bay in Okinawa, all the thousands of faces over the years driving or working in restaurants, and countless numbers of memories that escape me from time to time. I've lived a very full life so far, and it was time to stop worrying about things and just relax for a while. My rent was all inclusive, most of my bills were caught up, I had a good job where I can pay my child support, and I was tired of life. I needed a break, and I was set to take one now. I had some great racing games, and I could sit and watch movies. Not to mention a three-thousand-dollar collection of magic cards I could look at and play. I was all set and I planned on enjoying a little rest. Don't forget watching my favorite driver on NASCAR each week.

This went really good for me for a while, but I knew shortly after that this couldn't be it for me or at least I hoped it wouldn't be. Work was going well, and my plan, even though it was flawed, was working. Everything was very relaxed. Back at work, you remember that we had a lot of regulars there, and I happened to see one was here who came in all the time with her daughter, so I approached to say hi. As I came around the bench to my surprise it wasn't her daughter. "Who's this pretty young lady?" I said after noticing a beautiful young lady with a shy look in her face as I spoke. I fumbled in an awkward hello because I was taken aback by this beautiful girl who had replaced her daughter for a spell. I don't recall the conversation but heard the name Robin in all of this. I remember that she was shy that day, but it was our first meeting, and I don't think anything came of it because I figured a nice person like Robin would never go for someone like me.

It wasn't till later at another time after that meeting that she came in again and was meeting some friends for dinner that hadn't arrived yet. I finally had the gumption to talk with her and give proper introductions. I couldn't believe how nervous I was over this simple meeting, but the servers in the pantry were picking on me because they knew me, and according to them I was as red as an apple. I tried to look very businesslike so I wouldn't seem too infatuated with her, and as the conversation gave life to itself, we built a mutual interest in each other. I was also doing my best not to ramble as I spoke to her. I have a tendency to do that as you know. It was also important for me to make sure I let her talk too, because sometimes I don't let people get a word in edgewise. It's not intentional as I said earlier, but I have a lot to say, and I was really trying to impress her to see if this may go somewhere. She was so pretty, and she had this laugh every time I said something funny to her. She was actually laughing with me and enjoying the conversation, which in its own way had never happened to me.

We basically talked about where we worked, our homes, and a little about who she was meeting with that day. She had mentioned that she had horses, so I came back with the fact that I could fix her fence if she ever needed me to. Little did I know then how much fence we needed to fix. That obviously wasn't why we fell for each other, but a funny afterthought. I found out she worked at the hospital and was a therapist; then we just talked of simple things that I don't remember all the conversation but knew I really wanted to go out with her and knew I needed to ask her before her friends arrived. Luckily, without worrying about what she might say do to the fact that I was so infatuated with her so quickly I just said, "You want to have a drink with me so we can talk more while I'm not working?" The servers that day can tell you how excited I was that she said yes.

Because she worked Saturday in the morning, we decided on that afternoon at a restaurant in the mall. I was so excited I don't think I slept the whole time till that day. I couldn't wait to see her. I went a little early so I could be there when she arrived and had a shot of tequila to calm my nerves before, and there she was. Prettier than I remembered from a few days before. She ordered a glass of wine, and I can't even remember what I ordered, I was so nervous. Part of me wanted to impress her, but the part of me that wanted to just be myself won out.

The whole evening we talked of simple pleasures and what we liked or didn't like. I felt relaxed very quickly as we spoke more and more to each other. I did my best to let her talk, but I'm sure I probably rambled a time or two. We spent a good portion of our time speaking of what we wanted in life, and I think I made it pretty clear that I was tired and just wanted to relax and enjoy life for the rest of the time I had here on this world. She spoke a lot about her animals and how much they meant to her. She also told me about her mother and how she spent a good portion of her week helping her with shopping and spending quality time with her whenever she could. The conversation seemed to flow so easily through us. We were connecting very well and just enjoying our time so much that time itself seemed irrelevant.

I couldn't tell you how it ended that night, but the time went by so fast, I wanted to see her as soon as possible, again. She agreed, and for the next few weeks, we spent that time at my little apartment just talking and getting to know each other as good as we could. One thing that sticks out was telling her how I felt she had a lot of love and passion bottled up inside her, and it would take a strong man to be able to realize all that love she had. I think she believed me and slowly saw what I meant by the way she treated me on a daily basis. I felt our love building with every kiss and each smile from her. But I have to admit that I got scared, and I let my pride get the best of me.

Robin by far was the most intelligent woman I think I had ever known in my life. She had done something I personally could never do. She had her master's degree and was a therapist at a hospital here in Duluth. I had the utmost respect for her and her colleagues that helped out these children all around the area. I personally couldn't see why she would have any interest in me considering the background I had. Like six kids, many relationships, back child support, bankruptcy, and we all know the list goes on. She, on the other hand, had a good education, a stable life, a great job that she made over twice what I made, owned her own home, and owned her car. I had nothing but debt, but as time went on, she saw past that and was falling in love with me for who I am. And as I said before, she had a lot of love to give.

Even through all this, I was the one who wasn't sure of me, and after a few weeks, I called things off between us. I didn't have the self-confidence to see past the material things I was feeling. I was an idiot, but thank God Robin saw past that and two weeks later called me; we talked for hours and at this point for the first time in my life, I truly felt a woman was in love with me. Listening to the way she talked about her feelings solidified my love for her also. I don't think I had ever felt the unconditional love that we shared for each other. In the past there were so many things that kept me from truly being in love, and things never worked for me. I also believed this was the first love that had a passion for me and I felt weak in the knees like they talk about in movies and love stories. We have that for each other. She also, very shortly, fell in love with NASCAR with me. That to this day is something we share.

The way I see it, there is someone out there for everyone, but it isn't easy to find. All the distractions have a tendency to ruin that chance encounter where you meet that on true love. The person that you truly are inside, a lot of times gets hidden underneath and doesn't surface till later on in life. Jumping the gun too early will distort your soul and make it difficult to find you in all of the mess. Remember when I said, "I would help *you* find *you* by looking at the basics of you"? This is what you need to find, to have that Mrs. or Mr. Right. That isn't mentioning you need to find yourself so that you can be happy in your life. It will also give you the strength to see inside your Mr. Right and find what you both are looking for. "If you don't know yourself how can you find Mr. or Mrs. Right?"

I know that it's possible that I was meant to find Robin, but Michal and Randy started me on a different path when I was in the sixth grade. Guess who was right downstairs from me in that school so many years ago? You guessed it, the young girl named Robin was right there with me. As you'll recall, I was way too afraid of girls, or anyone for that matter, to see her there at the lunchroom or in the halls. I feel that the encounters I had back then distracted me from the path I should have been on all this time. Don't forget though, I still wouldn't change a thing for the sake of my children. But it is an interesting thought. We both went on difficult paths, but love did conquer all, and here we are together at last. Nothing will ever change that now.

With that said, we did end up moving in together, and my first meal with her family was at Thanksgiving that year. It was the perfect opportunity to let them get to know me, and I did very well with her mother who I look up to greatly. She and

Robin were very close, and we took care of her together from that day forth. That Christmas was a real treat for Robin and her mother, I'd like to say, because of me and my eccentric view of Christmas. Remember me and making sure there were lots of things to open? This was not the usual for Robin's family. They traded gifts; they just didn't go overboard like me with it. Then I found out Robin hadn't had a tree in her house for a long time because it was depressing being by herself, so we got a beautiful tree, and we didn't take it down for the whole year. She loved her Christmas now. I do go a little overboard, but I don't think I can change that.

Robin and I started thinking about how much we love each other and how we couldn't imagine life any other way now and told her mother in passing about it. Soon later she gave her ring that her father gave her for us, and we knew we were going to get married, but I hadn't asked her yet officially. That Valentine, I set up a reservation at a beautiful restaurant close to Two Harbors for a beautiful dinner and a great chance to make the woman I love my wife. I wanted to make everything as memorable as possible. So I snuck the ring out of the box and left the box in plain sight so she wouldn't know I had it and we started the wonderful drive up the coast to our nice dinner.

The restaurant was beautiful but a little open for my taste, meaning the space was like having a bunch of tables in a gymnasium. We did have a window set though, and it was very well placed. We both talked of love and things that were going on, and when the time was right, I grabbed her hand gently and proposed in a way that explained how much love I felt for her and that the love she showed me was beyond anything I had ever imagined and pulled her hand to my heart and said, "This is yours and only yours, and it beats only for you." The neat thing was that the ring was in the pocket over my heart and she said yes in a voice that could melt the moon. I knew our love was a forever kind of love. I was her strength and she was mine.

Some of her family and friends weren't too sure about this, but I think in time everyone will see the love is stronger than any material on earth and that none of those things are an issue to two people in love. I would never hurt Robin or do anything to harm her, and we will always be at each other's side. I will always open doors for her and sit beside her in the restaurants. We still to this day do everything together and always will.

A few quick things before I move on: animals, which are our family now. When we started our relationship, she had Hot Shot and Willie, who were her kids. Hot Shot is a paint and Willie an Appaloosa. When I first came along, the pecking order to them put me at the bottom, and Hot Shot and I went round and round for the longest time. We still push each other around now, but he knows who's boss . . . Robin. Then of course you always have are Pomeranian, Cocoa is his name. He was in charge of the house. She raised all of them including our two cats, Baby Grey and Shadow, from babies, except Willie. It was obvious even from the first days I met her that they were her life before me. They were her serenity.

Remember I joked about a fence at her place when I met her? *Oh my God*, I'm sure part of the reaction is the fact that I was a fence contractor that believed the only good fence is a new fence, but, boy, did this thing need work. Robin had twenty acres or so with no fence, and the front eight acres had a falling-down fence and one good acre or so had a good electrical fence. She wanted to have a fence on the back twenty someday if she could and knew the front pasture was falling apart. I told her that I wasn't fond of electric fence and showed her pictures of a Buck & Rail fence from my fencing years. "Is it sturdy? Hot Shot likes to get out of fence."

"Honey, it would be difficult to drive a truck through this kind of fence, not to mention horses won't try to jump it because of their depth perception. That was why they used them so much, especially out West," I said with a smile on my face. See, it did kind of bother me that I had nothing more to offer her then myself, but as things progressed, my knowledge of so many things from being a jack-of-all-trades made life on a small hobby ranch more exciting.

"Heck, I can build that fence on my own and use the trees on our property to build it, which will help clear the fields very nicely. Kill two birds with one stone essentially."

That spring, I started on the field and without going through it all got the pasture done this year, and the first year; 1,500 feet in the twenty acres got done. The one thing I will say about that is the full sense of being when you're working on the ranch and seeing the fruits of your labor, there is no better feeling. I can see the pride of our ancestors as I worked the fields out there on our property. I've been so lucky to feel and see these kinds of things all through my life. So many days in the field building fence, it is a great feeling to be sure. Life makes so much better sense when you have to go out there in the elements to take care of your home and your family.

Life had become a beautiful thing for us. My prayer was for happiness and stability, Robin's, at almost the same time, was for a good caring man who would love her forever. We have had some difficult times, but nothing will ever take away the love we share with each other. I went through hard times before us, as did she, and we finally are both happy about our future. Robin lost a father and a brother. I also lost a father and a grandson, and I'm sure this could go on forever, but books, sooner or later have to end, but to us it's the beginning again. I hope for all of you, as you read the last chapter, that in some ways it will be a beginning for you also. I do appreciate you taking the time to share my stories with you and hope they help you in some way.

What Robin and I are doing now is like catching up to our past and looking towards the future. I feel in some ways we were cheated in life from that small school so many years ago. I have no regrets at this point in life. I finally found the one I know I was intended to be with, and that is enough for me. The love we have is what made this book. There is no chance in heck I would have ever taken the time or had the patience to tell my story. If Robin wouldn't have pushed me to write all this down, it would've never come to be. I was meant to go through all this so I could give all of you this story. I hope and pray that it will help all of you. Especially all of you, Nickolas, Jason, Christopher, Zachery, Madison, Trenton, and the grandkids—I never meant to cause any of you pain and hope someday all of you will forgive me.

"Wisdom and intelligence cannot be used to tell someone who they should be or shouldn't be. Everyone's meaning in life is their own. We have to stop letting people push us around into thinking their way."

CHAPTER 65

Celebrating a Life
And
Life in Retrospect

He was born in '65, 65 chapters. Trust me, I didn't plan that. It is kind of neat though. This book has been very difficult in some ways but extremely easy in others. Oh, I think it was my last birthday; Robin gave me a small folder to start a manuscript for my kids. What you see now as the introduction was the notes I scribbled on the folder. I do talk a lot, and working in the restaurant does give me a chance to make people laugh and smile for just that small moment in time. That said, it doesn't escape the fact that I see so much pain, distraction, and empty looks on people's faces each and every day. With all the stories and experience, I found that in that moment I can give them a little serenity. It may only be a fleeting moment, but maybe it set up their whole day to just be a little more memorable. Just one day in an otherwise difficult life can mean the world to someone. Robin could see something in me that no one ever really paid attention to; the strength to be positive and to keep the cup half-full all the time. "You should tell people your story, Jim, and maybe they'll listen to you if it's coming from someone who doesn't have the distractions of life itself." One lady said she liked what she read because "it's raw life, no whistles and bells." I hope you all see that.

Another person who I think saw that in me was Robin's mother. She said "You make me reminisce very well, Jim." I didn't get to spend my life with her, but I truly got to see Robin a little closer through her mother. Robin had, in the past, taken the time to do this neat book where you ask your parents or grandparents all these neat questions about life and write their answers down for posterity. We also bought Mom a small recorder to tell stories when they came to mind, but she wasn't much for technology so she never figured out how to use it. But the notebook she found gave her many memories to write down. You have to realize she was eighty-four or so at the time she was doing this, so she had more memories than any of us could ever imagine.

With all of this talk, I was excited to do this book but then things turned for Robin and her family. Her mother started getting sick, and time seemed to be running out for us. Now I'm not going to get too detailed about something as personal as this, but I will tell you that going through this with Robin was the most difficult thing I could have ever imagined. This was Robin's mother, who she spent many hours taking care of and watching over for so many years. Robin would say she was watching over her but seeing them two together, it was a mutual thing. Oh, sure I saw a few arguments in the past, but the love they had in the sense of mother to daughter was huge. The love was intense, for lack of a better word.

After many tests and long nights of anxiety for Robin, it was official, Mom's cancer had returned. Yes, they had already been through this before and got it into remission. Once they found it, then there seemed to be test after test after test to see how far along this was going to be. We spent every moment we could watching over her and taking care of her every need. At one point, the doctors suggested a nursing home to make it easier to watch over her and keep her in an environment that had nurses and doctors looking after her. It seemed very logical to us at the time, but no one could have foreseen how quickly things can change.

While she was at the nursing home, Robin spent so much time there her mother and I had to almost force her to go home each day to rest. With her anxiety as high as it was it made it very difficult. On a lighter note, though Robin and I have some very fond and wonderful memories of all the talks we had and inside jokes about things that Mom said that will always be our secrets. Having the time we had made things easier then if something would have happened so we couldn't say good-bye. For me personally, I couldn't do that again like my dad. Robin's mother had become mine, and I cared for her dearly. It was there at the nursing home that I had a resounding moment with her with no one around.

I'm not sure how the conversation started, but she started thinking about her time as a child during World War II. Y'all know how I feel about the military and war, so you know this was a big moment for me. She was a young girl I think in Helsinki during the war, and they bombed her home town a lot. The thing that stuck out for her was them collecting the bodies of the fallen, and she helped to clean them before they buried them. As she spoke of the burials, she broke into tears and, with a voice like a child speaking to her father, said, "I really don't want to talk about that anymore." Her voice sounded so distraught, and I couldn't help but share those tears with her as she hid them away in her napkin, almost like trying to hide the pain in that little napkin. Moments later she seemed to have just turned it off, and with her red eyes, she looked at me and said, "Jim, please take care of her for me. She is my little girl, and I can't let anything ever hurt her, Promise me," "With all my heart."

A little while after that day, we had an appointment with a specialist, and he made things seem like we had made a bad decision about the nursing home at first but then explained how fast the cancer was spreading and then put her back in the hospital. We made the necessary phone calls to her sister and brother, and shortly after, Mom told us she wanted to go home. So Robin and I finally put our foot down and brought her to our home to go away peacefully.

Little did we know that we only had a few days. They were precious to Robin and me and would never change our decision to let her go in peace. The last thing I heard her mother say was "thank you, Robin."

Why would I end a book in this way? Because the time that I spent listening to her mom over the past few months before this happened is the inspiration to write my story down for your kids and all of you reading this. She had an inspiring life that needed to be told to her children. I want you to have a record of my thoughts like the ones that she wrote down in her book. I didn't get to spend my whole life with all of you as Robin did with her mother so I needed to do this. What little I saw showed me how much of an influence she had on her and her siblings. I remembered the day we talked all night after dad died and got to be there with him through all that. I wanted to be sure and tell y'all my story also. I have more I wished I could say, but maybe I'll work on that some other time.

Inside this life I've shown you I have felt a great deal of emotions. A simple song that you'll have to look up, called "All this Joy" by John Denver say's it the best. It wasn't till I wrote this book that I started feeling the words in this song from way down in the depths of my soul. I too don't know where that originated from. Sadly, he passed before I could ask him. We had our difficulties, but he was still my father.

Writing this book has been an inspiration to me in so many different ways that you couldn't even imagine how good it feels writing these last few pages. I started this with the simple task of telling my children my side of the story and then it became this passion to say all this to everyone out there that has been in my life. My meaning in life is to live, nothing more, nothing less. In society, we all have something to offer whether it's a doctor, a bartender, a truck driver, a cowboy, a man on the moon, a therapist, a governor, the president, a dancer, a mill worker, an inventor, a father, a mother, and so many millions of things that help each other. The one job that everyone seems to want is the judge. It is not our job to judge someone. Thinking that wisdom or intelligence is a way to judge a person is ludicrous. There is no point in doing so. Wisdom and intelligence cannot be used to tell someone who they should be or shouldn't be. Everyone's meaning in life is their own. We have to stop letting people push us around into thinking their way.

I hope I don't come across as someone who is telling you what *you* should be but helping you to see that what you are is what you choose to be, nothing more, nothing less. If people make an evil choice then shame on them, and society has laws in place to combat anarchy. Don't get confused by this and think I'm saying, "Do whatever you want." That isn't the point. We all are here to work together to make a peaceful life for all of us. "Do unto others as you would have done to you," makes a lot of sense here. Does anyone want people to treat you like crap because you're not in style or listen to the right music? No, they don't feel that way. Being kind is so much easier than trying to figure out a way to hurt someone else. Don't be the one who kills the bug or tears at the tree. Just be a human being and show some kindness. People don't gain a thing from destroying someone else.

Now that you have read my book, whether you're my kids or anyone else out there that wants to enjoy life, spend a day with a smile and a handshake to the people around you. You may scare someone at first, but they and you will be the better for it. If each one of you would get yourself away from this unnatural reality that our society has built and open your eyes to the "forest for the trees", then the rest will fix itself.

I don't think life was made to be so difficult. I think greed is what made life difficult. Greedy people really believe they are owed that money they steal from us. Because of people's kindness, it makes it easier to steal from all of us. There is a whole world out there full of animals who don't try to screw each other. They only go after what they need for survival. There is no point in survival that says they need to take more than we need. Remember the analogy I used about the whale and all that open space and the fact that he didn't take more then he needs? Don't be so cruel to them people around you. We are all here together, and we should do our best to help your neighbor.

Make sure all of you try to see the "simple things in life that save us all." The best medicine in life is your own experiences in life, and so many of the simple things have been forgotten in our day-to-day life. Just yesterday I was sitting at Taco Bell and watching the crowd of youngsters who only looked at others in laughter for what they did or didn't do or how they were dressed. Something as simple as respect seemed to not even cross their minds. They were to busy being cool in front of their friends. Not one of them boys took their hat of or showed any respect for the girls around them. No one opened the door for the older couple that was leaving as they stood by the door. Instead they muscled their way through the doorway. One boy with his pants halfway down his legs told his woman what he wanted and walked away trying, "in what I thought was a weird way", to look cool. The sad thing was the young girl did this for him and never even flinched at the way this punk treated her. Is this the world we want for our children? Where did he learn this behavior? What parent in their right mind would let their kid act this way?

A lot of these kids never saw their parents because they were to busy buying them baggy pants he wore. An unseen phantom of society raised that child. A reality that shouldn't exist made them the way they are. Morals and ethics have become a memory of a society that has lost its way in greed and self hoarding. I know that we can get them morals and ethics back. It has to start with you. Take a good look at yourself and realize the potential to just be a good person. Don't let this so-called reality take control of the little things in your heart. This goes for my kids and all the way up to the politicians and bosses out there and down to those who supposedly are unwise and unintelligent. We all live here on this earth and need to get back to the basics.

What are wisdom and intelligence? Sometimes I think there a way to judge someone. Then in another breath, I would say they are experience. I couldn't tell you the dictionaries' view of it and for the sake of the book I won't look it up. If I split the two, Intelligence is the three Rs: reading, righting, and arithmetic.

Wisdom is the knowledge of life or our experience's in life. Then the problem would be which is the more important.

Wisdom is humankinds' growth through time, and in our time it seems to be pretty low. Intelligence gives human kind strength, but without wisdom, it is a nasty route to destruction. There are some very intelligent people out there leading us down that path, getting worse and worse with each generation. Wisdom will always outweigh intelligence, but it is necessary to work together. We need the simple things in life back, to ground society before things get to far. Like Bruce Lee said in the movie, *Enter the Dragon*. A simple thing like water can move mountains. A simple thing like a tree can save all of us. Kids, I hope you can start seeing the "forest for the trees" and make life a little better for yourself and hopefully all of you that read this book that aren't my children can find yourselves.

Thank you for your time, and I hope the best for all of you out there who took the time to read this book. It means a lot to me to share my story and to hopefully give all of you the strength to see yourselves for what you are and what you may become. We need to get the world to see the little things that mean everything to our survival and everything to the meaning of life.

In the beginning
The rest of the chapters are yours
Make it a good story that you'll be proud to pass on

Get Published, Inc!
Thorofare, NJ 08086
17 February, 2010
BA2010048